D0230786

70001482644 9

Sweet Revenge

by the same author

BLIND EYE TO MURDER
KLAUS BARBIE
THE PAPERCLIP CONSPIRACY
RED WEB
MAXWELL: THE OUTSIDER
TINY ROWLAND
THE PERFECT ENGLISH SPY
HEROES OF WORLD WAR II
MAXWELL: THE FINAL VERDICT
NAZI GOLD
BLOOD MONEY
FAYED
BRANSON
THE PAYMASTER
BROKEN DREAMS
CONRAD AND LADY BLACK
THE SQUEEZE
NO ANGEL

Sweet Revenge

The Intimate Life of Simon Cowell

TOM BOWER

First published in 2012
by Faber and Faber Ltd
Bloomsbury House
74–77 Great Russell Street
London WC1B 3DA

Typeset by Ian Bahrami
Printed in England by CPI Group (UK) Ltd, Croydon CR0 4YY

A CIP record for this book
is available from the British Library

ISBN 978-0-571-27835-0

2 4 6 8 10 9 7 5 3 1

To Veronica

'He who seeks revenge should remember to dig two graves.'

Chinese proverb

Contents

Introduction

Marvin Gaye's 'Ain't No Mountain High Enough' was blaring across the dark Mediterranean as Simon Cowell pulled on his Kool cigarette. 'Today was an eye-opener,' he reflected, swigging a freezing Sapporo beer. 'I'm disappointed.'

At 2.30 a.m. on 5 August 2011, Cowell had returned to *Slipstream*, his 193-foot chartered yacht, from Le Bâoli, a brash restaurant in Cannes' harbour. 'I hate this place,' Cowell had told his friends. 'Getting in was trouble. I expected an elbow in my eye.' Offensive doormen had temporarily blocked his entrance after failing to recognise their famous guest.

After eating only a single course, Cowell had unexpectedly risen and declared, 'Let's go.' The group's exit had been delayed by a dozen tourists from Essex asking for a photograph. As usual, Cowell politely obliged – some would say his politeness was manipulation, but he believed in being pleasant to everyone – and then strode past the restaurant's bouncers, across the quay and stepped onto *Take Five*, a new VanDutch speedboat, his summer toy. Taking control from the ship hand, he pushed the throttle forward sharply. Speed was an easy cure for his stress. Zooming across the flat sea at 45 mph, he steered into the darkness beyond the harbour walls. The exhilaration provoked a smile and he swung the boat towards his gleaming gin palace, a haven of privacy from the mob.

Sitting on *Slipstream*'s spacious aft deck, Cowell glanced at the latest text messages from Los Angeles. 'Not good,' he announced. Casting aside the nearly full bottle of beer, he ordered, 'Another cold one,' and took a swig before heading for his suite. In Los Angeles, everyone was still awake. He needed a post-mortem. He anticipated making telephone calls until daybreak.

Seven hours earlier, Cowell had been linked by satellite from the yacht's lounge to Los Angeles, where 250 television critics had gathered for the industry's showcase of the upcoming autumn season. 'This is the big one,' Cowell had told Fox's executives. After thirty years in the music business, he was gambling his fate on *The X Factor*'s successful launch in America.

'I only play to win,' he volunteered. He had repeatedly re-edited a glitzy twelve-minute promotion tape highlighting the *X Factor* USA auditions recently held in Pasadena. His pursuit of the tape's editors in Los Angeles was a foretaste of how he would pressure them to produce flawless programmes. 'They'll get it in the neck like canaries in a mine,' he had promised. Perfectionism and unpredictability were his gospel.

'We all love this tape and this is going to be a great launch,' he enthused about the mixture of tantrums, tears and seductive singing to be shown to the journalists.

In Pasadena, he had picked Stacy Francis, a forty-two-year-old single mother, as the competition's probable winner. 'She'll be bigger than Susan Boyle,' he predicted privately. After Stacy, his next favourite was Rachel Crow, a frizzy-haired thirteen-year-old from a remote farm in Colorado. 'Both back-stories are special,' he said with daunting self-confidence, adding to his friends on the yacht, 'I'll be worried if the audience doesn't get to 30 million plus.' His ambitious target for *The X Factor* USA, he said, would humble *American Idol*'s 2011 average of 23 million viewers.

Attacking *Idol* was not a sideshow. Ridiculing the programme which had made him famous in America had become an all-consuming passion. To keep him happy, Fox had just broadcast a controversial promotional teaser for *The X Factor* USA in the middle of the All Stars baseball game. The commercial featured Cowell waking from a nightmare in which he was still working on *American Idol*. The promise was that *The X Factor* would push the 'bland' *Idol* aside. Many viewers were baffled, but none more so than *Idol*'s producers. After all, their programme was also broadcast by Fox. Fevered critics spoke about cannibalism and self-destruction as they witnessed the calculated gamble taken by Fox executives to stage *The X Factor* USA.

Fox's rivals had watched the recent turmoil surrounding Cheryl Cole's acrimonious departure from the US show with glee and had intensified their plots to usurp Cowell's supremacy. Fractured relationships always undermined self-confidence, and the promo tape during the baseball game was an own goal. 'I felt zero when I saw it,' admitted Cowell two months later. 'It was too clever and aimed at women, when the audience was all male.' Three months later, he would describe his strategy as 'a blunder'. That afternoon's satellite presentation from the yacht to the journalists in Los Angeles was a premonition of fate.

'*The X Factor* is like nothing you've seen before,' he began. 'We're throwing everything in to win – to make the best TV show in the world.' *The X Factor* USA, he declared unambiguously, would be better than *American Idol*. 'We're looking for contestants with star quality whom we can turn into stars.' *The X Factor* USA had not been launched, he answered one journalist, 'to win the silver medal', and there was an unprecedented $5-million prize. 'I want to show that the process is honest – warts and all,' he pledged, aiming to silence the repeated accusations about behind-the-scenes manipulation and deception. The journalists had not been told that he was broadcasting from the Mediterranean and, as he spoke, Cowell cursed the three-second delay to his voice. 'Are you the PR puppet *meister*?'

asked a woman. 'No,' he replied. 'It's not our intention to be mean. That's just within us.'

Sitting in the Los Angeles studio, Paula Abdul, the singer and dancer, described her reaction at being invited by Cowell to become an *X Factor* USA judge. 'I felt harrowed and elated and I cried for days after,' she said, three years in the wilderness at an end. 'Well, I give everyone a third chance,' cut in Cowell smugly. Nicole Scherzinger's voice followed, but the words of Cheryl Cole's replacement were incomprehensible down a deteriorating sound feed. 'Nicole's selfish,' Cowell chipped in 'live', reflecting his niggle that the former Pussycat Doll was focused solely on self-glorification – and also his pleasure of expressing blunt truths.

'We've got a problem,' rattled the TV technician's voice across *Slipstream*'s plush interior. The sound had been cut. Next, the screen went black. Technology was sabotaging the master of control. 'That's it,' announced the production manager on the yacht. To Cowell's disgust, the same manager whom he blamed for the disaster now asked for a photograph of the two of them together, but, always graceful, he smoothly fulfilled the chore and then hurried to his private suite. 'The feed was bad, the production was bad and we had no leadership,' Cowell lambasted his producers in Los Angeles. The happy spell on the pristine yacht had been broken. Doubtless all would be forgotten after a night's sleep, but new problems were certain to arise the following day.

Cowell had arrived on the Côte d'Azur on a private jet from Los Angeles after stopping in New York to collect his favourite holiday companions. Three couples had been invited to take care of his needs and join in the fun.

One guest was his best friend, Paul McKenna, the hypnotist and self-improvement guru, who was accompanied by Sam, an attractive English woman. The others were Andrew Silverman, a New York property developer and the owner of a casino in Panama, and his wife Lauren; and Kelly Bergantz, employed by Cowell as an executive producer, and her boyfriend, a hedge-fund manager. All the women were glamorous, high-octane players willing to pander to Cowell's innocent whims. They were joined by Sinitta, his former girlfriend, whose song 'So Macho' was Cowell's first hit in 1986. To widespread bewilderment – including that of Julie Cowell, his eighty-six-year-old mother – Cowell's former flames remained his closest friends, united by their jealousy towards each other while competing for his attention.

The notable absentee from the party was Mezhgan Hussainy, Cowell's Afghani fiancée. To his mother's relief, he had quietly cancelled his wedding to the make-up artist. 'I'm shattered by the way she behaves,' Julie Cowell had told her son after Hussainy had stormed from the dining room in his Los Angeles home and slammed the bedroom door. Although Hussainy had worked with Cowell in the studio, she had not understood the stresses in his life. She was unsympathetic, both Julie and Simon agreed, to his love of uncertainty and change and his 'relentless, relentless, relentless' competitiveness.

'We came to the conclusion that I'm a hopeless boyfriend, and I don't blame her,' said Cowell, gazing across the Mediterranean. He had agreed there would have to be compensation – 'When you make a promise to someone you have to support her' – and to minimise any damage he was reluctantly considering giving her his $8-million hilltop home in Beverly Hills. For the moment, their separation remained unpublicised. Although he had found another woman, who would board the yacht later, Cowell was mindful that any paparazzi photograph would embarrass the proud lady. To frustrate the intrusive cameras along the Riviera, he would party – and sleep – alone until he reached Sardinia.

The break-up did not surprise Paul McKenna, who at

forty-seven was another unmarried Los Angeles personality. 'We've got commitment phobia,' McKenna concluded about their common resistance to permanent relationships and children. Loving dogs and the 'people business' – or, more pertinently, 'people deconstruction' – was their common interest. Another was just having fun.

'I want to be happy, have good people around me,' agreed Cowell. 'I want to be free and I don't want to be bored.' After McKenna disappeared into his cabin, Cowell reflected on his own unwillingness to marry: 'I'm attracted to crazy women. I encourage crazy behaviour and I make them crazy. I'm attracted to certain personalities who are difficult to control, so there are tantrums, tears and fights, which is all part of the drama. My life is really odd. Every girl wants to be number one, and they're very territorial. I like the fight because otherwise I'd have a dull group of girlfriends.'

To his most intimate associates on the yacht, Cowell was the most generous friend but also, as a world-famous icon, an occasionally lonely man whose greatest comfort was lying on a couch between Lauren Silverman and Kelly Bergantz, watching a film and grazing on nursery food.

The fifty-one-year-old's career had reached a crossroads. Chartering *Slipstream* for one month at a cost of £2 million reflected his new tastes. During his first twenty years in the music business, Cowell had been regarded as an amusing sideshow, renowned for surviving endless humiliation before eventually emerging as a successful producer. Only in spring 2001, after moving hesitantly out of the record industry's shadows to become a television personality, did he finally achieve his ambition of becoming the Godfather of celebrity culture.

Six months earlier, in winter 2010–11, he had felt exhausted and on the verge of giving up. 'Then I got my mojo back and decided to crack on,' he said, taking a Kool cigarette lit by a member of the crew. Describing himself as a rebel, keen to define the vitality of his own era, he spoke energetically about his search for immortality.

Celebrity and shameless vanity have become Cowell's vehicle of subversion. On the yacht he flaunted his self-love and his personal admiration of those who were equally self-indulgent. Between beers, he revealed his negotiations with a Swiss company to freeze and store his corpse for £100,000, in the expectation that scientists will one day invent reanimation. 'I trust them,' he said. In the meantime, he spared no expense in order to prolong his life and looks.

Stubbing out his cigarette, at 4 a.m. he headed for bed.

'The best tomato sauce in the world on a pizza was Pizzaland's in Windsor,' Cowell declared soon after emerging for the first time the following day at three o'clock in the afternoon. McKenna nodded. 'I wonder if Geoff can make it for us,' continued Cowell, summoning *Slipstream*'s chef. Cowell expected the yacht's fourteen crew to satisfy his every whim, however trivial, and now he wanted Pizzaland's recipe to be instantly reproduced. Geoff agreed to make the calls. Twenty minutes later, he returned. Pizzaland, Geoff reported, was defunct, but he had tracked down the franchise's owner in Abu Dhabi. 'He's giving nothing away, but that's no problem.' On the basis that the charterer's request had to be satisfied, Geoff emerged forty minutes later with a fresh pizza inside a box decorated with Pizzaland's coloured motif, which had been copied from the Internet. 'Brilliant,' said Cowell, handing the shrivelled pastry to McKenna. 'Now, our favourite meal,' he announced as three hostesses brought Cumberland sausages, mashed potatoes and Daddies sauce. 'PG Tips with a dash of cardamom,' requested Cowell, as scones with cream and cucumber sandwiches made with sliced white bread filled the table.

With his annual income heading towards $70 million (£45 million), Cowell no longer stinted on luxuries, but nothing rivalled plain English comfort food. Over the combined meal of breakfast, lunch and tea, he and McKenna discussed the latest gossip – a competition the previous night between two billionaires' sons at a St-Tropez nightclub over how many bottles of champagne they could order. An Indonesian had won with twenty-two magnums costing $1.2 million (£800,000). 'I hate that,' said Cowell, who dislikes vulgarity, before switching the conversation to what he called 'my life balance' – pumping himself with vitamins to cancel out the damage caused by nicotine.

Twice every year, Dr Jean-Louis Sebagh, a French doctor based in London's Wimpole Street, injected Cowell with Botox. 'This is better than vitamins,' the doctor had advised. 'To me, Botox is no more unusual than toothpaste,' Cowell repeated to his friends, who shared his obsession. 'It simply works. You do it twice a year. Who cares? And it balances my smoking and drinking.'

Cowell travels everywhere with at least two large suitcases filled with potions – eye drops, face creams, bath salts, milk lotions and 'wash and go' shampoo. He visits Harrods regularly to buy the latest products. Women in his entourage always know his bathroom contains the best selection of cosmetics, which they are welcome to borrow. 'I am definitely vain, but to be honest with you I can't think of one person on TV who isn't,' Cowell admitted. No one would be allowed to spot him with 'bed head', that undesirable just-got-out-of-bed look; and, equally, when he awoke he disliked seeing his girlfriends before they were properly groomed. Appearances were critical and he liked to see women with their 'face' done.

Always willing to try a new idea to prolong his youthful appearance, he had recently fired a half-deaf woman who had visited weekly to cover him with oil, wrap him in cellophane and squeeze him into a tube with the promise that the paralysing discomfort and itching were guaranteed to detoxify and oxygenate him. After he tired of her loud monosyllabic proposals for a new TV show, he seized on another recommendation: HB Health anti-ageing clinic in Beauchamp Place, Knightsbridge. A friend's half-sentence description was sufficient for Cowell to splash out £5,000 for one hour's treatment in a 'bubble'. Three men had carried a contraption to his bedroom on the first floor of his London house which promised to detox, help weight loss and prolong life. 'I hated it,' he exclaimed, complaining that the German applying the treatment had spent the entire hour promoting his ideas for new TV shows, with the captive patient forced to listen.

The ultimate treatment was introduced to Cowell by Dannii Minogue in 2008. Dr Wendy Denning, an attractive British GP advertising her speciality as 'The Integration of Traditional and Complementary Medicine', recommended Cowell to have blood tests four times a year, 'the full blood work' every six months during his health checks at UCLA hospital in Los Angeles, and vitamins injected once a week. The twenty-minute injection contained magnesium, all the B vitamins and pure vitamin C. Whenever he was in America, Cowell received the same mixture via a thirty-minute intravenous drip in his bedroom every Saturday afternoon. On Denning's recommendation, he took a saucer of tablets daily, travelled with bottles of supplements and drank two smoothies each day – one red and one green – made from expensive rare fruits.

Plates of untouched food were cleared and the group started to play Balderdash, which has the strapline 'The Bluffing Game. The game you can win without knowing anything' on the box. Next, Cowell and McKenna checked Facebook. One year earlier, both had invented characters and bet on who would have the fewest friends after six months. Cowell's character was Derek

Bates, whose password was 'hairyballs69'. Logging on, he discovered no 'friends'. McKenna's invention, Jeremy Pipkin, had one friend, another person invented by McKenna. Both were genuinely disappointed by the failure of their ruse.

Immersed over the next four weeks in his billionaire's splendour, Cowell and his friends sailed across the Mediterranean from St-Tropez searching for fun. Their first port of call was Portofino, and then on to Sardinia to enjoy ex-Formula One boss Flavio Briatore's Billionaire club, one of the Mediterranean's best sanctuaries for the rich and famous to meet beautiful women.

Cowell's entrance with his friends provoked a frisson among the diners and dancers. Good-looking, rich, famous and, above all, unmarried, he was a potential catch for glamorous manhunters. And, most importantly, he was a willing target for a particular type. He certainly wasn't looking for intellect or strong characters; just uncomplicated, uninhibited, sometimes trashy girls. Despite his fastidious concern about personal hygiene, classy vulgarity excited the man. In his quest for transitory enjoyment, those defects were tolerated. His search was rarely in vain, with women quite literally throwing themselves in his path. One-night stands were ideal for a man resistant to commitment, even when they occasionally ended with theft and worse by girls whose motives were not immediately apparent. The stop in Billionaire had no such dramatic outcome.

After two days, *Slipstream* headed to Capri. Philip Green, the billionaire retailer and a close friend and adviser, was racing on his yacht from Turkey, while Natalie Imbruglia, an exciting, sexy Australian singer and songwriter, was waiting for Cowell to pick her up at a hotel on the island. The sassy entertainer, who had starred as a judge on Australia's *The X Factor*, came on board, according to one of the guests on the boat, intent, it seemed to her, on 'hooking up with Cowell after an earlier encounter'. For his part, Cowell also hoped to forge a relationship. His female friends were puzzled. 'Natalie's not very interesting,' whispered one. Cowell's charisma and fame, she knew, often overpowered the women he dated, not least because he rarely chased self-confident women who could resist the attractions of celebrity. Imbruglia, Cowell thought, was among the few who could spark something real. Instead, unsure about her host's fleeting intentions and his unwillingness to offer a relationship, she decided after four days to disembark.

'It didn't go anywhere,' Lauren Silverman concluded.

'Just a K&C,' agreed another pal, meaning 'a kiss and a cuddle'.

'I wanted another fling, and she didn't,' Cowell laughed. Rejection was irrelevant. He felt remarkably liberated.

'I don't care,' he announced at dinner soon after. 'This year I've cut out the darkness. I've cut out all the people I've hated.'

Lauren Silverman understood. For too long, Cowell had been shackled to his former partner turned rival and the owner of the *American Idol* format, Simon Fuller, and, as Cowell put it, his 'Moonies'.

'All day, every day,' Cowell recounted about his years on *American Idol*, 'they'd be watching me. Watching and watching. And then tapping and tapping all day long, sending Moonie reports back to Fuller. It was disgusting.' Silverman, his close confidante, nodded sympathetically.

Even while on holiday, Cowell spent no less than six hours a day on the telephone to London, New York and Los Angeles. In between, he spent hours watching DVDs of *The X Factor* and the programmes based on the *Britain's Got Talent* format broadcast in over forty countries. By any reckoning, he was unrivalled among the world's TV and music producers. His priority that August was *The X Factor* USA's launch on 21 September. Each episode would cost a record $3 million to produce, but in return advertisers were agreeing to pay Fox $400,000 for a thirty-second spot on the basis of guaranteed audiences. His focus was on reaching the stratosphere as America's most powerful TV star, a quest which was electrified by the events of 20 July.

In the Houses of Parliament in London, Rupert and James Murdoch had just been humiliated by politicians investigating their employees' illegal hacking of celebrities' telephone messages. Sensing weakness, Simon Fuller, Cowell's bitterest enemy, chose that day to issue a writ in the Los Angeles Superior Court against Fox Broadcasting. Carefully choreographed publicity ensured that Fuller's writ produced headlines from Los Angeles to London. The former owner of *American Idol* was suing his ex-partner. Fuller's declaration of war against Fox and indirectly also against Cowell demonstrated the British producer's bid to reassert his influence over the music industry.

Greed, ego and money are Hollywood's common currency, and causing conflict can often bring rich rewards. On *Slipstream*, Cowell spotted only Fuller's weaknesses. 'My fame is driving him crazy,' he smiled. For ten years, Fuller had waged legal and psychological warfare to confirm his supremacy over Cowell, and had extracted Cowell's meek acquiescence that *American Idol* had been Fuller's exclusive creation. For ten years, Cowell had gone along with what he believed was untrue, and now he felt Fuller wanted to extract more blood. He wanted a credit on *The X Factor* as 'executive producer', although Cowell was certain that he had not participated in any aspect of the programme. 'No one asks for a credit on a failure,' John Ferriter, a Hollywood agent, reassured Cowell as he reported Fuller's apparent anguish. A Hollywood broker of influence feared being frozen out. 'Desperate publicity-seeking' was Cowell's hostile comment.

It was no coincidence that the issue of Hollywood bible *Variety* that reported Fuller's writ was dominated by twelve pages of congratulations to Jamie King, the choreographer who had teamed up with Fuller to find talented musicians for a new show to be called *¡Q'Viva! The Chosen*, which was described as 'a search across the Americas for Latino artistry'. So far Fuller had not found a major American network to finance his prospective show, which had been instantly stymied by the announcement that its stars, Jennifer Lopez and Marc Anthony, were divorcing. In a city where a writ can sometimes be used as a negotiator's tool and both sides in a dispute can be seen eating amicably in the same restaurant, Fuller's blast was nevertheless regarded by some as out of the ordinary. 'We won't pay and we won't negotiate,' Cowell was told by Fox executives. Fuller, he felt, had shot himself in the foot. Their ten-year feud was coming to a climax. Andrew Lloyd Webber's famous response to the question 'Which Simon do you love more?' was 'My money is on Simon.' Cowell hoped the equivocation would soon be over. His revenge would be complete.

With little effort, Cowell's mask concealed any hint of those violent emotions. Despite endless media scrutiny, his critics' attempts to penetrate his defences and expose the reality of his passion and jealousy, or the existence of self-doubt and decadence, had proven fruitless. Fearing exposure, Cowell presented himself as the antithesis of debauchery: he was a man who never pronounced on morality and seemingly never committed a moral wrong. To some, he inhabited an identity but resisted being defined by it.

High-minded critics have dismissed Cowell's world of mindless pleasure as middle-class philistinism. Those debunkers have portrayed his pedestrian disregard of human complexity as proof of a man who is neither moral nor immoral, just superbly sterile. Yet, behind the mask, his confidants listen to confessions of torment, not least about his public image.

Like all subversives, he is terrified of others using his own armoury against him. Troubled by the hatred he has generated, he has grasped that his own fortune rests on resisting the same humiliation as he has heaped on others. For years he suffered mockery, and for the past eleven years he has sought revenge against those sneerers. 'This is the make-or-break year,' he admitted on *Slipstream*. By Christmas, he would know whether he had scaled new heights or been universally lampooned. A biographer wrote of Oscar Wilde, 'You drift beautifully on the surface and you will die unbeautifully in the depths.' Cowell hoped to avoid that fate.

By the end of the trip, he had also decided against freezing his corpse after all. A chance conversation during the voyage had revealed that the Swiss 'clinic', after receiving the corpse of a basketball player, had cut off and only frozen the head. 'Imagine', said Cowell, laughing uncontrollably, 'what all my ex-girlfriends would do if they just looked at my dead head. No way!'

1
The Creation

Laughter and parties were the bedrock of Simon Cowell's childhood. Both his mother Julie, a former Soho show dancer, and his father Eric, a property manager, were generous hosts who promoted enjoyment rather than academic study for their children. Guests at their successive homes on the western fringes of London could not have imagined that the Cowells were concealing a tangled succession of relationships preceding their own happy union. Once the dust had settled, among those invited for long Sunday lunches were not only four children from their previous relationships, but also their various grandchildren. They would later on be acknowledged in Eric's last will.

Eric Cowell, born in February 1918 in London's East End, could trace his father's family back to the eighteenth century. In 1770, William Cowell had been a rope manufacturer. The family business continued in the East End for over a hundred years until it was inherited by Joseph Cowell, Simon's great-grandfather. In 1890, Joseph, an Anglican, married Nancy Levy, a Jew, in Whitechapel. Their eldest son, also named Joseph, was born the following year and automatically took his mother's religion. The family business ended in the early twentieth century.

Soon after the outbreak of World War I in 1914, Joseph, then twenty-three years old, volunteered to join the Middlesex Regiment, serving as a private. The following year, he married Esther Malinsky, a twenty-nine-year-old Jewess who had been born in Poland. Esther's father, a cap maker, had fled to England to escape the Polish government's persecution of the Jews and set up his business in the premises of a mantle maker in the East End. The family home was two rooms at 22 Pelham Street, a Jewish area in Spitalfields.

After the war, Joseph became an office clerk and moved with Esther to Ilford, an east London suburb. When the second of their three sons, Eric Selig Philip Cowell, was born, Joseph was employed as an inspector on London's buses, checking passengers' tickets. On subsequent legal documents, Eric would describe his father as a 'transport manager'.

By 1939, Eric had qualified as a chartered surveyor. Soon after the outbreak of World War II, he joined the Middlesex Regiment and was posted to Calcutta as a commercial clerk. In 1943, promoted by then to captain in the 19th Hyderabad Regiment, he married Enid Proudfoot in Bombay's Anglican cathedral. Enid, the granddaughter of a native Indian, was unaware that her husband was Jewish. Misleadingly, he had described himself on the marriage certificate as 'Congregational'.

Life for British officers in India, the jewel of the British empire, was relatively blissful and Eric made the last year of the war even more comfortable by serving as a magistrate in Calcutta. His leisurely life of parties, privilege and servants ended in August 1946 and he retired from the army as an honorary major and returned alone to Britain to set up business as a surveyor, living near his mother, by then a widow, in Ilford. Enid, his wife, arrived in Britain some months later, but the marriage broke down and she returned to India.

Eric had already embarked on a relationship with Jeanette Sevier, a baker's daughter eight years younger than himself who occasionally modelled in Bristol. Renting a flat in Kensington, they remained unmarried but had a son, Anthony John, in 1948. Soon after, Eric found employment as a property manager for Barratts, the shoe manufacturer and retailer, and they moved temporarily to Stafford. In 1950, their daughter June was born.

Two years later, after returning to Kensington, Eric apparently obtained a divorce from Enid – no official British record can be found – and married Jeanette in Fulham, but within a year their marriage was floundering.

As part of his work, Eric travelled regularly at weekends between London and Northampton. Returning on the same train to London every Monday, he spotted an attractive woman, Julie Dalglish.

Born in November 1925, Julie was the only child of Robert Dalglish, a Birmingham garage mechanic and chauffeur whose Scottish family had for generations been lithographers. At the age of twelve, and despite her strict father's opposition, Julie, accompanied by her mother Winifred, had successfully auditioned to dance on the West End stage in London. She left Birmingham with three other girls for six weeks of rehearsals for *Goody Two Shoes* before the performances began at Christmas, running until Easter 1938. Living with the group in west London, she passed the exams for the Royal Academy of Dancing and during the war was a member of a dance troupe, touring Britain's seaside resorts to entertain tourists and the military.

After the war, alternately using the stage names Josie or Julie Brett, she returned to London to work twice every night as the lead dancer in the cancan and other routines with Joe Loss's Big Band in Pigalle, a dinner and dancing nightclub off Piccadilly. Aged twenty, she fell in love with Bertram Scrase, an actor, dancer and singer who was married to Elaine, another dancer. For years, Bertram and Elaine had performed a tap routine across England as the White Aces, but that had ended with Elaine's pregnancy in 1944. In summer 1945, after his daughter's birth in Brighton, Bertram abandoned Elaine and headed for Blackpool. The White Aces resumed with Julie Dalglish, and Scrase never returned to his wife.

Julie had fallen for a professional womaniser whose charm,

stories and looks had seduced endless women. Performing with Bertram, she toured Britain until she became pregnant. In 1946, while travelling with him to Dublin, she gave birth to Michael. To Julie's fury, Elaine refused Bertram's request for a divorce.

Over the following years, troubled by Bertram's endless affairs, Julie left Michael with her parents in Birmingham and continued dancing in London. Although their relationship had disintegrated, she had a second son with Bertram in 1950. Some would say that Bertram had disappeared with another woman, while others suggested that Julie had met another man. Julie would say that her relationship with Bertram Scrase was 'disastrous', and to some she would add, 'It didn't work. I thought, "Why did I get into this marriage?"' Since she was professionally known as Julie Brett, some assumed she was married to 'Mr Brett'.

Amid the austerity of the post-war era, the simultaneous task of bringing up two children while still working to become a famous dancer was exhausting, not least because Bertram was financially unreliable and, having set up a new home with Dorothy, a waitress in Bognor Regis, had abandoned contact with his two sons. To avoid destitution, Julie left her boys with her mother in Birmingham while she continued to dance at the Pigalle. Every weekend she travelled by train to the Midlands, returning to London on Monday evenings.

During these journeys, Julie spotted Eric Cowell boarding her train at Northampton after his regular visit to Barratts' headquarters. One day, in 1954, he approached her in the dining car.

'Would you care for a drink with me?' he asked.

'It's my birthday,' she replied, 'so yes.'

It was the start, she would say, of 'a long, platonic relationship in London' which developed because she found him 'very interesting, well read and he had a sense of humour'.

By then, Eric's relationship with Jeanette was in trouble.

Although they had only just married, he had continued to conceal his past. Neither of his children had met his brothers, sister or his mother. Unhappy in his marriage, he abandoned Jeanette to pursue Julie, a more attractive woman.

Julie had every reason to succumb to a man offering a solid relationship. But he wanted more. Soon after they moved into a flat in Richmond, she came under pressure to have more children. 'I thought we had four between us and that was enough,' she said, 'but Eric delivered an ultimatum.' After successive miscarriages, a son was born in Brighton in 1958. Due to complications in the last stages of pregnancy, the child, registered as 'Stephen Cowell/Scarse', died three weeks later. The following year, on 7 October 1959, Simon Cowell was born in south London. His parents were unmarried, according to Julie, because 'I was scared.'

Soon after Simon's birth, Eric introduced Julie to his sixty-nine-year-old mother Esther. Unusually, she was invited to stay in their Richmond home at the same time as Winifred Dalglish.

'My mother's from Poland,' said Eric, without providing any more information.

'Eric's family is Jewish,' Winifred told her daughter during that visit.

'Do you think you're Jewish?' Julie challenged her partner.

'I could be,' Eric replied. 'I don't know,' and then added, 'No, I'm certainly not.'

Julie thought no more about it, but she did conclude that Eric's mother was 'awkward and frightening'.

In June 1961, Esther died and the chance of Eric's Jewish background being revealed during his lifetime receded. By then, Julie was again pregnant and wanted to regularise her status. After searching for a bigger home, Eric had bought an unmodernised three-bedroom house at 34 Barham Avenue in Elstree, north of London. In March 1961, their second son,

Nicholas, was born, although unusually his birth was only registered in June. Three months later, on 26 September, Jeanette obtained a divorce from Eric on the grounds of his adultery with 'Julie Brett', and, on 24 October, Eric and Julie were married at Caxton Hall in Westminster, later celebrating with friends at the Savoy. Although Julie registered her address as 28 Culross Street in central London, they had already moved to Barham Avenue, where Eric had opened an estate agency.

Amid the leafy suburbs, Eric and Julie buried much of their past. Thereafter, questions about their previous relationships were brushed aside. Determined to enjoy a happy marriage in a fun-loving atmosphere surrounded by dogs, they revealed little about their past to their six children.

Humorous, gentle and generous, Eric spoke only about his happy days as a major in India but never mentioned his childhood or first marriage. His two children with Jeanette were forbidden by their mother to meet Julie. Instead, they enjoyed excursions on Saturday afternoons to Battersea funfair and holidays alone with their father, unaware of his new family.

Similarly, Simon Cowell was not told about his grandparents' past, his father's childhood and religion, or about his uncles, aunts and cousins, who all lived near by. Nor did his mother reveal much about Bertram Scrase, although both sons, Michael and Tony, who had lived with their grandmother, moved into Barham Avenue. Having lost contact with Bertram, Tony regarded Eric as his father, but Michael resented his stepfather's discipline and eventually, after many arguments, left and broke all contact with his mother, only meeting his real father in 1971 after Bertram appeared on a television programme. At the end of his life, Bertram was calling numbers in a bingo hall. Details such as these were either unknown or not mentioned in the Cowells' home.

Only much later did Simon realise that his parents were

unmarried when he was born, but his family never discussed the adulterous relationships. Eric and Julie saw no reason to disrupt happy childhoods. For them, nothing was more important than giving their family a secure, happy home, which neither had provided in their previous relationships.

Soon after Nicholas's birth, Eric spotted Abbotsmead, an eight-bedroom ruin in Elstree. Since trading his own homes provided additional tax-free profits, he bought the run-down house with large grounds for £10,000, a considerable amount at the time. The renovation was completed just after Simon's second birthday, and the family adopted a luxurious lifestyle.

In the post-war boom, Eric's business was expanding and, to take advantage of rising property prices, he opened a new estate agency in central London. Leaving home in the mornings, he sped down the gravel drive in a convertible E-Type Jag, smoking a Havana cigar and leaving behind a gardener, cook and nanny to help Julie care for the four children and their friends. Although Eric was never seriously wealthy, he had sufficient money to host large Sunday family lunches, where Julie, theatrical and charming, could be heard calling everyone 'Darling' and approving of men who applied make-up to conceal blemishes. 'Your personal appearance makes a big difference,' Julie would say.

Not only was the large house buzzing with children and, later, grandchildren, but the Cowells enjoyed an increasingly full social life thanks to Gerry Blatner, their prized neighbour, who was the head of Warner Brothers studios in Elstree. The mogul, living close to Britain's principal film studios, enjoyed Eric's entertaining anecdotes and indulged Julie's showbiz passion by introducing her to visiting film stars and producers or those living temporarily in their community. Thanks to Blatner, the Cowells met Bette Davis, Trevor Howard and Robert Mitchum.

After working for twenty years in show business, Julie plunged into the semblance of a Hollywood lifestyle. She rarely appeared for breakfast in the morning without her face being fully made-up and would certainly never leave home without perfecting her appearance. An elegant dresser, she was thrilled when Eric bought her her first mink stole. 'Mummy looks like a poodle' was Simon's appreciative comment when Julie asked her four-year-old to admire her appearance before she left for another of Blatner's parties. Cowell adored his mother's theatricality and vanity, which some would endearingly call 'camp'. Posing for effect and addressing people as 'Darling' epitomised Julie's gospel about the importance of charming people, deflecting criticism and offering generous hospitality. Rudeness and aggression were unwelcome in the Cowell household, and the universal response to visitors was warmth. Professionally, Julie Cowell had craved attention, and she did the same socially. 'The stars soon became our friends and neighbours,' wrote Simon Cowell in a grossly exaggerated 2003 account of those childhood events, 'and whenever they were in town I got to rub shoulders with the cream of Hollywood, as long as I could squeeze my way past my mum . . .' The highlight for Cowell was sitting on Bette Davis's lap. Theatricality was Julie's oxygen and at an impressionable age it affected, even infected, her son. Life, he learned, was best when 'one was noticed'.

Among the famous neighbours was Stanley Kubrick, the film director and producer. He regularly pestered Eric to sell Abbotsmead, finally raising his offer to a price which Eric could not refuse. Since selling property was Eric's business, Julie reluctantly agreed and in turn was thrilled by his new purchase. The Warren, in Radlett, four miles from Elstree, was smaller but had potential for expansion and would subsequently be resold. Although they left Abbotsmead after just four years, they retained the relationships with Blatner and other film personalities and would meet, among others, Roger Moore, Elizabeth Taylor and Richard Burton – although not, as described in previous accounts, over their neighbouring fence.

The move to Radlett coincided with Simon and Nicholas leaving the local private prep school and starting at St Columba's boys' school in St Albans. Taught by monks in their robes, the decent men were bewildered by the Cowells' indiscipline. At home Simon dressed up as Captain Scarlet, while at school he behaved as if he was a master of the universe, fashioning his personality as a self-assured youth whose criteria for success would be to fail exams, an attitude fed by Eric's encouragement of a relaxed atmosphere in the house. No member of his family had gone to university and none of his children were under pressure to read or excel at school. Success would not be judged by scholastic achievement but by having fun and making money.

Resistant to diligent study, Simon was disruptive in class, enjoyed playing pranks on other schoolchildren and the teachers and, when reprimanded, relished challenging authority. To his teachers' fury, chastisement did not cause contrition but hilarity. The troublemaker, they realised, was an unashamed attention-seeker intent on disturbing the class. The punishment meted out involved Cowell hanging from the wall bars in the gymnasium, but the process merely encouraged his rebellion at school, which was a continuation of the mayhem at home.

Living in a permanently messy bedroom, Cowell's love of pranks was little short of anarchy: he had shaved the top of his younger brother's head so that his hair was styled like an inverted Mohican; after finding a Father Christmas outfit hidden at the top of the house, he had set fire to the beard and left it smouldering, which nearly caused a huge catastrophe; and he had held a toy pistol at a bus driver's head, ordering, 'Take me to Watford,' which ended in his temporary arrest after the terrified driver called the police. Nothing, however, equalled his reckless enjoyment of driving his father's cars down the drive and onto the road. Outraged by the boys' poor behaviour and lack of discipline, Julie frequently hit Simon, but his nonchalant disregard, amounting to subversion, infuriated her. 'It was a mental battle with a strong woman,' said Cowell. 'Always fractious.'

'I was the dragoness,' Julie later admitted. Her appeals to Eric were greeted with a smile. 'I nagged him, "Have you done something?" But he usually didn't.' At moments of crisis, she would wait anxiously for Eric's return home, give him a gin and tonic and, when he had 'settled in', say, 'The boys are playing up.'

'I'll take care of it,' Eric would reply quietly before going upstairs. Invariably, his sons were listening to a Beatles LP. 'Tell your mother I gave you a jolly good rollicking,' he would say to his smiling children. After closing their bedroom door, he would report sternly that he had 'read them the riot act' and, sipping his gin, resume the *Daily Telegraph* crossword. Twenty years later, he confessed to his ruse.

'I was', Simon would admit, 'outspoken, obnoxious, cheeky and bored very easily. A strong-willed little brat.' He was shaped by his teachers' universal criticism of his arrogance and inadequacies. 'Giving lip' at school and at home was his revenge for his humiliation by the teachers' caustic put-downs, accompanied by their stares, threats, silences, contempt, ridicule, scoffs, mock disbelief and jokes at his expense. Gradually, he absorbed their performance as a model for delivering his own snap judgements of friends.

His emotional survival depended upon cultivating a sense of superiority over those who mocked him. 'I have an absolute hatred of losing,' he later admitted. 'Even losing at Monopoly as a kid. I just want to beat the competition.' Aggravated by his imminent humiliation, he would tip the Monopoly board over the moment he sensed defeat, rather than concede gracefully. Cowell would describe that behaviour as 'competitiveness'; others would say he was shamelessly spoiled.

An intelligent boy, he was frustrated by his academic failure and inability to find a remedy. Frequently, he avoided school by faking illness, sometimes placing a hot teapot on his forehead. Those who would later mock his 'Mummy, look at me!' attention-seeking could not pinpoint the characteristic underlying the son's relationship with his mother, except that her critical love gave him unusual, even unjustified, self-confidence.

New wealth allowed Eric to indulge his children. Through contacts, he was appointed in the late 1960s as a director of EMI music corporation, with responsibility for its property portfolio, a task similar to the one he had undertaken for Barratts. After selling his estate agency, he flourished on a high salary and good expenses. His children were spoiled by regular excursions to fairs and historic sites, and holidays in Spain, which at the time was unusual for English families. He bought a debenture on box 60 at the Ascot race course to entertain his friends and family on Saturdays, and encouraged his sons to miss school for big races during Royal Ascot week.

While delighted by the constant improvement in her fortunes, Julie forbade Eric to give her sons pocket money. Accustomed to earning her living as a teenager, she insisted that 'They should earn their own money.' Simon regularly washed neighbours' cars and windows, looked after their children and mowed their lawns. During holidays he picked up stones at a local farm and worked in a shop. Before he reached his teens, his sole ambition was 'to get rich'.

Although his sons could have progressed to the senior school, St Columba's Sacred Heart, Eric decided to move. He had received a good offer for the house in Radlett and bought a house about thirty miles south in Fulmer, near Maidenhead. Simon, aged twelve, and his brother were enrolled at the local Licensed Victuallers' School established for the children of publicans.

'It's really bad,' Simon told his parents in a rare observation about the quality of his education. His parents were unconcerned. Instead, they encouraged their sons to have fun. A self-contained flat within the new house was assigned to the two young boys and became the centre of their school friends' social life. There they played records, drank and smoked, and many attractive girls, including Paula Hamilton, a future model, drifted into the flat after school.

One year later, Eric realised his mistake and, on the recommendation of a friend, immediately transferred Nicholas to Dover College, a traditional boarding school in the Channel port. Nicholas's messages to his parents were not encouraging. 'It's dreadful. Awful,' he wrote. The school's strict regime included fagging, whereby the older boys expected him to do their cleaning and worse. Even George Matthews, his house master, described the seventy-five borders as living 'crushed like rats in small cages'.

Forewarned by his brother, Simon arrived later with the single ambition to leave the oppressive environment as soon as possible. He joined no clubs, played no sport and disliked the drab grey herringbone uniform. Having learned that the school motto, '*Non recuso laborem*,' meant 'I shun no work,' the only Latin he perfected was the opposite, '*Recuso semper laborem*,' 'I always shun work.' His behaviour won him just two admirers among the staff: the matron and George Matthews's wife.

'I couldn't bear the discipline and the boredom,' he said. 'I just wanted to get out and earn money.' In a letter home he wrote, 'Dear Mum and Dad, I hope you're happy to finally have got rid of me. I also hope you're happy in your centrally heated warm house and you have a lot to eat. Because I am lying in a dormitory which has icicles on the inside, and there's nothing to eat. I'm freezing cold and hungry. I hope you're finally satisfied.' In reply, he received two letters. The long one from his mother encouraged her son to study and remember his father's sacrifice in paying the school fees. The thinner letter from his father in an EMI envelope included a £50 note. The response encouraged Simon to send regular complaints and await the identical replies to finance his frequent forays to the local pub to drink and, particularly, to smoke.

By then, he had identified Mickie Most, a judge of a television talent competition called *New Faces*, as his hero. In the programme, Most, a record producer who counted The Animals, Herman's Hermits and Donovan among the successes on his own record label, joined other famous producers and singers to judge the performance of young artists auditioning in the studio. Unlike *Opportunity Knocks*, another television talent competition in which the audience decided which acts would progress to the next round, the contestants on *New Faces* relied on the panel's decisions. It was the humiliation meted out by the judges rather than the contestants' music that excited Cowell, and Most ranked among the most acerbically judgemental. Pertinently, Cowell was not particularly interested in the deluge of original songs produced in the 1960s and 1970s. Occasionally he went to concerts, and he often played records, but his favourite preoccupation at the end of every school day was smoking with friends and, on Sunday evenings, expressing his dread of going back to school the following day. At sixteen, in the weeks before taking O levels, the first public examinations which would determine his fate, he was never seen studying.

After taking the exams, Cowell's popularity and unauthorised presence in the pub prompted George Matthews to suspend the unruly boy for the last two weeks of the summer term. 'I did him a favour, I suppose,' Matthews later realised. 'Sending him home was the opposite of punishment.' Matthews recommended that he did not return for A levels. Unlike other pupils who would obtain high grades in eight or nine O levels, Cowell passed just two at the lowest grades. He was unconcerned. Content, he returned home, albeit to a new house.

Eric had completed another sale and repurchase, and the family moved into a new mock Edwardian house in nearby Pinkneys

Green which had been abandoned in mid-development by a bankrupt builder. After the construction work was completed, Eric intended to resell the house. Simon was enrolled at Windsor Technical College to resit his exams and eventually obtained three basic passes. His only achievement at the college was meeting Debbie Spears, his first serious girlfriend. At seventeen, he fell in love and during their eighteen-month relationship lost his virginity. The affair ended, he said, when he found her kissing a tutor at a party. The following day he telephoned her. 'Can I have my crash helmet back?' he asked. But the more serious challenge was to decide upon a career.

Regardless of his academic failure, Eric indulged his son. He was allowed to drive the family car, with the promise of a car of his own in the near future, and he was given ample food and clothes and taken every weekend for a family lunch to a local Indian restaurant. Only occasionally did Eric mention to his son his grim career prospects. After disastrous employment as a waiter and another job at the local Brillo factory, Cowell spent his days at home in some despair. Isolated from regular routine, he became a loner, spending his days reading *The Beano*, *The Hotspur* and other boys' comics, interspersed by the odd Flashman book, the adventures of a ruthless cad.

'With no qualifications and no talents', he admitted, 'my prospects were poor.' Encouraged by Julie to work, he found menial work at a warehouse and invited the boy who was driving the forklift truck home. Over dinner they compared their family lives. 'I never realised how lucky I am,' Cowell admitted afterwards. 'I've taken a lot for granted.' His next job was working behind the counter of Laskys, a hi-fi shop on London's Tottenham Court Road. The only 'buzz', he volunteered, was getting the pay cheque at the end of the week: 'I love getting money. I want to make money. Real money. Pocket money isn't enough. I want to be rich.'

Good-humouredly, Eric suggested his son become a quantity surveyor and follow him into the property business. With Cowell's poor O levels, that was a forlorn suggestion. Next, Eric drove his son to a building site in Birmingham. After walking for two hours in rubble and mud, the seventeen-year-old exploded, 'Are you completely mad?' and insisted they return to London. Eric next used his contacts to arrange interviews for his son as a management trainee at Tesco and a civil servant. Both ended in disaster because of Cowell's refusal to consider working in a structured environment. He returned home defeated but still buoyant. Despite his plight, he indulged his sole talent – entertaining his friends at parties – using his charm and good looks to attract girls. 'I lost my virginity to Simon Cowell,' Paula Hamilton admitted. 'He was very, very protective of me and he was funny and rebellious.'

Exasperated by her son's luxury-seeking lifestyle, Julie urged Eric to use his influence again. Finally, even Cowell realised that the offer engineered by his father of working in EMI's post room for £25 per week could not be rejected. 'I'll work my way up,' he promised.

'Always be polite and charming to people,' Julie urged on his first day in 1976. 'Manners maketh the man. They cost nothing. Courtesy is the hallmark of the civilised.' Eric, by then his best friend, added his own wisdom: 'Everyone you work with has an invisible sign on their head which says, "Make me feel important." Be polite to everyone.'

Delivering the post to offices occupied by energetic young men and women pursuing ambitions denied to himself was humiliating. His fleeting appearances were casually accepted and swiftly forgotten. At the bottom of the chain, he regularly pushed a cart along the pavement from EMI's headquarters in Charing Cross Road to a subsidiary in Dean Street, Soho. During those turgid months, there was one memorable moment: after entering the building, a youth his own age made a derogatory comment about the 'post boy pushing the trolley'. Cowell was stung. The glib remark highlighted his failure. Protected from poverty and worthlessness by his parents' safety net, he had been taught to conceal his feelings. The daily drudgery was Cowell's Rubicon, the moment of epiphany when he realised the consequence of his indiscipline. But now he silently pledged, 'Right, I'll show you.' In that cathartic moment he finally shed all traces of obnoxious behaviour and became ambitious overnight. He changed his appearance and manner to assimilate the culture at EMI. Holding his cigarette at head height, he started to address people as 'Darling', began wearing V-neck T-shirts cut to show more skin and had his long hair permed. His vanity was no longer only to attract girls but also to become part of the music world. He bought a crude sun lamp but, frustrated by the slow progress to become tanned, remained in front of the light longer than recommended, and without safety goggles. Soon he was screaming in agony. He was rushed to hospital with burnt eyes by his mother, who feared during the week his eyes were covered in bandages that his sight could be damaged. Vanity had triumphed where all the teachers' reprimands had failed.

Life outside the post room had improved. His brother Nicholas, prospering in a position his father had arranged as a junior in an estate agency, had moved into an empty flat in North Audley Street, Mayfair, loaned to him by a friend. Simon followed him there and the duo enjoyed evenings at Samantha's, a club in New Burlington Street, and threw parties in the flat. His new girlfriend, Lee Watts, a skinny elfin, was the victim when Paula Hamilton arrived in a jealous fit. 'She's gorgeous but crazy,' Cowell told his brother in the aftermath of a bitter argument.

Two weeks later, Cowell returned to live with his parents. While supporting him financially, Eric became exasperated by his son's careless driving. The speed nut repeatedly crashed his father's cars. Once he drove through the central reservation on a dual carriageway in Maidenhead – 'Simon swerved and saved my life,' Nick was ordered to say – and soon after he took his father's new Rover and again crashed at top speed. To disguise his culpability, he positioned the car against the wall of the family's house to make it seem that Julie had forgotten to apply the handbrake and watched, without comment, as Eric admonished his bewildered wife. After more scrapes and dents, in a bid to protect his own car Eric bought his son an old Citroën, followed soon after by a Lancia convertible. Like all Cowell's cars, the floor was soon covered with discarded cigarette packets, beer bottles and sweet wrappers, reflecting his unruly existence.

After eighteen months in the post room, Cowell confidently applied for promotion, hoping to work for a record label. He was abruptly rejected. He lacked any knowledge about music, he was told, a judgement he could not deny. His personal record collection was limited to The Beatles, The Rolling Stones and other mainstream groups, and he never attended gigs or concerts. Frustrated, he left EMI and, with the help of his cousin Malcolm Christopher, a production manager, was employed as a runner on a TV series being shot at Elstree for £15 a week. 'I was a slave to everyone,' he said. 'Whatever I was asked, I'd say "yes" and did it.' Once the production was completed, his cousin arranged another job for him as a runner, this time on Stanley Kubrick's *The Shining*. Days later, he was told that Kubrick didn't want runners. Unemployed, he asked Eric to intercede. His father telephoned Kubrick and reminded him about the house sale. 'Why didn't you offer my son a job?' he asked. Kubrick relented, but just then another string pulled by Eric produced a better prospect.

Eric was friendly with Ron White, the head of EMI's music-publishing division. At the heart of the music business, the record companies maximised their income by licensing the copyright of popular songs and music to artists. White offered Cowell an opportunity to begin a solid career but, just when all seemed set, he disappeared to Australia and Cowell was again sitting unemployed at home in Englefield Green, their latest home, near Maidstone.

Devoid of ideas, Cowell was impressed by his brother's fate. After just two years, Nicholas was earning £250 per week, driving a company car and had bought a flat. Reluctantly, Simon asked his father to arrange a job for him in the property business. Once again, Eric drew on his contacts, and his son was employed in the shops department of Hillier Parker, a leading firm of London estate agents. Within hours of his first day, Cowell had realised his mistake. 'They're toffee-nosed public-school twits,' he told Nicholas. Having been dispatched to compose a list of all the shops along Oxford Street, Cowell confessed his misery to his parents at the end of the first day.

'I want to work in music,' he said.

'I know you're unhappy,' said Julie, 'but you must give it time and settle in.'

However, Cowell insisted on resigning immediately.

'I don't think that's a good idea, but you must be happy in what you do,' said Eric, firmly establishing himself as the bigger influence. Unlike Julie, who was upset about her son's poor school record and directionless life, Eric offered solutions and uncomplicated advice. Cowell agreed to stay for another three months, continuously confiding to Eric about 'my screw-ups'. At the end of that period, Cowell was once again unemployed and sitting in his family home considering his future.

'He looks crestfallen,' Julie told Eric.

2

Rise and Fall

Unemployment did not dent Cowell's enjoyment of clubs, dancing and girls. On 15 May 1982, he went with Mel Medalie, a music producer, and others to Morton's, an expensive Mayfair club. Cowell was Medalie's unpaid runner, and was hoping for a paid job. Glancing across the room he spotted Jackie St Clair, a stunning young woman famous, he would later discover, for posing nude in top-shelf magazines.

Handsome, charming and persistent, he persuaded Medalie to make an introduction and later persuaded St Clair to come for dinner at Rags, a private members club in Chesterfield Street, Mayfair. Without money, he relied on his father arranging that he could sign the bill as a member. The beautiful Miss Nude UK was unimpressed, especially with his insistence that she eat some peanuts. 'I'm allergic,' she hissed, throwing the bowl in his face. Although she was 'too expensive for me', as he told his brother Nick, there was finally a brief affair. St Clair, however, preferred men who did not rely on their fathers to pay the bill.

While Julie lamented her son's unemployment, he spent the weekends with his brother and a gang of friends drinking and picking up girls in London's cheaper clubs, including Peppermint Park, Dial 9, Pizza Pomodoro and the Hippodrome. Simon and Nicholas would be sent to 'pull the girls' from the bar or the dance floor, while the others ordered champagne and Amaretto for their table. 'Young guys operating' was Nicholas's description of a group 'working and playing hard'. From there, they often headed at Nick's suggestion to lap-dancing clubs. Initially, they enjoyed For Your Eyes Only in Hammersmith, and then moved to Stringfellows in Covent Garden. To some, lap dancing was vulgar, but in Cowell's eyes it was fun wrapped up with a flash of showbiz, and his life's purpose was enjoyment.

Cowell's forlorn days at his parents' home temporarily ended after Ron White, the head of EMI's music-publishing division, unexpectedly returned from Australia. At Eric's behest, White summoned Cowell for an interview. 'It doesn't mean you'll get the job,' warned Julie as her son, dressed in a suit for once, returned home wracked by nerves. 'I'd give my right arm to get back into the music business,' he admitted. At 8 p.m., White called. 'You've got the job.'

Eric Cowell's advice on the eve of Simon's first day was unexceptional: 'Spot people who can teach you and stick to those you can learn from.' Unexpectedly, his son would follow that suggestion scrupulously for the next thirty years.

Excitedly, Cowell returned to EMI. To his horror, he was greeted by silence. Everyone knew that Eric had fixed the appointment for his unqualified son. Undeterred by the hostility, Cowell relied on his immediate supervisor, Ellis Rich, who bore no resentment, to explain his task. 'Search through the catalogues of music owned by EMI,' he was told, 'and match suitable songs to popular singers. Then persuade their agents during personal visits to use EMI's music.'

Cowell finally discovered his undoubted talent. Personable and entertaining, he ingratiated himself by following Eric's advice: 'In business always make sure that you make the other person feel important. Always shake hands and say "hello".' Easy in conversation and charmingly polite, he formed solid relationships with agents but was irked by all the A&R – Artists and Repertoire – men who scoured pubs, basement gigs and concerts across Britain for new talent. 'The biggest arseholes in the music business,' Cowell declared, identifying the gulf between himself and genuine music aficionados. Those pursuing art in music, he scoffed, were 'snobs'. Unaccustomed to diligent, methodical research and also to their bravura, he disliked the A&R men's self-importance after signing new clients. The middle-class interloper also felt alienated by their drug-infested lifestyle. 'I'm bored by them,' he told friends about a combative clique that brassily supervised their artists' careers by choosing producers, finding new songs and overseeing recordings.

Unable to conform, Cowell was attracted after a year to Ellis Rich's suggestion that they leave EMI and set up their own music-publishing business to 'make a lot of money'. Without first securing a commitment from songwriters, they left EMI, rented an office in Soho Square and began operating as E&S Music. 'Within a day of moving into our new offices,' Cowell admitted, 'I realised I had made a big mistake. We didn't have the funding to do it properly. We couldn't get the business off the ground, and many of the fundamentals of running an independent business were foreign to us.' Without telling Rich, Cowell asked Ron White whether he could return. 'No,' replied White. 'I was going to groom you for the top, but you've betrayed my trust.'

Moaning that he had been misled, over the following months Cowell persisted with Rich in developing the business in Britain and America. A doomed visit to Los Angeles incited him to blame Rich for the disaster, and relations between the two men deteriorated. 'When you're young you're paranoid,' Cowell later reflected. 'I was jumpy, insecure and worried. It was not a good time.' Their finances were going downhill. The upside was being on a steep learning curve about the music business. 'It's amazing,' he told his father. 'The bits of plastic cost fifty pence to make and you can sell them for £8.'

Making and selling, he decided, was more lucrative. In 1983, after a year of arguments, he left Rich. Much later, he conceded, 'Ellis was right. Publishing is a long, slow business which he understood. I would have earned millions, much more than I've got now, if I had stayed. The money was in music publishing and back catalogues. Ellis was disappointed that I didn't stick with him.'

That was not quite the recollection of E&S Music's landlord at 46 South Molton Street, Iain Burton, the sharp and ambitious owner of Ferroway Ltd, a music-production company whose own offices were in the same building. They had first met when Cowell, dressed in hot pants, had arrived on rollerblades at Burton's West End office with Mandy Perryment, an actress, and Simon's brother Nicholas, her close friend.

Although he was seven years older, Burton had become part of the weekend gang that included Nicholas Cowell, who by then was earning about £2,000 a month selling luxury properties in north-west London. Together they toured the clubs, drinking and looking for girls. Eager to be known as the 'Crazy Gang', the Cowell brothers liked impressing other clubbers, although the bill was often paid by Burton, who at the end of the night would invite everyone back to his penthouse in Onslow Gardens, Kensington.

Burton, a former dancer, had broken into the music business producing *Keep in Shape System* (*KISS*), a fitness instruction video starring Arlene Phillips, the choreographer of dance troupe Hot Gossip. Based on Jane Fonda's series of videos, Burton claimed to have sold half a million tapes of the attractive woman dressed in a body-hugging Lycra suit to the first generation of keep-fit enthusiasts. Astute and hard-working, he combined generosity to his staff with a determination not to allow anyone other than himself and his partner Stephen Goldberg to earn a profit from his deals.

Burton watched as E&S Music floundered and spent time with Cowell during his return to the wilderness searching for work. In that forlorn period, he became Cowell's inseparable best friend. 'He was ultra-confident, very funny and super-charming' was Burton's sentiment. Besides a shared interest in pop music and girls, he recognised a kindred spirit in Cowell. 'In those days', he recalled, 'none of us had any problem with being a little camp.' During one of the Cowells' Sunday lunches, he was persuaded by Eric to offer Cowell a job selling books published by Fanfare, a subsidiary of Ferroway, and also exploring how he could develop Fanfare Records, Burton's fledgling music label.

Burton allocated a desk in his office to Cowell, who worked for about £10,000 per annum as he learned the business and found new artists. 'An amazing break,' gushed Cowell, acknowledging his debt after being rescued from 'the bottom of the heap'. On reflection he acknowledged, 'From the post room up, the first fifteen years in the entertainment industry was about learning. I always worked on the basis of being patient and if you work hard it will come to you.' At twenty-six, he could finally afford to move out of his parents' home and rent a flat in Fulham. But he left reluctantly: 'I liked my bedroom and I liked the house.' He took with him a well-read copy of the *Guinness Book of British Hit Singles*.

Burton had already signed a deal to sell Rondò Veneziano, a successful Italian orchestra that played a fusion of contemporary and baroque music. On Burton's instructions, Cowell hired Nigel Wright, a young studio producer who was fast and imaginative, to supervise a remix. 'Get the music played on TV,' Burton told Cowell, aware of how television boosted sales. Cowell endlessly and unsuccessfully harassed television producers to use Rondo's music. 'Don't take "no" for an answer,' Burton told his disorganised employee. 'Keep trying until you get it.' In Burton's opinion, he was mentoring his best friend and junior. 'Watch and listen to me,' he told Cowell. 'Sit opposite me and learn from what I do.'

Eventually, Cowell heard that *Crossroads*, the TV soap, was to be set in Venice for one week, and he successfully harassed the show's producer to use Rondò Veneziano's 'Venezia 2000' as the theme music for that week. On the back of that, over 100,000 albums were sold. Thereafter, Fanfare was always profitable. Only commercial music, Burton decided, was worth promoting. 'What's the next fad going to be?' Cowell asked Nigel Wright, a question he would repeat endlessly.

In the quest for profits, in early 1982 Cowell visited Fairlight, a German laboratory specialising in manufacturing sounds. Among their products was a dog barking a song in tune. 'I think I can make this a hit,' said Cowell. Back in England, with help he turned the Fairlight sound into 'Ruff Mix', sung by Snap, the Wonder Dog. To promote the single, he targeted the producers of the BBC's *Top of the Pops*, television's most important pop-music programme. The wheeze, he explained, would feature a 'singer' dressed in a dog's outfit miming 'Snap's song'. The producers fell for the novelty and the valuable slot was secured for early September. Gung-ho, Cowell arrived at the BBC's studios to discover his 'singer' slumped by several empty beer bottles. 'I'm not doing it,' he slurred. To save the slot, Cowell drank a couple of beers to give himself courage, dressed as the dog and told the producer, 'I'll do the act.'

'Walk onto the stage,' he was told by the studio manager, 'turn left, then turn right and walk past the camera to the middle and then sit down.' On cue, Cowell stumbled across the floor, fell over children in the audience and unsteadily sat down by a table as the single was played. After a chaotic mime, he staggered off the studio floor and was told, 'You're banned for life.' Unfazed, he anticipated earning 'a fortune' from the record and a TV series.

To boost sales, he had commissioned Hanna-Barbera, the animation studio, to draw a cartoon for the album's cover. Days after the record's release, Disney threatened legal proceedings because the cover was a copy of a Disney design. The successful launch was curtailed and the album was withdrawn, but Cowell's legacy in the music industry was fixed. He now inhabited his own world. His weakness was his personal poverty. Unable to earn enough money, he still depended on his father.

To survive, most players in the music business attempted to profit from the current fashion, and at the time some of the best money was earned from subversive, violent rock music. Unlike the traditional A&R men racing between six gigs every night, Cowell could not nurture personal relationships with the opinionated, druggy rock groups performing in bars and clubs. Although he rebelled at school, he sympathised with his family's genteel lifestyle rather than the rockers' cultural resentment. Fanfare also lacked the finance to promote successors to The Beatles and the Stones. Stuck on the fringe, looking for a break to earn money rather than create art, his good fortune was an introduction made by his brother. Sharing a flat in Chilton Street with a friend, Nicholas was dating a Welsh ballerina, while his flatmate was going out with Sinitta, an eighteen-year-old aspiring dancer and the dusky daughter of Michael 'Miquel' Brown, a well-known Canadian singer. During the affair, Sinitta had appeared as a dancer on TV and once in a West End musical. Occasionally she drank and danced at the clubs visited by the Cowell brothers and was invited to spend weekends at the Cowell family home.

In 1982, after Eric had retired and moved with Julie to Majorca, Sinitta travelled as Nick's girlfriend to the island for a holiday. Shortly after, and not for the last time, Simon inherited one of Nick's cast-offs. 'It's their naughty face which attracts me,' Cowell said about girls with dark skin. He had first dated one at the Licensed Victuallers' School.

In late 1984, after another family holiday in Spain, Sinitta suggested to Cowell that he should listen to her recording of 'So Macho', which had been written by George Hargreaves. Excited by the music and with nothing else in prospect, Cowell offered her a contract. Just then, Burton telephoned to announce that he was pulling out of Sinitta's record to invest his money in a new project. 'I'm begging you,' implored Cowell, 'please don't close this down. Just give me some money and I'll make this record a hit.' Burton, proud of his reputation of 'nailing' his commercial adversaries 'to the floor', relented and gave Cowell £5,000. 'But that's it. Final,' he warned.

By industry standards, it was a pitiful amount. The following day, Cowell started the weary routine of touring all the radio producers in a bid to get airtime for his new artist. Despite being welcomed for his charm and humour, the record was universally rejected as falling outside mainstream pop. His only hope was to target gay men at a time when homosexuality was only legal between consenting adults meeting privately.

To understand the gay market and its twilight dance clubs, Cowell met with Ian Levine, an overt homosexual whose successful career in disco music took off after he left school in 1975 and discovered and promoted Evelyn Thomas, a soul singer from Chicago. Thomas's first record, in 1976, had been a modest success. Next, Levine wrote and produced Michael 'Miquel' Brown's hit song 'So Many Men, So Little Time', a song about a woman sleeping with countless men and waking in the morning unaware of the name of the person sharing her bed. Initially, Brown's record appealed uniquely to the gay community in North America, and especially New York, and then spread to gay dance clubs in the north of England. Levine's challenge was to persuade Radio 1 producers in London to overcome their prejudice against gay music and the north. Real success, however, depended on achieving 'the crossover': when a record which was popular among gays but unknown to mainstream music fans was suddenly demanded by heterosexuals in record shops across the country. If those sales were sufficiently high, the record would rise in the commercial record charts and automatically be played on Radio 1. 'So Many Men, So Little Time' achieved the crossover and became a major hit.

Cowell needed to understand how Levine had scored the rare jackpot which eluded so many producers. He found the producer working at Record Shack, a shop selling imported American gay records in Berwick Street, Soho. Levine's was a familiar story in the music business. At the height of his success in 1979, he had been crushed by catastrophic financial problems. Scarred by the experience, he began working behind a shop counter, but on Saturday nights he was the principal DJ at Heaven, a gay club near Charing Cross station. Every weekend, over 2,000 men packed the place and danced frantically until daybreak. In that small community, Levine had become influential by importing ideas from the Sanctuary club in New York. In particular, he mixed music between turntables and promoted the sale of records through Radio Shack. In 1983, he used his influence at Heaven and Radio Shack to promote his own record, 'Taking It Straight', which went on to sell 2 million copies in Britain, France and America. For the second time, he had achieved the crossover.

Cowell walked into Record Shack and introduced himself. Wearing a V-neck white T-shirt exposing his hairy chest and high-waisted red trousers, Cowell asked Levine to play Sinitta's 'So Macho' at Heaven and produce a record with Arlene Phillips and Hot Gossip singing 'Break Me into Little Pieces'. Sinitta, he added, should be included in the group.

After an hour's rehearsal at a recording studio, Levine booked Leroy Osbourne, a black man with a voice like Marvin Gaye, as the lead singer. Cowell arrived to watch Levine mix the tracks at the Trident studios in Wardour Street. Normally, Levine would need four hours for a mix, but Cowell's interference prolonged the process. 'That's fabulous, darling, but . . .' Cowell sighed, urging more drums, bass or vocals, each suggestion cancelling the previous 'improvement'. 'I'm pulling my hair out,' screamed Levine as he reached for another Kool cigarette, an American menthol brand bought by his parents. As Cowell introduced himself to them – it was never clear whether the attraction was the taste or the name – he urged Levine, 'Darling, can we have a bit more treble . . .' Fourteen hours later, the mix was completed but, despite Levine's efforts at Heaven, the record flopped. Eventually, the losses were mitigated by its use in a Japanese advertisement.

Failure did not dent Cowell's self-confidence nor his trust in Levine, whom he embraced as 'hilarious, conceited and very talented'. On the next occasion, Cowell entered Record Shack with his chest shaved. 'Don't you think it's more defined?' he asked. To Levine, Cowell appeared as 'a camp, silly, indecisive record executive who was catty and judgemental', yet they often spent time together at a Japanese restaurant near Cowell's office. During those meals in South Molton Street, Levine suggested that Cowell revive the black disco music popular in the 1970s using James and Susan Wells, an American brother-and-sister duo. 'They're great,' said Levine. 'You sign them up, I'll make the records.' Cowell arranged for the two to fly to London, and during 1984 Levine recorded three records: 'RSVP', 'Mirror Image' and 'No Care for Me'. With Levine's help, all were successful in the gay clubs but none reached the charts. 'Everything Levine's producing is hot,' Cowell realised, 'but we're not making any money.'

Sitting in his office, gazing at a large mirror on the wall – a gift from Sinitta, who had adorned the top with an inscription: 'Yes, Simon darling, you look beautiful' – Cowell contemplated how to copy Levine's recent successful crossover launches. Sensitive to the taste of gay men at Heaven, Levine had noticed that dancers now wanted music with more beats per minute than normal disco records. In the underground, even the term 'disco' had been ditched in favour of 'Boytown'. Levine had redefined the gay market by recording Evelyn Thomas's up-tempo 'High Energy'. Played by DJs in gay clubs across the US and Europe, the new release achieved the crossover, hitting number one in some charts and selling over 5 million copies across the world.

Thomas's success coincided with another hit, 'Whatever I Do', sung by Hazell Dean and produced by Pete Waterman. A hugely talented but still unrecognised producer, Waterman's next record was 'You Think You're a Man' by Divine, a drag queen with a huge following among gay and transvestite clubbers in America. 'For a man who started his career eating dog shit,' *Melody Maker* commented about the singer, 'this record is a step in the right direction.' Like Levine, Waterman's formula matched Cowell's ambitions. 'I'm aiming for the gay market,' he later told Cowell, 'because we can't afford to go anywhere else.' Without any money for promotion, and occasionally not even for a pint of beer, the producer told Cowell, 'It's a market where money can still be made if a massive hit in the underground creeps into the mainstream in the bigger shops.'

They had first met when Cowell, employed by EMI, visited Waterman's primitive studio in Camden, north London, and then later in Waterman's studio at the rear of the Marquee club in Dean Street, Soho. Waterman's skill, Cowell recognised, was not just 'like a DJ at a wedding, always knowing what music people wanted to dance to'; with his two partners, Mike Stock and Matt Aitken, he also possessed all the talent required to produce pop music. Combined, they could write songs, master the technical wizardry in the studio and promote their records perfectly. By 1984, after Waterman had built a modern studio off Marshalsea Road in south London, Cowell acknowledged Waterman 'as my point of contact. He knew what a song should sound like. We had a lot in common.' Pop music, Waterman told his admirers, was difficult to write. 'Either it's pure sugar or it's under-colour. And both are not liked.'

Fascinated by Waterman's challenge to the A&R snobs and the major record labels, Cowell relished an anti-hero who was neither fashionable nor cared what people thought, an unusual combination in show business. Clutching Sinitta's twelve-inch single, Cowell sought Waterman's opinion about 'So Macho'. 'You've got a hit,' said Waterman generously. 'She can chirrup a tune.'

'Would you do the follow-up?' asked Cowell.

'I'm too busy,' replied Waterman.

'Doing what?' asked Cowell cheekily.

Since his fate depended on making Sinitta a star, and remembering Iain Burton's mantra 'Never take no for an answer', he returned twice every week to Waterman's studios to watch the recording sessions, learn about the business and meet his rivals. 'I followed Waterman around like a dog,' admitted Cowell. Rushing through his offices, Waterman saw a man who was 'ambitious and great fun'. He also described him as infatuated by Sinitta and 'the most stylised human I'd ever met. Always the same hair, wearing a singlet and carrying cigarettes. He was always the same.' Behind the smile, Cowell was aggressively absorbing Waterman's promotional techniques. 'Music is showbiz,' Cowell was told. 'People steal your lines. Do the same.'

Nearly every weekend, from Friday until Monday night, Waterman drove Hazell Dean to five gigs a night in Mecca halls and private gay clubs across the north of England. Racing between the venues – starting at 9 p.m. in Hull, on the east coast, and ending at 2 a.m. in Liverpool, on the west coast – Waterman dived into grimy premises fearing that his car might be gone by the time he emerged. In that closed shop, the club owners and DJs, who never paid, believed they were doing the promoters a favour. 'They have to like you,' Waterman told Cowell, knowing that even charm could occasionally fail to win over the bouncers on the door. Once inside, Dean either sang to a backing track or mimed to the record if the club had no microphone. 'It's all frontier stuff,' Waterman told Cowell.

Financed by Iain Burton's credit card, Cowell regularly drove Sinitta to club gigs in Blackpool, Barnsley, Newcastle, Edinburgh and Birmingham, popping into regional radio stations during the day. Between stops, he called from telephone boxes to confirm the arrangements and book a damp bed in a run-down hotel. Copying Waterman and also posing as 'Disco Duck', a talent scout for a music magazine, he checked specialist shops in Soho daily to see whether a new trend had emerged, if any imported records were selling well and whether Fanfare could buy the rights. The drudgery was depressing but the alternative was unemployment.

In early 1985, Cowell's frustrations grew. A second launch for 'So Macho' had seen it enter the charts at number forty, only to stall and crash. 'Why aren't the kids interested?' he asked Waterman. 'The market is not stupid,' replied the producer, delivering the scripture. 'Gays like a particular type of music but don't want a badge put on it. You can't make a gay record and say it's gay. You must make a record for the market and be serious about it.' Cowell nodded.

'He wants to be the most famous man in the universe,' Waterman told an assistant. 'But he's shambolic, indecisive and not focused, except on fame. He doesn't know how to get there.'

Aware of Waterman's criticism, Cowell pledged to prove him wrong by obeying another of Waterman's homilies: 'You can hype a record if it's got legs. You can give it longer legs if it's stuck between forty and fifty in the charts by remixing it to give it a boost. But then you need radio or TV play to get real sales.' To improve Sinitta's record, Cowell spent the last pounds of Burton's budget on a third remix, commissioned a video to excite teenagers for £1,500 – a paltry sum compared to the slick American videos costing $1 million – and hired a plugger to get the record played on Radio 1. Cowell and the plugger waited for an hour to see the Radio 1 producer. The record was placed on the turntable. Ten seconds later, the producer said, 'No,' and bid the two men farewell. The station's institutional hostility towards pop music was reaffirmed.

'My records don't fit,' Cowell lamented, wondering just how a producer could get a record played on Radio 1. Some believed American-style payola operated within the station, with DJs pocketing wads of cash. To reach the radio producers, Cowell began inviting their secretaries for lunch and to nightclubs, only to discover that British payola amounted to giving the producers dinner with good wine. 'You had to play by the BBC's rules,' he accepted, but since there was only one producer on *Top of the Pops* and one on each Radio 1 programme, everyone was entertaining the same people and his 'soft bribery' failed.

The irritation was watching others' success, in particular that of Tom Watkins, a brash gay record producer who had become the manager of the Pet Shop Boys in 1985. Later that year, Watkins negotiated the re-release of 'West End Girls', a record popular in gay clubs in America and Britain. By the end of the year, Watkins had achieved the crossover and the record was number one across the world. Capitalising on his new wealth, Watkins rebuilt a large house with a swimming pool in Holland Park, began hosting riotous parties for boys and spoke about the 'knack of the gay market'. That was the elusive magic Cowell was seeking.

Having criss-crossed northern England and financed two remixes, Cowell was 'desperate'. Burton had declared that Fanfare was unable to pay its bills, making 'So Macho' a 'life or death issue'. Even getting a play at Heaven had become 'critical', and irritatingly his relations with Ian Levine had deteriorated after Cowell had succumbed to an irrepressible urge to humiliate the producer with what he called 'a prank'.

At the recent Midem, the music industry's annual exhibition in Cannes, Cowell and Marvin Howell, a friend, had meddled with the stall rented by Record Shack at the entrance to the exhibition hall. Prior to the opening, Levine had adorned the stand with framed records, the industry's memorial tablets testifying to his glowing record of hits, but, early in the morning of the first day, Cowell and Howell entered the hall and rehung the records at extreme angles and upside down. 'We've destroyed his stand,' laughed Cowell, as he hid to watch Levine's reaction. Levine was more distraught than anticipated. 'Cowell!' he screamed, instantly identifying the culprit. He then began searching frantically for the delinquents, eventually finding them collapsed on the floor shedding tears of laughter.

Levine's revenge was brutal: he refused to play 'So Macho' at Heaven. 'I won't,' he said. 'It's too naff. I've banned it.'

'I've done you so many favours,' retorted Cowell angrily, suspecting Levine's anger was fuelled by an unexplained resentment linked to his relationship with Sinitta's mother.

Determined to secure a play, one Saturday evening Cowell walked into Heaven with Sinitta and a copy of the record. Two thousand men, many stripped to the waist, were dancing.

'Play it,' he ordered Levine.

'I won't,' replied the DJ. 'It's a pile of shit.'

After an angry exchange, Cowell pulled a record off the turntable and put on his own twelve-inch. Puffing indignation, Levine snatched the record and smashed it over Cowell's head. Amid a shower of broken vinyl, the club fell into an eerie silence. 'Mr Piggy, you're a . . . ,' screeched Sinitta, hurling abuse at the obese man.

Days later, the two men met accidentally at the Hippodrome in Leicester Square, which was owned by Peter Stringfellow.

Four times a week, the Cowell brothers and their friends took two tables on the first floor. 'Why didn't you play my record?' Cowell asked Levine. As Sinitta watched, Levine gently slapped Cowell's face. In return, Cowell delivered a mighty punch to Levine's cheek.

Petulantly, Levine refused to retreat. His weapon was *The Street*, a weekly music magazine. In 'Eurobeat Bitch Session', Levine's gossip column, he sniped about the encounter at Midem:

It was almost spoilt for me somewhat by the presence of the awfully camp Simon Cowell . . . The reason for my anger at the dreadful little man is that I produced a track for Fanfare called 'No Cure for Me from Love's Insanity' for James and Susan Wells. Despite promising to release it, Simon has not as yet, and doesn't seem about to, as he still bears a bitter grudge against me for not playing his poxy Sinitta records . . . I also hear that Cowell – who reminds me of the Wicked Queen in Snow White, in front of [Sinitta's] mirror all day – plans to use the track on a segued compilation LP . . . sandwiched between two Sinitta tracks [which] makes me feel nauseous, a feeling which is overpowered only by the queasiness I feel imagining Simon in front of his mirror every morning: 'Mirror, mirror on the wall who is the fairest of them all?' Not you, you vain old queen.

The following week, Fanfare released 'So Macho' for the third time, but only after Cowell masterminded a ruse. Instead of allowing PRT, the distributor, to supply copies of the record to shops on demand, he had arranged for PRT to take the orders but to withhold supplies for three months, with the excuse that 'due to excessive demand it is out of stock'. As the orders accumulated, Fanfare released the records in one go in March 1986. The surge of sales was officially acknowledged in the industry's regular Tuesday charts: 'So Macho' was in the top twenty. Cowell immediately called the BBC producers to announce that the record had broken through and offer his inferior video. After three attempts, his ploy worked and, with a play on Radio 1, Cowell had finally achieved the crossover, selling 900,000 copies and pushing the record to number two. Fanfare's profits were heading towards £500,000.

Flushed with his triumph, Cowell replied to Levine's attack in *The Street.* Without considering the consequences, he compared his own 'beautiful body' to Levine's overweight figure, which 'vain people like myself find repulsive' but which, he said, guaranteed Levine victory in the 'Mr Barrage Balloon' competition. As a postscript, and as an indication of the level to which the exchange had sunk, he added, 'Which reminds me, do you want any more introductions to Escort Agencies? I know how much you enjoyed your last visit.'

Puzzled about Cowell's sexuality, in his column Levine replied, 'With all the time you spend looking at yourself in the mirror and shaving your chest, I doubt whether you get much chance to involve yourself in the music business, do you?' His outburst reflected the gay community's antagonism towards Cowell's musical taste. 'I hate you so much,' Levine told Cowell. 'You'd be as happy selling Andrex lavatory paper as records. Nothing is too crass for you.'

There had been carping about Cowell's camp mannerisms – 'He's light in his loafers,' sniggered one music executive – but Levine lacked any evidence that Cowell was not completely heterosexual. Yet he could not resist sniping in another column about 'some very personal things' involving Cowell, and that 'anyone who shaves his chest so regularly in order to look more hunky in a M&S singlet can hardly criticise anyone else'.

Unwilling to desist once Sinitta's fame was established, Levine resumed his attack by recalling the spat at the Hippodrome, when 'She [Cowell] was so outraged at something I said that she squealed, straightened her singlet and slapped me in the face. Naturally I slapped her back, and she slapped me back. (This went on for some time.)' In the same week, irritated by 'So Macho''s continuing success, Levine reported his 'horror' after discovering the record in a batch to be played at Heaven. 'In somewhat similar fashion to Dracula backing away from the Crucifix – I refused to enter the DJ box until I was sure that the record had been completely destroyed. Some people can be so cruel . . .'

Levine's misfortune was that Pete Waterman, by then established as a star for producing with his partners nearly thirty number-one hits in a short period for the likes of Donna Summer, Dead or Alive and Bananarama, disagreed. London's leading studio was in the midst of producing 300 hit songs. Cowell knew his fate would be turned by persuading Waterman to hand him just one of them for Sinitta. His plan was partly undermined by Sinitta herself. Having won a part in *Mutiny*, a West End stage show, she began an affair with David Essex, the star. The opportunity of a relationship with her childhood heart-throb, whose poster had been on her bedroom wall, was too good to miss.

'I've been dumped,' Cowell told his brother, clearly distressed.

'He'd been playing around,' said Sinitta, 'and when I said we should marry, he said, "No."'

Cowell was also stymied by Waterman. 'Will you help me?' he pleaded.

'I'm too busy,' Waterman snapped.

With no music to promote, Cowell was seconded to Iain Burton's other businesses, selling primitive currency converters and taped guides for museums, and visiting shops to promote Burton's latest business, 'Books-in-the-Bag', a do-it-yourself kit to grow vegetables which included seeds and a book. Pertinently, he also sold hi-fis and electronic equipment manufactured by Audio Fidelity, a public company which Burton had bought in 1986. Ferroway, which by then was earning about £4 million a year, had been 'reversed' by Burton into Audio Fidelity to cancel the company's continuing losses. Burton regarded his ownership of a £10-million public company as 'brilliant', and Cowell had no reason to doubt his friend's decision. He did not oppose the injection of his 25 per cent stake in Fanfare into the company.

'It's a great relationship,' Burton would say about Cowell. 'We're best of friends. I was very successful and we had a great time partying together.' Gradually, the only absentee would be Burton's live-in girlfriend, Vanya Seager, an exotic Indonesian topless model born to Chinese parents whom Cowell judged to be 'the most beautiful girl in the world'. Increasingly unhappy in her relationship with Burton, she remained at her home in Wimbledon. Cowell, observed Maurice Veronique, a friend who also worked at Fanfare, was 'sniffing around Vanya', but that was not, in Veronique's opinion, surprising: 'Simon always went after his friends' ex-girlfriends because he wasn't good at picking girls up himself.'

In early 1987, Cowell's relationship with Sinitta had resumed, albeit on more of a professional than an emotional level, as both wanted to capitalise on her fame. Waterman's help, Cowell knew, would be decisive, but could only be triggered by an irresistible tease.

'Have you seen it?' asked Cowell excitedly. 'Look at today's *News of the World* story about Sinitta going out with a young man who they've called a Toy Boy. Can you write a song for Sinitta called "Toy Boy"?'

'You've pulled a clever stroke,' Waterman told him, convinced the feature was contrived by Cowell. 'You've made Sinitta look like Madonna.'

The call coincided with Waterman's recent visit to Henry Africa's, a raunchy club in Wigan. Screaming women had been stuffing five-pound notes into the G-strings of muscular boys dancing on the bar and frenziedly trying to pull their thongs off. Inspired by 'a whim and a fancy', he floated Cowell's idea by his partners. 'Let's have a song called "Toy Boy",' he told Mike Stock, and asked Matt Aitken to write the music. Twenty-four hours later the song was written, but by then Waterman wanted Mandy Smith, the sixteen-year-old girlfriend of his friend, Rolling Stones bassist Bill Wyman, to be the singer.

'It's meant to be for Sinitta,' Cowell pleaded.

'She's arrogant,' replied Waterman. 'She doesn't impress me and there's no pleasure in working with her.'

In the music business, Cowell had discovered, the intensity of success and failure on a grand scale depended so much on personal relationships. Under pressure, Waterman finally buckled. 'Get Sinitta down here,' he ordered. 'She can sing "Toy Boy" for one hour and then go away. I don't want you telling me what to do. Sit outside the studio.'

Mike Stock, Waterman's fellow songwriter and studio producer, enjoyed his reputation as 'the saviour for strugglers'. Famous for writing a hit song every day and then mastering its recording and production, he rarely celebrated success, although his music regularly appeared on *Top of the Pops*. 'Toy Boy' was churned out like his other hits, yet he unexpectedly enjoyed the introduction to Sinitta and 'her shapely legs', and also to Cowell, who was 'so dapper and smooth'. There was a lot to like, thought Stock, about someone resembling 'an old-school gentleman so far out of our world'. At the end of the session, Cowell declared Stock's work 'perfect'.

His next priority was to hire Ron McCreight, a plugger and promoter universally liked and used by Waterman. Among McCreight's talents was persuading BBC producers to play records lacking in any merit. Like rival pluggers, he knew the only payola was the BBC producers' enjoyment of a good meal, the best wine and occasionally a night at the greyhound races. By then, McCreight could not help but know Cowell. At Waterman's frequent parties to celebrate another number-one record, Cowell could always be seen circulating around the room in a state that appeared to McCreight as bordering on desperation, arousing suspicion as to why he put so much energy into networking.

'I'll get "Toy Boy" a play,' promised McCreight before its release in July 1987. Shortly afterwards, he reported, 'It's guaranteed on Radio 1. Happy days.' That exposure made arranging Sinitta's appearance on *Top of the Pops* much easier. The record hit number four and stayed in the charts for over three months. Cowell's lament was Radio 1's reluctance thereafter to continue playing Sinitta's songs, reflecting the producers' implacable hostility to pop music.

Finally, Cowell had established himself in the business, but the cost was a fractured relationship with Sinitta. He was obsessed by details and image rather than the music, and both were opinionated, not least about the ideal clothes she should have worn on *Top of the Pops*. Their arguments grew and their relationship deteriorated as Sinitta's worldwide success began to influence her behaviour. Among those disenchanted by the singer was Waterman. 'She's overconfident,' he told Cowell. Nevertheless, Waterman included her in a forty-day tour of clubs, concert halls and ballrooms across Britain with Jason Donovan and other Stock, Aitken and Waterman stars. Sponsored by Coca-Cola and Iceland Foods, the tour was soon disrupted by what Waterman described to Cowell as 'a diva nightmare': in Dundee, Sinitta and a group of friends kicked down a toilet door; there were regular disputes in hotels; and finally she demanded her own bus. Knowing that what was going on behind the scenes was often ugly, Cowell paid all the bills, relieved that the disruption remained unknown to the public, but the real cost was Waterman's refusal to assign another of his best songs to Sinitta.

'All the best hits come from Pete,' Cowell told Sinitta. 'I feel physically sick when I hear Donna Summer because after "Toy Boy" I can't get those songs for you. Only Pete and no one else can give you that quality of material.'

Pete Waterman's veto sealed Sinitta's fate, and Cowell casually began searching for new artists. Inevitably, he sought advice from Ron McCreight. 'Getting pop played on Radio 1 is a nightmare,' McCreight confessed. 'Even Kylie is ignored.' The publicist's salvation was television shows. He frequently accompanied Kylie Minogue to TV studios and was bemused by how often Cowell tagged along to meet the producers, using the opportunity to promote artists whose names would later elude him. After considerable effort, McCreight arranged for a boy and girl duo to appear live on Saturday-morning television. Cowell carefully choreographed their dance routine and dictated their clothes, including a hat for the boy. Watching the programme at home, Cowell saw the hat fall off and the performance collapse into chaos.

'A fucking disaster,' he told McCreight.

'You chose what they should wear,' replied McCreight. 'Another punt that's gone wrong.'

Cowell appeared untroubled. He was enjoying his moment in the sun, the universal dream of those involved in the music business. Fanfare had earned over £1 million from Sinitta, hardly enough to pay off its debts, but that was of little concern to Cowell. If there was cash, he would spend it. 'I thought I was Jack the lad,' he would admit. He borrowed money to buy a plush flat in Maltings Place in Fulham and a second-hand black Porsche 911, and paid for endless entertainment on his company credit card. Encouraged by Iain Burton and trusting his employer's acumen to compensate for his own commercial naïvety, he also bought shares in Audio Fidelity, Burton's manufacturer of hi-fi equipment. To pay for the shares, Cowell borrowed £250,000 from the Midland Bank. There seemed no reason not to trust Burton.

The only cloud was his dependence on Stock, Aitken and Waterman, by then established among the most successful production teams in music history. To Korda Marshall and other A&R veterans who noticed him, Cowell was a sponge lacking originality but adept at regurgitating his mentor's insights. In the music industry, he ranked as an outsider in a community still boasting about its successful invasion of America during the 1970s in the wake of The Beatles and The Rolling Stones. Groups including 10cc and Genesis had signalled that Britain had cast off its colonial dependence on American music, but that independence was ending.

During the 1980s, many of the industry's heroes were self-destructing. Daily, messengers would arrive at London's music corporations to deliver packages of 'champagne and flowers' – a euphemism for cocaine – for the A&R men to take to that evening's gigs. The drug had become an essential and dangerous currency that was wrecking the industry's finances. Beyond the carnage and phoney accounting stood Cowell, frequently spotted driving his convertible Porsche, wearing Ray-Bans and with a voluptuous girl in the passenger seat. To Lucian Grainge, a rising star at PolyGram, Cowell was 'not credible. He looked like he was in charge of Easter eggs and separate from the most fertile period of British music: Wham!, Eurythmics, Duran Duran, Spandau Ballet – a fantastic time and all Cowell does is Sinitta and a few dodgy records.' Later, Cowell could not disagree. 'I wouldn't have been able to spot a good rock band and I couldn't sign good commercial music.'

In that latter genre, he suffered consistent failure. Sinitta was slipping into the past and, unable to find other hit artists, Cowell risked being ranked as a one-trick pony. Like a leech, he clung to Waterman for a break, signing groups with no prospects except as useful fodder to appear on *The Hit Man and Her*, a TV music programme which Waterman hosted in Manchester on Saturday nights between midnight and 2 a.m. 'It's the lowest end of the market,' admitted Waterman, who was targeting people coming home drunk to watch live pop music, interspersed by the host playing his own records to over a thousand clubbers. Waterman would regularly call Cowell on Friday mornings.

'Have you got an act for Saturday night?' he would ask.

'No, but I will in an hour,' Cowell would promise.

Singers eager to receive Waterman's blessing travelled by coach from St Pancras at lunchtime, returning to London at 6 a.m. To keep in touch, Cowell copied Waterman by acting as a DJ in gay nightclubs in northern towns and presenting his own singles. None were hits and he foolishly rejected opportunities, including one request from Waterman.

One week in 1987, he asked Cowell to listen to Kylie Minogue singing 'Locomotion', a hit in Australia. 'You'd be doing me a favour if you put it out,' he said.

'I quite like it,' said Cowell, 'but will you let us do the follow-up?'

'No,' replied Waterman, concealing his agenda.

'Then there's no point,' concluded Cowell.

The song would enter the charts at number two, selling 440,000 copies in England and exposing Cowell's limited understanding even of pop music.

Minogue had arrived in England that same week and, as ordered by her agent, had gone on Monday morning to Stock, Aitken and Waterman's studio. Throughout the week, she sat in the reception area, ignored by everyone. By late on Friday afternoon, Kylie was still refusing to move. As a throwaway gesture, Waterman told her to record 'I Should Be So Lucky', another song just churned out by the newly dubbed 'Hit Factory'. As she headed for the recording studio, Waterman went home for the night.

Cowell, meanwhile, was fretting about the dearth of new talent. He placed some hope on Fanfare's Christmas party, the pinnacle of his year. He invited about 300 guests, including all the top personalities in the industry, to the *Villa Cesari*, a boat moored on the Thames near Dolphin Square. After midnight there was a second party, to which he invited London's best-looking models. Together with Jackie St Clair, he had scoured the agency catalogues, picking those he liked and excluding those who were not his type. The cost, borne by Burton, was ignored. 'I believed in spending money I didn't have,' said Cowell, echoing a common sentiment among Margaret Thatcher's children, not that he was remotely interested in Thatcher or politics. His agenda was undisguised: 'The parties were good for business.'

Buttering up Waterman was critical: 'If Pete had a good night out, we had a chance of a record, so he and Mike [Stock] and Matt [Aitken] got the best tables. Anything you could prise out of him was good for your artists. I didn't want the crumbs. I wanted the cake. Everyone asked Pete for his best songs.'

An opportunity arose during the party. Waterman handed the DJ a record and 'I Should Be So Lucky', Kylie's new song, boomed across the boat. Cowell was thunderstruck. He began searching for Waterman. 'How did that happen?' he asked. Waterman explained that after Kylie had been ignored all week, she was about to be tossed out of the studio. 'Someone said to me, "That's unfair," so as an act of charity I let her record "I Should Be So Lucky", which Mike wrote in forty minutes while she was waiting. Out of pity. But I've only just heard it. Same time as you.'

'I'll offer £250,000 for the Kylie contract,' said Cowell.

'No,' replied Waterman.

'£300,000?' offered Cowell.

'No,' said Waterman. 'We'll take the risk.'

The record would be a worldwide number-one hit, but only reached number twenty-eight in the US.

As a consolation, Waterman agreed Cowell could have the song 'Instant Replay' for Yell!, a boy duo created by Cowell.

It reached number eight in the charts. The duo's popularity then dipped, and Cowell began beseeching Waterman to allow Fanfare to produce *The Hit Factory* 2, the second compilation album of Stock, Aitken and Waterman hits. The kudos for Cowell was that the record companies agreed for their hit songs to be included on the album and therefore, by default, on Fanfare's label, so Cowell could claim to have Kylie, Donna Summer and other stars under contract. The only hiccup was a successful legal action by George Michael against Cowell for misusing his music in a mix.

Cowell was still scratching for crumbs. Among them was Waterman's success with the lacklustre Sonia, which Waterman privately realised was ending.

'How did you manage that?' Cowell asked Ron McCreight.

'TV's doing it,' replied McCreight, showing Cowell the list of TV shows.

'I didn't realise there were so many,' said Cowell, more intrigued than ever by the process. There was no graduate entry scheme to the music industry. Access for music producers to TV depended increasingly on fantasy statements like 'We've got a £400,000 promotional budget for this record,' in the hope that the producer would reply, 'Wow, we'd better look at this.' Cowell's problem was credibility. Fanfare could never afford an impressive budget and, other than agreeing with Waterman to produce another *Hit Factory* album, Cowell had failed to find a new star.

Like so many independent labels, Fanfare had hit the buffers. They could no longer afford to buy any good music, even from Waterman. Their only recent success, Yell!'s 'Let's Go Round Again', had produced insufficient profits. Fanfare was struggling, sparking the deterioration of Cowell's relations with Burton.

'You should realise', Burton told a relative of Cowell's during one of his many visits to Cowell's family home, 'that Simon would be useless without me.' Over Sunday lunch, he told Julie Cowell, 'Your son owes everything to me.'

Burton won her gratitude for that generosity, although he didn't reveal that his business's borrowings had run out of control. All of Fanfare's capital was being diverted by Burton to sustain Audio Fidelity, a disastrous investment which was sliding towards insolvency. Burton needed cash, and the threat by a major shareholder at a board meeting in their new offices in St John's Wood to pull out had caused Cowell new fears. Burton had literally locked the office door to prevent the shareholder leaving. 'We need the money, and you can't leave without committing yourself,' Burton had said. After witnessing a ferocious argument, Cowell and the others were astounded as the shareholder climbed out of a window and ran.

Maurice Veronique, a close friend of both Cowell brothers from Windsor Technical College and also employed at Fanfare, warned Cowell of the company's predicament. 'Burton's driven,' he said. 'It's all heading for collapse.' In particular, Veronique was surprised by the company's finances, which were beyond Cowell's understanding. 'It's getting very messy,' he warned Cowell, whose financial acumen amounted to spending everything he earned. 'Iain knows how to play all the games,' added Veronique. 'I'm getting out.'

With £250,000 tied up in the company's worthless shares, Cowell had little option but to stay, although he would remain permanently baffled by Burton's financial engineering. His naïvety was secondary to his resentment towards Burton. His relationship with him remained close but was tinged with anger that his employer's egoism was holding him back. As the face of Fanfare Records, he had been transformed from the humiliated loner into an A&R man commanding some respect. But now their financial predicament had been aggravated, not least by a telephone call made by Sinitta to Burton.

In Burton's version, Sinitta had argued with Cowell and had decided on payback: 'Something was really bugging her.' She then told Burton, 'Simon's been having an affair with Vanya for at least a year.'

'Don't be ridiculous,' said Burton, later describing himself as 'simply dumbstruck and unable to breathe. It hit me like a thunderbolt.' Although his relationship with Vanya had already come to a painful end, he did not imagine that his best friend, whom he loved, would get into his old bed. In Burton's melodramatic words, 'Simon stabbed me in the back. In one go I lost the woman I loved and my best friend. They're the two people I love most in the world. It's so painful.'

'Why did he do it?' he asked Sinitta.

'Don't you understand?' replied Sinitta in Burton's colourful version. 'He wants to be you.'

As Burton's financial troubles increased, he did not dare mention his anger and hurt about Vanya to Cowell. Although the tension of working in the same office as Cowell was, in Burton's opinion, unbearable, he needed Cowell's support to survive. 'It was the beginning of the end,' said Burton. 'Our relationship was irreparably damaged.'

Dismissive of the financial meltdown, Cowell travelled to Acapulco for a holiday and ignored Burton's pleas for support in the boardroom battle to save the company. On his return to London, he arranged a champagne party on the *Villa Cesari* with a crowd of attractive girls to celebrate his second *Hit Factory* album, released in time for Christmas 1989. Waterman had been amenable to the deal. The previous album had earned good profits and, as he left the party enjoying 'all the froth', Waterman expected the same again.

Soon after the profits – at least £500,000 – began to roll in, Burton lost his battle to save Audio Fidelity. 'I didn't know what was happening,' Cowell would tell Waterman. 'It was a shock when it ended quickly.' Although Burton had separated Fanfare from Audio Fidelity, Waterman's expected income from the album, about £250,000, had disappeared into the debt-ridden public company.

More seriously, Cowell lost all the money he had borrowed from the bank to buy Audio Fidelity shares. His flat and his Porsche had also been bought on credit, and overnight the glamorous lifestyle financed through borrowing crashed. Unable to pay his mortgage, Cowell suddenly lost his home and car, and could not repay the loan for the worthless shares. 'Successful but broke,' Sinitta commented about her own situation, bewildered by Burton's financial management.

'I've lost everything,' thirty-three-year-old Cowell told his father, 'and I've lost my car.' As an afterthought he added, 'I've also lost my flat. I'll have to rent.'

'We have a spare room here. Come and live with us,' said Eric, who was renting a flat in Swiss Cottage from his son Nick, who lived with his family in a large house. Eric, who had just returned to London after nearly five years spent in retirement in Majorca, also bought Simon a red TR6 for £7,000. 'I'll never borrow money again,' pledged Cowell.

The family safety net had once again saved him from a life of poverty. With a loan from his father, he lived on about £200 a week and was dating Maria Rice-Mundy, a beautiful brunette introduced to him by Kim Cowell, Nick's first wife. Rice-Mundy, a hostess on TV quiz show *Sale of the Century*, went on holiday with Cowell and his parents to Thailand, but soon Cowell was complaining that 'She's too clingy.' He had enjoyed the chase but, having succeeded, became uninterested.

On his return, to resolve his £250,000 debt for the worthless shares, he negotiated with the Midland Bank to repay £60,000 over four years using a loan offered by NatWest against his father's guarantee. To everyone, Cowell appeared relaxed about his fate. 'I feel almost a sense of release in a strange way,' he told his father. 'Like all these burdens have suddenly disappeared, and I genuinely don't miss any of them.' The facade concealed his real fear. 'I haven't ever been more unhappy than now,' he told a friend. 'I've always been fairly jittery, but this is bad.' In turn, the pressure suffocated Rice-Mundy. 'I've never believed this is going to last for ever,' he told her. Like other women, she would find that his generous gifts and endless attention counted for little once he decided the commitment was too onerous. After six months, she flew to Hong Kong, leaving behind a man unwilling to face the prospect of unemployment: 'I literally had to start again with nothing. It was a pretty awful time.'

Burton had extricated Fanfare from Audio Fidelity before the crash and hoped to continue in business with Cowell. Inevitably, there were strains. Partly this was down to Cowell's relationship with Vanya but, more importantly, Burton had re-engaged with the music business, which had become Cowell's domain. Ignoring the simmering tension, they opened an office in Putney and made plans to launch 'Ritmo de la Noche', a Brazilian dance track. Fighting for his turf, Cowell resisted Burton's choice of singers and dancers. 'I've discovered this fabulous sexy Brazilian girl called Karen,' enthused Cowell, 'and she'll be brilliant.' Burton agreed and ploughed £50,000 into promoting the record, including a stunning video of Karen leading the group, Mystic, in a song-and-dance routine. In reality, Karen was miming to words sung by a Spanish vocalist. Eight TV appearances had been arranged, and the pair were thrilled by the market buzz. 'We'll earn £1 million from this,' predicted Burton. 'It'll be the summer hit. We'll be saved.'

One Sunday morning, on the eve of the launch in spring 1990, Cowell was roused from his sleep by Liz Webb, an investor in the project.

'Have you seen today's *News of the World*?' she raged.

'No,' replied Cowell blearily.

'Well, your Karen is all over the front page. She's a hooker. She offered her services to a reporter, and that's blown everything.'

Suddenly Cowell understood why Karen kept disappearing into the corner of his office to take calls on her mobile phone. Now it was all over, and he was to blame. Burton accused Cowell of having sacrificed his judgement because of a sexual relationship with the prostitute. 'Not really,' replied Cowell sheepishly. 'It was just a K&C' – a kiss and a cuddle.

That loss was compounded by Cowell trying to relaunch Sinitta with a song from Pete Waterman. Without faith in the project, Burton had agreed to press 5,000 singles, but an invoice arrived for 60,000 records. Just why Cowell had wasted so much money on an inevitable flop was never explained. By then, however, he had decided that 'there were two birds in the nest, and there wasn't room for both of us'. The only solution, they agreed, was to sell Fanfare.

Offers were invited from David Munns at PolyGram (which would become Universal) and John Preston, the chairman of BMG, which was owned by the German Bertelsmann Group and was the fifth-largest record company after PolyGram, EMI, Sony (CBS) and Warner. To Cowell's irritation, Munns rejected the offer to buy Fanfare despite, in Cowell's opinion, 'my great presentation'. In revenge, Cowell would later refuse Munns's offer to give him the Man of the Year award at a music event in July 2004.

Burton began negotiations with Preston, a level-headed businessman appointed to reverse the music business's decade of cocaine use and financial profligacy. The counter-revolution, Preston decided, should include promoting the pop and dance music beloved by white middle-class boys like Cowell and ignored by most of the independent companies. Cowell's friendships with television producers added to Preston's interest in a man with a reputation for having a magnetic personality and who habitually refused to take 'no' for an answer. His strategy was decided while Cowell and Burton were in his office pitching for BMG subsidiary RCA's investment in Fanfare.

Preston's telephone rang. 'Is Simon there?' asked Pete Waterman.

'Pop music's God is telephoning for Cowell,' thought Preston and his interest in Burton evaporated. In Preston's mind, the decision of whether to finance Fanfare or not had resolved itself.

For a different reason, Cowell's relations with Burton also finally cracked. Dissatisfied with his financial management, Cowell was angry that his employer intended to sell Fanfare without dividing the proceeds, despite his 25 per cent stake. 'If you don't give me my share,' warned Cowell, 'I'll go without you.' Burton ignored the ultimatum.

To Burton's surprise, he arrived on Monday morning and discovered that Cowell had abandoned their office. 'He's walked off without saying goodbye,' he fumed. Throughout that week, Cowell ignored Burton's calls and, to avoid confrontation, ran away when Burton approached him in the street.

'Iain never thought I would leave,' recalled Cowell, pleased to have taken the career-defining move.

'I can't blame Simon for thinking about himself,' Burton said years later. 'The situation was messy and not of Simon's making. But he could have been loyal as a friend.'

Cowell had already set up IQ Records, his own company, as a consultant A&R man for John Preston. Assigned to the RCA label for £50,000 per annum, he was guaranteed a 50 per cent share of the profits in a joint venture if he delivered a certain number of records and sales over the following year. In Preston's view, 'I fired Burton,' but he was unaware of the unresolved litigation between Cowell and Burton.

The issue was a contract Fanfare signed in early 1990 to

produce 'I'm Going to Stand and Fight', a record by Nigel Benn, the WBO middleweight boxing champion also known as 'The Dark Destroyer'. Britain's most popular boxer was due to defend his title in November against Chris Eubank in Birmingham. In anticipation of Benn's inevitable victory, 60,000 records had been pre-sold and total sales were predicted to be huge. During their 'divorce', Burton insisted that the Benn single belonged to him, a notion Cowell denied. In the days before the fight, Burton issued an injunction in the High Court, which Cowell, despite being penniless, decided to contest. Victory in the court – because of the certainty of huge sales – would wipe out his debts but, as he approached the courtroom doors, Cowell was tapped on the shoulder. 'I think we can do a deal,' said Burton.

With Cowell taking the bigger share of the profits, he headed for the Birmingham arena, stopping only at a betting shop. 'Eubank to win,' said the grizzled punter ahead of him. 'A madman,' thought Cowell. Shortly afterwards, sitting near the ring, Cowell watched the promised epic end in Benn's defeat when the fight was stopped in the ninth round. Cowell would join RCA in 1991 with a battered reputation.

'I never saw him again,' said Burton. 'He couldn't face me. His priority was to be successful and in the limelight no matter what the cost or risk to the bottom line. And, in the end, Simon exhibited an utterly ruthless streak and showed no sense of personal loyalty towards me.' Cowell preferred not to reply to that accusation. Burton would go on to create Aspinaloflondon, a successful luxury-goods retailer with no connection to John Aspinall, the famous owner of a Mayfair gambling club. 'I couldn't resist the name,' he explained.

Cowell's comfort was Waterman's forgiveness over his own £250,000 loss. Cowell did not apologise and, in Waterman's opinion, 'He didn't need to. He didn't do it on purpose. He was a mate. I've lost more and didn't care. I liked Simon and just moved on to make more hits and more money.' Waterman's only comment at the time was a homily to Cowell about his predicament: 'If you're not at the top, you're going nowhere.'

3

Endless Humiliation

John Preston had thrown Cowell a lifeline, but Cowell suffered no illusions. In the music industry, success was worshipped exaggeratedly and failure was punished by swift expulsion. 'My job was precarious because I was thirty-three and I hadn't signed "the big group",' said Cowell. 'I had failed because I wasn't good enough at that time. I wasn't stupid about my situation.'

After setting up IQ Records' office in George Street with Tony Lascelle, the accountant employed at Audio Fidelity, Cowell tried to operate as RCA's consultant, but his plight merely got worse. Among the first visitors to his office was Nigel Martin-Smith, the manager of Take That, a boy band which had got together in 1989. Over the previous two years, the group's songs had flopped. Among their critics was Pete Waterman, who had damned the group on *The Hit Man and Her*, his TV show, as 'tacky'. Martin-Smith needed a major record company to risk £1 million on relaunching the group. Like all major music corporations, RCA gambled their revenue from their back catalogue on nurturing new talent, accepting that bankrolling failure was a necessary risk. Artists would be cast off once they were no longer worth the bet.

Cowell was faced with a dilemma. Risking £1 million in the first weeks of his consultancy on a group unkindly described as 'pure gay porn' was unnatural and, without Burton's guidance, Cowell's uncertainty exposed him as indecisive. Eventually, after listening again to two new songs, Cowell told Martin-Smith, 'I don't like the lead singer, he's too fat' – a reference to Gary Barlow – 'but I would be interested without him.'

'Over my dead body,' replied Martin-Smith. Cowell was not disappointed: he didn't believe in the group.

Soon after, Cowell parted from Lascelle and moved into RCA's building in Fulham Palace Road. Walking around the office dressed in his normal uniform – a white T-shirt and high-waisted trousers – and leading Harry, a bad-natured Yorkshire terrier belonging to Sinitta, he introduced himself and his assistant Vanya Seager, his on–off girlfriend, who had previously lived with Iain Burton. The former topless model had no office experience – she couldn't even type – but she needed an income. She would be loyal, Cowell reasoned, and, according to friends, 'handy' in the office.

Their recent reunion had been accidental. Entering Mr Sing's, a Chinese restaurant in Earl's Court, he had been taken to a table where Vanya was waiting for 'Mr Cowell'. To Cowell's surprise, she was waiting for his brother, whom she was also dating. The brothers enjoyed swapping girlfriends, and Simon stepped in. Soon after, he complained to Denise Beighton, RCA's national sales manager, that 'She's too possessive. She's driving me nuts.' He needed his personal space but resisted firing her. Seager covered for his unpunctuality, disorganised diary and endless loss of car keys, papers, CDs and glasses. Before he left the office, she always made sure he was holding his mobile telephone, a packet of cigarettes and Anadin Extra tablets to relieve his frequent migraines, and every day she would cross the road to buy his lunch at the local greasy spoon. In return, he bought her endless gifts.

'Could you tell Simon I'd like the bag that so-and-so has got in the magazine,' Seager would tell Beighton, referring to a celebrity star, and he usually obliged. In their fiery relationship, which provoked curiosity in the office, Seager tolerated her boyfriend/employer enjoying himself at lap-dancing clubs, but complained bitterly when he bought a dancer a Gucci coat for

£3,000. 'I hate him going off with other girls,' she complained whenever they separated. His happiness with a woman regarded by others as sleazy irritated even a former page-three girl. 'Can you find out who he went out with last night?' she frequently asked Beighton, who in turn would be asked a similar question by Cowell: 'She's being so secretive. What did she do last night?'

The jealousy was bewildering even for Beighton, who was forging a close friendship with Cowell: 'He was terribly camp and there was no sexiness about him.' To those who speculated to Beighton that 'Simon's gay', she would reply, 'He's not gay. He sleeps with girls.' But she was puzzled by his 'girliness', and he visibly winced if a woman's period was mentioned. 'Girls with a period', he told Beighton jokingly, 'should be locked in a room with straw on the floor.' Beighton concluded that her new friend was 'complex' and 'had an intimacy problem'. After watching him for some months, she decided that he loved and chased beautiful women but disliked the detail of their lives.

Cowell's priority was to ingratiate himself with RCA's other A&R men, a competitive group. As in all music companies, he was working in an environment in which the use of recreational drugs – marijuana and cocaine – was common, with some people also using amphetamines and acid. Despite Preston's ambitions in an era of diminishing scandal and rebellion, drugs and sex remained intertwined in the building's culture.

Preston, wearing the brightest green leather shoes, expected RCA to sign between seven and ten artists a year, hoping that two cash cows would support the dross. To survive, Cowell needed to find one of the successes in an alien atmosphere.

RCA's head of A&R was Korda Marshall, a rock-music fundamentalist whose staff were told to 'search for talent at gigs, pubs, rehearsals, sports centres, youth clubs and at the end of the pier'. During their weekly meetings, Marshall expected his six A&R men to discuss the charts and the opportunities for new signings. His handicap against giants like Warner, who had £60 million to spend, was his limited budget of £9 million. In his cut-throat world, Marshall understood that his own survival depended on the performance of his A&R men. Knowing that the casualty rate to justify the money at stake was high, Marshall did not warm to the new arrival, who joked that while the 'cool people' went to 'two or three smelly gigs every night, I do my A&R watching TV at home'. In Marshall's words, 'Cowell doesn't go to clubs where his feet stick to the floor – he stands on glass for showbiz.' Sensing the discord between the two, Preston diverted Cowell in a new direction.

Cowell's arrival coincided with the decision to rejuvenate the Arista label as a platform for Clive Davis, the legendary New York producer, to resume business after his dismissal as president of CBS Records amid accusations of fraud. Famous for acts like the Grateful Dead, Dionne Warwick, Whitney Houston and many others, Davis regarded the London operation as 'my gateway into Europe to sell my records'. He expected Diana Graham, Arista's new managing director in London, to also massage his ego and supply music which he could sell in the US. If she failed to deliver within three years, she would be dismissed. The principal drawback was Arista's lack of artists, a problem which Cowell was expected to cure. His moment in the sun with Sinitta had passed, but Preston, trusting that Cowell possessed the relationships to promote pop music, urged Graham to rely on the maverick.

Initially, Cowell found Davis's backwater a welcome sanctuary. Pertinently, neither Preston nor Graham was aware of Cowell's financial plight. Concealing his emotions, he lived by his parents' mantra of 'get on with it' and smothered his bosses with charm. In the roller-coaster music world it was usual to be up one minute and down the next, and being penniless was not necessarily a stigma. Survival in the business depended, some insiders would say, on 'woodshedding' – the accumulation of expertise. To rise from the bottom and survive, Cowell had listened to awful music, until he had focused on a strand which he could justify as commercially viable. Next, he had forged connections and relationships with those he rated as trustworthy and talented. Others called it the 'kiss up, kick down' technique. That was the 'woodshedding' dynamic which transformed indecisive men into those who were confident about their judgement. The only pitfall Cowell had not anticipated was that Preston, against Graham's wishes, would appoint Nigel Grainge and Chris Hill as Arista's A&R team for rock music.

Grainge and Hill had earned credibility in the business. Working at the cutting edge with Chris Blackwell and Island Records, and later at their own company, Ensign Records, they had produced Eddy Grant, the Boomtown Rats, 10cc, the Waterboys, Sinead O'Connor and other hit artists. After selling Ensign to Chrysalis Records in 1986, Grainge felt he 'had a pretty hot reputation'. He was a proud purist in the rock scene and disdained Arista as barren. 'It's got no culture,' he announced. 'It's got to be created by a new A&R team, which is me.'

Like most rock A&R men, Grainge would race between gigs every night and listen to demo tapes during the day. Looking across the large open-plan office he noticed Cowell in 'a cubby hole'. Opinionated about music and placing his judgement above the need for commercial profits, Grainge was dismissive about a man floating in a comfort zone without cultural credibility. Cowell was infamous for worshipping Frank Sinatra – a decidedly uncool affliction – and disparaging most modern music, which he hardly played. 'I love Sinatra's music and his way of life, especially the drinking and smoking,' admitted Cowell.

In an introductory conversation, Grainge gave an honest opinion about Cowell's past records. 'Your stuff is shit,' he declared loudly. 'We're on different planets. We've had success and you haven't.' The chance of an amicable relationship seeped away as Grainge kicked Cowell's credibility, leaving him struggling for breath.

Cowell tried first to revive Sinitta once again. Although he was penniless, he paid £300 a month for her hair extensions and would patiently listen to her frustrated tirades on the telephone, occasionally putting the receiver down to light a cigarette while she ranted. Then, ignoring their turbulent relationship, he hired Ian Levine to produce a recording of 'Love Is the Only Solution' by Maxine Nightingale and watched Levine's mix at the studios in Chiswick. 'I love it,' he declared. The following day, Vanya Seager reported that 'He loves it so much that he's playing it all the time. He's been dancing around his office.' Levine was thrilled. Cowell was notorious for stopping disagreeable records after seconds. However, twenty-four hours later, Cowell changed his mind. The recording was abandoned and he released another song by Sinitta, which flopped.

Next he signed Sonia, the twenty-year-old from Lancashire made famous in 1989 by Waterman's production of 'You'll Never Stop Me Loving You'. Although the song hit number one and there were other successes, they had parted in 1991. Cowell hired Nigel Wright to produce 'Only Fools Never Fall in Love' for her. Signing a Waterman product, Cowell imagined, propelled him into a higher league, but he had ignored the reason for Waterman's decision: Sonia was short, looked dumpy on television and rejected advice on what to wear. After reaching number ten with Cowell, her career declined. 'I don't know what to do with her,' Cowell told Beighton, and cast her adrift.

His next hope was Allison Jordan, an attractive blonde whom he was also chasing romantically. He persuaded BBC TV's *That's Life* to stage a talent show, and Jordan became his favourite to win. Promoting her popularity and propelling her to victory in

May 1992 singing 'Boy from New York City' was not difficult, and in an extraordinary eight-minute plug the BBC featured Cowell, among others, predicting a top-five hit. 'The record's cheap and nasty,' Beighton told Cowell. 'Those sort don't sell.' Even Jordan spotted the tackiness. Holding the cover on television, she announced, 'They've spelt my name wrong.' Allison had been spelt with one 'l'. The record reached number twenty-three in the charts and disappeared. Some time later, Cowell recalled, 'We had a brief thing. She'd done her boobs.'

In the midst of those forlorn productions, Cowell heard some terrible news. Six months after he had rejected Take That, Korda Marshall was negotiating with Nigel Martin-Smith to sign the group for RCA and invest over £1 million. To avoid the potential embarrassment, Cowell called Martin-Smith and made an offer. 'Fuck off,' replied the manager, just days before he signed with RCA. Martin-Smith, Cowell realised, would make sure that Marshall knew about Cowell's rejection.

The backwash intensified Grainge's antagonism. Cowell was damned for massaging TV producers and newspaper journalists to promote forgettable pop. 'Nothing seems fast enough for him,' carped a man proud of nurturing artistic genius who had sympathisers at RCA, not least Korda Marshall. Cowell, Marshall agreed, was 'unashamedly a pop tart with appalling taste, and blatantly commercial'. In an unusual burst of anger, Cowell snapped back, 'Korda's so up his own ass.' His anger was really with himself for rejecting Take That. 'I'm feeling sick,' Cowell confessed to his father. 'I lost a good signing.' His father, he hoped, would explain why things were going wrong, but even Eric, he realised, could not teach judgement. 'I was bruised and frustrated,' said Cowell later. 'I had to toughen myself up.'

To compensate for his mistake, Cowell began searching for another boy band. The idea was not new. Every decade, a new cycle of music producers scrutinised sexy young men flashing

Ultrabrite smiles while they danced and sang pop in the hope they would appeal to a new generation of teenage girls who disliked rock. The producers' trick was to find teenage boys blessed with delicate good looks who could be packaged to flatter the cult of youth. In the 1960s, there had been The Beatles and The Monkees; in the 1970s, The Osmonds and The Bay City Rollers; and, in the 1980s, Wham! and New Kids on the Block. In 1992, at a studio in Chertsey, Cowell began auditioning a group of black teenage dancers for a boy band to be called Chaos. Nigel Wright, the producer, looked forlorn. None could sing. 'You're making a fool of yourself,' Ian Levine told Cowell when asked for help.

Levine then organised an audition at the Pineapple studios, for which a hundred young black singers showed up. 'Crap, you're no good,' cursed Levine, dispensing with most applicants after less than a minute.

'You're heartless,' gasped Cowell, standing in the background.

'I'm not going to waste my time,' replied Levine, who chose Haydon Eshun, a nine-year-old, to lead the group of five and brought Billy Griffin from America to add vocals to the new record. By the time it was completed, Cowell was dejected. Uncertain about his judgement, he decided on a whim to abandon Chaos.

'I just didn't get the feel for it,' he explained. 'There was no momentum. I was pushing uphill.'

Chaos would be relaunched as Ultimate Kaos by another producer. Their modest hits embarrassed Cowell.

'Cowell's been fabulously unsuccessful,' Levine chortled.

'I didn't know what I was doing,' Cowell would admit. 'It's incredible how stupid I was through lack of experience.' His only consolation was that despite Korda Marshall spending £1 million on Take That, commissioning two songs from Levine, the group still languished. He was not disappointed when Preston fired Marshall. In a desperate bid to rescue RCA from total disaster, Preston risked another £1 million on the group.

The mood in Fulham, Marshall would say after he departed, matched Hunter S. Thompson's description of 'a long plastic hallway where thieves and pimps run free and good men die like dogs, for no good reason'. Being spat out of RCA, he admitted bitterly, was 'a salient learning curve in the shallow, bullshitting music business'. The same vitriol was directed by the management at the survivors inside RCA, including Cowell.

BMG's German directors regularly held three-day conferences for sixty A&R men summoned from America and Europe to present their best recordings and receive either congratulations or a 'run down' for bad offerings. At the Excelsior hotel in Rome, Cowell presented his latest from Worlds Apart, a boy band that he had created. Within minutes of hearing the track, his rivals had renamed the group 'Cheeks Apart'. Cowell deflected the criticism by joking about 'scary Germans' and was soon embraced as entertaining. Unusually in the music business, his self-confidence was untainted by crushing arrogance.

Back in London, Cowell spoke about 'that ghastly convention, which I despised', and was blasted by Grainge. 'I can't stand your shit pop,' he told Cowell. 'Signing camp boy bands and worshipping remixes of Barry Manilow . . .!' Arista's reputation was bad enough, he continued, and they would fail to win respect 'if we're contaminated by pop and Roland Rat'.

Cast as the Antichrist, Cowell appeared to let the hostility wash over his head. Only a fool, he knew, revealed his weaknesses to an enemy. His apparent helplessness was a source of strength. Grainge, he accepted, was 'into serious music', and he laughed off a drunken accounts employee telling him loudly at the Christmas party, 'Oh, you're that idiot who signs all that shit.' But, in the new year, his plight worsened.

Three singles by Worlds Apart released during 1993 only

reached between twenty and fifty-one in the charts, reinvigorating Grainge's regular denunciations. 'I'm not putting out any more of this shit,' said a man who boasted about being 'pretty strict' about his values and enjoyed, as his brother, PolyGram's Lucian Grainge, would reveal, 'battle-scarring people'.

As his self-confidence eroded, Cowell was grateful for sympathy from Keith Blackhurst, the founder of the Deconstruction label, which had just been bought by BMG. 'They're brothers without rhythm,' Blackhurst told Cowell. 'They're the most arrogant people I've ever met.'

The consolation was temporary. By the end of his second year, as his boy bands failed to gel, the ridicule had crushed Cowell. 'I felt very alone,' he confessed. 'I was empty, desperate. If enough people tell you you're an idiot, you start to believe it. It was typical in the A&R culture that if it's not a great time commercially, you lose your self-confidence. It was a miserable time.'

Looking over her domain, Diana Graham concluded that 'Arista has become a full-scale battle. The atmosphere is foul.' She was Cowell's only ally at the label. 'He's absolutely charming,' said Graham about an employee who at least was generating some turnover, although no profits, unlike Grainge and Hill, who had lots to say but produced only losses. Her affection inflamed Hill's irritation at a man who habitually arrived late driving 'a flash car': 'I can't understand his relationship with women. Cowell just schmoozes with them.' Like others, he was puzzled that Cowell was dating beautiful women, yet still aroused speculation about his sexuality. Even Graham shared a bystander's observation about Cowell's aggression: 'He can be a total bitch about people. He keeps saying a person is "so ugly". He wants everyone to be good-looking.'

As news of the warfare leaked out, Jonathan King, a music-industry grandee who published the influential *Tip Sheet*, initiated peace talks over lunch. Grainge and Hill reluctantly arrived at a Chinese restaurant in Whiteleys, the shopping emporium on Queensway, to meet Cowell and King. 'You are three people I really like,' said King, 'and I want you to get on.' Cowell smiled approvingly. He was adept at dispelling hostility in a showbiz way and could charm anyone, including Grainge momentarily. By the end of the meal, the combination of King's salesmanship and Cowell's charisma appeared to have reconciled the former enemies.

The peace was short-lived. At the next weekly marketing meeting, he played another Roland Rat record. 'Oh my God,' spluttered Grainge. 'You may laugh at this,' continued Cowell, playing hillbilly music, 'but I've got seven TV stations lined up this weekend.' The following week he offered 'Sound of the Universe', an African dance record. 'I can sell some of these,' he said. 'You should be head of TV promotions,' mocked Hill, irked that Cowell had even placed a record on the BBC's six o'clock news. 'Let's do this by Nik Kershaw,' suggested Cowell, referring to a reissue of Kershaw's 1980s hit 'Wouldn't It Be Good'. After fifteen seconds, Grainge turned off the machine and drew a zero on his flip chart. 'This isn't art,' he spat. 'Well, I don't know how you would promote what you've just played,' countered Cowell. Teamwork, he cursed, was 'a big lie to me'.

Broken for the day, he headed for comfort to Denise Beighton and Vanya Seager. 'Why do these people hate me? What have I done to them?' At the next meeting, he resolved to secretly carry a tape recorder.

'I'm hard done by,' Cowell complained to Diana Graham, a woman so frightened by Grainge that she had walked into Cowell's office as he was listening to a proposed song and smiled, 'Simon, don't even think of signing that.' The humiliation, Cowell felt, was total. 'The records aren't selling the way I want,' he countered. Arista's publicity machine could not promote pop music. Unlike other A&R men, Cowell attended every

RCA marketing meeting to understand the business culture. Big sales, the circumspect inquisitor believed, were more important than art. Repeatedly he argued with Arista's lacklustre publicists about their failure to place his music on radio or television.

To prove his point, he once waited until they admitted their failure to place Whitney Houston's 'I Will Always Love You' on radio and TV. Then he arranged mass coverage for the new track in the media. The embarrassed publicists were not allowed to forget their rescue. In the music business, he knew, no one enjoyed someone else's success. Everyone shared the fate of an ungenerous career which ended either on the up or on the skids.

'You're not helping,' Grainge snapped at Cowell, irritated that there was again no new rock record to offer Clive Davis on his next visit.

Davis's A&R conventions were a living hell. After ordering the room temperature to be reduced to near-freezing to keep his staff awake – and some brought blankets – Davis would play his latest R&B records and extol their virtues in excruciating detail. 'They're hits,' he would emphasise, before expressing dismay that Cowell's records did not 'cross over' to Europe or America and that a proposed rockabilly album could never sell in America and would not even be released in England because it was so bad. And he lambasted Grainge for failing to unearth a new group. The criticism hurt. 'Arista is awful,' Grainge complained. 'It's lost its way.'

Cowell's continued presence made it worse. Grainge wanted Cowell out, and Cowell's own conduct merely reinforced his campaign. 'In the middle of a really tedious presentation at a weird off-site meeting I just lost it and started laughing,' Cowell would admit. 'And I couldn't stop laughing. And a guy actually told me in front of about twenty people to leave the room. Like I was a six-year-old. And at that point I just thought, "I can't do this." But I was fearful that if I didn't toe the line, they would fire me.' Pete Waterman understood the ambivalence Cowell excited: 'Simon can be offensive because he thinks it's funny.' The renewed blistering arguments prompted Graham to appeal for help to John Preston. 'Hold on and see what happens,' he replied. The battles entrenched Cowell's attitudes against those 'cynical and snobby people in the music business whom I despise'. Arista's office, he concluded, was 'a space – physically and mentally – where everyone has become the enemy'.

Cowell's strength was to conceal his emotions. He was rarely rude, even to his critics, and frequently generous. At the end of lunch in the neighbouring Pizza Express, he would pay for the table – sometimes a dozen people – despite his financial plight. 'I had a unique ability to ride lows,' he explained. 'When things went wrong, I realised it was my fault and I had to repair it.' Ever since his near-bankruptcy, Cowell had accepted that 'actually it's me that gets myself into a situation'. The paradox of his struggle against adversity at Arista was that, with Eric's support, his self-confidence strengthened. Relying on his father's advice did not end after he had moved out of his parents' flat and bought Coombe Kanata, a house on Kingston Hill in west London for £800,000. In their frequent conversations, Eric encouraged his son to stick to his convictions. 'Be patient,' advised the permanent optimist. 'Expect to cock things up and believe that you can work things out.' His fault, Cowell realised, was 'to believe my own hype and, while going through a sticky patch, start blaming the world'. Musically, he still loved Frank Sinatra and little else. Asked at a BMG meeting how he discovered new music, he replied, to unanimous disdain, 'I read the *Sun* to see what people want.'

Although his successful competitors were earning high profits as a result of what he called their 'obsession' to sign new rock groups, he sat at home watching TV and asking, 'How can I turn this into a record?' In spring 1992, he noticed that within one hour of the American World Wrestling Federation announcing a show at Wembley, 62,000 tickets had been sold, two-thirds of the stadium's capacity. Sky's broadcast of the show attracted an audience of 600,000. Somewhere, he thought, there was a market, and so he arranged breakfast in Holland Park with the show's manager. By the end of the meal he had identified a new idea: instead of arranging for a musician to appear on TV, he would use TV stars to make a record. The same afternoon, he called Vince McMahon, the WWF boss in New York. Ignoring the probability that none of the wrestlers could sing, he told McMahon that Arista wanted to make an album. 'Come over to talk about it,' agreed McMahon. At a regular A&R ideas meeting, Cowell announced his plan. 'Fanatical kids watch the show and they'll buy the album,' he said, enjoying Grainge's predictable outrage. 'So long as one of the wrestlers can sing, we can do the rest.' Even Diana Graham was aghast. 'She went on her knees and begged me not to do it,' Cowell told Waterman as they flew to New York.

Waterman went for the ride because there was money to be earned and he sympathised with his friend's plight: 'He was categorised as a novelty merchant. The industry had put him in a box, pushed him to one side and thrown away the key. They hoped he could be buried. No one had time for Simon, and he wasn't happy.' Nor was Waterman happy after they entered the WWF's headquarters in upstate New York. Greeted by seriously heavy characters exuding menace, Cowell made a charming introduction and then, without warning, announced, 'Pete will tell you about it. Over to you, Pete.' Flummoxed but never lost for words, Waterman spoke about his talents and success, fearing that any flaw risked an exit in a lead coffin or his premature end in a concrete overcoat. 'OK,' said McMahon, 'done.'

With the contract signed, the group's tracks were mixed by

Mike Stock in London. The single, released in September 1992, was a British number-three hit. The subsequent album, released the following year, was accompanied by a *Slam Jam Music Video*, featuring wrestlers dressed in garish clothes and dark glasses leaping or being thrown from great heights onto a canvas ring to an accompaniment of loud music. The album would sell over 1.3 million copies and reach number four in the British charts, although it failed in America.

Success emboldened Cowell. He needed to escape Grainge's outrage, get out of Arista and get his revenge. His target was 'People who have taken advantage of me in the past. I have a long memory and I'm very patient. One day I'll get my revenge by being more successful than them.'

Diana Graham agreed. 'He should join the boys,' she said, and suggested that Cowell should move across to his fun-loving contemporaries at RCA. His path was helped by Jonathan King. 'You should take on Simon,' he urged Jeremy Marsh and Hugh Goldsmith, the stars at RCA. 'He's good.' Cowell's priority, explained King, was commercial value rather than 'cool acts', and that inevitably meant the music was unworthy and untrendy, but Cowell appealed to the silent majority who bought two or three records a year. King's plea was transmitted to John Preston.

'I can't bear this environment any more,' Cowell confirmed to Preston. 'If I've got to stay with the arty set and music snobs, I'm leaving.' Convinced that Cowell possessed unique qualities, BMG's chairman decided to accommodate a mercurial character who resisted house-training.

Finding a solution depended on Marsh, Goldsmith and others at RCA agreeing that they wanted to work with Cowell. He had rejected Take That, who, after risking a fortune, they had turned into a massive hit. The ideal test, they agreed, would be their Easter skiing holiday in Val d'Isère, France. Sharing rooms with Cowell in a small hotel, Marsh and Goldsmith recognised a man who was 'bruised, desperate and crestfallen'. Cowell's wit gradually dissolved the doubts, while his limited skiing skills added to the hilarity. Dressed in a Crombie coat, his interest was plainly in clothing rather than sport. Stiff-hipped, unwilling to bend his knees and unable to carve the corners, he had difficulty even on the gentle blue runs and steered away from the more challenging trails. At the end of the holiday, the seven RCA employees held an Oscar ceremony, including one award for the week's most boring comment. Cowell won for describing the changing of tyres at Formula One races.

'You've passed the test,' said Mike McCormack, a fellow producer at RCA. 'You'll be our Gary Lineker. Just stand by the goal and when the ball comes along nod it into the back of the net. But first take six months off to get your mojo back. Come in when you've found what you want to do.'

'I'm really going to fit in here,' replied Cowell. 'I never want to be that miserable again.'

'I'm very grateful,' he would later tell Jonathan King. The experience hardened his resolve to surround himself in the future only with people who would nod and fall into line.

4

A Hit – At Last

Although he had supposedly moved from hell into showbiz heaven, he remained the man who had rejected Take That. At RCA's six-monthly A&R conference, he sat through the band's new single, 'It Only Takes a Minute', which won applause, and was then asked to play Worlds Apart's latest track, 'Together'.

Diligently, he had arranged for the group to be taught to dance and launched onto the club circuit, fixed photo shoots for teen magazines and charmed TV producers to book them on Saturday-morning slots. His hype was predicted to get Worlds Apart's record to number three in the British charts. Instead, it reached number eighty-eight and disappeared. The song was beaten by Take That at number one, while East 17, managed by his old rival Tom Watkins, were at number two with 'Around the World', which would go on to sell 3 million copies. 'It's a failure,' Cowell admitted. 'Sitting here is agony.'

Equally excruciating was the fact that Ultimate Kaos's song 'Some Girls' hit number nine in the British charts. 'Another very bad time,' admitted Cowell. 'After that, I dreaded the presentations at the annual marketing meetings because Take That would come up and make me feel sick.' His attempts to compensate for his mistake compounded his error. Insecure about his fate, he regularly asked Denise Beighton to walk with him from meetings to his office at the end of the corridor. 'He hates being seen alone as he passes the secretaries,' thought Beighton, sympathetic to his anxiety. 'I love him to bits, even though he's a laughing stock.'

The cure, Cowell decided, was safety and success in his unique area of expertise: 'manufactured pop' based on TV shows. No other A&R man sat watching children's television and relied on salesmen in retail shops. No other music producer would have enjoyed the *Mighty Morphin Power Rangers*, a new American programme featuring teams of violent, superhuman, costumed heroes. His problem was not to persuade John Preston that an album based on the show could produce serious profits but that he could secure the rights. 'Get on a plane and sign up the Power Rangers,' Preston ordered. Cowell flew to Los Angeles fearing that failure could mean his dismissal from RCA.

'The deal's not going to happen,' Cowell told himself thirty minutes after entering Saban Entertainment's headquarters. An executive employed by the billion-dollar children's-entertainment empire had derided his offer and was, in Hollywood's brutal manner, forcefully bidding Cowell farewell. As he opened the door, the executive's telephone rang. Haim Saban, the owner of the corporation, was asking in Hebrew who was in the room. 'Go up and see him,' Cowell was told.

'How much will you give?' Saban asked, referring to the rights.

'Not much,' admitted Cowell, laughing, 'but it would be a number-one hit.'

'What's the big deal about a number one?' asked Saban. 'I've just earned half a million dollars by putting the Power Rangers on chewing-gum paper, so why should I take your pennies?'

'Because you haven't got a gold record on your wall,' replied Cowell.

'OK,' laughed Saban, offering his hand. 'You've got a deal.' Saban would end up doing even better, fixing a platinum disc on his wall.

'Wherever there's a TV audience, I need to be there,' Cowell recited. 'Youth-cult tie-ins' was his new buzz phrase. Television programmes, he asserted, produced high sales by stoking emotions. With the production of the Power Rangers album under way, Cowell contracted one for Zig and Zag, two furry TV puppets from the planet Zog who featured in different TV shows. Their song 'Them Girls Them Girls' hit number five in the British charts in January 1995. He celebrated his 'huge victory' with friends at Knightsbridge eatery Mr Chow, although beyond that group, he knew, he remained 'a freak'. 'I felt that I was latching on to something unique that could potentially grow into a fantastic business,' Cowell would write later. 'I would always say to people during this period, "Laugh all you want. This is my target practice."'

To conceal his frustrations, he gave a convincing impression of fearless unconcern about failure and disdain for the mockery, while he dreamt of becoming a celebrity like Clive Davis or even Phil Spector. Darting in and out of the adjacent national sales office, he would always ask the same question of an office rival: 'How many records has he sold?'

'He's always angry about others' success,' scoffed Keith Blackhurst, a skiing companion who had brought Kylie Minogue to RCA after she fell out with Pete Waterman. 'He's good at one-line put-downs of others after they've put in ten months' hard work. He's the biggest cuckoo in the building.'

The competitiveness camouflaged Cowell's insecurity, but he was delighted to chortle about 'Those imbeciles at Arista, most of whom are out of the business today.' Grainge and Hill had been paid off, Diana Graham had also departed and Arista in Britain was defunct. Yet, despite the acrimonious contest, he made unusually few enemies. By defining his own market, he had detached himself from the street fight among his competitors, who were seemingly heading towards a dead end. At the beginning of that year's skiing trip to Flims, Cowell self-confidently moved out of the group's inferior rooms with pull-down bunks and took a bedroom in a nearby five-star hotel. He wanted comfort and style. All that eluded him was a surplus of wealth to finance all his wishes.

Momentary success was followed by what seemed to be permanent failure. Searching for another gimmick in 1995, Cowell signed Curiosity Killed the Cat, a four-man group led by Ben Volpeliere-Pierrot whose unusual mix of jazzy and funky pop shot them to fame in 1986, with Andy Warhol appearing in the video of their hit 'Misfit'. Cowell was planning their ill-conceived revival with 'I Need Your Lovin'' when Denise Beighton walked into his office soon after he arrived at 11 a.m. one Wednesday. Her brief message, delivered in her Brummie accent, changed Cowell's life.

'I watched *Soldier, Soldier* last night, and it had me sobbing like a baby,' she said, referring to an ITV drama series based on an army regiment languishing in the aftermath of the cold war. 'If it can get to a hard bitch like me, you should take a look at it.'

The hook, explained Beighton, was the two stars, Robson Green and Jerome Flynn, singing 'Unchained Melody', the 1955 hit revived by The Righteous Brothers in 1965 and which had also featured in *Ghost*, a Hollywood blockbuster, in 1990. 'You should get them to make a recording,' suggested Beighton. 'I'll make some calls,' said Cowell. At lunchtime he entered Beighton's office. 'ITV don't want to co-operate and the actors say they won't make a record. So that's it.'

Two days later, Beighton returned: 'Simon, you need to think again. I could have sold 100,000 singles today. The buyers for the high-street shops haven't stopped asking whether RCA could supply a recording by the two actors. The public want it. It'll be a definite number one.' Her prediction of a chart-topping hit changed Cowell's attitude. His biggest dream, more than money and fame, was a number-one hit. However, his instant enthusiasm to produce a record by the actors was dampened by Jeremy Marsh, RCA's chief executive, and John Preston. Both doubted Cowell's prediction that the song, which would take months to release, could be successful. Prompted by Beighton, Cowell ignored his superiors. Beighton's taste, he often said, was typical of the average man in the street – exactly the people he was targeting. 'I only understood the real importance of TV after Robson and Jerome were suggested to me,' Cowell would say. Aged thirty-six, this was the decisive moment that saw Cowell switching from opportunistic survival to a more considered strategy. The combination of experience and inspiration propelled him to bet everything on Beighton's idea. His fate depended on getting a number-one hit.

The scepticism within RCA was puny compared to Robson Green's vehement rejection of Cowell's calls. Cowell was repeatedly repelled by the actors, and later by their agent uttering threats of legal action. Using the 'never take "no" for an answer' attitude learned during the Fanfare era, Cowell switched his efforts to Green's mother, until the actor finally telephoned to complain about harassment.

'Why won't you talk to me?' asked Cowell.

'Because I'm not interested.'

'Why?'

'Because I don't want to appear on *Top of the Pops*,' replied Green.

Cowell cut to the chase: 'Listen to me. You both will get £50,000 for just two hours' work to record the song, even if it doesn't sell.'

After a pause Green asked, 'Are you prepared to put that in writing?'

On the eve of the two actors' arrival in Pete Waterman's studio, Cowell was inspired while driving down the Westway spur towards Shepherd's Bush to add a twist. The media was in full cry about a free concert in Hyde Park to celebrate the fiftieth anniversary of VE Day. The star of the show would be Vera Lynn, the military's sweetheart during World War II, who rallied the troops in 1942 by singing 'White Cliffs of Dover'.

'We'll put that on the B-side of a "special",' he decided.

'You're mad,' Beighton told Cowell, who needed to persuade Robson and Jerome to record the second song.

Waterman was, however, impressed. 'He never goes into a room thinking he knows the answers. He goes in with his ears open, fires a rocket and sees who salutes it.'

Soldier, Soldier had been forgotten by viewers by the time Cowell arranged his first meeting with the actors to sign the contracts. 'I don't know what Robson looks like,' he confessed to Beighton. 'I've never watched the programme.' To avoid embarrassment, they agreed that she would greet Robson Green first. In preparation, the night before Cowell watched an England football match. Green, he knew, was a passionate supporter, and he wanted material for a conversation.

After a successful meeting, Cowell began plotting how to revive an old song and make it a number-one hit. Much depended on Mike Stock in Waterman's studios. He was paid £180,000 to produce and mix the track so that it sounded like a $1-million Hollywood production. Stock ranked among the world's best producers and was dismissive of the A&R man – or the 'Um and Ah' man as he subsequently described Cowell – who didn't understand his art. So after delivering Robson and Jerome to Borough Road, Cowell did not stay for the recording. Two hours later, after the actors had left and the mixing began, Stock decided that some of the vocals could be improved. As usual, he hired Des Dyer, the lead singer of Jigsaw, as a session singer to 'ghost' a few words, for which he was paid £10,000. Handing over the completed tape, Stock told Cowell, 'You can make your fortune from this.' Both laughed, although Cowell dreaded the sceptics within RCA eager for his failure: 'I bet the house on Robson and Jerome, but after the wrestlers and Power Rangers I knew what I was doing.' The record was due to be released in November 1995, six months after the original TV programme.

At 9 a.m. every Monday morning, BMG's twenty managers met in the boardroom. Beighton was at one meeting at the beginning of November, as usual, and was 'taking the flak for Simon, who never arrived before 11 a.m.'.

'How's our team of solicitors?' asked Preston, referring to Robson and Jerome. 'Denise, I really don't think we should release it.'

'We should,' insisted Beighton, infuriated by the sniggers and scepticism, 'because it's going to be a number one.'

Cowell, she knew, had deliberately avoided the meeting because he was 'paranoid and hated even thinking about people laughing about him'. Preston's scepticism was supported by Clive Rich, BMG's business manager. 'This guy's a liability,' Rich told the meeting. 'Simon's costing us too much.' Rich's accounts showed that even Cowell's chart successes had been loss-makers. He spent so much in acquiring the artists and promoting the records that the profits disappeared. Now, Rich warned, Cowell was repeating his profligacy. Beighton ignored the doom-mongers.

In the pre-launch marketing, Cowell called in every favour from his media friends in order to get Robson and Jerome on radio and television, including *Top of the Pops*. His efforts failed. Both actors, unwilling to demean themselves as mere singers, rejected all offers, except for one programme: Cilla Black's *Surprise, Surprise*.

Cowell also waged a blitz on newspapers and magazines, and

was roundly ignored by everyone except Piers Morgan, the pop columnist at the *Mirror*, who agreed to write a double-page plug for the record. Cowell also commissioned a slick video based on the film *Brief Encounter*. In anticipation of his success, he even renegotiated his contract with BMG to remove the limit on his bonus. Preston agreed because he doubted that the public would buy the record.

In 1995, songs became hits by selling about 150,000 copies during the first week. The independent shops, RCA's salesmen reported, were refusing to stock 'Unchained Melody', but Beighton, responsible for selling to the chain stores, called in favours and sold 100,000 copies.

The night before the launch, 22 million people watched Robson and Jerome perform the song on *Surprise, Surprise*. Cowell's fate now depended on whether the viewers' excitement from eight months earlier would be rekindled. The following morning, he nervously awaited news of the first day's sales. At lunchtime, he saw on the computer that RCA was shipping 350,000 copies and there were outstanding orders for nearly a million more. Overnight, he had personally earned £1 million.

'Oh, darling,' Cowell gushed to Beighton, 'I want to buy you something.'

'My electric toothbrush broke this morning,' replied his staunchest ally.

Cowell returned that afternoon with a Cartier watch and a Dunhill lighter.

That weekend, he went with his father to the local Curry's store in Swiss Cottage. 'Unchained Melody' suddenly wafted from the shop's tannoy. 'My son here made that,' Eric told the sales assistant. Cowell protested his embarrassment, probably for the last time.

As sales rose towards 3 million copies, he had won credibility among some but criticism from the purists for 'shameless commercialism and raw populism'. The more perceptive realised that Cowell had 'shifted the goal posts'. Television, he proved, could produce stars as popular as those nurtured by the traditionalists, and they could earn as much money as 'genuine artists', even though they lacked credibility in the music world and would leave no legacy. In his euphoria, Cowell dismissed the carping 'arty snobs'. He craved fame but was satisfied with notoriety. Success was his revenge against his enemies. 'I've become more than confident,' he told a friend. 'I don't care what everyone in the room is saying – if they're against me, I tell them they're wrong.' He spoke about enjoying every moment and taking nothing too seriously. 'The thrill', he would say, 'is not the money but the game.'

The only shadow was a dispute started by Des Dyer. After 'Unchained Melody' became a hit, the session singer had asked Stock for a share of the unexpected bonanza – possibly 2 per cent of the profits. The demand surfaced amid rumours that Dyer's voice rather than Robson Green's was on the record. Angry session singers are a familiar noose around studios' necks but, instead of placating Dyer, Stock faced him down. Undeterred, the singer approached RCA. Initially, Preston ignored the allegation. After all, Nigel Wright, the producer of Robson and Jerome's first album, reported that 'both can sing and I don't need session singers. Just a bit of tuning and editing.' Cowell confronted Dyer personally. 'I don't believe you,' he said. But once the singer approached a tabloid newspaper in the week before Christmas to say 'I'm the voice of Robson and Jerome,' Cowell feared that a scandal would ruin his triumph. 'This has become the worst week of my life,' he told Stock melodramatically. 'It's ridiculous to say Robson and Jerome can't sing. They sang on TV. I don't even believe you needed a session singer. You just brought up the backing during the mix.'

Nevertheless, he urged Preston to capitulate. Cowell's

misfortune was the historic animosity between Stock and Preston. The producer had accused Preston, as head of the BPI, the music industry's trade organisation, of having 'rigged the market' to keep Stock, Aitken and Waterman's records out of the charts. Preston vehemently denied the allegation but acknowledged that other record companies had sent teams to the shops to buy their own records and thus push them up the charts, as was common practice in those days, or had 'bought up' space in the shops to exclude the independent labels. Even Brian Epstein admitted buying a chart place for The Beatles' first single back in 1962. BMG, insisted Preston, was innocent of that ruse, and he had defeated Stock's litigation against the BPI. In that soured relationship, co-operation between Preston and Stock was impossible, even after they heard that the tabloid was about to publish Dyer's allegations. At his own expense, on 20 December Stock obtained an injunction against Dyer, but Preston, at Cowell's behest, decided to buy peace. Since money was not a problem, he paid Dyer about £75,000, which was deducted from Stock's royalties.

With the problem resolved, Cowell focused on the follow-up to his big hit. After leading the now eager Robson and Jerome back into the studio in early 1995 to record 'I Believe', he persuaded the producer of the BBC's National Lottery programme to broadcast the duo singing their next song, 'Up on the Roof', for the 16 million viewers. The record beat Oasis's 'Wonderwall' to number one with the sale of another million records, and was followed by another chart-topper, 'What Becomes of the Broken-Hearted'. To keep the tap flowing, in 1997 Cowell offered the duo £3 million for another album. 'Simon,' replied Green, 'you've made us a lot of money and we enjoyed it, but we're actors and this time we're going to say goodbye.'

Green, the son of a miner, appeared to be bitter about the wealth Cowell had personally earned from the duo's success and the estimated £20 million in profits accumulated by RCA. Relations crumbled further after Cowell spotted Green and Vanya Seager kissing behind the curtains on a TV set. He felt deceived and also feared a public backlash against the married actor.

'We're having an affair,' Seager confessed to Beighton.

'You'll have to tell Simon the truth,' Beighton urged.

One morning, Seager did not arrive for work. Unbeknown to Cowell, she was pregnant and was about to marry Green. Beighton watched Cowell's shocked reaction when he finally heard the news. 'Simon, you've been very generous to Vanya and her daughter and you haven't been treated fairly,' she consoled her friend. His personal relationship with Green was terminated but, in consolation, he did at least possess enough tracks to produce a series of profitable Robson and Jerome compilation albums. He would next meet Green and Seager by coincidence in Mauritius over Christmas 2005, and they would celebrate the new year together.

Nothing could now hinder a raft of new projects. With production-line creativity, Cowell began commissioning the casts of TV soaps to sing pop songs. First up was 'Hillbilly Rock, Hillbilly Roll' by the Woolpackers, a group of actors from *Emmerdale Farm*; next came 'Where Did Our Love Go?', the Supremes hit, sung by Tricia Penrose, the actress playing the barmaid in *Heartbeat*; then the cast of *Coronation Street* 'sang' a compilation album; and, finally, ITV's Gladiators sang Thin Lizzy's 'The Boys Are Back in Town'.

Millions of records had been sold when Cowell heard in 1997 that the BBC was selling the recording rights to *Teletubbies*, a popular children's programme. RCA was quickly outbid by Telstar and Sony, prompting Cowell to arrive at the BBC's offices. 'What's the highest bid so far?' he asked. '£350,000,' he was told. 'Get all the lawyers in here. I'm offering £500,000,' he told the bemused group, 'and I'll sign today.' The public corporation could not refuse. 'Some people will love these records,' Cowell believed, 'others will loathe them. But as long as enough want to buy them, they serve their purpose.' He personally visited the Woolworth's buyer and pre-sold half a million records to score another hit.

Cowell's pop and dance records, John Preston trilled, were 'a brilliant strategy'. RCA's market share had risen from 2 to 8 per cent, prompting the label's managers to claim credit for their inspired support in signing Robson and Jerome. They also rewrote Cowell's contract to increase his royalties, bonuses and raises based on sales. The prospective sum, admitted an RCA manager, amounted to 'a fantastic blue-sky package, with the danger that he could earn more than Preston'. With his new fortune, Cowell bought himself a black Jaguar XK8 and began looking for a house in Holland Park, one of London's most expensive areas.

To expand his niche and stymie rival labels – in particular, Universal Music – he next signed a £1-million agreement with Simon Jones, who managed the business affairs of two major ITV companies, to own the rights to any artists under contract to the broadcaster. Next, he flew with Mike Stock to Hollywood. 'We'll only do number ones now,' he declared as he sought out the managers of Eddie Murphy, Antonio Banderas and other stars. Every approach was rejected. He returned to London to hear that a Stock-produced record by *London's Burning*'s John Alford, the so-called 'singing fireman', had flopped, costing £100,000, and that Curiosity's latest offering had also crashed.

'A real donkey,' said Korda Marshall, who was among many still mocking the opinionated A&R man frequently seated at Mr Chow in Knightsbridge, holding a Kool cigarette high in the air, wearing trousers pulled up high over his waist as usual and exposing his hairy chest. 'He always wants to come to the party but he's either not invited or comes and leaves early,' added Marshall. His opinion was shared by Lucian Grainge, Cowell's rival at Universal: 'Simon's not a credible A&R person. He's got a good name for concepts like Teletubbies and Zig and Zag, but he's a nebbish in the professional sense. Too clunky with artists and he can't talk to talent.' In an industry employing at most 500 people in key positions, somewhat like a private club, Cowell was flustered by his peers' continuing derision.

In desperation, he invited promoter and plugger Ron McCreight for lunch. Expecting a good meal, McCreight found himself in a dingy cafe on the Putney Road with a cup of tea and a sandwich, listening to Cowell's lament about a recent BMG conference. As usual, Cowell explained, he had played an amusing prank – surreptitiously taking out of the player a rival A&R man's CD of a cool rock band and inserting the Village People's 'YMCA', which had won many laughs – but the bottom line was that BMG's German directors had not applauded his commercial success. Seeking reassurance, he wanted an explanation. McCreight was genuinely flummoxed. Surely, said McCreight, he was appreciated in London, and that was enough? Cowell demurred.

His consolers were the close-knit group of skiers. Keith Blackhurst, Jeremy Marsh, Hugh Goldsmith and Mike McCormack were attractive to a man who was inquisitive and happiest when surrounded by energetic people who satisfied his short attention span. During their regular evening routine – gigs at the Wembley Arena and the Hammersmith Apollo, followed by dinner at La Familia in Kensington and then Tramp or Annabel's, the Mayfair nightclubs – the group noticed how easily Cowell walked through those establishments, like Jason King in *Department S* or Oliver Tobias in *The Stud*. To his friends, he appeared a handsome playboy rather than a sex symbol, and, while enjoying banter with girls, he was easily bored. Marriage, they agreed, was unlikely for a man who dared to be different and attracted 'no jealousy because he's loveable but too selfish'.

Louise Payne, a well-built topless model who had featured in the *Sun*, disturbed their preconceptions. In 1996, Cowell had spotted the blonde arriving at a music party with Bernard Cribbins, an actor famous for singing 'Right Said Fred' and 'Hole in the Ground'. 'I've got to meet that girl,' Cowell told Jackie St Clair, who was accustomed to executing introductions on Cowell's behalf. When that operation failed, Cowell bribed Kim, his sister-in-law, with a ridiculously expensive handbag to bring Payne, a friend from her modelling work, to his home.

Volatile but not strikingly intelligent, Payne did not fit with Cowell's usual taste for exotic, dark-skinned beauties. She was attractive but not stunning, but she had the right figure, was street-smart, liked his type of fun and fitted in with his friends. 'I'm in love,' he told Beighton, insisting that she meet Payne at a Chelsea hotel.

Over the following weeks, he complained that 'She's driving me nuts. She's playing me so well.' Payne was refusing to have sex with Cowell, although she eventually relented at the Four Seasons hotel during a trip to New York. In his excitement, he proposed marriage and bought a large diamond ring, and she agreed to move into his house. A few weeks later, while 'adoring her', he decided the commitment was too much and cancelled the wedding, and Payne moved out to live with her mother. Three weeks later, Cowell telephoned from a holiday in Thailand. On reflection, he said, he missed her. 'I can't believe you have the nerve to call me,' Payne said, but eventually agreed to resume the relationship.

Life together in Kingston Hill was filled with fun despite the constant presence of Sinitta and Jackie St Clair. Payne found the ex-girlfriends 'awkward' but accepted that Cowell required their presence for his self-confidence. As Denis Ingoldsby, a record producer, told Payne, 'Simon's insecure. He needs all the attention.' Unusually, Cowell also appeared to have settled on which woman he loved, although Payne's qualities, he decided, were on the limited side. When his parents were invited for tea to his house, Payne made an effort, despite Cowell's disencouragement, to arrange the cups and saucers, milk and biscuits and carry them into the living room on a tray. Cowell held his breath as his mother tilted the pot to pour. 'You seem to have forgotten the water,' smiled Julie.

5

Respectability

In the small car park in west London, the white van outside the headquarters of Brilliant!, a new publicity agency, could easily have been ignored if only the rumours about the five girls inside had not aroused Cowell's curiosity. It was 1995, and Cowell had been visiting Nicki Chapman, a former promoter at RCA, who mentioned that the girls, members of a group called Spice, were exceptional. 'Hi, girls,' said Cowell, opening the van's door and effortlessly persuading them to play the tape of their new song. Within seconds of the start of 'Wannabe', Cowell was electrified. 'Thanks, bye,' he said, racing back to his office.

Months earlier, at a regular A&R meeting, Cowell had asked Jeremy Marsh whether anyone had heard about Spice. The nervous looks terminated the conversation. Since then, he had heard nothing, so on his return to Fulham he called the girls' manager, Simon Fuller. The two Simons had first met about ten years earlier, when Cowell had asked Paul Hardcastle, Fuller's client, to write a track for Sinitta's album. Since then, they had met occasionally at music-industry parties. 'Have you had any offers for Spice?' Cowell asked. 'Because we'll double whatever you've been offered.' 'I've already signed them to Virgin,' replied Fuller. Cowell was irritated about a missed opportunity. Fuller's abrupt termination of the conversation was not surprising: they were neither friends nor kindred spirits.

Born in Cyprus in 1960, Fuller had then moved with his family to Africa, where his father managed schools, before coming to Britain for his secondary education. Unlike Cowell, he had used his schooldays in Hastings, Sussex, to become a businessman: first, by booking groups to play at the school on weekends; and, later, by acting as an agent for the groups, arranging performances in clubs along the Sussex coast and in London. After leaving school, he became an A&R man at Chrysalis and then set up alone. His success, unlike Cowell's, had been swift.

In April 1985, Paul Hardcastle, his client, sold 6 million copies of his song '19' worldwide, inspiring Fuller to name his management company 19 Entertainment. Fuller would also take on Annie Lennox, whom he transformed into a global star. Rich and clearly exceptional, he had first heard about Spice from Marc Fox, a music publisher employed by BMG, in 1995.

The group was the brainchild of Chris Herbert, who began his career by managing school friends keen to become professional musicians. After some success, his father, an accountant, suggested they jointly create Safe Management and, after various managerial mishaps, they decided in 1993 to form a group. Scrutinising the innumerable boy bands, Herbert made a radical choice: he would form a girl band. In the auditions he was searching for characters with sex appeal to attract boys and 'attitude' to appeal to girls. Eventually he chose five women and, at his own expense, drilled and rehearsed them for nearly a year in a rented house. The next stage was to find a creative team by 'showcasing' Spice, in November 1994, at the Nomis studios in Shepherd's Bush to an audience of producers, songwriters and music publishers. 'Everyone's blown out,' thought Herbert afterwards, convinced that he would soon be offered a recording contract.

Unbeknown to him, his group were dissatisfied with his plans and were seeking alternative management. Displaying their artistic 'integrity', the five girls had identified their ideal music and image, pinpointing Marc Fox as an ally. Fox brought Spice to meet his colleagues at RCA's office. As the ebullient visitors 'nicked my drink, sat on my lap, danced across the room and caused mayhem, the whole building came to a halt,' Fox recalled.

By March 1995, at Herbert's expense, Spice had recorded 'Wannabe', which they had written with two professional songwriters, but Herbert suspected his relationship with the girls was fracturing. The bad news was delivered in a telephone call by Geri Halliwell and Mel B announcing his dismissal. 'It's a kick in the teeth,' said Herbert about the betrayal. 'I've spent one year, day in, day out, creating them. I'm gutted.' He would find no sympathy in the industry for his loss. Loyalty was rare among artists who selfishly pursued their own interests.

Ambitious to participate in the group's career as their A&R man, Fox had by then introduced the girls to Simon Fuller at 19's office. Fox had two good reasons for selecting Fuller: his track record, not least with Annie Lennox, was widely acclaimed; and he was also contractually retained as a consultant by RCA, which was part of the BMG group.

'When I left the girls at 19,' recalled Fox, 'I thought BMG and RCA would have the rights to Spice, and also believed Fuller's assurance that I would be the group's A&R man.' Fox's earlier introduction of Spice to RCA's Jeremy Marsh had prompted Marsh to arrange an audition of the girls one afternoon in February 1995 at his own house in Brook Green, west London. Naturally he invited his friend and RCA's consultant Simon Fuller to accompany the girls. Sitting in Marsh's kitchen, Spice sang 'Wannabe'. At the end, Marsh's team – Hugh Goldsmith and Mike McCormack – immediately agreed to sign a contract with the girls, who had every reason to expect things to go smoothly: Annie Lennox was an RCA artist, RCA's management of Take That was widely acclaimed, and Fuller, their friend, was contracted to RCA. BMG's chairman, John Preston, approved making an offer.

Negotiations began but, after a short time, to Preston's and

Marsh's surprise the ground shifted. Fuller declared that he had become the girls' manager, and as such he was no longer restricted by his consultancy agreement with RCA, which specified his role as a 'production company'. As their manager, he added, his demands for the girls were complicated. Although Fuller was demanding more money than any other hitherto unknown group had received in music history, Marsh believed that their friendship and the consultancy made an agreement inevitable. After all, the distinction between 'manager' and 'production company' was purely semantic. Fuller disabused him of that notion. As their 'manager', said Fuller, he was expected to obtain the best deal, which was impossible if he were to act as their 'production company'. He could not be forced into a conflict of interests. Nevertheless, the RCA team still did not anticipate any problems.

'We can expect to do the business with Simon,' said Hugh Goldsmith. But as Fuller's costly demands increased and he mentioned that Virgin was eager to oblige, Marsh and Goldsmith smelled a lawyer's games. 'Simon knows how to bend it,' said Goldsmith. 'He's wriggling out of an obligation.'

As the news percolated up to John Preston that Fuller was, like many in the industry, getting around his consultancy contract, the BMG chairman angrily insisted that Marsh and Goldsmith use their personal relationship with Fuller to enforce it. 'Fuller's cutthroat and ruthless,' Preston complained. Everything depended upon Marsh. Blowing hot and cold, he eventually told Preston that although he personally felt betrayed by Fuller, he did not believe that the consultancy contract could be legally enforced.

By then, Fuller was exploiting his undoubted talents and auditioning the girls in Los Angeles. The reaction was positive, especially from John Ferriter, an agent who also persuaded Fuller to rename the group. 'Spice in America means drugs,' said Ferriter, 'so why not call them Spice Girls?'

Fuller returned to London, rejected RCA's offers and signed with Virgin. Preston's suspicions about Marsh and his own staff grew. His unease was aggravated after 'Wannabe' was released in 1996 and became the most successful single in the US that year. The Spice Girls' first album would sell 30 million copies, making them the most successful girl group in history. Their triumph, reflected Preston, was helped by Nicki Chapman and another former RCA promotions executive lured by Fuller.

'I was very unhappy,' Preston would say. 'I was pretty miffed. I couldn't know whom I could rely on.'

'The whole building had a right to feel betrayed by Fuller,' agreed Marc Fox. 'I went to him at the beginning because of our mutual contractual relationship.'

Among Chris Herbert's friends, 'Scavenger' was among the more polite labels given to Fuller.

Cowell watched Fuller's glory with envy. A rival's success always gnawed at him, especially as Fuller's fame was global – including a 1997 trip with the group to meet Nelson Mandela. Cowell's only consolation, as the accolades accumulated, was the news that the group had decided, while Fuller was recuperating from back surgery in Italy, to sack their manager. Some suspected the disputed rumours about his alleged affair with Emma 'Baby Spice' Bunton had contributed to the split. At that defining moment, and devastated by the women's disloyalty, Fuller might have reflected on the sentiments of Chris Herbert, Marc Fox and John Preston about his own conduct.

His dismissal by the Spice Girls encouraged Cowell to meet Fuller. The idea, proposed by Mike McCormack, was that they should travel to the house Fuller had rented from Franco Zeffirelli in Positano, Italy. McCormack had no doubt that Cowell was 'jealous of Fuller', but that was not a barrier in brokering the first real meeting between two mavericks with complementary talents. Fuller was visionary, brave and excelled in pragmatically moulding an artist's ideas into stardom, while Cowell was a big personality, even a show-off, who pursued his own understanding of the public's taste regardless of criticism. However, the bottom line remained that Cowell, unlike Fuller, had not created a star, let alone a global phenomenon like the Spice Girls.

Over two days, the men discussed possible co-operation. Fuller had taken a year off to consider new ideas and artists, and offered Cowell the chance to work with the groups he was signing, including 21st Century Girls and S.O.A.P.. Fuller also invited Cowell to invest in his latest Internet idea, Pop World. 'I expect to earn about £300 million from it,' predicted Fuller confidently, although, according to Cowell, he would end up losing about £12 million. At the end of the visit, neither the ideas nor the chemistry, in particular, gelled. Crudely, in Zeffirelli's magnificent house Cowell felt inferior to Fuller. Not only had Fuller managed world-class artists, while Cowell was merely a TV spin-off merchant, but he was much wealthier, and money counted for both men. Equally important, Fuller's sophisticated approach to business reflected his better education.

By coincidence, the two next met the following Christmas at the Royal Palm hotel in Mauritius. Cowell was impressed that he and Fuller were reading the same book. Although in his mind he could imagine saying to Fuller, 'I would be proud to walk onto the stage and say you were a partner,' he resisted formalising a relationship.

By then, Fuller was speaking about shedding his reliance on unpredictable artists, or anyone else for that matter. Instead, he was planning a multimedia business which would include S Club, seven young people from a TV adventure show on which they regularly broke into song. He planned to sell the brand through the show, records, tours and memorabilia. His offer to Cowell of an undefined job was again rejected. 'I'm happy at RCA,' Cowell explained.

By the time they next met in London, Fuller was planning to launch the Pop World website with Bob Sillerman, an American entertainment mogul. Over dinner, Fuller again offered Cowell a job launching records from the online show, but Cowell, unconvinced about the stability of a business based on the Internet, rejected the idea. He did not reveal that he was immersed in a scheme to match the Spice Girls' success.

One year earlier, Hugh Goldsmith had arranged a meeting between Chris Herbert, still searching for salvation after the Spice Girls' betrayal, and Cowell. They agreed to create Five, or 5ive, a new boy band. In the jargon, the prospective group would 'cross-appeal' to boys and girls and should sound, Cowell told Herbert, 'something like the Pepsi Max commercial. Like urban sport, a sound for the boys.' He added, 'Don't show me anything until you're ready.'

Inspired by Cowell, newspapers reported on the spring 1997 auditions to find the so-called 'Spice Boys'. Nearly 3,000 hopefuls appeared. A few weeks later, Herbert rented the Nomis studios to reduce the best twelve to the final five for Cowell to hear at the end of the day. 'Great,' Cowell pronounced, instantly offering the group a recording contract, with Herbert as their manager. In his own mind, Cowell intended finally to establish himself as a credible A&R man.

With that settled, Cowell went skiing with the RCA gang to La Clusaz. On the second day, he raced on mini-skis in the dark against two Italian air hostesses and crashed into a tree, tearing a knee ligament. Hobbling, he returned to London to hear that Herbert had rented a three-bedroom house in Camberley, Surrey, and was planning singing and dancing lessons for Five. 'Forget that,' said Cowell. 'I've got an idea.'

An A&R man's success, Cowell knew, depended on persuading writers to sell their best material, and Pete Waterman had introduced Cowell to Denniz Pop, a Swedish executive producer at the Cheiron Studios in Stockholm. Known as the 'Hit House', the studios were famous for being the haunt of Max Martin and Herbie Crichlow, who ranked among the world's best songwriters. Crichlow flew to London to play Cowell a tape of 'Clap Your Hands', his new composition. 'I like the music but not the lyrics,' Cowell told the writer. 'Give me some other words.' An hour later, Crichlow's lyrics had become 'Slam Dunk (Da Funk)'. Ecstatic, Cowell ordered Five to fly to Sweden for six months and begin recording. During regular visits, Cowell supervised the production and micro-managed their return to Britain to play in the 'newcomer' slot of *Smash Hits* magazine's national tour. Cowell watched every live performance scrupulously and ordered improvements in the build-up to the fans' vote for the 'best newcomer' at the end of the competition in the Docklands Arena. Five won.

Heady with success, Cowell organised a massive launch party at 5 p.m. on 5 November 1997 on the fifth floor of Harvey Nichols, the Knightsbridge store. Arriving in the packed room with his girlfriend, Louise Payne, Cowell played his media contacts to secure widespread coverage, including a page in the *News of the World* by Rav Singh, a friendly journalist. The results in the charts were less impressive. The record only reached number ten in Britain and failed in America. Cowell became jittery.

The atmosphere in the RCA office was tense. Preston had not satisfied BMG's desperation for hits, and the Spice Girls' fortunes fed his suspicions about Jeremy Marsh's ambition. The time had come, he believed, to leave, and his disenchantment was mutual. At BMG's German headquarters, the company's president, Rudi Gassner, had identified Richard Griffiths, a British executive with mixed accomplishments in America, as Preston's successor. In the days before the handover, Cowell nervously hoped that Preston, whom he regarded as his mentor, would speak positively about him to Griffiths. He had reason for concern: standing outside Preston's office, Cowell had overheard the chairman snipe, 'Everything which is shit in this building is caused by Simon Cowell.' Some insiders would say that Preston, a corporate animal, misunderstood the maverick.

Griffiths was in no doubt that Preston's advice on the night before his departure was that he should dismiss Cowell. 'He's an embarrassment . . . an impediment,' he recalled Preston saying. Preston would deny that sentiment and assert that Griffiths was 'bigging himself up' to present himself as Cowell's saviour. Preston did, however, recommend that Cowell's latest demand for a new £5-million contract as a joint venture in a 'label deal' was 'too expensive'. He told Griffiths, 'I'm tight-fisted and I'm not sure he's worth it.' On that basis, Preston added, 'Simon is expendable.'

Jonathan King remembers calling Griffiths. 'Simon's the one person you should keep on,' said King. 'Don't listen to John Preston.'

Griffiths was open-minded. With a background in rock, he had no taste for Cowell's pop music and little sympathy for his position in the music business, but he recognised that the sale of 4 million Robson and Jerome records and Five's debut had 'changed Cowell's game plan'.

On his first morning, he walked into Cowell's office. 'Have you got any hits?' he asked breezily. Cowell lifted a tape: 'Five's new single, and it's great.' Charming and with impeccable manners, Cowell could not conceal his trepidation. 'I know you're nervous about me,' said Griffiths, 'but I've made even worse records than you have. Let's hear what you've got.' The sound was good, and Cowell visibly relaxed. Griffiths gave Cowell the deal he demanded: a shared venture in S Records, Cowell's own music label, thus transforming him into a serious music executive.

Success for Five in America depended on Clive Davis's interest, so Cowell flew to New York with Chris Herbert and Louise Payne. Davis was keen and, with his support, the group did an eight-day tour of the US, appeared repeatedly on TV, performed in Times Square, hit the US top ten and scored more hits across the world. To celebrate, Cowell bought Louise an MG sports car, but soon after he decided the commitment was suffocating him. Amid some recrimination, the relationship was again suspended. Unperturbed and on a high, Cowell was already planning Five's next record.

Davis, he discovered, had rejected Max Martin's latest song, 'Hit Me Baby One More Time', on the orders of one of his groups, TLC. 'Can I hear it?' Cowell asked Davis. Cowell was electrified. Every year, he knew, the world's songwriters only produced three or four 'exceptional' pop songs which guaranteed success for an artist. Martin's latest was one of them.

'I've now given it to a new girl called Britney Spears,' said Martin.

'Never heard of her,' said Cowell. 'You're mad. No one can be successful with a name like that.' Then he added, 'I'll give you a new Merc 500SL if I can have that song. It costs £95,000.'

'No, it's contracted,' replied Martin, convinced that Spears would make him much richer.

Cowell was left with a problem. Five needed a Martin song, but fortunately the writer agreed to work with them in New York. 'I don't want any complaints before I've finished,' he stipulated.

'Absolutely,' promised Cowell, setting aside time to deliver a stiff warning to the group. The song Martin had written in his 'factory' was 'Bye, Bye, Bye'.

'What a bag of shit,' said one of the Five as Martin played the tape. 'Crap,' agreed another, fuelling a chorus of vitriol. Martin was outraged. After castigating the five boys for their rudeness, Cowell asked Martin to forgive them. 'No,' snapped the writer.

The song went on to launch 'N Sync across the world. Five began sliding in America and, beneath the smiling exterior, Cowell was incandescent. He had fallen victim to the A&R man's familiar misfortune: he had created stars who, he believed, had become ungrateful, self-deluded monsters suicidally convinced about their own genius. His only salvation would be their swift demise.

At that moment, he was called by Louis Walsh, a genial manager from Mayo in the Irish Republic. The second-oldest son of a poor Catholic taxi driver with nine children, for years he had struggled between football and failed musical ventures, until he created Boyzone in 1993. Ever since, Walsh's group was in the news, either because of their successive hits or because the manager was concocting colourful stories, including one about the group crash-landing in the Australian bush. 'I give the media stories and they use them,' said Walsh. 'They don't always have to be based on truth, but at least they're plausible. The one about the plane crash in Australia I made up, but who's going to know or check?'

In his initial attempt to secure a recording contract for Boyzone, Walsh had telephoned Cowell, but his calls had been ignored. Instead, he had signed with Lucian Grainge at Universal. Now, he called Cowell again about Westlife, a new boy group he had created. 'Simon was a hustler, ambitious and the one to watch,' Walsh would recall, 'and unlike EMI and Virgin, who were snobby, RCA liked pop music.' Again, Cowell repeatedly refused to take his calls. They finally met while Cowell was visiting Dublin one Saturday evening with a group that was booked to appear on a TV programme – proof of the exceptional care he offered his artists.

'Why don't you take my calls?' Walsh asked Cowell in the studio's green room. 'You could have made millions with Boyzone.'

'Darling,' replied Cowell, waving his cigarette, 'we'll work something out.'

Walsh was undeterred. 'I've got a new group you should see,' he continued. Six singers were waiting in a huge hotel suite for an audition. 'I've called them Westlife,' said Walsh, hoping that Cowell could provide the grooming and marketing, and a winning song.

Cowell agreed to meet the group at the hotel, despite his new cynicism about boy bands. He had come to hate the vapid young men with plastic, virginal prettiness targeted at young girls and gay men. 'If you want to be a singer and can't play an instrument, you join a boy band,' he believed. 'A lot of people are doing it just to be famous. There's nothing more nauseating than seeing a boy with a ghastly haircut and fake smile singing an insincere song.' Yet Take That, on their way to producing eight number-one singles, were proving the contrary.

At the end of the audition Cowell was blunt. 'Two of them have good voices, but they all look terrible. I hate them. You need to recast the group.' The lead singer, added Cowell, should definitely be excluded. 'No way,' replied Walsh.

Cowell returned to London convinced about his own judgement. 'I was good at spotting who was in a different league in a group's early days,' he would later reflect.

Two months later, in June 1998, Walsh called again. 'I've changed Westlife a lot,' he said. 'Come back to Dublin.' The call came at the right moment. Five had failed to match either the Spice Girls or Take That and were causing trouble. The next day, Cowell returned to the Dublin hotel. After listening for thirty seconds, he called out, 'Stop.' Walsh feared the worst. 'I'll sign them,' said Cowell. 'They'll be international stars.' Walsh was astonished. 'I've got the producers lined up,' added Cowell. As he would later admit, after seventeen years of mixed fortunes, 'I wanted to prove a point after the Spice Girls and Take That.'

The group would be launched singing 'Swear It Again', produced by Pete Waterman. Cowell groomed the group meticulously and organised the promotional campaign. 'You can't sell many records if they're rubbish,' he often said. There was only one ingredient he could not fix: the luck of delivering the right sound at the opportune moment. The release was set for the second week of April 1999. His fate within RCA would depend on the midweek charts published on Tuesday 20 April.

Two days before that, Cowell flew to Boston for the annual BMG conference, anticipating the certainty of embarrassment at listening to the latest Take That hit, the gut-wrenching egoism of Clive Davis offering his latest global hit and the familiar scoffs about the Teletubbies. At least the detested grilling had been partially mitigated by Five's past success. But to the world he remained the promo guy who got lucky, lacking credibility as a serious player. Westlife would be his revenge against the doubters.

Early on Tuesday morning, he called London. 'It's at number one,' he was told. Bubbling with excitement, he telephoned his parents, who were by then living in Brighton. 'You'll never believe it . . .' he started. Unusually, his mother's voice was strained. 'Well done,' she said. 'I'll call you back.' Mindful of Eric's homily – 'Let him enjoy his day' – she resisted revealing the previous evening's events.

As usual, Eric had sat with his gin and tonic completing the *Daily Telegraph* crossword, a ritual he had followed for over fifty years. 'Have you noticed these crosses in the crossword?' he asked Julie.

'I can't see anything,' she replied.

'Yes, there is a pattern of four crosses.'

'Yes,' agreed Julie, unconvinced, 'I can see them. I'll go and make dinner.'

Minutes later, she found Eric slumped in the lavatory, dead after a heart attack. The following day, her son's call from Boston had interrupted the gloom as the family gathered at her house. Unsure how to break the news, especially when her son was on a high 3,000 miles away, she remained paralysed and near-silent.

After she replaced the receiver, the Reverend Martin Morgan, a family friend who was in the room, advised that Simon should be told. Nicholas Cowell made the call, catching his brother in his hotel room. Simon was devastated. Unable to conceal his despair, he went down to the hotel lobby in tears. After years of anguish, embarrassment and failure, his *consigliere* and best friend had missed the moment of his triumph. Arrangements were made for him to fly to New York and travel on to London by Concorde.

Infuriatingly, the supersonic jet broke down, but after some delay he finally reached Brighton. Tony, his half-brother, was arranging the funeral. Simon, he noticed, was distraught. He could not deal with his father's death, just as he had been unwilling over the previous two years to cope with his father's obvious decline. At a family lunch some months earlier, Eric had signalled that his heart problems were insuperable and that he had given up hope, but Simon had ignored the reality. He had been unable to accept his father's mortality.

'Eric's death is an eye-opener that people don't live for ever,' Tony told Simon after Eric's Christian funeral.

'I thought both my parents would,' replied Cowell.

Only in the following days were some of his father's secrets revealed: namely, that he was Jewish and that his first marriage in India had gone unmentioned. At that moment there was much to ask, but the opportunity to hear answers had been lost. No attempt was made to approach the other members of Eric's immediate family, and his self-imposed isolation was preserved.

For Cowell, the sadness was tempered by Westlife's success. Walsh joked that he had even ordered the group to sign agreements not to marry for five years, but on serious matters he deferred to Cowell. He had little choice. Whenever Walsh gave an opinion, Cowell walked away without a comment. 'Yes,

Simon,' Walsh learned to say. Cowell had taken control and was listening to no one. After Pete Waterman repeated a suggestion offered by Walsh, he was abruptly silenced: 'You speak to nobody. Only me. I decide. It's what I think that counts.'

'Simon's become frighteningly focused,' Waterman reported, bemused by Cowell's extremes. 'He's totally absorbed. Totally wrapped up in it.'

Cowell had identified 'Flying Without Wings', written by Steve Mac and Wayne Hector, as Westlife's next song. 'I badly needed it,' he admitted later. 'I felt total sickness, afraid I couldn't get it.'

Both writers were persuaded to come to his office to play their tape. Cowell locked the office door. 'I had the bit between my teeth,' he would admit. 'Just the same focus as on Robson and Jerome.' Two hours later, they agreed to sell the song to the group. It was an instant number-one hit.

Inevitably, success sparked obstinacy among the group. Previously, Cowell had been influenced by his artists, but now he was intransigent, unwilling to allow any interference, especially regarding the choice of songs. Ferocious arguments erupted. 'Get into the studio,' Cowell ordered, exploiting the group's personal limitations. 'Do it my way or go to your lawyer and check your contract. You'll get a writ.' Like lambs, they obeyed. The trick in the music business, Cowell had learned, was getting difficult people to do things they don't want to do. Resistance, he decided, should be crushed.

Walsh, an affable Irishman, dodged the blows. He was not the sharpest manager, but he understood better than most the internal politics of record companies. He had chosen Cowell, and he stepped back as Rav Singh, the *News of the World*'s showbiz reporter, 'exposed' Stephen Gately, a member of Walsh's protégés Boyzone, as gay. Stars rarely 'came out', and Singh invited Cowell to celebrate his scoop in a Mayfair nightclub.

Walsh was uninvolved in that operation, and stood back once

again as Cowell planned Westlife's first American tour. Recent attempts by British groups to sell in the US had not been encouraging. Unlike the 1980s, when Irish performers including U2 and Sinead O'Connor had stormed the country, the following decade saw British acts including Oasis and Five flop on the other side of the Atlantic. To compete with the Backstreet Boys and 'N Sync, Westlife needed a sharper edge with harder music. Only Cowell, Walsh knew, could fashion the high-cost promotional blitz. During the autumn of 1999, Walsh congratulated himself on choosing Cowell, as the A&R man choreographed Westlife's release of 'If I Let You Go' in America into a number-one hit, with their next two singles also topping the charts.

Cowell spoke about milestone birthdays as watersheds in his life, and that October saw his fortieth come around. The celebrations started with Hugh Goldsmith hosting lunch at San Lorenzo in Knightsbridge for the RCA crowd, followed by go-karting. In the evening, Jackie St Clair hosted a surprise party at Mirabelle in Mayfair. Forty guests arrived wearing wigs and with their faces covered in foam. As gifts for Cowell they brought bottles of Grecian 2000. During the meal, a 'monstergram' – a big-bosomed woman acting as an S&M-style stripper – appeared and 'assaulted' the birthday boy. Beside him sat Svetlana, a Russian beauty wearing a wedding veil. Finally, the same friends and family partied at Mr Chow. Cowell was on a roll as he mixed with a collection of gossipy pop journalists, including Piers Morgan and Andy Coulson, the showbiz editor at the *News of the World*; music executives, including Lucian Grainge; and a clutch of former girlfriends all supportive of a man who had finally established himself.

Westlife transformed RCA's fortunes overnight. The group dominated the *Smash Hits* tour and within three weeks Cowell delivered 'I Have a Dream', Westlife's Christmas song, which would beat Cliff Richard's 'The Millennium Prayer' to number one and score the year's highest record sales. 'He looks like the cat who got the cream,' carped one of his RCA rivals. 'I'm on a high,' admitted Cowell. 'So now it's confident Simon.' Pete Waterman, whose company had produced the records, was ebullient: 'Simon is Mars and Venus. He's one man pulling all the strings and has taken everyone to the cleaners. They now hate him because of his hits.' Steve Redmond, the editor of *Music Week*, discarded his own jaundiced opinion: 'He's no longer the promo guy who got lucky. He's created new success. He's qualified to sit at BMG's table.' Cowell's music, he believed, had made the rock A&R men look 'old-fashioned and pedestrian'.

Redmond was chairing his magazine's annual awards ceremony at the Grosvenor House hotel in Park Lane in December 1999, the perfect venue to make a statement to the industry. Nearly a thousand music executives and artists were packed into the ballroom. Like fighters at a boxing match, the contenders for the prestigious record of the year award were bunched in the corners of the room. At Universal's table, Lucian Grainge was expecting Boyzone's Ronan Keating to step onto the stage. Instead, Westlife won. The applause was followed by Redmond blessing Cowell's success by naming him Executive of the Year and BMG as Corporation of the Year. He anticipated a humorous, mixed reaction but was staggered by the outburst as 'the A&R geniuses screamed howls of derision because Cowell was regarded as an upstart plugger and he'd refused to flog around pubs looking for talent. They liked to think they were a higher calling, what they called "art".'

In the battle between art and business, Cowell had won. His triumph was a decisive turning point in his life. His only defeat would be inflicted by Naima Belkhiati, a member of girl group Honeyz. For weeks, Cowell had relentlessly pursued the beautiful singer. 'I've got a big crush on you,' he had announced as he plied her with gifts of clothes and jewellery. Fearful of his pursuit, Belkhiati asked Denis Ingoldsby, her manager, to intercede.

'Simon, please leave her alone,' asked Ingoldsby, who was critical of Cowell's treatment of Louise Payne. 'She's very young and she doesn't fancy you.'

'I can't,' replied Cowell. 'I'm obsessed by her.' She resisted, he later concluded, because 'she suspected that after I got her, that would be it. And she wasn't wrong.'

There were compensations to her rejection, with Lucian Grainge making the first attempt to lure Cowell from BMG. The executive who would become head of Universal Music in Los Angeles, the world's biggest music corporation, was cursing himself for rejecting Westlife after Walsh had called to announce his latest creation. 'Westlife? It's low-life,' Grainge had replied as he himself was struggling to save Boyzone. Ronan Keating, Boyzone's lead singer, wanted to manage Westlife simultaneously, seemingly unbothered about whether his own group fell apart. In the midst of his battle against Keating, Grainge had watched Westlife 'take off like a rocket', in so doing transforming Cowell, a man whom he had earlier regarded as 'a nebbish', into someone serious.

Cowell was invited for dinner at Julie's in Holland Park and offered 'a sensational deal' as head of Mercury Records. The package, said Grainge, was worth between £5 million and £7 million, including the royalties which Cowell would receive on Westlife. Cowell's cool reaction reflected his new emotional maturity. He would use the offer to leverage a better deal from RCA. Grainge did not, however, anticipate Cowell's speed. The very next day, BMG boss Rudi Gassner flew from Germany to meet Richard Griffiths and Tony Russell, Cowell's trusted lawyer and minder, at One Aldwych, a bar on The Strand.

Griffiths's hand was weak. Cowell's importance to BMG's credibility had become of more value than the profits. During the negotiations, Cowell waited impatiently. The details regarding royalties, rights and incentives were of less interest to a man who sought cash in the bank. 'He's looking for a simple equation,' realised one of the RCA team. 'A cheque in his hand to see what he's got, and he'll sulk if he doesn't get what he wants.' 'He's a big fish in a small pond,' said Gassner, as he trumped Grainge's offer, 'and he stays in our pond.' Cowell was finally flush with money.

Over the previous eleven months, he had been living at Jackie St Clair's while his new house in Holland Park was renovated. Originally he had moved in for 'just six weeks', but his constant changes to the house's design had prolonged St Clair's agony. Frustrated that St Clair would not allow him to use her bigger bath, instead compelling him to use a small bathroom, during his twice-daily baths to get himself 'minty fresh and squeaky clean using lots of gels' he allowed the water to run, unaware that the overflow was dripping through the ceiling. On top of that, he regularly threw away all the small silver spoons along with his empty yogurt containers, had burnt the sofas with cigarette ash, started a fire in the living room and destroyed an electric oven, filling the kitchen with smoke.

There were other strange habits. Before leaving for the office in the late morning, he regularly ate shepherd's pie and watched cartoons, but occasionally was still so bleary that he would crash his Ferrari into the neighbour's wall. 'The eleven months felt like eleven years,' St Clair complained later, presenting 'the visitor from hell' with a bill for over £100,000. His mother sought to have the final word. 'As you grow older', Julie Cowell told her son, who smoked heavily and ate junk food, 'you need to look after your appearance. You've only got one body.' He ignored her advice and similarly was deaf to her pleas about his clothes, buying only white and grey T-shirts and black and grey sweaters. 'I'm bored with your T-shirts,' Julie told him, 'I like it when you wear suits. You look nice in suits.'

St Clair sought to change her guest's appearance by introducing him to regular weekends at spas and by taking him to Richard Anderson, the Savile Row tailor, Berluti in Conduit Street for his shoes, Rod McNeil for his teeth and George Trumper for West Indian lime cologne. He would spare no expense to own the best of everything.

At forty, Cowell believed he was unbeatable and even untouchable. He was wealthy, had status in the music world and was enjoying one-night stands, while maintaining an on–off relationship with Louise Payne. Foolishly smug, he was unknowingly heading towards a fall.

6

Double Disaster

Cowell's mood on arrival in Mauritius for a family Christmas holiday and the millennium celebrations was still affected by Eric's death. There was no compensation for losing his best friend.

On the plane from London were his mother Julie; his brother Nick, with his Russian girlfriend following his separation from his wife Kim; Sinitta and a boyfriend; and Cowell's latest girlfriend, Lisa Forward, a blonde lap dancer, with her four-year-old son. 'She's an erotic dancer,' Cowell told his startled fellow guests at The Residence, a five-star hotel. Jeremy Marsh, also staying at the hotel, watched Cowell quickly become irritated by his companion. First, Cowell told shocked guests that the woman was 'rubbish' in bed. Next, he looked on open-mouthed as her son, dressed as Batman and waving a toy Keyblade, charged around the restaurant demanding sausages and chips. Finally, the woman committed the cardinal sin: she was boring.

'I've just heard', Cowell told Forward, 'that I've got to fly today to New York for a business meeting.' After dispatching the girl and her child on the next flight to London, at his expense, he continued his holiday. The clear sunlight over the Indian Ocean on the eve of a new century reinforced Cowell's conviction that, professionally, everything was perfect. He had created a slew of new groups which, in combination with Westlife's four number-one records and US launch with a new album, suggested limitless opportunities.

Heading his new ventures was Mero, created during spring

1999. The male duo – Derek McDonald and Tommy Clark – had been launched that July as RCA's 'biggest project in a decade'. McDonald's song 'It Must Be Love' was recorded in Los Angeles and a promotional video shot in Miami. In the autumn, Cowell predicted that Mero would beat Wham! and the Spice Girls. 'We had to fight off a lot of competition from the other labels,' he told the *Sun*'s showbiz journalist, 'because when a band like this comes along everybody gets wind of it.' On his return to London he even spoke about Mero outdoing Westlife. 'They will become our worldwide priority act,' he puffed in anticipation of the release of the single in March 2000.

The record flopped. 'It's a disaster,' Cowell moaned. 'I wasn't involved enough,' he later confessed. 'I had no feeling for the band.' His disengagement, he admitted, had grown as he focused on his ultimate challenge to Simon Fuller and the Spice Girls.

By 2000, the Spice Girls had sold over 38 million albums, but their girlie image had become tainted by torrid relationships and unexpected babies. Cowell's conviction that there was 'a gap in the market', as he told BMG's Richard Griffiths, had been shared over the previous year by thirty-two rival A&R men who, like Cowell, calculated that the Spice Girls' 'popularity was over' and who had launched girl bands with the line 'It's time for somebody new.' The image Cowell sought to manufacture was again drawn from a Pepsi Max commercial, this time featuring five women embodying 'girl power' and excelling in various extreme sports. He relied once more on Chris Herbert to produce the new stars. Both were motivated by getting their revenge on Simon Fuller. Herbert blamed Fuller for his losing the Spice Girls, and for Cowell 'beating Fuller had become a preoccupation'. 'Girl Thing was a cynical attempt to copy the Spice Girls,' admitted Cowell. 'The dust had settled enough for us to do it without looking like we were bitter,' said Herbert.

Five girls were recruited after auditions and began rehearsing together in a suburban house under Herbert's direction. In his vision, the new 'Five' would not utter gimmicky girl-power slogans but deliver a 'fresh, funky, bubble-gum rap' sound. Using the Pepsi advertisement as the blueprint, they hired the same songwriters for what Herbert hoped would be 'the ultimate girl band'. Despite his entrenched doubts about manufactured bands, Cowell believed that while it was almost impossible to create an original group, Girl Thing could be, he told Griffiths, 'The biggest ever. We'll overtake the Spice Girls.'

Impressed by Cowell's detailed scrutiny for the autumn campaign, Griffiths approved a £1.5-million budget. 'I've got a great feeling about this,' Cowell told the showbiz writer Rav Singh. Much of the budget was spent recording specially written songs, among them 'Pure and Simple', but Cowell chose 'Last One Standing' to launch the group. The only hiccup was the significant loss of Pete Waterman. 'I've got to get off the gravy boat because success is drowning me,' he told Cowell before disappearing.

Keith Blackhurst, the chief executive of BMG's Deconstruction label and responsible for marketing the new group, regularly refused Cowell's requests for more money, especially for the promotional video. Shying away from confrontation, Cowell smiled and headed straight for Griffiths, who approved the extra amounts. Budgets were obstacles Cowell would not tolerate. Blackhurst, who had brought Kylie Minogue to RCA after her split with Waterman, was bemused. 'Girl Thing is just Kylie by numbers,' he laughed. The comparison did not deter Cowell. After all, Kylie had become a global sensation before Griffiths, wrongly believing that her best days had passed, terminated her contract. Griffiths believed in Girl Thing, and Cowell was more committed than ever. In his endless pre-launch interviews, he presented himself as the brilliant producer of Five and Westlife who was challenging Fuller and the Spice Girls in co-operation with Chris Herbert, who was certain he could beat his original invention.

'The amount of hype is unprecedented,' bubbled John McKie, the *Smash Hits* editor, excitedly. 'There's a real buzz about them. They are five gorgeous girls, and the song is great. People want something new and in-your-face, and they definitely fit the bill.' Few journalists could resist the story.

Drawing on every relationship, Cowell placed the group on nearly forty TV and radio shows before unveiling the climax of an unprecedented promotional campaign at the Eiffel Tower. About 400 European and American music executives, journalists and celebrities were invited at RCA's expense to travel to Paris.

By the time half of them arrived on the Eurostar train from London, most were 'well-oiled', reported one promotions executive. The girls' flamboyant live performance before lunch in the tower's second-floor restaurant was greeted rapturously by the journalists, who then travelled across the city to a five-star hotel for dinner and a party. Most felt obliged to write gushing prose, and Cowell returned to London expecting an instant number-one hit.

'Last One Standing' was released in July 2000, with 200,000 copies distributed to the shops. The factory was on stand-by to manufacture hundreds of thousands more. At 10 a.m. on Tuesday morning, Cowell arrived unusually early in his office, waiting for the head of sales to deliver the 'midweeks' sales sheet. His stomach churned as he looked down the list to find Girl Thing at number eight. 'Complete disaster,' he muttered in shock. 'Black Tuesday,' said Blackhurst, saddened by the blow.

Cowell dreaded Griffiths's call. Griffiths believed in only backing winners. 'He could have destroyed me,' admitted Cowell later. 'He could have said, "You fucking idiot, you've blown all this money. You're not as good as you think you are."' Instead, Griffiths delivered a considered judgement: 'All I will say to you,

Simon, is that this is the best thing that will ever happen in your career.' And he put down the phone.

Cowell waited two hours before entering Griffiths's office. 'My ego is out of control, isn't it?' he asked.

'Yes, Simon,' replied Griffiths.

'I've made a huge, huge mistake,' groaned Cowell, retreating in depression.

The group also flopped in the US. Crushed by failure, Cowell knew that the music village and, especially, Fuller were thrilled about his humiliation. The self-styled genius feared being swept away by public exposure. He hated his enemies describing him as a mediocrity. In the blame game, he first regretted 'surrounding myself with "yes men"'. Next, he cursed Waterman's absence. Finally, he blamed 'my own stupid mistakes'. It was, he conceded, 'hard to settle down. Until then, my earlier failures could be blamed on others, and I was quite retaliatory. But this time I couldn't blame anyone else. I had made the bad decisions. The Girl Thing song wasn't good enough. The cynical attempt to copy the Spice Girls had crashed because they were still doing so well and there wasn't a gap in the market. It was a very difficult few weeks to get my confidence back. I was responsible for an expensive flop. After Westlife I had believed my own hype.'

The crisis of confidence was compounded by realising that he had hit a plateau. Pop music had hit a buffer. Neither Waterman nor the Swedes were mass-producing new hit songs, and Cowell could 'no longer plan the next twenty years with confidence'. Despite their phenomenal success, purists were even attacking Westlife. 'A bunch of karaoke monkeys barely able to scratch their empty testicles,' commented one newspaper. Cowell believed in hits rather than artists, but he needed a twist in his career to find the stars.

The seeds were sown over dinner at the Ivy in Beverly Hills soon after the Girl Thing flop. Cowell and Griffiths were entertaining Stephen Ferrera, the producer of Shakespear's Sister, an award-winning pop-rock band. Inevitably, the three men were dissecting their recent misfortune. 'All you do is great and makes a lot of money,' Griffiths told Cowell, 'but if you want a legacy in the A&R world you need to sign artists who have credibility.' Cowell disagreed: 'To me the future of the music business is tied to TV, and TV in America has not been a platform to drive music like in Britain.' He outlined his vision for a television programme with music, which Ferrera would later swear bore similarities to *American Idol*: 'Nostradamus, because it was just as he said.' On his return to London, Cowell discussed his ideas with Jonathan King, whose influential *Tip Sheet* made him a prime candidate in November 2000 to become EMI's chief executive. However, days later, King's career imploded when he was arrested for engaging in sexual activity with underaged boys. Among his calls from the police station seeking sureties to be released on bail was one to Cowell.

'Right, I'll do it,' promised Cowell instantly.

'Don't you want to know how much?' asked King.

'I said I'll do it, just tell me where I go,' said Cowell, who would pledge £50,000.

'It won't do you any good,' said King apologetically.

'That's what friends are for,' insisted Cowell, who would later deny any knowledge of the reason for King's arrest.

'Simon's the last of the non-gay queens,' King would say.

To raise his spirits, Cowell decided to revive Girl Thing. On reflection, number eight in the charts did not spell doom. All they needed was a brilliant follow-up. 'We shouldn't have cloned the Spice Girls,' said Herbert, constantly working with Cowell to recraft the group's image during a lengthy tour of Britain. Atomic Kitten's fate was encouraging. The all-girl hit group had recently been on the verge of disbanding when a new song,

'Whole Again', restored their fortunes. The same, they hoped, could happen to Girl Thing.

Cowell's first thought was 'Pure and Simple', a song written by a team created by him and Herbert. RCA had spent a huge sum on hundreds of mixes to perfect the recording. As a test, the record was released in Asia, but it flopped. 'We'll try it here,' Cowell sighed, until Griffiths argued persuasively that the record would fail in Britain too. Cowell dithered and, during the following days, the song slipped from his control into the hands of his rivals in a succession of events which would change many careers and television history.

Weeks earlier, Cowell had been invited for lunch at J. Sheekey's, off St Martin's Lane in London, by Nigel Lythgoe, a successful producer of TV entertainment shows. Cowell arrived with Denise Beighton. Lythgoe explained that his son, living in Australia, had sent him a video of *Popstars*, a show on a local station about the creation of a pop group. The Australians, continued Lythgoe, had adapted a similar programme produced by Jonathan Dowling in 1999 in New Zealand.

Dowling's programme, itself based on *Opportunity Knocks*, the ITV blockbuster which started in 1956, featured a panel of two men whittling through 500 contestants to produce five girls to be fashioned into a group. The show's magic lay in the auditions, the contestants' rags-to-riches stories and the climax – a recording contract for the winners. TrueBliss, the winners in New Zealand, had gone on to score some success.

Now, continued Lythgoe, Claudia Rosencrantz of ITV had commissioned a British version of the programme to be shown in two parts. First, thousands of aspiring young singers would be auditioned and reduced to a talented handful. The second part was a documentary series featuring the chosen five rehearsing as a group in preparation for the release of their single and their launch into stardom. The new group would be called Hear'Say.

Coming to the point of the lunch, Lythgoe continued, 'One of the three judges will be a record executive. It could either be you or Lucian Grainge.' Instantly, Cowell expressed his interest.

But then, slowly, the tone began to change. Lythgoe boasted about his achievements, the size of his office and even the perks which he enjoyed. Cowell counter-boasted, and soon Denise Beighton's mouth dropped: 'Two gladiators were fighting without a reason. It was shocking.' At the end of the meal, Cowell accepted the offer. His only condition was that RCA would be given the recording rights for the group.

During their return to Fulham, however, his interest dissipated. 'I can't work with that man,' he told Beighton. 'He's an egomaniac, a nightmare.'

'Simon, it was both of you. It was a clash of egos. I've never seen you like that. You reacted badly.'

'Well, I can't see it working.'

'You'd be absolutely crazy not to do the programme,' replied Beighton, before adding, 'In Australia the programme made a number-one hit.'

There was a long silence. Then, 'OK, I'll do it.'

Cowell's acceptance triggered Simon Jones, an ITV business manager, to begin negotiations to formulate a contract. The two had known each other since Cowell, on RCA/Arista's behalf, had bought all the rights to Granada's music programmes. As their discussions progressed, Cowell again equivocated. Indecisive at best, he was racked by uncertainty. Cowell imagined the programme would be vaguely similar to the American MTV channel's *Making the Band*, appealing to a fringe audience. 'I don't see it,' he told Waterman. 'I can't see how it'll work.' Privately, he also feared public humiliation. 'I didn't want to fall on my face in front of millions in an uncertain format,' he would admit. 'I wouldn't be in control.' Instead of explaining those fears, he called Jones with a reasoned excuse. 'I don't think I can do it,' he said. 'I've got a band splitting up and I've got to dedicate my time to that.' He added that the music industry was a private world and, like magicians not revealing how someone was sawn in half, he needed to protect the secrets. 'If you made baked beans, you wouldn't show the public the ingredients.'

Jones was surprised by Cowell's about-turn. He had clearly failed to grasp the potential record sales. RCA, declared Jones, had automatically lost the record deal. 'Cowell's galled by that loss,' Jones later told Lythgoe. 'He was angry and hurt. Tough. Tell Universal that it's their deal and their executive will be on the show.'

Grainge was delighted but, as it was on the eve of him becoming Universal's deputy chairman, he refused the offer to appear on the show as inappropriate and, as he put it, 'bullied' Paul Adam to take his place.

Two others were needed for the panel. The previous year, Lythgoe had suggested Jonathan King. 'Over my dead body,' replied Rosencrantz, 'but what about you?' 'Done,' said Lythgoe, and put down the telephone. Lythgoe, Rosencrantz realised, seemed 'obsessed with being famous and being watched by millions'. He would be joined by Nicki Chapman, who had been encouraged by Simon Fuller to be a judge. Soon after, Cowell met Fuller at an industry dinner. He could not understand Fuller's excitement about *Popstars*, but persuaded Fuller that Chris Herbert should become Hear'Say's manager.

Naturally, Herbert was keen for Hear'Say to have a winning song. Noting Cowell's decision to abandon 'Pure and Simple', he discreetly brokered the song's sale to Paul Adam, Cowell's rival at Universal. Following standard industry practice, RCA had not formally signed a contract for the 'mechanical licence' with the writers of 'Pure and Simple', and Cowell was powerless to stop the deal. Normally, Cowell resisted confrontation and rarely lost his temper, but on that occasion his self-restraint disappeared.

'We spent time, money and energy on this song,' he screamed at Herbert, 'and now we don't have a single.' Eventually, Herbert would retreat: 'I was his protégé and I abused my alliance with Simon.' But by then it was too late. As a fallback, Cowell chose 'Girls on Top' for Girl Thing's relaunch in early 2001, to be followed by 'So You Wanna Have Sex'. Cowell's anger with Herbert was aggravated by the buzz in the RCA building about *Popstars* and Universal's excitement about 'Pure and Simple'. Even before the show's transmission, Cowell knew his Girl Thing errors were about to be compounded.

Cowell flew to St Lucia for Christmas with his family and Mandy Perryment, who had been married to Iain Burton for five years and then after the divorce had a brief 'fling' with Cowell in London and Miami. Also on the trip was Louise Payne, reunited once again with Cowell. 'Simon has a healthy appetite for my women,' Burton observed when he heard about the party. 'First he goes off with my live-in, and then he's off with my ex-wife.'

Their conventional beach holiday in St Lucia ended after a hotel refused him admission because he was wearing a T-shirt. Standing outside, he met Michael Winner, the film producer.

'You should come to Barbados,' suggested Winner. 'It's much better than St Lucia and I've got six empty rooms at the Royal Pavilion which you can use.' The extra expense was no trouble. Cowell was spending on 'a reward basis: I was buying everything I wanted but kept back enough for a bad day', and Barbados was an introduction to a new way of life. 'I like the people, the restaurants and hotels,' he declared.

Throughout his holiday he was tormented about hitting a plateau. Past glories had faded and he could not imagine his own and the industry's future. 'The normal system has failed,' he said. The only solo star of substance to have emerged in recent years was, in Cowell's opinion, Robbie Williams. Although he had been in Take That, a boy band of the kind Cowell was so adept at creating, Cowell struggled to imagine where he would find a similar artist. Pop music, he sensed, had reached the end of an era, and he needed to change. How, he wondered, could he plan his future when he probably would not secure any of the five blockbuster hit songs which would be written the following year? And how could he 'ever get any leverage to avoid dependence on a mad businessman', just when insiders were gossiping about falling record sales?

The dilemma was compounded by Cowell's unease with singer-songwriters over whom he could exercise little control. 'I don't like to put myself in a position where I am dependent on one individual's creative talent to bring what we need to make this company profitable,' he said. He preferred creating a star rather than nurturing someone who believed in their own abilities. Cowell confided his fears to Tony Prince, a friend who was also in Barbados and staying at the exclusive Sandy Lane hotel, and planned to outline his salvation to Louise. His on–off–on fiancée was eager to eat at Crane, a traditional restaurant right on the beach. 'OK,' said Cowell, 'so long as I can spend the evening describing my idea of *Pop Idol*.'

On his return to London he invited Simon Jones for lunch in Fulham. 'I've got a great idea for a TV show,' he said. 'I'm changing jobs to Pearson TV,' replied Jones. 'Tell me after I get there.'

Cowell's fears were worse than he imagined. On 10 January 2001, he was staying with Louise at the Mandarin Oriental in Knightsbridge while his house was again being renovated. Both were watching the first episode of *Popstars*. Quickly he became agitated, not least because Louise, 'with the attention span of a gnat', was engrossed by the programme. Just before the end, he telephoned Pete Waterman, who at the time was sharing a hotel room in Cheshire with two girls. He was also watching *Popstars*.

'I've made a huge mistake,' moaned Cowell. 'My stomach dropped. That was great TV. Universal's going to sell a ton of records.' The programme reached 7.6 million viewers who had been riveted by Lythgoe's brutal honesty about awful performers. 'I'm sure there's a tune in there somewhere,' the self-styled 'Nasty Nigel' had carped.

The excited chat about *Popstars* in BMG's building over the following days magnified Cowell's irritation. The so-called TV expert, sniped his rivals, had rejected his biggest break. Cowell was contrite. He had failed, he confessed to Beighton, to understand TV's potency because his instinct was for selling instant packages rather than nurturing talent. To recover, he realised, he would need to launch his own TV programme. 'They've got it wrong,' he later told Waterman as they chatted about *Popstars*. 'It doesn't work. There's no pathos. There's no end. It's not real. It should be like real auditions. Bad and real. And it should be single singers, not groups. They should compete so there's a winner at the end. Are you in?'

His worries were aggravated by the fate of Girl Thing. Their new release had bombed at number twenty-five. 'It's not the best of times,' Cowell moaned.

'We'll cut and run,' agreed Griffiths. 'It's better to accept defeat and move on to the next war. But it's not all doom and gloom: Westlife is a success.'

Already murdered by the media, Cowell pulled the plug on Girl Thing. 'We were dropped. It was awful,' complained Michelle Barber, one of the group. 'When it went wrong, Simon just vanished in a puff of smoke. He melted away.'

Cowell admitted his error: 'I shouldn't have presented myself in public as a Svengali figure behind the band. I should have kept way in the background.'

There was a more fundamental fault: Cowell's short attention span subverted the essence of nurturing artists. Although he paid enormous attention to detail, he was interested in his artists' appearance, their songs and the marketing rather than the development of their characters. Just as his turnover of women was fast and unpredictable, he had shown limited patience when engaging with each girl in the group. His qualities were perfectly suited to television.

By then, Cowell had once again met Simon Jones, who had by now moved to Pearson TV, later to become FremantleMedia.* Over lunch, Jones heard Cowell's description of the talent competition which would become *Pop Idol*. 'And I'm just off to see Simon Fuller because he's good at these things,' said Cowell, acting on Richard Griffiths's advice that 'The two of you should do some work together.'

Over dinner with Fuller and Nicki Chapman at the Conran restaurant in the Fulham Road, Cowell admitted, 'I've made a mistake,' and laid out in detail his notion of *Pop Idol*, with himself as one of the judges looking to find a real star during a series of auditions. The idea, Fuller knew, was nearly as old as television itself, but he immediately offered Cowell a twist to the *Opportunity Knocks* format that he had been mulling over since 1998: 'The audience should decide the winner by telephone voting.'

'Brilliant,' said Cowell.

The next stage, they agreed, was to interest a broadcaster. Their ideal was Claudia Rosencrantz at ITV, but the likelihood of the network jettisoning *Popstars* for an untested programme was remote. Nevertheless, after a conversation, Lythgoe agreed to mention the refined idea to Rosencrantz, with him continuing as a judge.

'Good news,' Cowell told Jones. 'ITV have agreed to

* FremantleMedia is the content subsidiary of RTL, which is 90 per cent owned by BMG.

consider *Pop Idol*. We can pitch to ITV through you. I'll see you tomorrow.'

To Jones's surprise, Cowell arrived with Fuller. 'This is not a crappy TV producers and talent show,' said Cowell, dominating the discussion, 'but this is how I will find my next Robbie Williams or Cliff Richard.' Four judges, he explained, would hold real-time auditions and discuss the contestants' merits. The audience would be entertained not only by the contest, but also the music. 'The public loves hearing their old favourite songs,' he said, emphasising the importance of music for the show's success. 'And then the audience will vote by telephone for the winners.'

His motive, Cowell admitted, was to secure for BMG the worldwide rights to every record released by *Pop Idol*'s victor. Jones's task would be to compose the detailed presentation to ITV.

With Jones on board, Cowell now needed Griffiths's approval. He arrived for a meeting with Jones. As the two Simons entered the office, Griffiths shouted, 'I know your fucking game. You just want to be a TV star.'

In the division of labour, Cowell would produce the records, Fuller would manage the new star and FremantleMedia would create the show. In the agreement drafted by Jones in early February 2001, the creators and the owners of the show's format would receive 5 per cent of the production budget as a fee. Since there were three owners – Cowell, Fuller and FremantleMedia – Jones increased the fee to 6 per cent, to be divided equally. Fuller rejected that suggestion. He wanted ownership to be divided between himself and Cowell. Jones's insistence on one-third each finally prevailed. Ten years later, Fuller would say, 'I offered FremantleMedia one-third ownership for producing the show,' calling it 'the biggest Christmas present they'll ever have, ever, ever, ever'. Neither Jones nor Cowell recalled that interpretation of the discussion.

On Tuesday 13 February, Alan Boyd, an experienced producer of TV entertainment who would later be employed by FremantleMedia, was asked by Jones to meet himself and Cowell. To Boyd's surprise, Fuller also arrived. Once again dominating the presentation, Cowell explained, 'We've done a sketch of what we want. Now we want you to build it up.' The television professional was tasked with creating a bible describing the logistics for the studios, the video-taping facilities, the organisation of auditions for 50,000 contestants, the installation of a telephone system for voting, the running order and finally an estimate of the cost.

'On that day,' Boyd would later say, 'I had no idea who created the idea.' He made an appointment with a BBC executive who was eager to compete with ITV's *Popstars* on Saturday nights. But before Boyd, Cowell and Jones arrived at the BBC's headquarters, Claudia Rosencrantz called.

'Come and see me before you go to the BBC,' she said. Fearful that the BBC would gain an advantage, she was excited by gossip that the show featuring Hear'Say's recording of 'Pure and Simple' had secured a huge audience for the new show. Her excitement was mirrored at BMG, although not by Griffiths. He had been summarily replaced by Hassa Beitholt, whose focus was on BMG's loss of millions of pounds' worth of business to Universal.

Before pitching to the BBC and ITV, Cowell and Fuller sat down with their respective lawyers, Tony Russell and Andy Stinson. By the end they had orally concluded two critical agreements: first, that the income from selling the programme's format should be divided equally between Fuller and Cowell; second, that Fuller's company, 19 Entertainment, would manage the winners' careers, while Cowell and BMG owned the recording rights.

Soon after, Fuller called Cowell to propose a change. 'I've got an idea,' he said. 'To make it simple, you take the music rights and I'll take the TV rights. And both the rights are for life.' Cowell consulted Hassa Beitholt, but crucially neither understood the value of the intellectual property rights of television programmes or had experience of selling a TV format to foreign broadcasters. They only wanted to sell records and reproduce the phenomenal success of February's *Popstars* final. Trusting Fuller, Cowell accepted his suggestion and did not consider that their arrangement should be immediately formalised by a signed contract. There was naïvety, Cowell would later admit, but he also believed he had an oral agreement with Fuller. In the frenzy, Cowell's only concern was to persuade Rosencrantz to accept the programme as outlined in the twenty-page proposal.

'We won't be relying on music to make the show successful,' said Cowell, taking the lead while Fuller and Jones listened. 'It will be a soap opera.'

'I love it,' said Rosencrantz, committing ITV before the BBC could make a counter-offer.

While finalising the contracts, Fuller called Jones. 'I've agreed with Simon', he said, 'that I should have his third, so that means I have two-thirds.' Surprised, Jones called Cowell, who confirmed his arrangement with Fuller. Accordingly, and unbeknown to Cowell, Stinson negotiated on Fuller's behalf with Jones a far-reaching contract between ITV, FremantleMedia and Fuller's company 19 to make *Pop Idol.*

In sharing the royalties or income derived from owning the intellectual property rights of the programme across the world, FremantleMedia would own and be responsible in perpetuity for all of *Pop Idol*'s production and distribution rights and the merchandising of any products. In return, the company would give to Fuller 50 per cent of any income received from the US and 10 per cent from the rest of the world. In other words, if *Pop Idol* succeeded, Fuller would proceed to earn millions of pounds. Fuller also insisted that if the programme was sold in

America, he would receive a credit as 'executive producer'. In turn, Jones demanded the same. To increase his status further, Fuller stipulated another single credit at the end of the show stating, 'Created by Simon Fuller'.

Ten years later, Fuller gave his version of those events to Richard Rushfield, the author of *American Idol: The Untold Story*:

Simon [Cowell] has been a friend of mine forever. We both love music. We're both entrepreneurs. So when it came to me finessing this show, there were two things I needed. One was a record company, because I was a management company, to offer the prize and drive the show. Then also a kind of partner in crime, someone who could work with me, who knew artists, who could be on the panel.

Fuller claimed responsibility for choosing Cowell as the record-company executive. On being offered the job by Fuller, Cowell allegedly replied, 'Yes, I want to do the exact kind of show. I've got my vision to have some artists on my record label.'

Fuller continued, 'He was on the same page. We were very much two peas in a pod. It was a perfect combination. He'd be on the panel and my idea would come to fruition, we'd go conquer the world.'

Cowell's position was that he was unaware of both the agreement between Fuller and FremantleMedia and Fuller's interpretation of events. In his version, he was focused on developing the show with a team which included Nicki Chapman. Due to legal complications, Nigel Lythgoe was excluded, so Cowell suggested that Pete Waterman should be a judge.

'We're starting *Pop Idol* next Thursday at a conference centre in Manchester,' Cowell told his old mentor. 'They'll pay you £500 for each programme. Be there at nine o'clock.' The fourth judge was Neil Fox, a radio DJ.

The programme was unveiled on 22 March 2001. Prominent

at the presentation was Lythgoe, appointed as the executive producer. Talented and perceptive, he was seething. He had adored the fame of 'Nasty Nigel' and was furious about losing that role, especially to Cowell.

Two days after the programme was unveiled, Cowell received a shock. Hours after its release, Hear'Say's 'Pure and Simple' was already a chart sensation, heading towards 1.5 million sales. 'Have you seen these numbers?' he asked Simon Jones, quoting the midweeks. 'They're incredible.'

Daily, Cowell would stare at the statistics in disbelief, distressed that Hear'Say was outselling Westlife's new single by ten to one. The music industry's battle lines for the next decade were being drawn. The first blow was delivered soon after, at the industry's prestigious Brit awards in a Park Lane hotel.

'Oh, Lucifer,' Cowell sniped at Lucian Grainge backstage. Grainge had just been honoured for his work with Hear'Say, and Cowell had booed the loudest. 'Our success has killed you,' joked Grainge, chortling how he had successfully lobbied to secure votes in Universal's favour against BMG.

'OK, let's move on to the next thing,' Cowell said the following morning, seeking to reassert his status. 'I've sold 25 million albums and scored fifteen number-one singles over the past ten years. There's more to come.'

The hectic pace of producing a television show finally ended his relationship with Louise. 'You're going to die a very lonely man' were her parting words. 'I probably won't,' Cowell replied, appearing unconcerned. He did not like commitment, he wanted an unhindered choice of women; he did not want children, he wanted fun; and he did not want to retire at sixty-five, sitting bored on a beach with 'someone I wouldn't be speaking to'.

A few days later, his mood changed. Payne's warning 'hit home'. 'I could die lonely,' he admitted to himself. 'I need to fill the gap by building a career for myself.'

7

Moment of Truth

'We must go to America,' Cowell told Simon Jones in March 2001. Even before the first auditions of *Pop Idol* were taped, Cowell wanted the format sold to an American network as a vehicle to sell records. Fuller agreed, so Jones booked three business-class tickets to Los Angeles and reserved rooms at the Four Seasons. 'I'm flying first[-class],' said Fuller. Cowell was flummoxed. BMG refused to pay for an upgrade, so, to avoid humiliation, he personally paid the difference and flew first-class.

The day after arriving, the three Simons were due to meet several network producers. 'I'm staying by the pool,' announced Fuller. Neither Cowell nor Jones were suspicious. Instead, both set off to pitch *Pop Idol* enthusiastically to NBC, ABC, CBS and Fox. All four networks were looking for formats to reverse their sliding ratings. Cowell's pitch was that a talent show with live auditions and the public's vote offered viewers the chance to share in the American Dream.

'And what exactly do you think we're supposed to be doing for you?' asked a 'lippy' female executive dismissively at the end of Cowell's speech.

'Well actually, sweetheart,' Cowell replied, 'it's more a question of what I could be doing for you.'

The next meeting ended with the terminal 'Well, we'll get back to you.' At the third, Cowell was stopped in mid-flow. 'No,' said the executive. 'Why not?' asked Cowell. 'Because it's a music show,' came the response. Every music programme in America had flopped. In 2000, ABC's *Making the Band* – about creating a boy band – had failed to win a wider audience beyond young girls and was relegated to cable channel MTV, while another network had dropped *Popstars*, about the creation of an all-girl group, blaming low audiences. The shows' consistent failure persuaded Mike Darnell, the producer of Fox's alternative entertainment, to dispatch an underling to meet Cowell. 'It's not for us,' announced his 'wishy-washy' mouthpiece.

Sitting on the kerb of Pica Boulevard outside Fox's 20th Century complex, angry because he had forgotten to order a car to return to the hotel, Cowell lit a cigarette and tearfully moaned, 'That was the worst meeting I've ever been to.' Back at the hotel, Fuller appeared unconcerned – an odd stance, Cowell would later reflect, for a man whose position was that he had invented and owned the format. Together they flew back to Britain to film the first auditions in Manchester.

Amid inevitable disorganisation, the judges met for breakfast with Ant and Dec, the hosts who would introduce the show and provide continuity links. The producers had supplied just one camera for the audition, which was initially directed at the contestant. When he or she had finished singing and left the room, the camera would swing to record the judges' discussion. Then the contestant would be recalled to be told the result. Cowell had agreed that format with Nigel Lythgoe and Richard Holloway, an experienced producer of talent competitions, including *Opportunity Knocks*. At the last moment, Claire Horton, the producer, installed a glass desk in front of the judges. Beyond that, despite Alan Boyd's twenty-page proposal, the detail of the programme's content was as flexible as Cowell's original pitch. Cowell's only certainty was relying on the right mix of people to find a new star for S Records, his music label.

The first day was chaotic. The hesitant procession of contestants was followed by the judges' ponderous opinions and then the meeting with the performers to politely reveal the results. By lunchtime, Cowell had had enough: 'I'm dying here. We have to be ourselves and tell them the truth like in a real-life audition.'

'It's purgatory,' Pete Waterman agreed. 'We would never listen to these kids. We would throw them out before they've finished.'

'Why would you want to interrupt?' asked Lythgoe indignantly.

'Because they're crap,' said Waterman. 'We have to tell the performers to their faces what we think. They've come for a laugh. They're not being serious. We've just got to tell these boys and girls the truth. They're rubbish.'

'And we need two cameras,' added Cowell, 'one on the judges.'

Extra cameras were quickly installed and the contestants were asked to repeat their performances. Led by Waterman, the judges spoke unpleasant truths. Cruelty was good television, Cowell realised, soaking up Waterman's performance like a sponge. 'Simon only turned nasty', Waterman would say, 'when he saw how much fan mail I was getting after the first *Pop Idol*.'

To craft 'Nasty Simon' Cowell adapted the deadly one-liners familiar to those in the music business. Waterman was as bemused by Cowell's swift reinvention of himself as he was by Lythgoe's frustration. 'You're being bombastic,' Lythgoe complained. 'You shouldn't tell contestants to "piss off". You should be reasonable.'

'Nigel,' said Waterman, 'you want to script us? We've done this routine for fifteen years. Telling people they're complete assholes is usual in the business.'

'Wrap,' Holloway called at 3 a.m. the following morning.

'It's working better,' Cowell told Waterman. 'We're making it work.'

That first day shaped the demarcation which would permanently disfigure music reality shows in Britain and America over the next decade. Namely, who devised the detailed format of *Pop*

Idol? Cowell's supporters were Claudia Rosencrantz, Waterman and Claire Horton, while those who opposed him moved with Lythgoe into Fuller's camp.

Pertinently, Simon Fuller had not travelled to Manchester and was unaware of the programme's evolution. 'Just as well,' thought Waterman. 'There's a clash of personalities.' A beast was conceived that was neither one person's creation nor under one person's control. Nevertheless, ten years later Fuller would say, 'I was so fast off the mark because I'd already had it worked out . . . It's not so rare that I was ahead of the curve, but I was ready to go.'

Despite his invisibility at the critical moments of *Pop Idol*'s conception and execution in Manchester, Fuller's lawyers were hyperactive. During the programme's production, but before transmission, Cowell's lawyer Tony Russell called his client with alarming news. When BMG, said Russell, had started negotiating the recording rights with Andy Stinson, Fuller's lawyer, Stinson had replied that Fuller owned all the rights, including the recording rights in perpetuity.

'You've blown it,' Russell told Cowell. 'Do you want to go on or pull out?'

Cowell gulped. He thought he had a verbal agreement with Fuller to divide the income fifty–fifty, with the TV rights going to Fuller and Cowell keeping the music rights, but in the absence of a written contract he was left paralysed. 'We're really fucked here,' Cowell thought.

'I'd look like the biggest mug in the world if I pulled out,' he told Russell.

His priority was to sell records. He had even agreed to appear on the show without a fee because he knew that Universal would jump in if he withdrew. Other news from the BMG negotiator compounded his concern. One of Fuller's team was heard to say, 'We're going to punish Simon Cowell,' reflecting Fuller's depiction of Cowell as a junior partner who should be grateful for any participation in the deal.

'That was a moment of truth,' Cowell would later say. Reflecting on the previous months, he wondered whether he should have been suspicious about Fuller's lack of enthusiasm after Rosencrantz had approved the programme. 'There were no high fives from Simon. I was screwed right from the beginning,' Cowell concluded.

The best tactic, he decided, was to ignore Fuller's demands and allow the negotiations to continue while he immersed himself in the show. His teacher, Claudia Rosencrantz, was emphatic after viewing the first rushes: 'TV is an intimate medium and the viewer needs to empathise with the presenter. Be genuine and never let the viewer down, because you're in their homes. Panels thrive on dynamics. Know your characters and stick to them: Neil Fox is the professional, Nicki is the warm, kind mum, Pete's the mad man and you're the gladiator.' Lythgoe, the executive producer, added his own advice: 'You've got to take control of this show. Be the judge.'

Listening and watching carefully, Cowell fashioned himself on Mickie Most and Tony Hatch, famous during the 1970s for terrorising hopefuls on ITV's *New Faces* talent show. In the creation of this new soap opera, he offered himself variously as 'Nasty Simon' and 'Sarcastic Simon', whose withering criticism dashed dreams. To perfect his performance, he sat uncomplainingly through intensive all-night editing sessions to learn the craft from those making the programmes. Scrutinising his performance, he noticed how the angle of his head, the pursing of his lips and the blink of an eye were all magnified to give special meaning. To excel in television's drama, he needed to produce a flawless act, milking every moment, aware that acting is the art of perfecting the lie. That feat, he hoped, would also conceal his personal insecurity from his critics' scrutiny.

The media launch for the show was arranged at the Hard Rock Cafe in Old Park Lane, Mayfair. Before the fifteen-minute promotional tape was shown, Cowell sat smoking in a corner, ignored while the other judges were besieged. After the promo was shown and the ecstatic applause ended, he was mobbed. Noting the square jaw, perfect teeth, blow-dried hair and toned muscles, the journalists discovered a 'star' delighted by his instant celebrity and whose brutality in the programme contrasted sharply with his personal courtesy.

'Fame will not change me,' Cowell told Rosencrantz after a summons to her office. 'I've never really hungered to be in front of the camera,' he continued, but in truth he luxuriated in having realised an attention-seeker's dream.

Celebrity is a drug which can only be satisfied by nurturing relations with the media. Their mutual addiction feeds the celebrity's hunger for recognition and increases sales for newspapers and magazines, with the whole process managed by specialists such as Julian Henry. Henry, a publicist, had been hired by Simon Fuller to place interviews and glowing profiles of his client in several newspapers. Henry's brief was to position Fuller as a successful, magnetic and enigmatic personality who avoided publicity.

'Fame has its price,' Rosencrantz warned Cowell, introducing what she called 'my standard lecture'. 'It's a double-edged sword. After you've been seen by 15 million people, I will read about whatever skeletons you've got in the cupboard in next week's *News of the World*. So think about it.'

In the lucrative kiss-and-tell era, there would be women, Cowell knew, eager to cash in on their freewheeling encounters, so he decided to hire Max Clifford, an infamous publicist, to manage his reputation. To many, Clifford was an unattractive operator, known for his confessions as a serial adulterer and for being paid for tipping newspapers off about famous personalities' various peccadilloes. He was admired, though, for protecting his clients and offering what Cowell would describe as 'realistic advice'.

Clifford's work began hours after *Pop Idol* was launched on 5 October 2001. Cowell was no longer the unknown bachelor but the superstar stud. Every aspect of his life was to be amplified in the tabloid newspapers, including descriptions of his regular visits to lap-dancing clubs.

For months, Cowell had been a regular visitor to Stringfellows with his friends, including Rav Singh, the *News of the World*'s showbiz reporter. He enjoyed being 'swamped' by lap dancers whom he treated affectionately, rewarded with generous tips and occasionally took home at the end of the evening. The girls' attraction was their looks, their uninhibited nudity, the fun, the convenience and the lack of commitment. Some tabloid writers drew a different picture, hinting that his trips to Stringfellows were a smokescreen to cover his alleged homosexuality.

Amid the wave of initial publicity for *Pop Idol*, the *Mirror* published on its front page a photograph of Cowell scantily dressed in women's clothes, including frilly knickers, and with his arm around a man. The implication was that Cowell was gay. Cowell telephoned his mother. 'When the *Mirror* journalist came for an interview, did you give him the family photograph album?'

'Yes, dear. He was so nice and promised to send it back.'

His next call was to Piers Morgan, the *Mirror*'s editor. 'Do you know who the man next to me was?'

'Yes,' replied Morgan. 'It was your brother. We seem to have forgotten to mention that.'

'Did I come across as camp?' Cowell asked Denise Beighton hours after transmission of the first programme.

'You came across just as you are,' she replied diplomatically.

His mother was less polite. While shopping in Brighton, she was regularly attacked for her son's insolence on the programme. Even Nicholas Cowell called Simon to describe his torment in a dentist's waiting room, fearing he would be criticised for his brother's behaviour.

'I've made the biggest mistake of my life,' Cowell told Beighton over lunch at their local Pizza Express. 'My mother's been attacked. I shouldn't have done it.'

As the ratings rose, however, his fears disappeared. Britain was becoming excited by Cowell's snap brutality: 'You sound like Mickey Mouse on helium'; 'What if I told you you couldn't sing?'; 'I'm afraid to say that really hurt my ears'; and 'I don't believe you're a star. If you win, I'll believe we have failed.' The tabloids described the programme as 'brilliant TV' and rated his and Waterman's performances as better than the others'. 'Nicki Chapman's talent', wrote Ally Ross in the *Sun*, 'was to make sure Jason Orange found his way to the WC,' while Neil Fox, the fourth judge, was dismissed as 'no good'. In contrast, Waterman and Cowell were blessed as 'brilliant' for encouraging contestants to degrade themselves and for 'weeding out the freaks, the geeks, the Bolsheviks, the trade unionists, people with funny-shaped heads and all the other fruit bats that make this show so enjoyable'. Even Lythgoe joined the chorus: 'Cowell is really cruel. I mean, this guy was thrown out of the Gestapo for cruelty.'

The controversy about his rudeness – or his replicating the music business's honesty – fuelled the publicity. 'Having a tough time for two minutes on camera, so what?' he retorted. 'If you don't want that, go to another talent show.'

Cowell's vitriol was not limited to the contestants. Although he had tried since his schooldays to avoid confrontation, his competitive instincts spotted the benefit of provoking rivalry with two of the panellists during the show. He disliked Nicki

Chapman, whom he dismissed as Fuller's cipher, and ridiculed the fourth judge: 'Foxy, all you do is play bands' records on the radio, while I actually create these bands for the likes of you. Your remarks are unfair. Once you've created a band and made them into multimillion successes, then you can criticise me . . . Unless you have something constructive to say, don't. You're boring me.' In retaliation, Fox raged about Cowell's 'poisonous' put-downs as worthy of 'a pantomime dame'. Enjoying the gulf he had created, Cowell recalled, 'He really went for me. I was shocked. He called me a prat and I've never seen him like that before. He lost it.'

His brashness was fed by his possession of 'real money', which guaranteed freedom. Ever since doing childhood chores for pocket money, Cowell had longed to be rich. 'Money. I want as much money as I can get my hands on,' he unashamedly told *Rolling Stone* magazine when asked for his biggest wish. His regret, he added, was not to have been The Beatles' A&R man in the 1960s – not for the music, but for the royalties. At last he could afford the best homes and cars, and flew by helicopter to Blenheim Palace with Jackie St Clair to collect a new Aston Martin DB7 and support the manufacturer's publicity stunt.

One of the perils of fame was the hate mail and crank calls. 'You've fucking had it. I hate your fucking guts' was typical of the abuse. 'I just try to be honest with people,' he told the *Sun*, the newspaper he had identified as his favourite mouthpiece. 'Rejection is hard for some.'

By the end of November 2001, 'Sarcastic Simon' was hailed 'as the most outspoken dasher of dreams, reducing young hopefuls to tears with his blunt assessments of their talents'. The image he preferred was the fun-loving good guy who adored his mother, cared for his friends, enjoyed his Aston Martin and flashed his white teeth, which, he confessed, 'are not my own'.

'Women Fans Fall for Mr Nasty' was the *Sunday People*'s

headline. 'It's certainly come as a surprise,' Cowell said with a smile. 'I thought that by being outspoken it would create a lot of animosity, but it has had the opposite effect.' His camp behaviour, failure to marry and his interviews encouraged speculation about his sexuality. Cowell had the reputation of enjoying an easy, flirtatious relationship with women, especially his coterie of old girlfriends. But women who worked closely with him, even those he regarded as friends, spoke discreetly about how his narcissism prevented him from truly falling in love with anyone. Their suspicions gained credibility thanks to an interview he gave the *Mirror*: 'I've never had a girlfriend. I chased Naima from Honeyz for years, but she always turned me down. She is my dream woman.'

Such a self-deprecating, inaccurate answer was unusual for a star, but by then Cowell had mastered the chemistry of media manipulation. Understatement, teasing and the throwing up of a smokescreen, combined with a sprinkling of stardust, were crafting an aura of mystery. While nurturing his stardom, he was simultaneously creating an enduring veil to guard his privacy.

The strategy worked instantly. Rival tabloids portrayed the celebrity in contradictory guises. Some described him as a sad, single man living alone in Holland Park, hiring escort girls, wearing the same clothes and fearful of his mother's wrath for saying 'bollocks' to Waterman. Others gleefully described his 3 a.m. arrival at lap-dancing club Spearmint Rhino, where he chain-smoked and drank iced Amaretto while a stream of naked busty girls 'bumped' into him.

Soon Georgina Law, a twenty-three-year-old lap dancer from Huddersfield with whom he had spent the previous Christmas in Mauritius, was, with Clifford's help, identified as Cowell's favourite. 'She's a great girl,' Cowell declared honestly, 'but she'll never be a pop idol. If you've heard her sing in the shower you'll know what I mean. But she has tremendous talents in other areas. She's got a great body, and the moment I saw her I thought, "Wow!" She was a magnet for me – that's why I spend a lot of time in Spearmint Rhino.' Then he added, 'When we're with each other we don't think of anyone else.'

Within a day, more was discovered about Law's past. As a regular presenter of Playboy TV's adult channel, she was well known as the girl-on-girl queen in porn films who had said, 'I don't do men,' and who had featured in *Star Whores*, a lesbian romp. 'There's no point denying the truth,' advised Clifford.

Cowell was unabashed. 'She loves giving happiness wherever she can,' he commented about the new revelations. 'She has certainly been giving me a lot and I hope there's plenty more to come in 2002.' The following day, the *People* revealed that Law worked for the London–Paris Escort Service as a prostitute called Linda, charging £2,000 a day anywhere in the world so long as she flew first-class. She had also, asserted the newspaper, featured in 'vile lesbian porn films' in which she 'writhed in bondage and licked chocolate off other women and more'. Again, Cowell appeared unfazed: 'I have no problem with her blue movies. At least no men were involved in them – that I know of. Of course I have forgiven her. She is a great girl and I think the world of her.'

The antics of 'Mr Nasty' in Mauritius encouraged more women to sell their stories, enabling the tabloids to assess Cowell's sexual prowess. 'Is he a Bonk Idol or Flop Star?' the *News of the World* asked three women. For Cowell, the most memorable comment came from Debbie Corrigan, née Spears, his first girlfriend. 'Making love to Simon', she recalled, 'is like going on a cross-Channel ferry. He rolls on. He rolls off. And frankly I felt sick throughout . . . In words Simon will understand, he's not good enough. He's not a bedroom idol.' Asked to rate him between one and ten, she replied, 'I wouldn't even give him one.' 'She's bitter that I haven't called her' was Cowell's retort.

Once the tabloids had finished, Clifford urged his client to be interviewed by the *Guardian*. Posing as 'invincible, defiantly laddish and magnificently queenly', Cowell explained how *Pop Idol* had been devised by himself and Simon Fuller over dinner. Asked 'What makes you most happy?', the man who openly admitted getting easily bored with women, work and life replied, 'God, not a lot. I am quite miserable because I'm never satisfied with what I've got. You're always looking for the next high, and that is what I define as happiness. I go through mood swings and the highs don't last very long.' Celebrity, he knew, was an addictive quick-fix drug: 'When you're hot, you're hot.'

The return after Christmas for the *Pop Idol* final in February should have been a roller coaster to glory. Cowell had identified Gareth Gates, a stuttering seventeen-year-old music student from Yorkshire, as the winner and disparaged the other favourite, Will Young, a twenty-two-year-old studying musical theatre. A third 'favourite', Darius Danesh, with a goatee and ponytail, was cast as the wild card. The astutely edited show, boosted by the tabloids' exposure of the contestants' private lives, was attracting growing audiences as the competition headed for the Criterion theatre in the West End. Live programmes would be filmed there in which the final ten contestants would be chosen. The 'hook', ITV discovered, was to involve the viewers in deciding the contestants' fate.

'That's the end of the judges,' Nigel Lythgoe told Cowell.

'What do you mean?'

'It was never assumed you would judge this until the end. Now we just use the audience votes.'

'Of course it was,' snapped Cowell, outraged about the prospect of being excluded from the live shows. His relationship with Lythgoe, theatrical at best, had never recovered from Lythgoe's disappointment at being dropped from the screen. Like Tom and Jerry, they could be good friends who enjoyed dinners 'winding each other up', but Lythgoe's abrupt declaration, Cowell suspected, was personal revenge.

'He's been put in an awkward situation by Simon Fuller,' Cowell told Waterman. 'Simon's taking our publicity personally. His ego is one hundred times bigger than mine. I don't crave publicity.' Although sceptical about Cowell's professions of modesty, Waterman agreed they were heading for a showdown. 'He's definitely jacking up the ante,' he warned.

'I've sent the judges off on holiday,' Lythgoe told Claudia Rosencrantz. 'I beg your pardon?' Rosencrantz exploded. 'The fun of the show is whether the public agree with the judges. They must be in the studio. I'm calling them now. No judges and I'll pull the show.' Lythgoe retreated, but the atmosphere was poisoned. 'What should have finally been a good time has become awful,' complained Cowell. His simmering argument with Fuller was escalating into a call for 'battle stations'.

'Please come to my office now,' Cowell asked Simon Jones in an agitated tone. 'I can't believe it. Simon's trying to take the music rights off me. I need your help on this.'

Cowell was wracked by fear. His hopes of an amicable settlement had been dashed. Fuller, he reported, had told BMG's lawyers that their corporation lacked any written contract for the music rights to the *Pop Idol* winner, and he also denied any verbal agreement with Cowell. Now, continued Cowell, there was gossip that Lucian Grainge – Fuller's neighbour in Richmond who had recently signed Fuller's group S Club – was negotiating for Universal to sign the record deal for the *Pop Idol* winner. Although Cowell would say that Grainge 'is my best friend in the music business', the two were continually competing. Both marked every personal success by erecting an advertisement for their hit album outside the other's office. More seriously, Grainge was attempting to poach Sonny Takhar, Cowell's key music executive. Cowell had called Grainge from his bath: 'I've got to tell you, I respect competition, but you've crossed the line. Our friendship is at stake.'

'That's the way it is,' replied Grainge.

'Bastard,' snapped Cowell, who, with the offer of a lot of money, eventually talked Takhar out of leaving.

Although Grainge would deny discussing a deal with Fuller, Cowell was fearful of Universal repeating the Hear'Say bonanza.

Simon Jones was surprised by Cowell's news: not only about relations between 'the two Simons' breaking down, but also by Cowell's failure to sign a contract with Fuller. To broker a reconciliation, he called Fuller. 'Simon thinks he's the creative genius behind the show,' said Fuller, 'but he isn't. You can never believe what Simon says.' Relations, Jones realised, were indeed fractured. Advised by Stinson, Fuller's challenge – 'Don't fuck with me. We had a deal' – was delivered in a precise undertone. The skilled poker player had outwitted Cowell. 'I've been double-crossed,' claimed Cowell limply.

The argument rapidly infected the production staff. 'Back-stabbing and paranoia' was Claire Horton's verdict as she emerged from Cowell's office. She, Rosencrantz and others watched as Cowell, alternating between sulks and excitement about the programme, became aggravated by Fuller 'dragging out' the negotiations as the contest between Young and Gates gripped the nation in the week before the final.

By the end of January, 10 million Britons – 48 per cent of the TV audience – were watching the show and 90,000 had applied for tickets for the final, which would be held at Fountain studios in Wembley. Gates was tipped to be the victor after winning 62 per cent of the 1.3 million telephone votes in the semi-finals.

On screen, Cowell appeared unaffected by Fuller's tactics.

He even smiled as Ant and Dec appeared on the set wearing trousers up to their nipples to mock his characteristic style. 'It does look ridiculous,' Cowell admitted, and thereafter wore his T-shirt over his trousers. There were no other laughs during the final week. A record audience was expected to vote and, Cowell heard, 'pre-orders for the winner have gone through the roof'. Sales of over 1 million records were expected. Both Gates and Young had recorded a double A-side single, 'Evergreen' and 'Anything Is Possible', for a rush release. The loser's version would be jettisoned in an incinerator, but Fuller's intransigence was jeopardising Cowell's windfall.

'The show is on fire and everything is at risk,' Cowell told a meeting at BMG, by then part of Sony Music. The corporation's choice, advised the lawyers, was stark: either sue for the 50 per cent share of the show's income on the basis that a court would believe Cowell's version of his oral agreement with Fuller; or accept Fuller's offer of a four-year record deal for the winner and nothing else. Compared to Fuller's deal that all the finalists give 19 Entertainment a 20 per cent cut of their earnings for the following twelve years, BMG's and Cowell's profits would be limited.

On the morning of the final, 9 February 2002, nothing had been agreed. Arriving at the Fountain studios in Wembley, Claudia Rosencrantz sensed 'a horrible atmosphere. You could cut it with a knife.' Others spoke of witnessing 'a Shakespearean betrayal' as Lythgoe tore into Cowell, while Cowell attacked Nicki Chapman for supporting, on Fuller's instructions, Will Young rather than Gareth Gates. Horton spoke about 'the most exciting day ever'.

The bookies' favourite was Gates, whom Cowell hoped would win to become the 'new' David Cassidy or Cliff Richard, reaping the same profits as Hear'Say. Just before 19 million viewers – 59 per cent of the total TV audience – tuned in for what would be a national TV experience, Cowell capitulated and accepted

Cowell enjoyed inviting friends onto *Slipstream*, including Lauren Silverman and Kelly Bergantz (left), and in 2011, Mezhgan Hussainy, his fiancée. Below, left to right: (back row) Sinitta, Lauren Silverman; (front row) Andrew Silverman, Simon Cowell, Mezhgan Hussainy.

Simon Cowell's unusually close relationship with his father, Eric, sustained him throughout years of failure.

Julie, Simon's mother (far right), was a dancer at the West End's Pigalle club when she met Eric.

Cowell (left) and his younger brother Nick enjoyed a comfortable childhood in a very close-knit family. Initially, Simon's relationship with his mother (above right) was volatile. Now she is a critical supporter.

The Cowells celebrate Julie's seventieth birthday in 1995.

After years of frustration, Cowell finally scored his first hit with Sinitta, singing 'So Macho', in 1986. After further humiliation, he finally persuaded TV stars Robson and Jerome to record 'Unchained Melody', scoring a huge hit in 1995.

Cowell credited his success to Stock Aitken Waterman, London's best songwriters and producers. In 1988, Pete Waterman (second left) turned against Sinitta and Cowell's relationship with the singer became temporarily strained.

Cowell owed his break in the music business in 1983 to Iain Burton (second right), a friend of both Cowell brothers, who often partied with Jackie St Clair (bottom right).

Simon Fuller (left), the Spice Girls' manager, was Cowell's rival and then his partner until a commercial row over *Pop Idol* in 2001 made them enemies. Ever since, Cowell has pledged to get his revenge.

Fuller's success with the Spice Girls (below) fuelled Cowell's ambitions.

Westlife, created by Louis Walsh (above, centre), was Cowell's outstanding hit in 1999.

Girl Thing (right), created by Cowell in 2001 (to copy the Spice Girls) flopped.

Cowell was attracted to a certain type of girl, especially those who appeared topless or scantily dressed (clockwise from top left): Vanya Seager; Louise Payne, his first fiancée; Terri Seymour; Georgina Law and Jackie St Clair.

Fuller's offer of a four-year exclusive recording deal to release the winner's song on S Records, his label.

Unbeknown to Cowell, Fuller had also asked Rosencrantz to include a credit – 'Created by Simon Fuller' – at the end of the programme. However, his request was forgotten. 'I haven't seen him at a production meeting or single show,' scoffed Horton.

Across the country, people gathered in pubs, clubs and at private parties to celebrate the birth of a star. The telephone network crashed as 8.7 million votes were cast. 'Bad news,' said Cowell with undisguised fury. 'Will has won.' Young had secured 53.1 per cent of the vote.

Cowell headed for his dressing room to plan the promotion of Young's record. 'The whole night was horrific,' he complained. 'It was a miserable time. I felt sick to my stomach because I realised I'd made a mistake.' From down below, he could hear Claudia Rosencrantz and the two-hundred-strong production team celebrating wildly with champagne.

Will Young's 'Evergreen' sold over 1 million records in the first week and then a further 800,000. Cowell did not conceal his antagonism towards Young, indiscreetly ignoring the winner. 'Will is a great singer, but Gareth is a pop idol,' he said curtly.

The national excitement about Young did, however, alter Cowell's understanding of the show. Initially, he had focused on *Pop Idol* creating a star. After the final, he recognised the value of his own stardom.

'I've got to maximise what I've got,' he said. Using his new fame, Cowell railed against the 'snobs': that 'awful' congregation who attended the hateful Brit awards. 'Same people, same outfits, same gossip,' he said. He was equally dismissive of the artists: 'Our pop stars today have lost their sense of mystery. I think it's because they are too accessible. There is no frenzy over bands these days. Fans are not going crazy and fainting. It's all so boring.'

His success and jeers stirred the 'snobs'' animosity. Watching poor performers humiliate themselves for the audience's gratification and then for Cowell's staged vilification evoked accusations of exploitation and manipulation.

The anger was not misplaced. Lythgoe confessed to 'choreographing' the show. Producing the programme, he said, 'allowed me to screw around with emotions and manipulate. They say I'm a master manipulator. I love that. It's fun and we screwed around with people. But if you come on the show you know that you're going to get that. Every time someone knew which trick I'd used, I'd switch the trick.'

Established stars turned their hatred of *Pop Idol*'s manipulation against the star himself, Cowell. Their protests were championed by Elton John and Robbie Williams. 'Cruel television', said Williams, 'is fucking with people's lives for entertainment.' Their disapproval was supported by Tony Wadsworth, EMI's president, who had been excluded from all the TV spin-offs. 'I'd rather develop artists who cross borders and produce catalogues for the future,' said Wadsworth. 'Reality TV does neither.' The professional criticism of Cowell was supplemented by personal attacks. His glory, his critics prayed, would be short-lived.

Fame aggravated Cowell's occasional depression. In his professional career, Cowell would say, he rarely felt joy about something that had happened. He was more excited about future challenges. But twenty years in the music industry had taught him the cost of transient fame. Pop stars rarely prospered for more than two years, and only a handful of artists, like his beloved Frank Sinatra, survived for ever. Lacking sympathy for fading stars, he faced the same peril.

Unsure how long his own fame would last, he withdrew, living increasingly within his own world. Limiting his social life to trusted friends, he became sensitive about personal relationships and gossip. His reticence amplified the mystery surrounding him.

Retaining Max Clifford, and the unusual candour about Georgina Law and other lap dancers, had aroused suspicion that Cowell was concealing his homosexuality. The evidence was purely circumstantial. He was forty-two, unmarried, close to his mother, had provided security for Jonathan King's bail and behaved in a camp manner. His vanity, appearance and manner drowned for some the evidence of his serial heterosexual relationships. So while not a single man had approached a tabloid to sell a kiss-and-tell story about even so much as a suggestive approach from Cowell, detractors like Ian Levine continued to gossip despite a total absence of any supporting facts. The speculation grew in March when Will Young unexpectedly came out to Rav Singh, Cowell's friend at the *News of the World*.

At that moment, Louis Theroux, the TV documentary maker, was filming a profile of Max Clifford. Cowell's provocative explanation for hiring the publicist as 'protection' raised obvious questions, which Theroux tested in early 2002. Referring to Cowell, Theroux asked Clifford, 'Is he gay?'

'No,' replied Clifford.

'Would you tell me if he were?'

'No, I wouldn't if it was something that we were going to keep quiet.'

Cowell had agreed to participate in Clifford's vanity exercise and appeared to be surprised as he walked into the shot and was told by Theroux, 'Word on the street is that you're gay.' Cowell first laughed and then, as Theroux added, 'I had always assumed you were gay,' looked at the camera, annoyed. 'I deny it,' he said.

'That was very embarrassing,' Cowell told Clifford later. 'Music is a gay-friendly business and if I was gay there would be no reason to hide it. But I'm not.' After a few moments, he added, 'The film has made us all look stupid.' At the preview arranged by Theroux, Cowell exploded and asked for changes.

'No way,' replied Theroux, who had already obtained Cowell's signed consent. 'That wasn't the smartest thing I ever did,' conceded Cowell, angry about Clifford's voracious love for publicity.

His denial incensed people in the gay community. At the next London Music Radio Conference, Elton John was allowed to ask Cowell, who was sitting in the audience, 'When are you going to come out and admit you're gay?' Cowell looked flabbergasted by the singer's 'childish game' and responded, 'If it means I end up with you, Elton, then never.' Later, he would say he was joking: 'I didn't think much about it. A lot of my friends are gay. I work with gays.'

Thereafter, he avoided the singer whenever possible, even when they became neighbours in Beverly Hills. 'I can't stand being with Elton,' he would say. 'It's too heavy.'

In particular, Cowell disliked the slurs from some of Elton John's hangers-on, who cast homosexuality and cocaine as chic. In his opinion, gays dominated the music industry, but that group had not, in his opinion, sufficiently opposed the degenerate industry bosses who exploited the insecurity, frustrations and desolation of young artists who injured or killed themselves with overdoses. Equally, when John openly denigrated *The X Factor* and paraded his gifts to charity, Cowell offered an open challenge: 'Why don't you give money to starving musicians?' In self-justification, John issued a long statement, but in Cowell's opinion the singer forgot how he had booed Waterman in 1996 when he won his third Ivor Novello award for the best song of the year. John's anger, in Cowell's opinion, was jealousy, pure and simple.

The damage to Cowell's reputation among John's sympathisers was irreversible. Mention of Cowell's name often produced an automatic response that he was gay. Clumsily, Clifford sought to mitigate the accusations by arranging for Georgina Law to 'reveal' to a tabloid that Cowell had 'licked champagne from her body' during a 'forty-eight-hour non-stop sex session'. Clifford's ruse boomeranged after Spearmint Rhino, where Law performed, was revealed to be another of his clients. The only beneficiaries from the saga were the publicist, pocketing fees from Cowell, the club and Theroux himself.

'I was angry about it all,' said Cowell, not least because the spat was a distraction from his real battle with Fuller.

'Fuller's playing a different game of poker,' Pete Waterman warned, but Cowell misunderstood the message. Naïve about business, he was still blind to Fuller's claim to the format's ownership.

He did, however, understand that *Pop Idol* was challenging the music industry to behave like other entertainment businesses. Money was the priority. The 'snobs' were often uncommercial. Instead of agonising over whether to invest £1 million to nurture rock-and-roll artists singing about protest and rebellion, *Pop Idol* rewarded record companies who manufactured performers like Hear'Say and offered popular schmaltz, with a synergy between product placement, advertisers and the musicians. He was unashamed to lead the fight as the pop business took on art, but his real battle, he would discover, was against Fuller.

8
Global Star

Pleased by his contractual victory in Britain, Simon Fuller reassessed his commercial opportunities in the US. Unlike when Simon Cowell pitched to the American networks, he now possessed a tape recording of the format that was scoring exceptional audience ratings in the UK. His agent in Los Angeles sent the tapes featuring Cowell's success to re-engage the network bosses in a new reality series. To her surprise, the three major networks repeated their objections towards music formats, so finally she and Fuller returned to Mike Darnell at Fox.

Following the success of *24*, starring Kiefer Sutherland, Fox were established as the fourth network, but their fortunes depended on finding other hit shows. Their search was hindered by the turbulent aftermath of the 9/11 attacks on New York and Washington. Uncertain about the public's mood, the network needed appropriate programmes for the summer.

Just five foot two in Cuban-heeled boots, dressed like a child cowboy and often behaving like a jester, Darnell spoke frequently about his hunt for 'visceral emotions'. The result was a succession of eccentric reality shows, including *Temptation Island* and *Who Wants to Marry a Millionaire?*, although he had also rejected plans for a beauty show in a women's jail and a quiz featuring adopted children picking out their biological fathers from a line-up. His hits had outweighed the failures.

The faddish producer was converted by Cowell's caustic performance. *Pop Idol* was worth trying, but only if compatible with the network's financial straits. To secure the commission, explained Darnell, Fuller would need to waive his licence fee and also find sponsors to fund the production. Advertisers, both knew, were shying away from cable channels because viewers were using their TiVo to fast-forward past the commercials. Coca-Cola and Ford were possible backers, but others would be needed. While Fuller negotiated with the sponsors, Fox's owner, Rupert Murdoch, heard from Liz Murdoch, his daughter, about *Pop Idol*'s success in Britain.

'What's going on with this show *Pop Idol*?' Murdoch asked Peter Chernin, his deputy at News Corp. 'I spoke to Liz. It's a big hit in England, and she says it's great.'

'We're still looking at it,' replied Chernin.

'Don't look at it, buy it,' Murdoch ordered. 'Right now.'

Rather than wait for sponsors to finance eight programmes, Chernin ordered his staff to commission fifteen programmes financed by Fox. 'Just close the deal,' he said.

An essential part of the deal, Fuller was told, was Cowell appearing as a judge. Nigel Lythgoe made the approach. His telephone call caught Cowell by surprise: firstly, because Fuller's success exposed his own failure the previous year in Los Angeles; secondly, because Fuller had sold the format as his own; and, thirdly, because he was being offered an extraordinary opportunity. Every British star hankered for glory in Hollywood. As usual, though, he dithered. Over dinner, Fuller was dismissive of Cowell's hesitation and his fear of humiliation in America. 'Don't be such a drama queen,' he told Cowell. 'You've loved every second of it. The records are going to be big hits – America will love you.'

Unable to decide, Cowell flew to Germany to discuss the offer with Rolf Schmidt-Holtz, BMG's chairman. 'We're putting no pressure on you to go to the US,' said Schmidt-Holtz, a former television producer. 'It's your decision, but don't bother if you don't want to.' The German's lukewarm response was echoed by Bob Jamieson, RCA's president in New York. Jamieson was outright sceptical about the attraction of a television 'lark or game show' for the music business.

The 'push back' to this advice was orchestrated by Clive Davis, Cowell's champion. 'It's an opportunity to showcase our musical heritage,' said Davis, attacking Jamieson's blindness to the opportunity of introducing a new generation to classic pop songs, which in turn would encourage reissues by new artists – so-called 'covers' – and generate copyright fees. The friction propelled Jamieson's swift departure from RCA and Schmidt-Holtz's sudden enthusiasm for the idea. If Cowell accepted, said Schmidt-Holtz, BMG's partner, Sony, would require a four-year licence for the winners' records. But the corporation – unconvinced that the show would be a hit – refused to invest $1 million in the production in exchange for a share of the advertising revenue, and consequently would lose huge additional profits.

'Nasty Simon' making gullible people cry appealed to Darnell's appetite for shock and sensation, but he was resistant to adopting more of the British production, especially allowing the judges to perform without an agreed script. Spontaneity was judged too risky. 'Here's what I want to do,' he told Murdoch.

'You don't change a thing,' interrupted Murdoch, suspicious about Darnell's commitment. 'This show works in England. And you're going to make the same show they made in England. The problem with you Hollywood people is you always want to change things and you ruin everything.'

The programme would be called *American Idol* and, at Fuller's suggestion, be produced by Lythgoe and Ken Warwick, the producer of *Pop Idol*. Casting for another two judges and a host, Darnell hired Randy Jackson, a former bass player and successful A&R man for Columbia Records, and Paula Abdul, an outstanding choreographer and singer who had had four number-one singles, including the 1980s hit 'Opposites Attract', and whose first album, *Forever Your Girl*, had sold 12 million copies.

As host, Darnell chose Brian Dunkleman, a stand-up comic and minor actor. The appointment sparked a flood of telephone calls from John Ferriter, the agent.

'Mike, you've got to use Ryan Seacrest as a host too,' Ferriter implored, promoting an unknown DJ from Georgia with frosted hair. 'You can't just rely on one host. If there are technical problems, you'll need the same act as Ant and Dec.'

'No way,' said Darnell, putting the telephone down and leaving for lunch. Two hours later, he returned and found Ferriter in his office. The agent was dedicated to Seacrest's stardom and, after an hour, Darnell was persuaded to employ the handsome twenty-seven-year-old.

The final uncertainty was Cowell's attitude. Fox, he knew, was urging Fuller to secure his irreversible commitment. That alone was an incentive for Cowell to express more doubts, although not to Fuller. Having agreed to a one-year contract for just $150,000 per show, negotiated by his agent at CAA, he called Nigel Lythgoe and Ken Warwick and announced he was pulling out. His fear of failure was camouflaged by his misgivings about American TV executives. Their habitual interference, he told Warwick, would sterilise his performance.

'I'll look after you,' promised Warwick. 'It'll be just like England. You won't have to compromise what you do. You can be yourself.'

'What if the show isn't a hit? After two weeks, they'll pull it.'

'They've promised to stick with the show because it could take a few weeks,' Warwick replied.

Cowell was unpersuaded. 'Get me out of it,' he told Tony Russell, his lawyer. 'I don't want to do it.'

Next, he called Nicole Hill, the wife of Bucks Fizz's producer and a friend whose advice he trusted. 'I'm pulling out,' he announced.

'Hang on,' exclaimed Hill. 'Either way, if it fails or succeeds, you'll regret it. If the show is a hit without you, you're going to think you could have been part of that. And if it isn't a hit, you're going to think you could have made the difference.'

As so often, Cowell was influenced by those he trusted, and her advice swung his decision. 'Right, I'll take the risk. But no option for a second series. I want my freedom.'

'I'm not sure about this show of yours,' the estate agent told Cowell as they walked around the house Fox had rented for him in Beverly Hills. 'I wouldn't hold out too much hope.'

'Why?' asked Cowell.

'Because Fox has built in a month's break in the lease.'

Cowell's fears, he realised, were shared by Fox. No one anticipated that a British show featuring an unknown British music executive would attract a respectable audience, even as a summer filler.

At stake was Fox's money and Cowell's pride. He had already clashed with Gail Berman, Fox's number two.

'Aren't you lucky that Simon Fuller chose you to be a judge?' she smiled during lunch at a restaurant.

'I beg your pardon?' spluttered Cowell, putting down his soup spoon.

'Well, you know, he could have chosen anyone else to be on the show,' continued Berman, bursting into a viper's nest.

'You need to check your facts,' said Cowell, abandoning his meal and walking out of the restaurant.

Now, with hindsight, he understood what Fuller was saying to him when they had been reunited in Los Angeles. 'Don't contradict any description of myself as the sole inventor of *Pop Idol*,' Fuller had told Cowell. 'I invented it, I own it and you're just a performer.'

Ever since that frosty welcome to Los Angeles, Cowell had

noticed Fuller's endless self-promotion in the media as the unchallenged power broker. In an interview for the *Sun*, a journalist had written, 'Fuller is the supremo for *Pop Idol* – forget Cowell, Waterman and Nicki Chapman. Simon Fuller invented, controls and owns *Pop Idol* and has just sold rights to Fox and will start broadcasting in June.'

The defiance was incendiary. 'Crazed' was Cowell's reaction. 'I've decided I've got to start my own show,' he told friends in London.

The advance publicity for *American Idol* was calculated to shock. 'We are going to tell people who can't sing and have no talent that they have no talent,' promised Cowell. 'We're going to show the audition process as it really is. You're going to look through the keyhole at something people aren't normally allowed to see. Lots of useless people are going to be told that they're useless. I'm warning you now, you are about to enter the audition from hell.'

No one had warned Paula Abdul, the only famous personality among the four American presenters, what to expect. Like most Hollywood stars, her personal life had been rocky. Two marriages had failed, other relationships were messy and, following an airline crash and repeated surgery, she had become dependent on painkillers and other medicinal drugs. Her introduction to Cowell at the first audition at the Millennium Hotel in Manhattan was, in that familiar showbiz style, gushing. He was attracted to an unpredictable, temperamental, petite woman and assumed that she would soon succumb to a sexual relationship. On reflection, though, he decided to resist. 'It's the daytime test. We would have had to have a conversation afterwards,' he explained, 'and I don't know what we would have said.' Abdul's observation about Cowell would be more sardonic: 'He's a flirt but his hands usually end up on his own chest.'

The chance of seducing Abdul evaporated soon after the

auditions began. Attracted by the slogan 'Thousands sing, millions vote, one wins', none of the 10,000 people attending the auditions in seven cities had expected that their bid for stardom in Hollywood would be cruelly mocked by a vain English performer. Nor did Abdul.

At the end of the first contestant's song, Randy Jackson and Abdul uttered some polite comments.

'This singer is just awful,' Cowell lashed out. 'Not only do you look terrible but you sound terrible.'

'You can't talk to people like that,' Abdul exclaimed as the tearful contestant left the room.

'Yes, I can,' Cowell replied. 'In fact, I just did.'

'But this is America,' snapped Abdul.

'Yes. And?'

'And he's just a kid.'

'A kid who happens to sing terribly,' retorted Cowell, terminating the discussion.

Pioneering such crushing honesty was brave and, to many viewers, mesmerising. It was also addictive.

'You're a loser,' Cowell told the next contestant. 'That was terrible, seriously terrible.' At lunchtime, Cowell found a tearful Abdul dramatically threatening to quit. 'The purpose of the show is to be honest,' Cowell explained, 'like in the real world.' Abdul's distress was not assuaged. 'I think Paula is going to walk,' Cowell told Lythgoe. 'I don't think she's going to want to continue.' To broker the peace, Lythgoe sent Abdul away for a brief rest, while Cowell and Jackson continued without her.

'The tension', Cowell would later say, 'was unbelievable. The bad feeling was so strong. I really thought the entire show was in jeopardy.' The mood on the following day's flight to Atlanta, Cowell admitted, was 'horrific', but he refused to relent. The few talented contestants were rewarded by the chorus 'You're going to Hollywood,' but whenever Abdul soulfully encouraged a hopeless contestant, Cowell exploded. 'Why do you have to be so rude?' Abdul spat, as the television producers smiled at their prize. Lythgoe regularly placated Abdul, often by disparaging Cowell.

By the time of the audition in the third city, Abdul reluctantly acknowledged that the programme was about 'the truth'. She agreed to continue judging the auditions but refused to fly on the same plane or sit in the same car as Cowell. The star himself was unperturbed. 'She's a diva,' he thought, 'and she fancies me. I think she's in love with me, but the feelings are not mutual.' To generate publicity, he told a journalist that a Las Vegas beauty had offered to have sex with him in exchange for advancing to the next round. 'I would have accepted,' smirked Cowell, 'but my producer said "no".' Once the auditions were completed, Cowell returned to London to plan the second season of *Pop Idol*.

Fox broadcast the first recorded programme on 11 June 2002. At 3 p.m. the following afternoon, Cowell was called by a Fox producer in Los Angeles.

'Simon, this is amazing. It's a hit.'

'What are you talking about?' asked Cowell, caught unawares. 'What's a hit?'

'*American Idol*. We opened last night and the ratings are going through the roof.'

It turned out that 9.9 million people had watched the programme, the largest audience for an American TV show that night.

The results programme the following day, which reported the votes from the different time zones across the country and the consequent elimination of contestants, was watched by 11 million people. Fox executives, excited by the unexpected success, put the growth of the audience down to the 'water-cooler factor': Tuesday night's viewers had spoken about the programme the following day, encouraging more people to watch that Wednesday night. Overnight, Fox TV was no longer the underdog. *American Idol*'s audience was 40 per cent higher than that of its rivals.

Dozens of journalists called Cowell for interviews and, by the end of the week, newspapers and magazines across the US featured Cowell and the other judges on their front covers. On his return to Hollywood for the live shows to decide the nine finalists from the final thirty contestants, Cowell was mobbed on the streets. He was a Hollywood star. His quips – 'I'm afraid to say that really hurt my ears' – were being repeated like Shakespearean couplets. The criticism of himself as 'genuinely loathsome', 'arrogant', 'smug', 'snide', 'smarmy', 'obnoxious', 'rude', 'vain', 'mean' and 'prancing' increased his fame, thus matching his dream. 'Anyone who has experienced recognition is a liar if they say they don't enjoy celebrity,' he volunteered. 'It's easy to pick up girls, it's easy to book restaurants.' Every detail of his life was scrutinised, even his sharp exchange at the London Mandarin Oriental with tennis legend John McEnroe, whom he told in the lift to 'stop being rude to staff'. As they stepped into the lobby, they came close to a fist fight.

Returning to his house in Roxbury Drive, Beverly Hills, he took a telephone call from Terri Seymour, a twenty-eight-year-old English underwear model introduced to him eleven years earlier by Paula Hamilton. 'Call me if you come to Los Angeles,' he had said casually when they had last kissed at Tramp, the Mayfair nightclub. Seymour, a former co-host of ITV's *Wheel of Fortune*, had been dating his brother Nicholas before flying to Los Angeles to feature in an advertisement for shampoo. She telephoned Cowell for a drink, unaware of his new fame. One week later, instead of returning to London, she moved into his house, hoping that the relationship would lead to marriage and children. She had not heard Cowell's outburst to Denise Beighton earlier in the month when he read that Paul McCartney was to marry Heather Mills. 'Why on earth does he want to marry her?' he had exploded. 'He can have sex and blow jobs from her and buy her presents, but you don't marry her.' Beighton had been unsurprised. 'Terri's not like some of the others,' she told Cowell, adding, 'Not a hungry gold digger.'

'Yes, she's sweet,' replied Cowell, suggesting to Beighton more a brother and sister relationship. Normally, Beighton observed, he described women he was chasing as 'gorgeous'.

'*American Idol* is everywhere; it's taken over the country,' Cowell kept repeating to himself. Wherever he went, people called his name and grasped his hand, eager to meet the English lord who dashed the dreams of American lasses. To his amazement, he had become a national personality. Among his new fans was Lisa Gregorisch, the executive editor of *Extra*, a showbiz TV programme.

'Everything's great,' he volunteered, 'but my fee is way too low.'

A few days later, Gregorisch telephoned Cowell: 'Watch the show tomorrow and see what happens.'

A report the next day featured New Yorkers saying they loved *Idol*, mostly because of Cowell. In the wrap-up, the reporter confidently asserted that Cowell's success had prompted rival networks to offer him contracts. The following morning, a Fox executive called Cowell: 'We're planning to renegotiate your contract and offer you more money.' However, Cowell's total joy disappeared soon after, when the show went live.

Until then, he had apparently never watched the recorded programmes to the very end. But sitting in the CBS studio in West Hollywood until the conclusion of the first live show, Cowell froze as the production credits ended. The last caption read, 'Created by Simon Fuller'.

Furious, Cowell turned away. 'That was a knife in my stomach when I saw that for the first time,' he would admit. Fuller had failed to get that credit on British television because Claudia Rosencrantz and the other producers had disagreed with his assertion. But after his agreement with Cowell about his ownership of the format, Fuller's contention was legally irrefutable. Cowell discovered the result of this in the green room after the show in Los Angeles.

'So, when were you hired to be on the show?' a junior producer asked, clearly expecting Cowell to express his gratitude to Fuller. The final aggravation was Fuller's successful sales blitz of the show to foreign broadcasters. He refused to extend the music rights to Sony beyond *American Idol* as broadcast in the US. Instead, the rights for the *Idol* programmes in the rest of the world were sold to Universal.

Abdul noticed Cowell's 'agony'. Despite their fractious relationship, she resolved to 'talk to him over the credits because I knew it wasn't easy'. Festering silently behind the rictus smile, Cowell plotted his reprisals: 'I'm never happy about a competitor's success. I despise it when somebody who isn't working with me is successful on their own – it really upsets me. And I wish for their demise.' Fuller, Cowell admitted, 'has a lot of strengths I do not have' – as proved by Fuller securing the Fox contract for *Idol.* He regarded Fuller's career as the benchmark he would use in advancing from a music producer and pantomime villain into a global television executive. But first he wanted the cash to buy Los Angeles's best lifestyle.

Cowell's biggest asset was a half share in S Records, the joint venture he established in 2000 with BMG. Rolf Schmidt-Holtz, BMG's chairman, agreed to pay just over £12 million for Cowell's share of all the income from the records linked to *American Idol.* Provocatively, a newspaper reported that Cowell received a 'rumoured £25 million'. Assured of cash to renovate his homes in Los Angeles and London and to finance his new ventures, his main aim now was to disprove Fuller's authorship of *Idol* and 'determine my own destiny, my own future'.

Fox had reportedly paid Fuller $35 million to license *American Idol* for the second series, and Cowell began thinking about creating a rival to *Idol*, with similar income from format sales, telephone voting and sponsorship deals. 'I'd be insane not to take advantage of my position,' he told Schmidt-Holtz.

'One good idea', advised Schmidt-Holtz sympathetically, 'will pay for your next ten years, so there's no need to rush out a project. You just need to sit back and look at the market and try to do something the public wants.'

Cowell's first idea, sold to ITV and ABC, was *Cupid*, a programme following couples who were dating. 'Workmanlike' was the kindest description of the inconsequential pilots filmed amid Cowell's battle with Fuller.

During the last weeks of *American Idol* in Los Angeles, Kelly Clarkson, a Texas cocktail waitress, began to emerge as the obvious winner. She was not only a talented singer and songwriter, but her 'journey' was the stuff of dreams. After appearing in school musicals, she headed for Hollywood, but returned home dejected, rehearsing in an empty room accompanied by a piano until she applied for the *American Idol* auditions. With huge sales anticipated for her first record after she won the final, Clarkson was sent to the Westlake studios in West Hollywood to record the song for Sony. Acting on Cowell's orders, Stephen Ferrera, the producer, began recording 'A Moment Like This' until Fuller arrived.

'Why are you doing this?' he asked Ferrera. 'She should be recording "Before Your Love". That's what I told you.' Cowell's orders, insisted her putative manager, should be ignored.

Ferrera was caught in a see-saw squabble replayed several times. With neither willing to concede, the compromise was a double A-side record. 'A match made in hell,' concluded the eyewitnesses. Some blamed egoism, while others spoke of Cowell's creativity competing against Fuller's strategic commercialism.

In the midst of that argument, Fox offered Cowell a contract for a second season. 'I'm helping the devil, Simon Fuller,' he seethed, forgetting the weakness of his legal position. Nevertheless, he accepted. On his behalf, his agent asked for $250,000 per episode. 'Are you out of your mind?' Sandy Grushow, Fox's head of entertainment, replied. Grushow offered $40–50,000 for each show – about $1 million for the series – which Cowell accepted, agreeing to start filming in January 2003 but refusing an option for a third season.

With Cowell committed, Fuller had little reason to placate his rival, especially on the night of the *American Idol* final in September 2002. Cowell and Paula Abdul arrived together at the Kodak theatre, and both searched for their familiar position behind a desk opposite the stage. 'Not here, up there,' ordered Lythgoe, pointing at a box without microphones on the highest balcony.

'What are we doing up here?' asked Abdul.

'We've been set up by Fuller,' seethed Cowell. 'They're humiliating us and letting Ryan Seacrest run the show.'

Lythgoe had obeyed Fuller, thought Cowell, and had forgotten about the £250,000 he had just borrowed from Cowell. 'Nigel works for Nigel,' a consoling voice told Cowell. 'He's a bitch,' volunteered another. The only consolation was Lythgoe's last-minute choice of 'A Moment Like This', which Clarkson sung in a thrilling show watched by 22.8 million people.

Without further comment, Cowell celebrated with Fuller that night and, after a long discussion at Fuller's house about commercialising their successful discovery of a real star, the two flew to New York to lobby Clive Davis for help. Although Clarkson's record was heading straight for number one, Davis's skill was to 'validate TV artists' by making the prize of a recording contract meaningful. In Cowell's words, 'Clive would give Kelly Clarkson credibility as a legitimate artist.'

Davis regarded his two visitors as 'apples and oranges'. He respected Fuller as an entrepreneur, while Cowell was 'smart for coming out of the A&R ranks and was a wise, shrewd observer of the contemporary music scene'. Davis gave both men the necessary assurances: 'I'm getting the best writers in the world for her album. I don't want music that has fallen off the airwaves. I want to secure lasting territory, not bubble-gum sounds.'

As Clarkson's agent, Fuller spearheaded the operation to turn the TV victor into a national star and dispatched her and the other contestants on a forty-city concert tour to promote a DVD of the programme. Adroitly, Fuller also arranged for Clarkson to sing the American national anthem to President George W. Bush at a public ceremony. Appropriately, Fuller would stand in the spotlight next to his new client.

Cowell watched the skilful refinement of Fuller's image. The 'publicity-shy' manager offered himself in interviews to the British and American tabloids as the genius who was crafting Kelly Clarkson with the same skills he used for the Spice Girls. 'I'm about empowering people and making their dreams come true,' he expounded. 'Kelly will last longer than most reality pop stars because she's an amazing talent,' he continued, adding, 'I'm thrilled by what's going on now.' Fuller's publicist had massaged the journalist, who had reciprocated by describing his paymaster as being trusted by 'hopefuls' because he is 'bright, amusing and appears to be disarmingly vulnerable'. That sentiment was endorsed by Fuller's self-deprecation: 'Critics probably don't like me because I'm so nice. I'm incredibly articulate, thoughtful and moral and think about what I do. I want to be known for doing something good. I'm not fucked up enough to want to be famous for doing bad things. My business is creating fame and celebrity, and I'm one of the best in the world. I know it to the finest detail. I reflect what's out there, and if there's a demand for something I recognise it. I don't think I'm crass. I stand by everything I do.'

Fuller's swagger reflected some concern about his image, since S Club and the Spice Girls had both ended on a sour note. His attempt to launch *World Idol*, a TV programme, had failed because the sixteen judges, including Cowell and Pete Waterman, divided by language and politics, appeared to be auditioning themselves for appearances on the British and American shows. 'This is a farce,' scoffed Cowell. 'Morons from Poland and idiots from Australia. It's disgusting. As wretched as you can make a show.' 'A joke,' agreed Waterman.

Fuller blamed Cowell for the flop. 'You could have made it work,' he said, believing that Cowell lacked his usual enthusiasm.

Another failure was Fuller's *American Juniors*, a series about 'youth culture' for six- to twelve-year-olds. Cowell enjoyed Fuller's setbacks, although they mirrored his own. *Cupid* was cancelled by CBS and ITV after one season. 'It performed well and got an average audience of 10 million in America and peaked at 7 million in Britain,' complained Cowell afterwards. 'It could have been improved. We had the wrong producers and production skills. I learned a lot from the experience.'

With women screaming his name around Hollywood, demanding his autograph and even passing him slips of paper with their telephone numbers, there was a disarming aspect to Cowell's self-promotion. 'Girls get fed up with me,' he told a journalist, describing how 'scary Hollywood women' were bored by him. He had been chatting up a girl at a bar, he explained, who had leant over and whispered slowly in his ear, 'You must have a very, very small dick.' He continued, 'I almost choked on my drink. I think I looked down at my crotch, felt very small, then left.'

Some were surprised he offered that anecdote to a journalist, but he saw it as 'amusing evidence of my humility'. Others suspected a tease but could not decide whether his target was men or women, or whether it was simply all down to his love of reading more about himself the following day.

Cowell enjoyed the celebrity but needed a more secure home to protect his privacy, so he rented a badly designed house on Loma Vista in Beverly Hills to share with Terri Seymour. For the moment, she was 'the one', although, fazed by her flat chest, he urged her to have 'a boob job'. She resisted. 'It would be a nice little treat for you,' urged Cowell.

'Life with him is amazing,' Seymour told friends. 'He's generous, energetic, charming and funny.' But there was a cost: he demanded her constant presence to discuss his work and needs; his moods changed; and fearful of failure and humiliation, he needed constant reassurance. As Seymour explained, 'Life is full-time hard work to keep up with him.' Usually ebullient and self-confident, on other occasions he became bored and fractious, even with Seymour. 'A minefield,' one friend concluded, unconvinced that Cowell was faithful to Seymour.

Cowell was reassessing his personal relationships. Fame and his absence from London had limited his friendship with some of his closest friends in the music industry. Inevitably, his regular Sunday lunches with his mother had ended, and he spoke less to his brother. He talked more often with agents, lawyers and television executives. Most important of all were his women friends, especially Jackie St Clair in London and girls from casual relationships started in clubs and elsewhere.

Juggling between work, family and friends was complicated by his requirement for 'my space'. Personal responsibilities were eschewed by a man who made little pretence of remaining faithful to one woman for long. His only commitment was to remain loyal so long as he was happy, but he insisted on the freedom to change if he preferred another woman. 'When the buzz has gone and it fizzles out,' he said, 'then it's time to move on.' A failed marriage would cost half of his assets, and risking his money was 'verging on insanity'. There would be no obstacles to his freedom, either children or marriage. He was too old, he insisted, for both. Like Peter Pan, his happiness depended on remaining at the centre of the universe, enjoying his fixed, fussy routine and never ageing.

Serving his habits began the minute he awoke, late in the morning. Breakfast had become a hallowed ritual perfected by Roxana Reyna, his housekeeper. Served on a tray while he remained in bed, it came in an agreed order: first oatmeal, followed by a smoothie, papaya, tea and toast. The tray regularly collapsed onto the bed, leaving Marmite smeared over the sheets.

Unashamedly hypochondriac, he swallowed a succession of vitamin and mineral pills before heading to his sizeable bathroom for his next ritual. Depending on his mood, after the long bath he turned off his telephone and would be massaged before a succession of creams – especially anti-ageing concoctions recommended by experts, newspapers and friends – were applied. Next, he agonised about what to wear, although the selection was deliberately limited.

In that self-centred world, Seymour found no space for her own cosmetics in the bathroom. 'I'm using yours,' she told him. So long as everything looked perfect, especially his image, he was satisfied. In the house, every painting was straightened, every object squared and every surface sparkling. Cleanliness was an obsession. Outside the house, his big cars gleamed with twelve coats of polish. If a hub was slightly scuffed while he drove carelessly fast, a replacement was procured immediately.

A Smart car he had ordered for delivery in London had been instantly rejected. 'Take it away,' Cowell told the salesman, fearing that its presence on the drive next to his Range Rover,

Rolls-Royce and Porsche was offensive to his image. 'They want to photograph me with the car,' he scoffed.

Paradoxically, he believed that gratuitously abusing the contestants enhanced his reputation. 'I'm conscious I can get away with rudeness,' he smiled. Others, he believed, lacked his charm: Chris Evans was damned as 'a rude, arrogant little prick. I just intensely despise the guy'; Jennifer Lopez was criticised by Cowell as 'a joke' for arriving at *Top of the Pops* with an entourage of seventy – 'I've never met her but I can't stand her'; and he dismissed Blur with 'Who cares what they think?'

To promote himself, he agreed that his maternal half-brother Tony Cowell, who had changed his surname from Scrase in 1996, should ghost-write his autobiography, which would be called *I Don't Mean to Be Rude, But . . .*. Approved by Cowell himself, it was the story of a self-confessed rich 'eternal egoist' blessed with the same talent, self-confidence and star power as Frank Sinatra and Madonna. Surprisingly, inserted into the book were confessions of repeated propositions from beautiful nude women and even one from a middle-aged man offering 'the most despised man in America' $100,000 to insult him while he made love to his wife. Unmentioned was his fear of failure, but he did approve a 'confession' about Fuller: 'Simon went on to create the format for *Pop Idol*.' The sentence was allegedly included on Fuller's insistence, and over the following years he would aggressively threaten litigation if Cowell dared to hint that *Pop Idol* was not completely Fuller's idea. 'I regret saying that,' Cowell admitted eight years later. It wasn't true, he complained. Occasionally he forgave Fuller, but he never forgot the humiliation. As his life crossed a new threshold, his anger fuelled his lust for revenge.

9

Sabotage

With guarantees that he would earn at least £5 million in 2003, Cowell jetted off to Barbados, mixing with some of Europe's richest businessmen, including Philip Green, a fifty-year-old billionaire retailer who had just sealed his reputation by successively acquiring about half of Britain's high-street clothing chains.

Cowell had first met Green while visiting Monaco for the Grand Prix and staying with Michael Tabor, the British racehorse owner. Green had come to *Thunder Gulch*, Tabor's yacht, for tea. In Barbados, listening to Green and other businessmen, Cowell began to understand the limit of his horizon. Beyond selling records and appearing on TV, there was a range of untapped commercial opportunities which he barely understood.

He returned enthusiastically to Los Angeles for the second series of *American Idol*, which began on 21 January 2003. Over 70,000 people had been auditioned, and the producers, after filming endless interviews and examining each contestant's 'back-story' to their life's 'journey', had decided the likely winners. They were also beginning to rely on talent scouts to scour clubs and bars to find potential stars.

An average of 21 million people watched the recorded programmes, which were edited to tilt the viewers towards the contestants favoured by the producers, regularly helped by Mike Darnell's injection of a scandalous item into the media's gossip columns: Vanessa Olivarez, a self-declared lesbian, enthusiastically followed the producers' script to humiliate Ryan Seacrest and was then publicly ejected; Fox's publicists leaked that strippers had threatened violence against Cowell; and another week's manufactured shock was that Frenchie Davis, a possible winner, had been dropped after the 'discovery' of her appearance on *Daddy's Little Girls*, a porn website. As Cowell's fame grew, Darnell contrived a poll asking, 'Is Cowell sexy or does he suck?' 'Suck' won with 58 per cent of the vote.

The producers were unconcerned about charges of manipulation. 'I hate rules. I absolutely despise them,' said Darnell to Cowell's glee, fearing the risk of the show becoming 'a little too safe and boring'. His cure was to 'drop a bomb on everything'. Darnell's impulse for popularity prompted the release after the US invasion of Iraq of a single featuring the contestants singing 'God Bless America'. It went to number one.

Encouraged to extremes, on one show Cowell called a white contestant 'a monkey'. Randy Jackson was outraged: 'Week after week you've been insulting people. You can't call people monkeys.'

'I can call people whatever I like,' replied Cowell.

'I have a problem,' said Jackson. 'This is America. You don't do that to people. You don't insult them like that.'

'Can we discuss this later?' asked Cowell.

The argument climaxed with Jackson standing up and challenging, 'You want to take this outside? Come on.'

Although compulsive television, it was apparently impossible to use 'monkey', so the argument was restaged replacing the term with 'loser'. As that argument waned, a new one erupted after a contestant alleged that he had enjoyed a secret sexual relationship with Paula Abdul during the competition. Energetically promoted by the ABC network, the evidence initially seemed credible, but after investigation Fox dismissed the allegation as unproven. The episode taught Cowell a lesson, and he would resist any temptation for an easy affair with the endless attractive and available females appearing on the show.

There was no doubt about the acerbic relationship between Cowell and Abdul. 'You're a jerk' was one of her more flattering comments to him during a programme. 'Paula's a brat,' Cowell told his confidants. 'She's got a combination of arrogance and insecurity. She even sits on four cushions to be the same height as me.' Feeble attempts were made to conceal their refusal to travel together. 'Paula's totally insincere and stuck-up,' Cowell continued. 'I can't stand her. She thinks she's royalty and has an entourage of eleven people. She hired a scriptwriter to try and get me back last time – but it was awful and she kept saying things that didn't make sense . . . She gives contestants false hopes. But when I challenge her to give up her time to help them she won't.'

To exploit the situation, the two were filmed enjoying a cosy dinner in Cowell's house. Unexpectedly, they ended up forming a close friendship. 'A lot of artists are difficult,' he said afterwards, 'but she became loyal and interesting.'

Media fascination with their arguments pushed the show's audience up to 26 million viewers. Cowell was acclaimed as 'the frank, villainous Brit . . . without whom the series would most likely have been on a voyage to the bottom of the Nielsen's [TV ratings]'. The praise encouraged Cowell's vitriol. 'The biggest insult of my career in music', he told a contestant, 'is that you even thought I would consider you to be a pop idol. Get out of here.' After hearing another contestant sing 'It's Raining Men', Cowell commented, 'I thought you did Ryan Seacrest's favourite song justice.'

To attract even more viewers, Seacrest was encouraged the following night to ridicule Cowell's personality, clothes and sexuality live on air.

'What is Simon's favourite song?' he was asked.

'I don't know,' Seacrest replied, 'but his favourite club is called Manhole, where they are listening to "YMCA".'

Seacrest's barb was picked up by Howard Stern, a shock jock

on American radio, with Graham Norton, a gay British comedian, claiming it was proof that Cowell was 'one of us'.

Being outed as homosexual was no longer a novelty, and Cowell's denial sounded weary: 'I've never fantasised about being with a man,' he told a newspaper. Both he and Seacrest were reprimanded by Fox's Standards and Practices department, but too late to halt ceaseless gossip that the two men were sexually involved. 'If our gayness is the big secret,' quipped Cowell, 'then why would we joke about it in front of 30 million people?' To silence the gossip, he addressed his alleged homosexuality in his ghosted autobiography. He had 'a more feminine side than most men', he admitted, adding, 'If I was gay why wouldn't I admit it? It wouldn't harm me . . . and my mother wouldn't freak out.' Unmentioned still was the pertinent fact that not a single man had offered any newspaper evidence of an advance by Cowell, despite the promise of enormous financial reward.

The gossip about a possible scandal compelled 33.7 million Americans to watch the final *Idol* programmes on 20 and 21 May. Twenty-four million votes were registered for the final two contestants, Clay Aiken and Ruben Studdard, with Studdard winning by just 130,000 votes. To avoid another argument between Cowell and Fuller about the winner's song, the task was assigned to Clive Davis, who was working from a bungalow at the Beverly Hilton. He would, he conceded, be producing a celebrity rather than an artist or star.

Both the finalists' singles were hits, selling over a million copies, although there was to be no artistic legacy. But there was no disappointment. *American Idol*, gushed Peter Chernin, had been responsible for 'the single most dramatic turnaround in Fox's history'. After a contrived flip expression of disinterest about renewing his contract, Fox offered Cowell $8 million a year for a new three-year contract, which he accepted.

*

Secure in America, Cowell told Claudia Rosencrantz, 'I definitely don't want to do a second series of *Pop Idol*.'

'You've got to consolidate,' Rosencrantz countered. 'We will work around your American commitments, but if you want to establish yourself against your rivals, you'd be mistaken not to keep going in Britain.'

The unmentioned rival was Fuller. Rosencrantz's advice, Cowell decided, was right. She was promising a power base for him to cement his popularity.

Rosencrantz's motive in luring Cowell back was not entirely altruistic. To fill the eighteen-month gap before *Pop Idol*'s return, she had commissioned *Popstars: The Rivals*, featuring Pete Waterman and Louis Walsh creating rival girl bands. Walsh had won the competition by creating Girls Aloud, featuring singer Cheryl Tweedy, but he had clashed with Nigel Lythgoe, the executive producer. 'Nigel's an ambitious fucker who will do anything to anybody to win,' thought Walsh bitterly. He described Fuller as 'small, well groomed, polite and nice', but, on reflection, added that 'Simon Cowell's got better teeth, better cars and better women.' Walsh urged Cowell to return for another season of *Pop Idol*, 'if only to get rid of Nigel'.

Cowell had just bought a new house in Holland Park for £5.6 million and had commissioned renovations. One more season, he decided, would not be fatal. He also employed Tony Adkins, a former royalty protection officer, as his bodyguard and driver. In March 2003, the contracts were signed and Cowell began commuting between Los Angeles and London. Rosencrantz was relieved by the certainty of huge ratings, while Fuller was delighted by the extra revenue from the use of the *Idol* format. The two men were doubly committed, with Cowell filming the *American Idol* auditions for part of the week and then, after jetting to Britain, recording the *Pop Idol* auditions for transmission at the end of the summer.

To promote the return of *Pop Idol*, ITV featured Cowell on billboards across the country and sold T-shirts with the slogan 'Simon says what I think'. Newspapers reported that the 'nastiest' waxwork had been installed at Madame Tussaud's. Cowell's only stipulation had been that the jumper on his effigy should hang over his trousers to avoid any ridicule of his high waists. Visitors were encouraged to sing, triggering Cowell's taped judgements, such as: 'That was my favourite song of all time. Not any more.'

Finally, ITV staged an episode of *This Is Your Life*, the very last of the series, to promote their star. In a weak production, there were many noticeable absentees from Cowell's life, including Iain Burton, Simon Fuller and any executive from the music industry, especially from RCA. Pete Waterman appeared with some glib praise and resisted repeating his off-air scepticism: '*Pop Idol* didn't make Gareth Gates and Will Young, it made Simon Cowell.'

Cowell returned to London seemingly committed to the series. Twenty thousand aspirants had been auditioned for fifty places in the final. 'I only like two so far,' he said ominously. True to form, he told a young male, 'There are 500 contestants left, so how come the chances of you winning are a million to one?' Other contestants heard lines such as 'I don't think anyone in London is as bad as you – and London is a big city,' and 'The bad news is, this is a singing contest.'

Away from recording the programme, in a drab hotel conference room Cowell targeted his venom against Nicki Chapman and Fuller. No one could ignore the arguments. Despite his constant winking, Cowell's anger, aggravated by the eleven-hour transatlantic commute, soured the atmosphere.

'It's terrible,' said Rosencrantz.

'There's real animosity between Fuller and Cowell,' agreed Claire Horton.

'Simon's dumping on *Pop Idol* to prove his power to Fuller,' snapped Waterman. 'They're at each other's throats.'

The focus of the 'unhappy ship' was Cowell's brazen championship of Michelle McManus as the winner. 'You're pushing a girl who started the show at twenty stones and is now heading towards twenty-five stones,' Waterman told Cowell angrily, 'and you're excluding real talent.' To Waterman's bewilderment, Cowell kept saying with a wink, 'Trust me, I've got it covered. It's all sorted.'

At first, Waterman only spoke about being 'so frustrated because the first series was such fun'. Next, he accused Cowell of being 'incredibly patronising to the British public'. Finally, he was puzzled that ITV would wilfully abandon its biggest show. 'Simon's sabotaging *Pop Idol*,' he told his confidants, 'because he resents Fuller's success. He's pushing for Michelle to kill the show.'

The headquarters of the revolt was Cowell's dressing room. '*Idol* was my idea,' said Cowell to his guests, including Jackie St Clair, Terri Seymour, Vanya Seager and Sonny Takhar, the manager of Cowell's record label. Fuller's credit as the creator of *Pop Idol* at the end of the show inflamed the mood.

Soon after Waterman arrived at the Fountain studios on 20 December 2003 for the final, he was seething. On air, Cowell was encouraging 14 million viewers to vote for an overweight woman wearing an ill-fitting red dress. 'You're mad,' Waterman told Cowell during an advertisement break. Not only was Cowell killing *Pop Idol*, but he was also undermining Fuller's chance of promoting a good client. 'He's killing it stone dead,' thought Waterman, 'saying to his enemies, "You think you're clever? Now see this. It's dead."'

Five minutes before the results of the 10.26 million voters were announced, Waterman stormed out of the studio, telling journalists, 'I've had enough of this farce. It's a bad show for freaks and geeks.' To his surprise, no one called his outburst into question. He suspected Max Clifford's malign influence, but in reality some believed that he was jealous about Cowell 'stealing' his nasty act. He left behind producers celebrating at a party without any stars. Fuller had disappeared and Cowell was fuming in his dressing room. The two Simons, Rosencrantz realised, were irreconcilable.

No fans were waiting for Cowell in the rain outside the studio. Stepping into his Rolls, he was content. His battle against Fuller was unknown to the media, and the public's enthusiasm remained high. The sporadic accusations the following day about his sabotage were denied. McManus, he said, was 'the only one with a decent voice and a personality, and there was no real talent this year'. It was, he insisted, 'a series without passion and an anti-climax'.

The more substantial criticism was led by Billy Connolly, the comedian. Lashing out at Cowell's theatre of cruelty, he charged, 'He's so typical of the slime that's in control of rock and roll . . . I think he's repulsive and I hate what he does. I want to slap him. I'd like to give him a big bitch slap.'

Cowell was unscathed. Attacks by politically correct mouthpieces were repulsed by a simple truth: *Pop Idol* existed to discover talent and then sell records. Money wasn't being spent to please those seeking universal admiration for dreadful singers. Connolly, he added, had never spent any of his money to support young people.

To complete the housekeeping, Cowell relied on Peter Fincham, the FremantleMedia executive, to confirm that there had been no sabotage. Votes could not be bought and, regardless of talent, Scotland always voted en masse for a Scottish contestant and so McManus had won. In the event, Waterman's scepticism would be justified. Michelle McManus's single, 'All This Time', sold only 118,000 copies and, after suffering miserable isolation in London, she faded away.

Cowell rarely cared about a failed artist's fate. Bumblers, whether singers or executives, received no pity. Music was a business for sharks. In his ego-driven world, talent came second to self-promotion. But even Cowell, during the aftermath of McManus's flop, was caught cold by Simon Fuller's latest interview. The businessman had persuaded a journalist to write about him: 'In the mid-1990s, he came across a struggling group called Spice that had spent 18 months dismally chasing success . . . He tweaked the name to Spice Girls . . . after noticing the trend called "girl power".' Chris Herbert, Cowell realised, had been airbrushed out of history just as he had been. Once again, the 'publicity-shy' executive whose publicist permanently intoned that his client refused to meet journalists had given an interview in return for being described as 'The most brilliant entrepreneur in the British music industry . . . Simon Fuller is to music what McDonald's is to fillet steak. He doesn't worry about obstacles or problems. He goes for it 100 per cent.' The profile contained a blow-back: Fuller's skills included 'the packaging of synthetic stars' like S Club, who were suing him, alleging that while he earned £50 million from their performances, he paid them just £2,000 per week. He was unapologetic. 'I could put cardboard cutouts of you on the stage,' he told them, 'and it wouldn't make any difference.' Like *Pop Idol* winners, his protégés' careers were short-lived. Even the exception, Posh Spice – alias Victoria Beckham – had been photographed the previous week shivering in Fuller's car park, humiliated as he arrived an hour late for their meeting.

That treatment precisely mirrored Cowell's feelings about his own relationship with Fuller.

American Idol's third season was due to start in January 2004. $8 million had secured Cowell's appearance, but his dissatisfaction had increased. Flying to Barbados for Christmas with Terri Seymour, he resolved once again to exact his revenge.

A kind of Caribbean 'Surrey-on-Sea', Barbados suited Cowell's simple tastes. Surrounded by serious tycoons and celebrities at the Sandy Lane hotel, he liked the plain food at the Lone Star restaurant and the absence of nightclubs. Combined with the sun and blue sea, his holiday should have been idyllic. Instead, he seethed about Fuller's credit on *American Idol*. 'I can do better than this,' he told Seymour daily while pondering his strategy.

Fuller, he suspected, was threatening to squeeze him out of TV. As flavour of the year, every new format Fuller suggested to the networks was instantly accepted. 'He can sell anything,' said Cowell, irritated that Fuller had sold *American Juniors* to Fox and excluded him from any income from the records. Fuller kept his counsel in the face of Cowell's aggressive criticisms.

Angered by Fuller's aggrandisement, Cowell had accepted an invitation to be interviewed on a New York TV programme and criticised Fuller's show. Hours later, he received a phone call in his hotel. 'We heard what you said,' screamed a Fox executive, 'and it was disgraceful. You're no longer part of the Fox family.'

Cowell flew to London convinced that he was about to be dismissed. Instead, Rupert Murdoch had directed his executives to reassure Cowell that his contract would be renewed. Unwilling to be exposed again to Fox's caprice, Cowell thought hard: 'I need some leverage.' Eventually, his ideas were formalised.

While he was plotting his revenge, Seymour had been begging Cowell to eat at the Cliff, the island's best restaurant. Cowell had resisted. The food, he griped, was pretentious and the ambience was disagreeable. However, he finally agreed, on one condition: 'We'll speak about general matters for the first five minutes and the rest of the time we'll speak about me.' Cowell's conditions were not unusual. Seymour's life was always about Simon, and these were the rules if you wanted to play with him. Over dinner, he outlined his idea for a new programme called *Star Wars*. The conversation helped Cowell articulate his plan.

Later that night, he called two *Pop Idol* producers, Nigel Hall and Siobhan 'Shu' Greene, his wife, in England. 'I want the judges to play a bigger role,' explained Cowell, repeatedly mentioning that the judges would be looking for 'the X factor'. Over the following days, the three developed his idea, which had been tentatively renamed *The Greatest*. On his return to London, he swiftly sold his idea to Sony executives. Escaping from Fuller would be good news and, with Cowell and Sony choosing all the songs for the programme, their profits would increase.

The next stage was to visit Claudia Rosencrantz. 'There's good news and bad news,' smiled Cowell, with more winks than usual. 'I'm not going to do *Pop Idol* again. However, I've got a new idea.' Cowell's description of his new format raised a problem. Although there were differences with *Pop Idol* – groups could compete as well as individuals, the age range would be wider and, most pertinently, the three (not four) judges would wrestle against each other as partisan mentors of the contestants to sensationalise the off-stage activities – Rosencrantz silently recognised the similarities. Her dilemma was palpable. If she failed to accept his idea, her star would move into the BBC's welcoming embrace, especially after *Fame Academy*, the corporation's competing programme, had flopped. Her only choice was to jettison Fuller, clinch Cowell and ignore the similarities between Cowell's idea and *Pop Idol*. After all, she reasoned, *Pop Idol* drew heavily on the Australian format originally delivered by Nigel Lythgoe, and fortunately the Australian owners, after protests, had settled their copyright claim against ITV on modest terms, with no payment after two days of arbitration. There was no reason to believe that Fuller's case in protecting his format from developing into *The Greatest* would be any stronger. In any event, since Rosencrantz was determined to keep Cowell, Fuller's interests were secondary. 'We love, love the idea,' she exclaimed on the spot.

The deal with ITV was done but would remain a secret until Cowell had overcome the next hurdle: persuading FremantleMedia, the producers who owned 50 per cent of *Pop Idol* and *American Idol*, also to abandon Fuller. The programme's title remained uncertain but he needed to return to America.

In Los Angeles, *American Idol*'s third season had broken new records. Eighty thousand had been auditioned and the producers had improved the show's appearance. Twenty-nine million people watched the opening contest on 19 January, the highest ever. Cowell's reaction was petulant: 'This is the worst day I've ever seen in judging this competition. A disgrace. I didn't want to come in today.'

In late February, Cowell returned briefly to London to present a dilemma to Tony Cohen, FremantleMedia's chief executive. 'I don't want to do the show any more,' Cowell told Cohen, 'but I've brought a proposal for a new programme which ITV has bought. After much agonising, I've decided to call it *The X Factor*.' He proffered a carefully crafted document. Cohen's predicament was greater than Rosencrantz's. *Pop Idol* had become a global brand bought by over thirty countries. His choice was either to embrace Simon Cowell and confront Fuller or lose the ITV slot in Britain. The money argument, Cohen gambled, was in Cowell's favour.

The new master of leverage did not anticipate Fuller's reaction. Outraged and perplexed by the news, Fuller repeatedly called Cohen from his office in Battersea.

'What are you doing?' he asked, urging that FremantleMedia comply with its contractual obligations to 19 Entertainment and take legal action against ITV and Cowell. 'We must litigate. We must protect ourselves. Everyone is against us.'

Cohen repeated that *The X Factor* was different to *Pop Idol*. 'You're our partner,' said Fuller, without raising his voice. 'You're switching horses in the race. It shouldn't happen. If ITV choose Cowell, then sell *Pop Idol* to another British broadcaster.'

Cohen refused.

'In that case, I expect you to sue yourselves,' said Fuller, conscious that he would be losing not only the licensing fee, but also the income from managing *X Factor*'s winner and the record royalties. The argument about money became part of the undertone.

Another contest now erupted: who was richer? Fuller or Cowell? The comparison became a clash of egos similar to two football managers who, before a match, shake hands to signal their symbolic respect and then commence a titanic battle. Previously, mutual friends had portrayed 'the two Simons' as wary but friendly towards each other. The raw emotions sparked by the television executives' decisions splintered that illusion.

In Los Angeles, Fox's senior executives feared Cowell's strategy. 'If *The X Factor* is a flop,' the network's chief told Cowell in a telephone conversation, 'everyone will assume that *Idol*'s success has nothing to do with you. And if it's a success, you'll want to bring it to the US, and that will annoy us at Fox.'

Cowell ignored the warning. The process was transforming him. He was no longer the puppet but the putative executive of a show he would personally edit. He regularly sat with Claire Horton, Nigel Hall, Shu Greene and Richard Holloway to develop the format and choose the panel. Louis Walsh, Boyzone's creator, was an easy choice. 'Wouldn't it be great if Sharon Osbourne did it?' asked a voice as they sat in Cowell's garden. Osbourne had recently come to public attention when she, her husband Ozzy Osbourne and her family had all appeared as stars of a reality show. 'Yes, but she won't want to,' replied another. 'Well, I've got her telephone number,' said Simon Jones, 'so I'll call her in Los Angeles now.'

Osbourne agreed immediately. Four days later, the deal was concluded.

Cowell had never met Sharon Osbourne but he appreciated her achievements. The fifty-one-year-old daughter of a self-styled gangster, she was a loud and vulgar entertainer whose confessions about life amid music, violence, drugs, alcohol, adultery and cancer commanded affection from women who had bought 2 million copies of her autobiography, despite her habit of sending excrement in a Tiffany box to special enemies. Cowell's first meeting with his new star at the Ivy in Los Angeles was complicated by his off-the-cuff comment in December 2003. When told that Ozzy Osbourne had had an accident, Cowell had quipped, 'He's probably done that to push his record to number one.' Later, he heard that the musician was in a coma. But since Sharon Osbourne wanted the job on *The X Factor*, she ignored the jibe and by the end of the meal was declaring, 'We love each other.'

The switch from star to executive producer triggered a change in Cowell's character. Fuller's commercial success, he realised, was born out of regimented organisation, the antithesis of Cowell's own chaos and dithering. To organise a television show he needed to discard the ill-disciplined lifestyle of a careless record executive and emulate Fuller's methodical ways. The man who rarely scrutinised documents and even as a schoolboy found difficulty focusing on detail began repeatedly making lists and forcing himself to write 'reminder notes'. Suddenly, he became appalled by the mess he inhabited. The detritus in his car – the empty cigarette packets, bottles and papers – disappeared; he cut down on junk food and followed a nutritionist's menu; his dirty clothes were no longer dumped on a chair in his bedroom but instead fastidiously cleaned and stored in wardrobes. And while he did not curtail his frequent shopping trips to Armani, he recruited a stylist to present a series of clothes and bought between five and ten identical shirts, suits, jeans and T-shirts.

At Loma Vista, his rented Beverly Hills home, the dressing room was transformed into a citadel of orderliness as he gradually filled the wardrobes with fifty pairs of identical trousers, nearly two hundred T-shirts, thirty suits and twenty white shirts. Discipline had finally entered his life.

In March 2004, the British team met at Cowell's house in Los Angeles to finalise *The X Factor*'s set, music, lighting, themes and structure. Cowell drove the debate to tweak, unpick and rebuild the format. Always listening and thinking, both his expectations and the budget grew. After twenty hours of discussions, the team returned to London, while Cowell prepared for the final of *American Idol* on 26 May.

Watched by 31.4 million viewers and with 65 million votes registered, Cowell told the winner, Fantasia Barrino, a black teenage single mother from South Carolina, 'I think you are, without question, the best contestant we've had on any competition.' Hyperbole came naturally to Cowell. Her single 'I Believe' went straight to number one but, while her career proved wrong those who argued that most talent-show victors disappeared, she did not live up to Cowell's hype. Eventually, another wannabe hit the dust. In contrast, Cowell's star was rising. *American Idol*'s ratings had risen by 13 per cent and the rate for a thirty-second advertisement slot was heading towards $400,000. 'The show's a cultural institution,' pronounced Rupert Murdoch, unaware that his star had fled Los Angeles to supervise the first *X Factor* auditions in London.

As the show's debut approached, Cowell became nervous about his appearance. Although the forty-four-year-old smoked and drank beer, he persuaded himself that exercise and vitamins were enough to counteract any risks to his health. The source of this convenient wisdom was newspaper reports and conversations with equally health-focused friends. The inevitable conclusion was that to preserve his looks, he should increase his vitamin intake.

On a friend's recommendation, he consulted Dr Jean-Louis Sebagh, a French doctor in London's Wimpole Street. 'We can do something better than that,' said Sebagh. 'When it comes to the skin, gravity is against us.' He recommended regular vitamin injections and Botox injections twice a year. After the first course of treatment, Cowell examined himself endlessly in the mirror and praised 'a miracle'.

He was less enthusiastic about the *X Factor* auditions. ITV's set designers had presented a scale model of the stage but, after listening to their description, Cowell began pulling at bits of cardboard, systematically destroying their work in front of their eyes. 'I'm demolishing it because I hate it,' he declared. 'It looks cheap. Dreadful.' The limited budget paid for little more, complained Cowell, than 'audition rooms which look like wooden shacks'.

At least Shu Greene had selected contestants who played to his instincts. Often from the north, the characters were, she assured him, 'twinkly, quirky, passionate fun people with a light shining out of them'. Despite his middle-class London roots, he loved the raw and uncontrived sense of humour typical of the north of England. The bad news followed quickly. Watching the edited version of the first two episodes, Cowell feared that the chemistry between himself, Walsh and Osbourne had failed to ignite the contestants. Editing, he hoped, would remove the weaknesses and magnify the drama. He desperately needed a polished show.

His consolation was Fuller's frequent telephone calls to Tony Cohen.

'What does *The X Factor* look like?' asked Fuller.

'It's not like *Idol*,' replied Cohen, fearful that because the same FremantleMedia team had been responsible for *Pop Idol*, he was vulnerable to litigation.

'Let me see it,' demanded Fuller.

'No, I can't,' replied Cohen.

The recorded auditions, introduced by Kate Thornton, a friend of many pop stars, were first aired on ITV on Saturday 4 September 2004.

'Literally anyone can win this show,' said Cowell.

Every debt and favour was called in to place stories on the front pages. Nothing, he decided, would be left to chance in his quest for revenge.

10

Simon v. Simon

Cowell was in his bath in Los Angeles one Sunday lunchtime when Peter Powell, his agent, called. The ratings for the first episode of *The X Factor*, reported Powell, were not good. Only 5 million had watched the first show, just 26 per cent of the audience. Ten million had watched its BBC rival, *Strictly Come Dancing*, hosted by Bruce Forsyth. Compared to the 10 million who had watched the first *Pop Idol*, continued Powell, it was a bad beginning. 'I felt really awful,' Cowell recalled.

Worse news arrived on Monday morning. Fuller had served a writ on ITV, BMG and FremantleMedia alleging unauthorised exploitation of the show he had created. Cowell was 'stunned. I never have been so angry in my life. I was absolutely so mad with Simon Fuller. The timing was horrific. His motive was to destabilise the show. My concern was how it would affect ratings.'

'When there's a hit there's a writ,' sang industry insiders. Although Cowell's lawyers were certain that 'Fuller doesn't have a cat in hell's chance or a prayer of succeeding', Cowell was 'paralysed by shock'. Even 'Sarcastic Simon' was careful about his safety. Fuller's audacity was unexpected, not least because he was litigating against FremantleMedia, his partner across the globe. His aggression even included tipping off the media in advance, especially the *Guardian*. 'He believes in reinterpreting his contractual position' was the opaque explanation provided by a Fuller insider.

'It's the worst week of my life,' Cowell lamented. The first show, he knew, was poor, but the next two episodes were better.

Everything depended on promotion to improve the ratings the following week. The risk was huge.

The following Sunday, he was holidaying in Mexico with Terri Seymour. He called Nigel and Shu Greene, who were both shopping in Oxford Street.

'The figures are up by half a million – 34 per cent of the audience,' Cowell was told. Smiling with relief, he celebrated Fuller's torpedo failing. Their relationship was in tatters, even though Cowell was in the midst of filming the auditions for *American Idol*'s fourth season.

Over the following weeks, *The X Factor*'s ratings steadily rose. Although *Strictly Come Dancing*'s audience remained loyal, each week *The X Factor* engaged an increasing number of viewers fascinated by the 'story-telling business' and hooked to the conviction that their votes would decide the universal dream. They were also attracted by Cowell's unpredictability. With a slight pause and movement of his head, he uttered spontaneous comments that were damned by some as breathtakingly rude but loved by others for their disarming charm. To shine, he suggested lines off camera for Louis Walsh to use and then crushed him for talking 'rubbish'. He also encouraged Walsh to attack him, hoping to create the same media interest as *American Idol* aroused in the US.

'I don't want to be like Cowell,' Walsh told the *Sun*. 'I don't dye my hair black. I don't do sun beds. I've had no Botox and I don't wear high waistbands.'

'Louis is the strangest man I've ever met,' Cowell countered, adoring the publicity.

'The show has drained me emotionally,' smiled Walsh, 'and I'll need one month to recover.'

After four weeks, American singer Lionel Richie, a guest on the programme, asked Cowell, 'What's the talent like?'

'It's not about them,' replied Cowell. 'It's about us.'

That was the defining difference between *The X Factor* and *American Idol.* Cowell's focus was on nasty competition between the judges and the brutal truth towards the contestants, while *Idol*'s judges were soft and reassuring.

In London, the favourites had emerged within five weeks, provoking the *Sun* to accuse Cowell of rigging the vote. 'Get the *Sun* on board,' producer Alan Boyd told Cowell.

One month after the writ was served, in the midst of Cowell's commute between Los Angeles and London the affidavits on which Fuller relied were delivered. He had three principal witnesses: Nigel Lythgoe, Nicki Chapman and Andy Stinson. Cowell took issue with Chapman's denial that she, Fuller and Cowell had ever met at the Conran restaurant to discuss the idea which became *Pop Idol.* His recollection was very different. Fuller also mentioned a historic document proving his sole authorship of *Pop Idol.* The document had never been seen by Cowell.

In affidavits sworn on Cowell's behalf by Pete Waterman, Claire Horton, Simon Jones and other producers, including those employed by FremantleMedia, all testified that *Pop Idol* had been developed from Cowell's, and not Fuller's, ideas. None could recall seeing Fuller's historic document. Pertinently, after his writ was delivered Fuller did not call those siding with Cowell.

One week later, he telephoned Cowell. 'Can we find a way to settle this?' he asked. Cowell was uncertain whether his adversary was belligerent or fearful. Knowing that Fuller was a better poker player, he was suspicious and felt vulnerable. If his gamble failed, Cowell knew, his image in America would be dented. In any case, he reasoned, his television days were numbered because 'people are going to be sick of me soon'. On the other hand, he felt emboldened. 'Fuller', he calculated, 'is clearly freaked out that I might bring *The X Factor* to America.'

To supplement his income, Cowell had launched other

ventures, with mixed results: a new TV show to be called *Mogul* had been rejected; a high-cost 'Rat Pack' album had lost money; and, after two years of fraught work, he had finally formed Il Divo, an opera boy band.

'I'd like you to listen to them before anyone else,' Cowell had beseeched a producer in New York.

'They'll never be successful,' the producer responded curtly.

Cowell fumed. 'I thought, "I'm never going to put my life in the hands of an idiot like that again."'

Fame, he had assumed, would terminate the patronising snubs. Instead, he felt that he had been betrayed by a partner. 'I am not happy about it,' Cowell bristled, uncertain of Il Divo's fate. 'Everything could crash.' Suddenly his destiny seemed precarious.

'None of this makes sense,' he concluded about Fuller's peace feeler. Toying between revenge and a settlement, he needed advice.

Lucian Grainge, his and Fuller's mutual friend, seemed an ideal *consigliere*. Cowell flew to the south of France to meet him. 'Find a commercial solution to litigation, not a legal one,' said Grainge, suggesting that they meet Philip Green.

'Come and stay with me on my boat for two days,' offered Green the following day. During his visit, Cowell described his conflict with Fuller over *The X Factor*'s ownership. 'Come up to the bridge,' said Green. Climbing to the top of *Lionheart*, his 206-foot yacht, Green waved his arm over his gin palace, which nestled among other billionaires' overbearing trophies. 'I didn't buy this yacht with a principle,' he said. 'I did it with a cheque. I've never gone to court. Is it worth going to court? You're an outsider on a massive learning curve. It's exciting. Fantastic. Can you work with Fuller? Move on.' Green outlined a compromise for BMG and Tony Russell to offer Fuller but, by then, the battleground had shifted.

The *X Factor* audience was rising and, with the programme's success, Fox feared that Cowell might leave *Idol* and launch *The X Factor* in America. Peter Chernin called Cowell. 'Is there anything I can do to help end the row?' Chernin's self-interest was shared by Fuller. Fearing the arrival of *The X Factor* and its impact on *Idol*, Fuller decided to sell 19 Entertainment and the *Idol* franchise to protect his investment. 'I've got leverage for once,' Cowell smiled. 'That was the gamble of the *X Factor* launch.'

The publicity in the run-up to the *X Factor* final on 11 December 2004 predicted that Steve Brookstein, a thirty-six-year-old amateur singer, would win. There were, Cowell now realised, two *X Factors*: the one on the screen and the one that featured in the tabloids. Carping criticism and a crisis generated front pages, and audiences rose. Stirring the pot increased the ratings.

'Steve's full of crap, and people need to know that,' said Sharon Osbourne, playing the game. 'He's even fooled Simon. He's a fake. I don't like people playing the victim.'

Understandably, Brookstein responded angrily to Osbourne and was equally incensed by Walsh comparing him to Fred West, the mass murderer. The argument hooked 6.7 million viewers. Although 8.6 million had watched the BBC's *Strictly Come Dancing*, Cowell had earned over £2 million from the record sales and the show was gaining ground.

Brookstein, Cowell was sure, was another celebrity rather than a star. Cowell's critics, championing genuine artists, would undoubtedly carp about the damage he caused to music, but no one complained that Hollywood was damaged by the production of bad films. *The X Factor* had given Brookstein a chance denied to him by the industry, but at a price, Walsh calculated: 'They're all disloyal monsters. They get angry about failure and they never appreciate success. People think we're using them but in truth they're using us.'

Beyond the cameras, the contestants' families and friends were worse. They attached themselves to the red carpet and expected drink and drugs. 'We're looking for stars,' Walsh told Cowell, 'and all we're getting is competition-winners with contrived stories. They want fame but don't want to work hard.'

Cowell was gliding above the fray. 'Louis doesn't get it,' he thought, but his real anger was towards Sharon Osbourne. Her aggression had become intolerable. 'I don't know if I can continue with Sharon,' he told Rosencrantz. Her rowdiness, he explained, discomforted him. 'I think she should go.'

'But she's good telly,' said Rosencrantz. 'Go to Barbados. Relax there and we'll sort it out when you get back.'

Days later, Cowell flew to the Caribbean and was joined at the Sandy Lane hotel by Nigel Lythgoe, who arrived, impressively, with former supermodel Jerry Hall and Ryan Seacrest. Cowell was doubly impressed after Hall was replaced by Raquel Welch, the actress, whose poster had been stuck on his bedroom wall when he was a teenager in Maidstone. Welch, Cowell persuaded himself, was being flirtatious, but she was soon being ignored as an argument erupted between himself and Seacrest over another girl Cowell was chasing.

His friendship with Seacrest, including trips together with Randy Jackson to Las Vegas, Miami and Cabo San Lucas in Mexico, reinforced his conviction that Seacrest was the buck intending to challenge the stag. 'Your Highness,' Seacrest had chided Cowell, putting his arm around Terri Seymour the moment he spotted photographers as they walked out of the Ivy restaurant in Los Angeles. To trump Seacrest's quest for publicity, Cowell dived to pat a passer-by's dog. To Seacrest's irritation, the photographers turned to snap a better picture, so he followed Cowell, snatched the lead and pulled the dog towards himself. The tomfoolery was part of Cowell's new friendship and part of Hollywood's unique lifestyle.

Agents, keen to boost their clients' profiles, frequently called Cowell to announce, 'I have a client who would like to meet you.' If Cowell agreed, a good-looking woman appeared. On one occasion, Denise Richards arrived, eight months pregnant and accompanied by a chihuahua. Some months later, she returned to watch *American Idol* in Cowell's house. In a similar social arrangement, Amanda Holden was introduced, only to announce coyly as she entered, 'I have a car arriving at 11 p.m.' She departed punctually.

The sybaritic life was in odd contrast to his passion for dogs. Before leaving Barbados, Cowell had visited the Hope Foundation, a charity that cared for abandoned dogs. Cradling the animals was a reflection of what he admitted were his 'odd' emotional relationships. As a patron of the Battersea Dogs Home, Cowell was known for walking dogs at night in London and for making appeals for animal charities, including the World Society for the Protection of Animals. After two hours in the Barbados sanctuary, he had left a cheque for £10,000.

Cowell returned to Los Angeles for the fourth season of *American Idol* with foreboding. 'I'm ignoring it,' he would say unconvincingly about the litigation. He was certainly avoiding Simon Fuller, who had been ungracious about *The X Factor* in an interview. 'ITV in their wisdom backed the talent,' he had said. 'But if they had been smart and worked out a way of keeping Simon and I together with *Pop Idol*, it would have been to their advantage. What they have lost is a global franchise. Instead they have a poor man's copy, with the rest of the world getting the real deal.'

American Idol, he enthused, had 'become definitive'. Thirty-second advertisement slots were selling for $395,000. Kelly Clarkson had sold 5 million copies of *Breakaway* in the US and 12 million worldwide, making it the third-biggest-selling album of

2005. Irritated by Fuller's assertion that viewers were more interested in watching *American Idol* than Cowell himself, Cowell's interest in the programme plummeted. Frequently, he arrived hours late for meetings, and during the taping of one poor contestant he turned away from the stage to gossip with Paula Abdul, who was by then under attack from Fox for her erratic behaviour.

Surrounded by a constantly changing entourage, Abdul was attracting the wrong headlines. She had failed to stop after a minor car accident, was occasionally reluctant to leave her dressing room for the studio and appeared to be drunk during television interviews, although she rightly insisted she was merely suffering from the side effects of painkillers. Her much-publicised misfortunes increased the numbers watching, not least to see her caustic relationship with Cowell. Bemused on the sidelines, Cowell watched with occasional sympathy as an unpredictable star struggled to survive.

As all that was going on, Cowell had spotted Carrie Underwood, a twenty-one-year-old farmer's daughter from Oklahoma whose back-story featured frustrated attempts as a teenager to become a professional singer. 'I resented that I'd have no investment in her development, so I said nothing about a probable star,' he later explained about the winner. The reward belonged to Fuller when Underwood attracted nearly 30 million viewers to watch the final on 25 May 2005. Fox's challenge no longer came from the opposing networks, whose midweek audiences had evaporated, but lay simply in persuading people to stay at home and watch the show rather than go out.

Underwood's fame as a country singer was a sideshow to the litigation with Fuller, but her popularity re-energised his negotiations to sell 19 Entertainment. Aged forty-five, he feared that twenty years' hard work could abruptly end without any residual value, just like the Spice Girls. He often referred to the unexpected demise of *Who Wants to Be a Millionaire?*. Overnight, the hit TV quiz show had crashed from meteoric ratings to insignificance. However much he derided *The X Factor*, Fuller could not be certain in a 'bubbly market' that *American Idol* would survive five more years. Repeatedly, he asked his expanding staff, 'What's the next big thing?' but no one came up with a significant pitch. Instead of risking his life's achievement, he negotiated to sell 19, including the *Idol* franchise and the management of the show's winners, to Bob Sillerman, a New York media billionaire and the owner of entertainment conglomerate CKX. Sillerman had never watched *American Idol*, but his eleven-year-old daughter and her friends raved about the show. That was not the only reason he was interested in Fuller's offer: he spotted a risk and smelled a bargain.

In his original scenario, Fuller envisaged pocketing $1 billion for 19, but *Idol*'s continuity in America was threatened by *The X Factor*, and 19's last annual operating profits were only £10 million out of a £48-million turnover. Playing a canny game of poker, in March 2005 Sillerman paid $158.3 million for the company. Fuller also received a six-year contract plus a percentage of the yearly net profits and an annual consultancy fee. In the erratic entertainment world, Sillerman judged Fuller's wish to cash in to be 'smart'. As the investor Bernard Baruch had quipped, 'No man went broke taking a profit.'

To his confidants, Fuller spoke about building an empire of 'bigger things' through combining Sillerman's wealth with his talents. He mentioned 'a match made in heaven' and called it 'a world-beater' of TV production houses. Talking about 'content is king', his genius would be to 'unlock the brand value of famous names', including Elton John's music catalogue and the estates of Elvis Presley, Marilyn Monroe and Muhammad Ali. Sealing the deal depended on settling the litigation, and the advance publicity for the new season of *The X Factor* raised the stakes.

Seventy-five thousand people had turned up for the latest

auditions, three times more than the previous year. Trumpeting the programme's idiosyncratic identity, Cowell said, 'The show's kind of a snapshot of this country: funny and sad in parts.' He did not parry those asking whether the show reflected madness or was exploiting it. 'Maybe a bit of both,' he said with deliberate uncertainty. 'It's looking at reality through a keyhole. Why sanitise it? I like to see the good, the fantastic and the terrible.' He had learned lessons from Steve Brookstein's sale of only 250,000 albums. 'Last year,' explained Cowell, 'it was a bit of a freak show. There were so many odd people there.'

'There isn't one single endearing trait in his entire body,' agreed Walsh about Brookstein, noting that G4, the runners-up, had gone double platinum with their record. Brookstein had been dumped ostensibly because of disagreements about his next album, but in reality it was for commercial reasons.

Brookstein disappeared, complaining that Cowell was 'very greedy'. Like all artists, he discovered that his contract allowed the record company to charge all his expenses against his income and royalties. The 'star' earned comparatively little. Few viewers had also realised that the owners of *The X Factor* were earning thirty-five pence on each telephone vote and that some telephone companies, such as Virgin Mobile, were charging eighty-five pence for each call. In addition, Cowell and his partners were earning a share of ITV's advertising revenue, royalties for the performance of each song and the opportunity to promote their own artists, such as Westlife. Not surprisingly, Cowell responded vaguely to questions about his income but, in reply to those confused by the focus on himself rather than the singing, he volunteered that he and the other judges were to blame for 'letting our egos get in the way of the contestants'. In reality, to increase the entertainment the crazy mix was refined for the second series.

Among the freakish contestants chosen by the producers were a male stripper, a porn star and a crazed crooner who, after screaming rather than singing, was told by Cowell, 'It's your weird smiles I don't like,' before being escorted off the stage by security. The friction between the judges also intensified. Sharon Osbourne fought with Cowell and then threw a glass of cola over Louis Walsh. Later, she encouraged the audience to boo Walsh for favouring four Irish sisters against her favourites. 'It's the Irish mafia,' she stormed. 'He says he's followed his heart but he's followed his passport.' In retaliation, Walsh called Osbourne 'a manipulative bitch', and, to Cowell's glee, Irish president Mary McAleese entered the fray, asserting that 'everyone in Ireland' was supporting Walsh.

To keep the publicity bandwagon rolling, Walsh confessed that Cowell's and Osbourne's ridicule had caused him 'sleepless nights'. Enquiring journalists were told by Walsh, 'I'm actually taking sleeping tablets to get some rest.' Mischievously, Cowell offered himself to ITV's *This Morning* show to describe Walsh as 'stupid' and 'reveal' Walsh's possible demise: 'The real problem is finding somebody bland enough to replace Louis. Where do you start? It's hard being stupid. It's definitely not as easy as it looks. But Louis does it brilliantly.' Later that day, Cowell added fuel to the fire by telling a newspaper, 'Louis is an idiot, he has been tremendously stupid. He came into this competition bragging he had a winner – that he had the show all sewn up. But with the wrong song choices and wrong management Louis has managed to muck it all up.'

Pleased with his performance, Cowell then flew to New York to settle the litigation with Fuller. His appetite for a court hearing had diminished after he'd assessed the risk. The costs would amount to at least $10 million, with Claudia Rosencrantz adding a further twist.

'I'm on neither side,' said the commissioning editor whom he regarded as a friend. 'My affidavit tells the truth, although I favoured *The X Factor* because ITV needed you.' Both sides, she said, could draw some comfort from her statement. Then she delivered the sting: 'Just think of the image of two hugely rich men arguing, and it will be you who will be more harmed because you're in the public eye.'

Pete Waterman also advised Cowell against 'going into court and showing the public your bag of marbles'. Combining this with Philip Green's similar advice, Cowell agreed to Fox brokering a settlement but, to devalue Fuller's stake, he told the *New York Times* that he might not sign again for *American Idol* because he would no longer have the music rights. Negotiations to broadcast *The X Factor* in America, he hinted, had started with ABC and NBC.

The countdown to a settlement involved what Cowell called 'rather stressful hard bargaining'. In exchange for him not selling *The X Factor* in America for five years, Fox offered Cowell a contract to star in *American Idol* for five seasons starting in January 2006 at $20 million per year, plus an escalating bonus based on ratings and additional payments if the production or the programmes were extended. Sony would own the US music rights for the artists. Cowell received none of the profits from *American Idol*, while Fuller obtained nothing if *The X Factor* was ever shown in America but did retain his 25 per cent share of *The X Factor*'s licensing fee in Britain. In Cowell's absence, the negotiations were finalised at the Regency hotel in New York on 26 November 2005.

In the midst of that hiatus, Cowell was advised to sell his 50 per cent stake in the TV programmes, including *The X Factor*, to Sony for about £60 million. Cowell understood the reason: 'We've got no business plan, no strategy, no structure and no purpose. We're winging it.' His focus remained on records, not the sale of TV formats. Critically, no one had explained to Cowell the value of merchandising the *X Factor* brand. Cowell agreed that Sony should become the sole owner of the distribution and music rights of *The X Factor* and any other programmes he invented, while FremantleMedia would own all the worldwide franchise rights in perpetuity. Simco, Cowell's trading company, would thereafter receive only a percentage of the profits, including income from the sale of records.

In the final hours after the agreement was concluded, but before Fox's executives had signed the mountain of documents, Tony Russell called Cowell. 'Keep your name out of the media for a few days,' he urged. One hour later, Cowell was told by a journalist that Louis Walsh, upset by Cowell's ridicule, had resigned from *The X Factor*. 'He didn't realise how sensitive I am,' Walsh had complained. 'I might be a clown on TV but I'm also a manager, and he affected my credibility.'

'He can't judge a hamster competition,' scoffed Cowell, and replaced the receiver. To him, Walsh was a loyal guy, 'like a spaniel or red setter – always wagging his tail'. If he sent a mildly critical text to Walsh, he could be certain that his insecurity would provoke an immediate telephone call. He also needed him on the show. But, on this occasion, Walsh ignored Cowell's calls. Walsh was inconsolable. 'I think Simon's very vain,' he told journalists as he flew home to Dublin. 'He wears platform shoes, has spray tans, wears make-up and dyes his hair. I've resigned. It's the straw that broke the camel's back.'

Suspecting that Cowell was reeling, Walsh gleefully started giving a running commentary to the media: 'Simon has so far sent five grovelling text messages begging me to come back to the show.' Eventually, Cowell grovelled sufficiently and he withdrew his resignation, but the respite was short-lived.

At 9 p.m. that same day, Max Clifford called Cowell. The front page of that night's *Sun*, he reported, featured a topless fat stripper spanking Cowell. The source of the photograph, taken at his fortieth birthday party, was a disgruntled relative of a Girl Thing singer. 'God, this is so embarrassing,' said Cowell, fearing that Fox would be repelled by his seedy image. 'We've got to stop it.' Clifford immediately called an executive at the *Sun*. 'If you run that snap you'll have no job tomorrow,' he warned, to no effect. Next, Cowell rang and repeated the same threat, but the presses were rolling and the editors at the newspaper's headquarters in Wapping appeared unbowed. Unable to reach Rebekah Wade, the editor, Cowell called Rupert Murdoch in New York. 'I'm pulling out of the Fox deal,' he said.

'What's up?' asked Murdoch. The news alarmed the News International chairman. 'How many are printed?' he then asked his executive at Wapping, before ordering, 'Stop the presses.' A new front page was rapidly composed and the offending newspapers pulped. In the trade between the tabloids and celebrities, Cowell had called in a favour, and he knew that if the photo had been more compromising, his request would have been resisted. But he was satisfied. The tabloid journalists, accustomed to his frequent calls to their mobile telephones, depended on him for stories. In return he expected loyalty.

His influence was extended by granting his favourites admission to his dressing room. Although he complained that too many people entered his small windowless 'office which drives me mad and I hate it', he still welcomed his retinue, including his mother – whom he treated like the Queen, despite her criticisms – and, recently, Philip Green and his daughter.

A love affair was developing between the billionaire and the star. 'I'm cheap,' Green replied after Cowell thanked him for his advice. 'I charge no fee.' He was among the 300 invited to Julie's surprise eightieth birthday party at the Savoy, where entertainment was provided by the cast of the West End musical *Rat Pack*. 'Simon's always seeking his mother's approval,' some guests observed warmly, adding that money was clearly no longer an issue. He had finally signed the five-year deal he had been offered to appear on *American Idol*.

Although privately he claimed a 75/25 victory in the litigation with Fuller, Cowell issued a graceful statement: 'Simon and I have shown just how well we work together in recent years. We have remained friends throughout this dispute and I think it was this friendship that allowed us to settle our differences.' Asked about his ambitions, Cowell replied, 'More money. If it could pour on me every day like a shower, I would lie in that shower for hours. I just love it.'

Those reading the sentiments recognised the reason for Cowell's elation. Until then, he was always in a bad mood, even sick, when newspapers' rich lists were published showing Fuller's superior position. Now there was a chance to get even, or go ahead. 'First he wanted to be a millionaire,' observed RCA boss Jeremy Marsh, 'then he wanted £10 million, and next £100 million. Now he's dreaming of being a billionaire.'

'That's true,' agreed Cowell.

Fuller also had good reason to be bullish. After paying off a 25 per cent shareholder, he was walking away with about $120 million to fund XIX, his new corporation, and to build a new empire in collaboration with Bob Sillerman. He won universal praise for securing a 'calling card for bragging rights'.

The new season of *American* Idol, starting on 17 January 2006, promised to be more successful than the previous four. The first episode of the show that combined awfulness, fame for the talented and rows among the judges was watched by 35.5 million people, another record. Reigniting hostilities, Fuller's fateful summary was damning: '*American Idol* is the powerhouse, not *The X Factor*.'

In Britain, *The X Factor* dominated the front pages. No other television show generated so many reports about infighting, scheming and tawdriness. The bitching between Sharon Osbourne and Louis Walsh thrilled Cowell. 'I encourage them to behave like brats,' he admitted. 'They're argumentative, spoilt, demanding but loveable.'

Thankfully, Osbourne provided stories for the tabloids in the countdown to the *X Factor* final on 17 December. First, about her recent 'breast job', because 'my nipples were looking down at the floor'; and then about Kelly, her daughter: 'She's not alcoholic . . . She's just been finding her feet and experimenting with drugs. She's just been trying to find herself and get comfortable in her own skin.'

Beyond the studio and the soundbites, a new maturity had transformed Cowell. Meetings to discuss every aspect of *The X Factor* – the music, the production and the commercial relationships – comprehensively were conducted with unyielding resolution. There was a steely focus to his every comment, order and question. The television producers, music executives and professional advisers that he had summoned were left under no illusion about Cowell's intransigence, which was based on bitter experience. Technically, he had unrivalled mastery of television and music production. No detail regarding lighting, camera movements, sound quality, set design, costumes, song choices or even an artist's make-up escaped his attention. Post-mortems ended with lengthy notes about future changes. His micro-detailed critique, delivered in clipped sentences – not a word was wasted – was foreign to those accustomed only to TV's 'Sarcastic Simon'. Triumph would only come, he knew, if he challenged every employee to scrutinise every detail exhaustively. No one there ever doubted that, for Cowell, showbiz was a serious business.

The reward was the 9.2 million viewers who watched Shayne Ward, the twenty-one-year-old son of Irish travellers, beat Andy Abraham, an ex-binman, in the final. The BBC's *Strictly Come Dancing* had pulled in 10.4 million viewers. 'The other show's repetitious,' said *Strictly*'s host, Bruce Forsyth, who declined to watch his competitor. The number of votes, over 10 million, was double the previous year, and Ward's record, 'That's My Goal', sold 732,000 copies in its first three days, becoming the Christmas number one.

The producers' original selection of contestants had ensured the shock factor, and the publicity continued long after the final with the revelations that Ward's father had just been jailed for eight years for raping a pensioner; two uncles and a cousin had been convicted for murder and gang rape; and his older brother had been arrested for the murder of a pregnant mother, although he was subsequently cleared.

Another winner was Louis Walsh, who became Ward's manager and forged a successful career for him. However, he was irritated to be paid half of Osbourne's £250,000 fee per series, and much less than Cowell. 'I had to point out how much they need me,' said Walsh, who was awarded an extra £100,000 for the third series.

The biggest winner was Cowell. 'I create the hype but don't ever believe it,' he said. For over twenty years he had relied on his own judgement, and he never underestimated the public's taste for trivial drama to increase ratings. 'When you do this kind of job,' he continued, 'the one thing you can't do is guess what other people would like. You have to do things that you like.' He had no pretensions about changing the world or leaving an artistic legacy. Just as he proudly asked for fish and chips in a top-rated French restaurant, the man who disliked 'cultural snobbery' and spoke about 'my very populist, incredibly juvenile tastes' adopted a plain manner to assert his supremacy over his staff, the network controllers and his rivals. Guaranteed to earn at least $300 million over the next five years, his ambition to defeat Fuller in America would be launched from Britain.

'I don't want to end my TV career and grow old on *American Idol*,' he said with a wink.

11

Supremacy

There was a lot on Simon Cowell's mind when he met Denise Beighton and her business partner for lunch at the usual pizza restaurant in Fulham. He had received about £2 million for selling *American Inventor*, a TV programme, to ABC; he had lost ITV's commission for *Star Duets* after the BBC started a similar idea – 'It was galling,' he said, with some suspicion; and, after arranging for Il Divo to perform on the Oprah Winfrey show, 5 million copies of their album had been sold. Flush with money, Cowell decided to pay $6 million for his first home in Los Angeles.

Cole Place, on top of one of the Beverly Hills, was a newly built 5,000-square-foot paradise overlooking the city. A housekeeper and a cook were employed to care for him. To finance his new lifestyle Cowell was plotting a bigger TV show so that, as he put it, 'I'll earn money while I sleep.' To Beighton's surprise, after speaking about the shows and music, Cowell switched the conversation to sex.

Every day, the tabloids published the most trivial reports about his life, sometimes real, occasionally fabricated, but always, in Max Clifford's judgement, beneficial to his client's image. 'Anything Simon puts his name to is bound to generate huge interest,' Clifford told the *Daily Telegraph*'s Celia Walden, in relation to an offer for Cowell to launch his own range of cosmetics. A recent *Sun* opinion poll had placed Cowell second after actor Daniel Craig as women's favourite fantasy while making love. The dream man was unsurprised: 'I would expect to be near the top as I'm obviously extremely attractive. I am interested to know where Louis Walsh came. Was he even in the top 100,000 or didn't they include the over-70s?'

Cowell's attitude towards women always puzzled Beighton. While she was convinced he remained unmarried because of his inability to commit himself to a relationship, Simon Jones, her homosexual business partner, was one of many who speculated that Cowell was gay. Both, however, were puzzled by Cowell's description during the meal of his new fantasy: 'A girl', he said, 'coming to my house dressed only in a fur coat and stockings.' Beighton, who had witnessed so much of Cowell's sex life, asked later, 'I wonder why he told us that?'

Shortly after, Richard Wallace, the editor of the *Daily Mirror*, received a series of explicit photos taken by a photographer hidden outside Cowell's west London home. They showed Jasmine Lennard, an attractive twenty-one-year-old woman, arriving at 9 p.m., dressed in a fur coat. Unusually for London, the temperature that summer's day had reached 81°F. The photographer would claim to have overheard Cowell, lying clasped with Jasmine on a hammock in the garden, speaking on the telephone to Terri Seymour in Los Angeles. The implication was that he had also heard sexual activity. Later, the photographer's flash caught Cowell's head peering around the front door as Lennard departed at 3 a.m. Naturally, Wallace wanted a comment from Cowell, not least because Lennard's father was known as the owner of a shoe chain and her mother had appeared in a James Bond film.

Clifford anticipated the editor's call. His client had already described his introduction to Lennard while eating at Cipriani's with Sharon Osbourne. 'I was set up,' he would complain, asking Clifford to minimise the damage by keeping the story out of the newspaper.

'Can we stop this?' Clifford asked Wallace. The *Mirror*, he knew, was less malleable than other newspapers because Cowell had a commercial relationship with their arch-rival, the *Sun*, owned, like Fox, by Rupert Murdoch's News Corporation.

'Why?' replied Wallace. 'I owe you nothing.'

In a world of smoke and mirrors where editors cursed a publicist who would sell even his own mother, the two agreed that the newspaper would quote 'Cowell's spokesman' explaining that the photograph merely recorded 'a meeting to discuss TV projects'.

The following day, after Cowell and the rest of the world had gazed at the front-page embarrassment and Louis Walsh was quoted saying how much he had 'laughed' at the photo, Cowell called Wallace.

'I can't control you, can I? When I have a problem with News International I call Peter Chernin at Fox and say, "Do you want a problem with your number-one star?" What can I say to you?'

'Not much,' smiled Wallace, who agreed to meet Cowell for lunch. The story, he suspected, had further to run.

Terri Seymour, Cowell's 'permanent' girlfriend in Los Angeles, was humiliated. She had suspected that Cowell had been unfaithful before, but, after confrontations, had always accepted his denials. At least that had remained private. Now she could not resist flying to London. Her noisy departure encouraged photographers to stalk Cowell, who, fearing Seymour's wrath, headed for Heathrow in his Rolls-Royce. As she emerged, Cowell shepherded his girlfriend away from the crowds to a Starbucks. For twenty-four hours Seymour was placated by his denials and expressions of affection, but then she read the tabloids and exploded. Cowell shuddered at the tears and tantrums from the woman whom his mother regarded as a daughter.

'I was set up,' pleaded the bachelor. 'I hate you asking questions. Nothing happened.'

'Life', retorted Seymour, 'is all about you, Simon. We never have a conversation about marriage.'

She wanted his commitment despite Julie Cowell warning, 'You're pushing too hard for marriage and kids. He won't.' His unfaithfulness, Seymour feared, spelled the end of their relationship.

'I have heard brilliant things about you,' said Cowell in a flattering performance when he met Richard Wallace. The editor was unmoved. He knew the deals Cowell made with his rivals: he was close to News International, cool with the *Daily Mail* and had done a deal with the Express group, which was owned by Richard Desmond, a discredited publisher of pornography.

'We aren't going to have a problem about Simon, are we?' Philip Green had asked Desmond, a friend on the social circuit.

'No,' replied Desmond, 'so long as he comes to my charity dinners.'

To insure himself, Cowell had sat with Desmond at that year's annual dinner for Norwood, an organisation caring for sick children. Wallace refused to give similar undertakings. One night, soon after their meeting, Cowell had called Wallace at 11 p.m.: 'Richard, you've been a naughty boy again. I'm just getting on a plane at LA, and you're doing an *X Factor* story which is not helpful.'

'I don't know what you're talking about,' replied Wallace. 'It's a five-par story of no consequence.'

'It's a critical time for me,' insisted Cowell.

'Well, it's not for me,' replied Wallace, who resented Cowell's passion for controlling people, even when he did it not by cajolery but by charm and generosity.

On his return to Los Angeles, Cowell resumed his life with Terri Seymour. By then, some gossiped that money had resolved his problems with the two women. Seymour was showered with gifts. To those who were suspicious, Cowell explained, 'I don't want to ever seem stingy. My father was generous too.' Just as he would not allow women to pick up the tab at restaurants, he would not allow disgruntled girls to sell 'kiss-and-tell' stories and jeopardise the burial of his past humiliations, especially just as he was enjoying his breakthrough in America. He only admitted the truth about the Lennard relationship two years later when, amid her tears, his relationship with Seymour ended.

In 2003, Cowell had bored himself watching *Fame Academy*, a BBC programme similar to *The X Factor*. 'I'd prefer to watch a dog performing than that,' he told Shu Greene. Hours later, he called Greene again. Dancing dogs, said the dog-lover, would be a great programme. After brainstorming for two days, Cowell pitched to Claudia Rosencrantz a talent show compèred by three judges for all ages of amateur entertainers, including singers, dancers and comedians. The resulting pilot was called *Paul O'Grady's Got Talent*.

'It's unwatchable,' moaned Cowell. 'It's so bad.' He disliked O'Grady and the programme lacked a live audience. Rosencrantz disagreed. 'It's the funniest show I've ever seen. A no-brainer smash hit.' A change in ITV's management ended the project. Fox also rejected the idea three times. Then, in 2005 – 'out of the blue', Cowell would say – an NBC producer asked to see the O'Grady pilot. To improve the programme, Cowell had edited the ninety minutes down to a sizzling seven minutes. At the end of his presentation at his home, the producer bought seven to nine episodes 'on the spot' as a filler for the 2006 summer season. 'It'll only work if you have sixteen episodes,' insisted Cowell, but his plea was rejected. Nine episodes of *America's Got Talent* were commissioned, starting with a two-hour show on 21 June 2006. Cowell chose singer Brandy Norwood, the ex-*Baywatch* actor David Hasselhoff and Piers Morgan as the judges.

Morgan had good reason to be grateful to Cowell. Ever since

he had helped Cowell launch Robson and Jerome, they had remained friends. In normal circumstances, that relationship could have been tested by a succession of scandals surrounding Morgan's career as the *Mirror*'s editor. Notoriously shameless, Morgan was suspected of involvement in a share-tipping conspiracy with his own journalists, who were subsequently convicted while Morgan was not prosecuted, and, to enhance his campaign against the invasion of Iraq, he had published fabricated photographs of British soldiers assaulting Iraqi civilians. Since his newspaper's circulation was also in free fall, he was, on an executive's orders, frog-marched from his office into the street. Later, even his best-selling diaries were criticised as unreliable, as were the questionable circumstances of his stories about celebrities.

Untroubled by his misconduct, Cowell had invited Morgan for lunch soon after his dismissal: firstly, to commiserate; and, secondly, to discuss the future. Ever since he had been interviewed by Morgan for *Tabloid Tales*, a TV programme about the stories behind the headlines, he had marked the charming aspiring celebrity down as perfect for delivering poisonous comments on his shows. Morgan would be ideal, he decided, for the first series of *America's Got Talent*.

Twelve million watched the first episode, which featured jugglers, acrobats, finger snappers, ventriloquists and singers. Morgan proved to be an inspired choice. The cheeky entertainer shaped his humiliation of the contestants on Cowell's model, reducing them to tears. 'Should he live or should he die?' he appealed to the audience, like a Roman consul in the Coliseum.

An ever-increasing audience watched Bianca Ryan, an eleven-year-old singer from Philadelphia, win $1 million in the finals in Los Angeles on 17 August. With that success, Cowell returned to ITV. '*Britain's Got Talent* is a no-brainer,' he told Paul Jackson, ITV's director of entertainment. Eventually the deal was agreed.

Contestants would appear before a live audience, with Ant and Dec as hosts. The winner would receive a cash prize and perform in front of the Queen at the annual Royal Variety Performance. Cowell insisted that Piers Morgan's success in America made him a natural choice for the British version.

The knave's resurrection was not universally welcomed. 'Piers Morgan, what an easy person to hate,' wrote Graham Norton. 'The penis on legs,' commented comedienne Maureen Lipman, describing a man horribly pleased with himself despite his unreliability. Morgan's notoriety encouraged Cowell's excitement. At the last moment, Amanda Holden was hired to join him and Morgan as the third judge.

Cowell's position in British television appeared unassailable. ITV's audiences were declining and advertising revenue had fallen by 9.6 per cent, but Cowell was the network's lifebelt. In response to Jackson's demand to 'reduce the budget' by 10 per cent, Cowell countered, 'We need bigger sets, better lighting and a bigger budget.' At meetings with his staff – Shu Greene, Nigel Hall, Andrew Llinares, Richard Holloway and his deputy, Claire Horton – Cowell regularly cast aside the product of two months' work or demanded 'twenty dancers', even though the budget was for six. 'And I want a helicopter shot,' he insisted. His restless demands for constant change were challenged only by Horton, who was protecting FremantleMedia's budget. His other staff sat in silent acquiescence. 'It's rare that he doesn't get his way,' Horton complained. 'Everyone is being treated as a facilitator of what he wants. It's too ridiculous. Everyone's failing to bring him back to reality.' Confident of his authority to edit his show and even dictate where it should appear in ITV's schedule, Cowell refused to attend meetings at the broadcaster's offices in south London and expected the executives to drive to his west London office at his convenience.

By limiting his £20-million contract in 2006 to forty hours of broadcast TV (*The X Factor* and *Britain's Got Talent*) over two years, with a pro rata automatic pay increase for each additional hour, Cowell provoked a bitter argument about his personal income. 'The devil is in the detail,' said Jackson during a dispute about Cowell's demand for 'overage' – extra payments for any work beyond the contracted hours – versus Jackson's desire to protect his shareholders. After bluff and counter-bluff, ITV's director of television, Simon Shaps, succumbed, and Cowell's fees and the budget were increased by 10 per cent. The repeated retreats did not signal weakness but reality. Cowell's genteel vulgarity was delivering record audiences.

In *The X Factor: Battle of the Stars*, a celebrity show starring James Hewitt, a former army officer who had enjoyed a secret affair with Princess Diana, and Rebecca Loos, famous for a recent fling with David Beckham, Sharon Osbourne goaded Loos after she sang. 'Was there something stuck in the back of your throat?' she enquired. As Loos's face fell, Osbourne added, 'And put some knickers on to warm your voice.' To everyone's glee, during the commercial break Loos beseeched Louis Walsh to 'Please stop Sharon doing this to me. Only you can help.' Instead, Osbourne, vowing a vendetta against the Beckhams, stormed off the set because Cowell refused to back her against Loos. Looking 'bored', Cowell encouraged the battle, but the following day he called Peter Powell, his agent. 'Get me off this show,' he insisted. 'We're all turning into prostitutes here.'

Battles were always welcome. In the next series of *The X Factor*, for which 100,000 had applied to audition, Cowell was thrilled as a rejected female contestant advanced towards Walsh with a glass of water. 'I saw her coming,' said Walsh, wiping his shirt, 'so I threw water at her first. She was the type who wasn't going to take "no" for an answer.' The tabloid hissiness and the pantomime nature of the show guaranteed that the audience would keep growing, but Cowell's attention had switched. Walsh, he decided, was dispensable. Cowell wanted change and Walsh was not only the weakness, but also the eyewitness to Cowell's failures as a music producer. He wanted the past expunged and his humiliations revenged, yet Walsh harped on those vulnerabilities, unwilling to appreciate Cowell's progression from the A&R era.

Their antagonism focused on the fate of Shayne Ward, the *X Factor* victor in 2005. Walsh enjoyed telling the world that Ward was his candidate and had been opposed by Cowell. 'Ever since then', Walsh complained to the tabloids, 'Simon has been trying to make my life hell.' The 'hell' was their continuing competition about the contestants' fate in the 2006 competition. 'Simon, you know nothing about guitars and real music, and everyone knows it,' snapped Walsh in one programme. 'He's petty and vindictive,' retorted Cowell. 'Simon,' Walsh hit back in front of millions of viewers, 'this song is dedicated to you. It's called "Does Your Mother Know?".' As the episode ended, Tony Adkins, Cowell's bodyguard, fearing violence, separated the two men. Cowell retreated to his dressing room and refused to leave. 'I want a quiet word with Louis,' he told an assistant. 'I'll give him a reality check.'

'You've gone too far,' seethed Walsh soon after, angered at hearing about Cowell's embarrassing criticisms of him to journalists. 'What Simon did', Walsh told the same writers, 'was absolutely disgraceful. Childish and silly. He has run off to nurse his bruised ego.' The newspaper reports of their tiff helped to generate 11.3 million viewers the following week.

Enjoying the argument and irritated by her exclusion from the publicity, Sharon Osbourne grabbed the spotlight during the next programme by licking Cowell's face and rubbing his nipples. 'Ooh, Simon loves a big haggis,' she gushed in what some viewers thought were 'horrible' antics. Cowell was furious.

Revolt was intolerable, unless he benefited. He wanted obedience. Instead, Walsh was carelessly digging his own grave by telling a newspaper, 'Simon's obnoxious, smug and really loves himself, but underneath that he's a really great guy.' After more backstage fights, Cowell stayed at a different hotel to Walsh during the programme's auditions in Cardiff. The Irishman, he concluded, was 'boring'. In Cowell's lexicon, the sentiment was fatal, particularly as, during the show, he had spotted a genuine star.

Although Leona Lewis, a twenty-two-year-old from Hackney in east London, was described as 'a receptionist', her father had spent £80,000 on his child's education at music and drama schools. After he 'sacrificed everything', Lewis had, at her own expense, recorded several songs before entering *The X Factor*. Long before she had reached the finals, Sony record producer Stephen Ferrera had called Cowell from New York. 'She's dynamite,' Ferrera said after watching Lewis on YouTube. 'She's clean-cut and wholesome, with international appeal. She should do an album with Clive.'

At the end of the second live programme, the show's guest performer, Rod Stewart, told Cowell, 'That girl's a star.' Shortly after, Clive Davis called Cowell. 'You may have a Whitney Houston on your hands. I will sign this girl whatever happens.' Long before the final, Ferrera was researching hundreds of songs to create Lewis's first album.

By mid-November, Lewis's irrefutable superiority was forcing Cowell to deny that the competition was fixed in her favour. 'I've bet £1,000 Ben will win,' he said about her fellow competitor Ben Mills. 'I genuinely think Ben will win,' he insisted about a man who would be eliminated before the final showdown. Some believed Cowell was dissimulating to conceal the producers' manipulation, while others questioned his judgement. Either way, he loved the publicity.

Some tabloids reported Lewis allegedly enjoying 'sex romps' with an ex-boyfriend; others found an uncle who was a convicted robber and a relative with a rape conviction; all reported her parents' separation; and, to stir the spice, Lewis denied that she would sleep with Cowell to win the show. Consistent with their relationship, Walsh parodied Lewis as 'dull and shy with no personality'. He hoped, he said, that Lewis would lose so 'I can see if Simon's face falls apart. He'd be gutted.'

In the three-hour final on 16 December, watched by 12.6 million viewers, Lewis beat Ray Quinn, singing the specially commissioned 'A Moment Like This'. Eight million voted, earning the four stakeholders – Simco, ITV, FremantleMedia and the telephone corporations – about £2.8 million. There was additional revenue from special merchandise, including video games, T-shirts, mugs, an *X Factor* karaoke machine and a Christmas record, which was downloaded over 50,000 times within the first three minutes of its release. To Green's surprise, Cowell would not develop the merchandising business.

The X Factor had delivered a genuine international star. Clive Davis welcomed Lewis to Los Angeles to be 'broken into the star-making machine'. The producer had arranged the same showcase as he had arranged for Whitney Houston. 'I invited top songwriters to watch Leona perform. I wanted to encourage them to write for her. I got "Bleeding Love" and "Better in Time". Both were number-one hits.' Producing the album with original material would take one year. He planned the launch of her debut album at 'my annual Grammy awards party – the hottest ticket in town – and on eighteen TV shows, on radio and a theatres tour'. The album – *Spirit* in Europe and *Forgive Me* in America – was destined to be a number one. By 2008, Lewis would be the world's highest-paid singer. A star had been born – or at least manufactured by the best producers. In turn, Cowell had become America's and Britain's highest-paid TV star.

Another victor was Richard Griffiths, Cowell's former boss, who had established a management company for singers. His agency was struggling until Cowell called. 'It's anarchy,' said Cowell. 'The judges are fighting to become the artists' managers. I want you to become the manager for all of *The X Factor*'s artists so it's a level playing field.' With Leona Lewis, Griffiths gratefully leapfrogged to success.

After a Christmas break in Barbados, where he socialised with Nigel Lythgoe and Philip Green, Cowell returned to Los Angeles for the start of *American Idol* on 16 January 2007. The prospect filled him with horror. 'I feel I'm in a prison,' Cowell said to himself. 'I've got to get out.' Lythgoe, he decided, was becoming unpleasant, a situation made worse by the hectic schedule and the programme's success, despite its poor contestants. Over 30 million viewers would be watching what the advance publicity promised would be a 'meaner' show, but the meagre highlights were Cowell being attacked by one contestant with a tub of hair gel, apologising to another for saying that she looked like a giraffe and making amends to a third for calling him 'a bush baby'. This was all profitable television for Fox, but was boring for him.

His irritation sparked a spate of arguments about *American Idol*'s content with Lythgoe, who, Cowell decided, seemed to be harassing him. After one public quarrel, Cowell told an eye-witness, 'I'm quite comfortable having a bust-up with people to their face. It kind of clears the air.' 'Simon blew Nigel out of the water,' sniggered Ryan Seacrest.

The stalemate needed resolution.

Cowell was belligerent when *The X Factor*'s senior producers arrived in Los Angeles from London to discuss the new series. Meeting in Cowell's home, they discovered a restless star impressed by Mike Darnell's mantra of constant renewal. Unlike other British TV producers, who looked for new shows rather than improving existing winners, Cowell spoke about 'raising the bar' and 'refreshing the show' to prevent *The X Factor* becoming stale and withering. His shopping list was exhaustive.

First, he wanted a bigger budget to improve the show's appearance. Inevitably, the ITV producer refused, but Claire Horton agreed to see whether his expectations of 'pushing the envelope' and tinkering with endless technical details could be met. 'I also want major changes,' Cowell told his visitors. Ben Elton's parody of Walsh and Osbourne as tired clichés in his book *Chart Throb* matched Cowell's own opinion. 'Louis', said Cowell, 'is exhausted. People I trust tell me he's become pointless.' Kate Thornton, the hostess, was unimpressive, he added. Both, he decided, should be fired. Some around the table were unconvinced but, sensing the mood, Shu Greene agreed. 'I think Louis should be replaced by Brian Friedman,' she suggested, recommending the choreographer who was directing a pilot of *Grease Is the Word*, a TV singing competition for couples to win a place in the West End musical. Although Friedman's charms lacked universal appeal, Greene's instincts commanded respect, and Cowell confirmed Friedman's selection. No one spoke in favour of Thornton. She would be replaced by former DJ Dermot O'Leary.

Responsibility for delivering the dismissals was assigned to Richard Holloway, a genial producer capable of delivering graceful executions. Everyone also agreed to Cowell's suggestion of an extra judge. He wanted Dannii Minogue, the thirty-five-year-old star of *Australia's Got Talent* and sister of Kylie, the hit singer. She had recently blamed her broken marriage, friendships and engagement on 'my hectic work schedules'. Female vulnerabilities attracted Cowell.

'I have bad news for you,' Holloway told Walsh, who was

standing in his Stockholm hotel room. One week earlier, after a meeting with Cowell in Los Angeles, he had been sent to Sweden to find new songs. 'I feel like I'm being stabbed in the back,' Walsh stuttered as Holloway revealed his fate. 'I'm really shocked.'

Minutes later, Cowell was called by a journalist to comment on Walsh's dismissal. Startled, he assumed that staff at ITV or FremantleMedia were paid by tabloid journalists for tips. 'It was ITV's decision,' he declared.

'I wasn't sacked,' Walsh told the first journalist to call. 'I made the decision to leave by myself.' But, after more leaks from the producers, he admitted, 'It seems I've been fired by Simon.' Then he added, 'I don't know where this rubbish about me being boring or dull has come from – it is completely untrue.'

Hearing that Walsh was distraught, Cowell called. 'It's nothing personal,' he said.

'I'm devastated,' admitted Walsh, looking at himself in the mirror. 'Am I too old? I know I haven't looked after myself properly. My teeth, my hair, my skin . . . they all need fixing.'

As he gabbled about his lack of self-confidence, Cowell assured him, 'It's just ITV's decision.'

By then, Holloway had personally visited Kate Thornton's home. In tears, the sacked presenter recalled how another producer had mentioned her 'bad teeth and bingo wings'. Now, she told Holloway, she felt doubly humiliated because Cowell had 'assured me privately and publicly that my job was safe'. She refused to take Cowell's telephone call.

The reaction in London stung Cowell. Both casualties attracted widespread sympathy. He hated being portrayed as disloyal. The parting, he told each journalist who telephoned, had been amicable, and he went further: 'I didn't fire Walsh or Kate. It was ITV . . . It was not my decision.' He had pleaded, he said, to keep both of them.

Walsh was incensed after the publication of Cowell's

sentiments. 'I have been completely shafted by Simon,' he told the *News of the World*, adding that Cowell, and not ITV, controlled everything. 'He has told me bare-faced lies about my future and, worst of all, he didn't have the balls to tell me personally that I was going.' Kate Thornton, he added, 'is very upset and feels really humiliated. She wants to speak to Simon, but he hasn't even called her to wish her well.' She, in turn, blamed the 'political cesspit at ITV'.

Paul Jackson and Simon Shaps were prepared to take the blame. To Shaps it seemed that Cowell regarded Walsh's dismissal as part of a 'guessing game of the panel's identity to generate media interest while the programme was off the air'. Cowell, he knew, enjoyed uncertainty.

To keep the story boiling, and in reply to Sharon Osbourne's accusation that he was 'a coward', Cowell summoned a *Sun* journalist to fly to Los Angeles. 'I should have told Louis myself he was sacked,' he explained. 'What he should know is that there was only one person defending him and that was me.' He added that he had nine new shows in development and in eighteen months hoped to have fifteen shows in production in the US and UK. Walsh was unimpressed. 'I'll never work with him again,' he told the *Sun*, sobbing about his 'heartless' sacking. 'He never even called me.' No one, it appeared, could unearth the truth, and Cowell had moved on.

The speculation about Walsh's replacement fuelled more welcome publicity. Agents pushed their clients' names into the spotlight, and Max Clifford stirred the pot. 'Donny Osmond is definitely in the frame,' said the publicist, 'but I'm not sure Simon would be keen on choosing someone younger and better-looking than him to be on the panel, so we'll see.' Even Sinitta threw herself into contention. 'I'm the rightful new judge because I've been groomed for the job,' she said, grateful for Cowell's continued support after her marriage in 2002. He had also backed her successful bid to adopt two babies after her surrogate pregnancy had failed.

In early April, Brian Friedman and Dannii Minogue were confirmed as the new judges. Cowell had taken pleasure from the saga. Control over his own kingdom was so much more fun than appearing on *American Idol*, especially during 2007's lack-lustre competition.

On 23 May of that year, Cowell arrived at the Kodak theatre in Los Angeles for the show's final. He was bemused by Paula Abdul, who had recently broken her nose, apparently by falling while avoiding Tulip, her dog. 'How's the dog?' he asked mis-chievously, knowing her fate on *Idol* was uncertain.

Early the previous year, the media had reported Abdul's late, tearful arrival at the Fox studios and her involvement in some brawls around Los Angeles. She blamed her painkillers, but Fox's producers questioned whether she was worth her $1.8-million annual fee and began considering replacements. The controversy had resurfaced during 2007. She had again called Cowell 'a jerk' and 'an asshole' after he covered his ears and mockingly told a man, 'You should be singing in a dress and stilettos'; then she had tried to slap him; and, finally, she had appeared on a Seattle TV show, jerking her head, slurring her speech and with glazed eyes.

Like Cowell, she was disillusioned by the inadequate contest-ants. Although, in 2006, 63.4 million votes had been registered for Taylor Hicks, a twenty-nine-year-old from Alabama, Cowell had derided the winner as 'a drunken father singing at a wed-ding'. Although Hicks's first record, 'Do I Make You Proud?', was a number-one hit, he was dropped the following year by Arista, as Cowell expected. The 2007 competition was even worse. Melinda Doolittle, who consistently won the most votes, had been voted off after a negative campaign organised by vote-fortheworst.com, making Jordin Sparks, a dull seventeen-year-old from Arizona, the probable winner.

The season's only highlight had been *Idol Gives Back*, a trip to Nairobi for the judges in a bid to raise $60 million for charity. Arranged by Richard Curtis, the screenwriter, Cowell spent three days in the Kenyan capital's biggest slum. 'The toughest three days of my life,' he told Curtis. 'I couldn't believe the extent of the poverty.' Nevertheless, to make it palatable to the US public, he persuaded Curtis that 50 per cent of the money raised should be given to American charities.

The worst moment that season had been a cutaway during a live programme of Cowell rolling his eyes while the others were mentioning the massacre of thirty-two students at Virginia Tech. The public furore threatened permanent damage to his reputation. 'It was damning,' admitted Cowell. 'An awful twenty-four hours and very frustrating because the Fox producers told me it had blown over and I should say nothing.' Cowell demanded the chance to explain that he had been speaking to Abdul, unaware of the discussion of the killings. 'I may not be the nicest person in the world,' he explained in a transmitted interview, 'but I would never, ever, ever disrespect those families or those victims, and I felt it was important to set the record straight.'

Looking bored on the finals night, his head resting on his arm, Cowell amused himself by reminding Abdul how before a previous programme he had told her, 'Ask me to tell the story about the moth and the melon.' When she obeyed, he had replied caustically, 'I don't know what you're talking about,' as the camera cut to Abdul's incredulous face. Abdul grimaced as Cowell glanced at the stage and noticed Trevor McDonald, the British TV presenter. Acting puzzled, he watched McDonald progress across the stage towards him holding a large red book. 'Simon Cowell, this is your life,' said McDonald as the audience roared. 'Is this a wind-up?' asked Cowell. 'I'm actually really embarrassed.' *This Is Your Life* would be taped in London after Sparks won a finale that was watched by 25 million Americans, compared to 36.3 million viewers in 2006. Sparks would sell about 3 million albums before her career declined.

Cowell was apprehensive about *This Is Your Life*. The same programme four years earlier 'wasn't great', he had admitted. 'It felt too early. I never watched it afterwards or read the book. Ally Ross had written in the *Sun* that it was hilarious watching Cowell with no friends. This time I hoped it would be better.' Inevitably, he knew in advance about ITV's plan to give an old format just one more chance, and had played his surprise perfectly.

Introduced as 'One of the most famous people on the planet, he is one of the most obnoxious men on TV, the Antichrist of the pop world,' Cowell's first guest was Louis Walsh. In the contrived drama, which Walsh would call 'Laurel and Hardy', as Walsh walked towards the leather sofa, Cowell said, 'This is going to get very uncomfortable.' 'Not for me,' snapped Walsh, who nevertheless gushed about their past collaboration.

'I humbly offer a grovelling apology, Louis,' laughed Cowell.

'All is forgiven but not forgotten,' replied Walsh.

Amid applause and clapping, Cowell said, 'And we'll do some other shows together.'

'I'm not sure about that,' replied Walsh.

'Nor am I,' said Cowell after a delay.

There were other tributes from Ant and Dec, Pete Waterman and Ben Elton, whose amusing monologue included the comment 'To Simon Cowell masturbation isn't about self-abuse, it's about fidelity.' Then, after his family and Andrew Lloyd Webber praised the hero, Ryan Seacrest and the *American Idol* judges stepped through the doors. 'Simon's the only person who calls out his own name during sex,' said Abdul, who got more laughs by adding, 'Looking at himself in the mirror is what Simon thinks is foreplay.' When Trevor McDonald mentioned 'girlfriend', Cowell jokingly said 'Linda . . .,' knowing that Terri

Seymour would walk in. She smiled, unaware of the barb. The show ended with Cowell standing aside from his guests and pushing the red book, with his name spelled in gold, towards the camera. He was pleased that the programme was better than the previous one: 'I made bloody sure this time that there would be more friends.'

After pocketing over $30 million plus his share of the royalties on Jordin Sparks's records, Cowell began intensive editing of *Britain's Got Talent*. The first series would start on 9 June 2007 and run daily for nine days. Simultaneously, he was editing *America's Got Talent*, introduced by Jerry Springer and with Sharon Osbourne as a judge, which would begin on 5 June. 'Each edit', Cowell told himself, 'improves the drama, music and presentation of the contestants.' His daily routine had changed too. Waking at noon, he worked seven days a week, sometimes until 5 a.m., with a nap in between. His restlessness had become relentless.

On the day the first of the recorded *Britain's Got Talent* programmes was transmitted, Cowell arrived at the Emirates stadium in north London, the new home of Arsenal football club. Eight thousand people had arrived for the first auditions of *The X Factor*, an unexpectedly high number. Cowell sat down with Sharon Osbourne, Dannii Minogue and Brian Friedman to hear the first contestant. Ten minutes later, he stopped and summoned Andrew Llinares, the producer. 'It's not working without Louis,' said Cowell. Llinares was surprised. 'I miss Louis,' Cowell told Claire Horton a few minutes later. 'Brian was a mistake.' After a brief attempt to start the auditions again, Cowell called a halt and went to his dressing room, a corporate box overlooking the football pitch. He telephoned Paul Jackson: 'I've got to have Louis back.' Shocked, Jackson urged, 'Can you at least finish today's auditions? I'll drive out to the stadium to meet you.'

Cowell, he later discovered, had not continued the auditions but instead had locked himself into the box. 'Without Louis,' Cowell explained, 'there's no one to feed the lines for me to make my sort of jokes.'

Even Osbourne was struggling. Cowell had stumbled on the truth that as the contestants became weaker, the show depended more on the judges. 'I need Louis,' he reiterated. 'He's fun. He's a court jester.' Cowell did not admit another reason: Walsh had regularly uttered excellent lines which Cowell repeated. In the edit, Walsh's original version was dropped and, by selecting the best shots of himself, Cowell perfected his own appearance. Not only did he need Walsh's return as a sparring partner, but Walsh had just threatened to transfer Westlife from Sony to Universal, with the group destined to sell over 40 million albums.

This was the stuff of madness, thought Jackson. Eight thousand contestants and over one hundred crew were standing idle while Cowell was pleading for the man he had fired. Cowell's financial wastefulness had reached new extremes. 'Your career is on the line,' said Jackson to Cowell. 'You're going down. You've lost the plot. The Walsh situation is causing chaos.'

'The show', Cowell replied, 'is more important than the contestants.'

'You're destroying the credibility of the show and you're making us all look stupid. The press will jump all over us for not knowing what we're doing,' concluded Jackson.

Cowell was unfazed. Recording was abandoned and he agreed to meet Simon Shaps. 'ITV think it's all doom and gloom,' thought Cowell. 'I can't understand why everyone is so scared about admitting a mistake.'

Unusually, he travelled to ITV's headquarters. To Jackson's and Shaps's surprise, he seemed to be enjoying the crisis.

'I'll take the responsibility in the press that we made a mistake,' he told Shaps.

'Simon likes to portray Walsh's firing and rehiring as drama, mischief,' thought Shaps.

Jackson was included in a conference call. 'Why do we want Louis back?' he asked. 'Is he the only option?'

'I've given you my reason,' said Cowell, ending the discussion. Shaps reluctantly agreed.

The same afternoon, Cowell telephoned Walsh: 'There's a chance you could come back.'

'My bags are packed,' replied Walsh.

'Don't say a word or it won't happen,' warned Cowell, knowing that the next problem was firing Brian Friedman, who was already injured by Cowell's decision to abandon *Grease Is the Word* during a press conference.

'Simon's smothering my creativity,' complained Friedman flamboyantly. 'I haven't signed a new contract yet. I need six months to clear my head.'

Within hours, the news had leaked. Cowell, reported the *Sun*, had begged Walsh to return, offering him £1 million, but Walsh had refused. Cowell was paralysed. 'The tabloids', he acknowledged, 'help you more than they harm you. They are promoting you, your shows and your artists . . . when I've had a bad time with the press I've normally deserved it.'

The X Factor's salvation would have to wait while he rescued *Britain's Got Talent*.

The reviews of the first *Britain's Got Talent* programme, watched by 5.2 million – 22 per cent of the audience – were poor. 'Ian Hyland's review in the *News of the World*', spluttered Cowell, 'is absolutely damning.' His publicist deflected the criticism by feeding trivia to TV reporters: Cowell had sat on two cushions because Piers Morgan was taller; Terri Seymour 'revealed' that Cowell did 300 push-ups a day to appear fit in his T-shirts, even when flying; and Amanda Holden was scripted to divulge her cure for Cowell and Morgan's 'squabbling'. She behaved like their mother and reminded them of their past humiliations: 'Neither has any social skills when it comes to saying something difficult without being rude. I ask Piers Morgan whether he was sacked from the *Mirror*, and I ask Cowell to tell me about Zig and Zag.'

Five days later, the mood turned. The audience grew and the critics spoke about a 'renaissance' as TV's Saturday-night graveyard was transformed into 'a golden age' by reminding the audience about English eccentricity. The emerging hero was Paul Potts, a thirty-seven-year-old mobile-phone salesman from south Wales who had spent £12,000 on singing lessons. On the final Saturday night, 11.45 million – 48 per cent of the audience – watched him win the vote with his performance of 'Nessun Dorma' from Puccini's *Turandot*. 'Oh God, not opera,' sighed Cowell.

Just as Potts gloried in the spotlight, Brian Friedman faced his eclipse. Cowell, he complained, had caused a personal crisis, a sentiment echoed by Dannii Minogue. 'I am at the end of my nerves,' she told the producers. 'I'm waking up thinking, "Am I next?"'

Cowell was unaffected by their worries. His success depended on exercising total control over his shows, the network controllers and his producers in two continents. Any weakness was intolerable. Louis Walsh's mixed fortunes did not leave a scratch on the Cowell brand. Turning his mistake into a soap opera was welcome publicity, and Max Clifford provided the tabloids with 'colour' as they covered their front pages with praise for the hapless Irishman's resurrection. On 22 June, Cowell and Walsh were photographed spending the day together at Ascot. The week's races were Cowell's comfort zone. Only his closest friends were invited to his box, and a different ex-girlfriend arrived every day. For Terri Seymour, Cowell's unusually close relationship with his former girlfriends was part of life. In return for his generosity and affection, they became trusted confidantes happy to endure a celebrity's introspective monologues. The only man prepared to offer similar therapy was Walsh, whom Cowell occasionally spoke of as 'my best male friend'. Like the other guests at Ascot, Walsh was unconditionally grateful to his host. Thanks to Cowell, his life would certainly improve.

To cover Walsh's return to *The X Factor*, Jackson and Cowell agreed to stage a scene in which Cowell would be filmed saying to Sharon Osbourne, 'Something's wrong and I can't put my finger on it,' to which Osbourne would reply, 'We miss Louis.' After the exchange had been reshot several times, everyone declared themselves satisfied, except Jackson. Aspects of the staged discussion made him 'cross'. Holloway refused to consider his objections: 'Simon has approved this, so if you want to change anything, you'll have to speak to him.' After a 'heavily charged' conversation with Cowell, Jackson ordered two seconds to be removed.

Considering Cowell's anger with those searching for evidence that *The X Factor* was rigged – and he hated the tabloids' use of the word 'fix' – staging the scene was a strange decision. He always fumed about complaints to Ofcom about the voting, which would trigger official investigations. Although no complaint was ever upheld, few doubted that the recorded programmes were distortions. Purists could moan, but reality television was by its very nature unreal.

The irrefutable reality was Cowell's ambition for supremacy. His success depended upon inspired producers unconditionally sympathising with his whims. Those failing the test automatically became less useful. The casualty of the summer's turmoil was Paul Jackson. His unease about Cowell's toing and froing with Walsh reduced his value. Cowell, Jackson suspected, enjoyed the excitement of casting a judge off the programme to give his show an additional boost. Public dismissals, the sceptic mused, could even become Cowell's trademark. Those heretical thoughts ended Cowell's complete trust in Jackson. He disliked being second-guessed, and he disliked Jackson's unwillingness to recognise his emergence as a global star. If the protester could not adjust, he was best edged out of the inner circle. Jackson would no longer be invited for Sunday breakfast in Holland Park or to enjoy banter in Cowell's dressing room. Cowell believed that he had drawn the best out of Jackson, and that his input had now become irritating.

12
Toys

'They're my toys,' thought Simon Cowell as he sat in the Mediterranean sunshine. He loved playing with women, especially those starring as judges on *American Idol* and *The X Factor*. Dannii Minogue added to his fun. 'She'll be the new toy in the show, and everyone will enjoy playing with her,' he mused.

In July 2007, Cowell had rented the appropriately named Villa SC near St-Tropez, with staff and a Ferrari Spider thrown in. Exhausted by the eleven-hour commute between Los Angeles and London, the frequent flights across the US and producing and appearing on two shows, he collapsed in the south of France with Paul McKenna and Sinitta, his loyal friends, who were joined by Kelly Bergantz and others employed by Sony. Terri Seymour was not invited.

A year earlier, Cowell had tired of Terri. As he explained to a confidant, 'I told her, "I don't want to sleep with you any more but I want you as a friend."' Tearfully, she accepted the inevitable and, despite the split, agreed to pretend their relationship was continuing.

'I felt liberated,' said Cowell, but he was 'embarrassed' after the news inevitably leaked. 'For the first time,' he grumbled, 'I've had to put out a press release to announce the end of a relationship.' The statement was delayed until he arrived in France. To cushion her embarrassment, Cowell volunteered, 'Terri dumped me in a text message.' He wanted neither marriage nor children, he said. 'I treat my shows as my babies.'

Seymour was suffering greater stress. Four years earlier, she had said, 'I am pretty secure. He's never given me a moment's worry. Simon has said he has been faithful, because there would be no point continuing the relationship if he were not.' After his denials, she had ignored the Jasmine Lennard awkwardness but was distressed by his refusal to commit. 'I said I wanted a baby,' Seymour explained, 'and Simon told me to buy a terrapin.' His most romantic gesture, she said, 'was to buy me a toothbrush'. Less romantic were the repeated arguments caused by his boredom, demand for 'space' and her accurate suspicions of unfaithfulness. After four years together, she sensed he was enjoying an affair in Los Angeles, possibly in an apartment he had recently bought nearer the city.

'The split is amicable,' Max Clifford announced. Seymour's pride was protected by providing an apt quote from her: 'Now I can use the mirror. He used to take for ever in the mornings.' The pain was mitigated financially: Cowell bought Seymour a Bentley, a Range Rover, a house for $4.6 million in Beverly Hills and covered the reconstruction and maintenance costs. Through Cowell, Seymour also landed a contract as a reporter on *Extra*, a celebrity show broadcast by a Los Angeles TV station.

Cowell's generosity, it appeared, ensured Seymour's continued discretion. Indeed, she never sold a kiss-and-tell story describing their relationship. As Denise Beighton had observed, Seymour's figure did not match Cowell's fantasy, yet they were good friends. Moreover, Terri and her mother were close to Julie Cowell, and that was important for Cowell. Without any other real friends in Los Angeles, he knew he could rely on her.

On cue, Sinitta stepped forward to quash new rumours about Cowell's sexuality and the reason for his generosity to ex-girlfriends. 'Sex is so important to Simon,' said Sinitta, 'that's his trouble. It clouds his judgement. But I know what he really wants. Someone to be his companion, his buddy, his mentor, but someone who can put up with his work ethic as well. I'm going to find him his perfect woman. He does have this problem though. It's called a roving eye.'

Among the friends he met in St-Tropez was Philip Green, anchored off the coast on *Lionheart*. Cowell used the opportunity to discuss his sale of 50 per cent of Simco to Sony two years earlier.

'Why did you do that?' asked Green.

'It was an adviser's idea, to raise cash,' replied Cowell.

Green shook his head. 'A mistake. You're not thinking about merchandising. That's where you'll make your money,' said Green, mapping out a sketch of a media empire.

'He's been one of my biggest mentors and is one of my closest friends,' Cowell praised Green. He was also grateful for one final suggestion: 'Get a yacht for your next summer holiday. It's more private and you can move around.'

The 2007 season of *America's Got Talent* had been extended to twelve two-hour programmes running from June until August, with Sharon Osbourne, Piers Morgan and David Hasselhoff as the judges and Jerry Springer as the host. The competition, won by Terry Fator, a ventriloquist, was consistently the summer's number-one show, helping sales of the format to other countries. At the same time, Cowell was preparing for the *X Factor* auditions in Britain. One hundred and fifty thousand hopefuls had applied and recordings would begin in mid-August, just after *American Idol*'s auditions began in San Diego. Criss-crossing the Atlantic, he couldn't resist casting the fly: 'I'm working on a secret project. Bigger than *American Idol*.' That was guaranteed to wind up Simon Fuller.

By mid-August, playing with his toys on *The X Factor* was providing more fun than he anticipated. 'Dannii Minogue and Sharon Osbourne are at loggerheads,' he rejoiced. 'When I sit next to one, the other sulks. I have to try to give each one equal attention.' To generate more tension, he slanted towards Minogue, describing Osbourne as the 'queen bee' who disliked the Australian 'strutting around as if she owns the place'. The closer he sat next to Minogue, the more Osbourne and Walsh suspected their employer's motives.

Playing with the two women fed his appetite for enjoying similar games with the contestants, and the producers had gathered a collection of freaks. Seventy-year-old Emily Bell-Hodgson was dressed in Michael Jackson-style clothes, with sunglasses and a cap to conceal her face and poor teeth. 'You're like something out of a horror movie,' observed Cowell. 'I urgently need dentistry,' she admitted, adding, 'I'm standing here like someone who actually has the X factor.' 'Yes, but not on planet Earth, darling,' cut in Cowell. Other put-downs were similarly original: 'If you sang like this 2,000 years ago, people would have stoned you'; and 'If your lifeguard duties were as good as your singing, a lot of people would be drowning.' Some thought the high point of his games was the crucifixion of an unemployed drug addict: 'You're lazy, deluded and talentless.' In reply, she screamed, 'Kiss my arse . . . the way you lot live your lives, you're all fucking shits.' She was then ejected from the studio by Cowell's bodyguard. 'She was the worst contestant I have ever met,' Cowell chortled to the *Sun*, encouraging the viewers to watch that night 'the amazing rant' of a woman revealed to be 'a £60 a time hooker in a massage parlour'.

Others marked the humiliation of Emma Chawner, a hugely overweight girl filmed with her similarly oversized family, as a highlight of Cowell's playfulness: 'That dress is all wrong and you sang out of tune and you sounded like a baby.' Tearfully, Chawner left the audition and was filmed telling her family that the dress was 'so good', followed by the family entering the room to complain to Cowell. 'Take a good look at yourselves,' replied Cowell robustly. 'You are the reason why this girl is disappointed. You have given her false hope.'

Critics would say Cowell and his producers had given the 'false hope', but he was unbowed, telling Katie, a successful contestant, that she had been subsequently excluded. 'You're pregnant,' he said. 'It's crazy because you'll give birth during the finals.'

No one was disappointed as she raged and her fiancé threatened to smash the camera. By the third programme in the series, over 10 million were watching, a massive 48.9 per cent of the total TV audience. And Cowell playing with his toys was keeping the figures high.

To Cowell's glee, in early September Sharon Osbourne threatened to resign. Tired by the weekly commute between Britain and America for *The X Factor* and *America's Got Talent*, she had become emotionally drained by her brother's disclosures to the *News of the World*. David Arden, a convicted criminal, had told the newspaper that his sister hated Cowell, was jealous of Dannii Minogue and was trying to sabotage *The X Factor*. Grabbing the priceless publicity, Cowell encouraged Osbourne to defend herself. 'My brother', said Osbourne, 'has lived off me for years, taking millions, but after I stopped the cheques he became bitter.'

She quickly withdrew her resignation, but her suspicions about Cowell and Dannii Minogue were revived when she and Walsh, sitting in their private plane on the tarmac, spotted the two getting into their own bigger jet. 'They're having it off,' she told Walsh, peering through the window.

Cowell denied her allegation but later confessed to a discreet affair. 'I had a crush on her. It was Dannii's hair, the sexy clothes and the tits. I was like a schoolboy. She was foxy. She was a real man's girl. Very feminine.' He loved the conquest of a star who was fun on the programme. Secrecy, he knew, was vital. Even after he was photographed holding Minogue's hand in the back of a limousine as they left the BBC studios, most speculated that the clasp was designed to bring another headline, although Cowell would admit, 'It was genuine love.' But there were limits. To his surprise, he found Minogue gloomy and, 'after Terri, I wasn't ready for another relationship'.

Osbourne's suspicions entrenched her jealousy of Minogue. Just why she cared about the fling was hard for Cowell to understand, but, amused by the screams delivered in a mid-Atlantic twang from her cosmetically enhanced face, he gladly stoked the fire by back-stabbing and spreading rumours about Osbourne's dubious family and large entourage. Provoked into retaliation, Osbourne delivered some dramatic spoilers during the programme. 'Fix!' she regularly screamed, which satisfied Cowell's critics. 'That's great TV,' agreed Cowell, 'but it's creating a daily drama for people management.'

Richard Holloway often hastened to Osbourne's dressing room to 'douse the fire' and urge the distraught woman to 'calm down'. 'You tell her it's not good enough,' Cowell said. 'It's all fixed, so who the fuck cares?' cursed Osbourne, whose spokesman talked about Cowell employing a call centre in India to get votes for the winners. Although the allegation was completely untrue, to Cowell Osbourne's outbursts were great sport. Playing with Minogue, he knew, incited her. 'I often ogle Dannii's bum,' he told the *Sun*, knowing that Osbourne was irritated by Minogue's flirtatious and frequent visits to Cowell's dressing room.

In October, Osbourne arrived for a live programme angling for a showdown. A journalist had tipped her off about Minogue's scoffs that Osbourne used plastic surgery to conceal her age. Shortly before the show started, Osbourne entered Minogue's dressing room. Not coincidentally, she chose Minogue's birthday for the confrontation. 'Happy birthday,' she seethed, and began to rant. Within seconds, the Australian was crying. As her make-up disintegrated, Holloway intervened. 'Fuck off,' screamed Osbourne. Five minutes before transmission, Claire Horton rushed into the room. 'I'm quitting,' yelled Osbourne.

Near by, Cowell sat in his room. 'I wasn't happy about it, but I didn't come out because I didn't want to get involved,' he said. With moments to go, Osbourne was shepherded into the studio, Minogue's make-up was repaired and Cowell emerged with a smile. 'I find girls fighting very amusing,' he said. 'The competition adds spice to the show, and the show is about the judges, not the contestants. Everyone is enjoying playing with the new toy.'

After the programme, which was watched by a record audience, Osbourne justified her outburst to a newspaper: 'I've had it up to here . . . It's like a bloody circus. It's a pantomime with the pyro, feathers, girls dancing and wiggling . . . But I've made a mistake. I don't know if they want me back.' The following day, she phoned Cowell to apologise. They met the following night. 'Stop fighting, stop flouncing . . . and stop getting on my nerves,' Cowell ordered sternly, anticipating a new peak in the ratings. Meekly, Osbourne complied.

In Cowell's world, success deserved a prize. The battle between the girls justified a reward for himself and nothing was more appropriate than a new dressing room in the shabby Wembley studios. On a higher floor were some dirty rooms, so he spent £20,000 of his own money to convert them and triple the size of his old suite. The walls were covered in slate-coloured leather tiles and enormous mirrors, the furniture was also leather and a bathroom was built with Spanish marble. From then on, one hour before the programme, while mayhem and screaming raged beneath him, Cowell would be soaking in a large hot bath watching *Strictly Come Dancing* 'to wind me up to do better'. Louis Walsh was suitably impressed. 'The funniest moment', he observed, 'is watching Simon doing his hair in the dressing room before every show. He loves looking in the mirror.'

The conversion of the dressing rooms was a mere trifle. Cowell had also bought a Bugatti Veyron, the world's most expensive car, for £750,000 and paid $400,000 for a Rolls-Royce Phantom Drophead Coupé with a cream leather interior. The bigger trophy would be a second house in Beverly Hills. Pressed for time, Cowell needed a friend to undertake the search. Naturally, he turned to Terri Seymour, who, with gentle coaching, had recovered from the split and became another trusted 'ex'.

Louis Walsh had sided with Osbourne in the Minogue battle, so, to generate publicity, Cowell encouraged Dannii to complain to a newspaper, 'Louis keeps grabbing my bum at work and I am like, that is wrong . . . please get off me.' Walsh denied the accusation and, at the next opportunity during a show, criticised Minogue's comments about a singer: 'How would you know? You've never had a hit.' As the show ended, Minogue rushed tearfully to Cowell's dressing room. Like an errant schoolboy, Walsh was summoned by Cowell. 'I'm in trouble,' Walsh thought as he entered the room and saw Minogue sobbing.

'You can't say that sort of thing to Dannii on live TV,' said Cowell. 'It's bullying.'

'But I did,' replied Walsh, believing that Cowell had loved the snub and was merely acting to please his lover. Controlling women gave him great pleasure.

'Well, it mustn't happen again,' smiled Cowell, getting up to give his hair a quick wash and then blow-drying it in front of the mirror while his visitors looked on. 'He tilts his head just like a woman,' thought Walsh. 'Anyway, it's all for show. We love slagging each other off and we try to out-bitch one another.'

The bust-ups raised the tension for the final on Saturday 15 December. 'Sharon's an old witch,' said Minogue in a loud whisper overheard by the studio audience during a break in the show.

'That was wonderful,' Cowell decided. 'Better than the singing.'

As planned, Sharon Osbourne was tipping towards an explosion. The speculation about the 'relationship' had been refuelled by Minogue's 'revelation' that while 'desperate for love', she preferred 'a man's man'. Although she flirted with Cowell, she admitted 'that man could flirt with a book, a wall, anything, and I don't fancy him'.

An invitation was arranged for Osbourne to appear on *The Graham Norton Show*. Asked about Minogue's 'contribution to the music industry', Osbourne spat that Minogue was only on the show 'because of her looks' and because she and Cowell 'are close'. Getting up, she turned her back to the camera, patted her backside and compared her ample behind with Minogue's Botoxed face. 'She's younger, she's better-looking, Simon wants her and he doesn't want me . . . thank God.' Minogue, Osbourne would add later, was cursed by 'appalling' plastic surgery and only stayed on *The X Factor* because she wanted sex with Cowell.

'A loose cannon,' said Cowell.

'A car crash,' agreed Walsh about a woman he adored.

While the 'toys played', Leon Jackson, a slight and pale eighteen-year-old Scotsman, had unexpectedly won the competition. Cowell mentioned that he was unimpressed by the karaoke-style novice, a Gap shop assistant who lacked star quality. Television audiences were proving to be curiously bad judges of stardom. Once again, the solid Scottish vote for their countryman had overwhelmed a better singer. 'I've been thrown a lifeline by God,' Jackson cried to 12.7 million viewers, with Dannii Minogue at his side. The £1-million Sony record contract and the TV exposure pushed his single, 'When You Believe', to number one for Christmas, but it sold only 630,000 copies. Briefly, he tasted the glamour of wearing a £2,000 Gucci jacket and living in a £500-a-night suite, and the excitement of women approaching him to say, 'You're fit.' 'Now he's going to be a superstar' was Walsh's prediction.

Cowell knew that Jackson was destined to follow the same trajectory as previous *X Factor* winner Steve Brookstein, who was by then singing in pubs and being regularly insulted about his downfall. Cowell had no qualms about the cruelty of show business, where it was up one day and out the next. Nor was he bothered by his critics' claim that Jackson's demise confirmed *The X Factor*'s dismal influence on the music industry. The show was never conceived of as a charity but as popular television designed to enrich Cowell and Sony by reducing the cost of finding and marketing stars and securing high sales of their music.

Snow Patrol, Kaiser Chiefs, Razorlight, Keane and Franz Ferdinand had all sold millions of albums in 2007, proving that *The X Factor* did not kill original music. Instead, the show provided the prospect of instant success to those lacking sufficient experience to complete the stiff ascent to the top. While many talent-show winners fizzled out, unable to sustain a career, some succeeded: Paul Potts sold 3 million albums and reached number one in seventeen countries; Will Young, the *Pop Idol* victor in 2002, maintained his success; Leona Lewis was on the cusp of international fame; and Kelly Clarkson was also selling millions of albums.

The nature of stardom had changed. The aura, mystique and mythology which had enthralled fans for years had been ripped apart by mass exposure. The isolation and idolisation of most stars was being replaced by stars being in thrall – even grateful – to fans. Despite the money invested in them, some *Idol* and *X Factor* victors would eventually be found entertaining passengers on cruise liners or turning on the Christmas lights in obscure villages. That was show business. 'A lot of people want you to fail,' sighed Cowell – and even he lived with the fear of his own humiliation, although not in the immediate future. His

American career was entering a new chapter. The end of his five-year contract with Fox was in sight. The success of *The X Factor* and *America's Got Talent* had altered all his relationships.

Cowell was more irritable than usual on his return to Los Angeles for the start of the seventh season of *American Idol* on 15 January 2008. His relations with Simon Fuller during their occasional conversations about the show remained coolly stable, but his dealings with Nigel Lythgoe had become intolerable. The auditions had again not thrown up a potential star, and Cowell was frustrated by his lack of influence. The hook to keep the audience, he believed, was to contrive arguments among the judges or to focus on the characters among the contestants. *Idol*'s talent scouts and producers were tasked to find not only great singers, but colourful back-stories. In Cowell's words, he wanted 'oddballs because they're entertaining'.

In February, he pinpointed Kyle Ensley, a computer nerd, as the 'geeky anti-hero' to satisfy his requirements.

'I can't let you have him,' said Lythgoe.

'I want him,' insisted Cowell. 'I want someone I can pick on.'

'No geeks this year,' replied Lythgoe, unconvincingly opposed to manipulating a 'victim'. *Idol*, he said, was about the contestants, not the judges. Cowell was equally adamant that slick entertainment required high production values. During their heated argument, Ensley's role as a curiosity became academic. Asserting his authority, Lythgoe loudly criticised Cowell's intention to 'wreck' the show's credibility and condemned his 'verbal assault'. 'The argument went on for a long, long time,' Cowell recalled. 'And I couldn't shake it off when we were filming.'

Appalled by Lythgoe's petulance, he cornered Mike Darnell. 'What's the problem?' he asked the producer.

'Everyone has voted against it,' explained Darnell. Not only Paula Abdul and Randy Jackson, but also Cécile Frot-Coutaz,

FremantleMedia's purposeful chief executive for North America, were opposed to Ensley remaining. Cowell backed off, telling Ensley in front of over 25 million viewers that his expulsion was regrettable.

Cowell suspected Lythgoe's victory reflected Fuller's influence. He assumed that Fuller, still fuming about the litigation and irritated by Cowell's growing success, had rekindled Lythgoe's resentment, festering since 2002, about his fame. 'This has all left a sour taste,' Cowell told Darnell. 'This is a decisive moment. I'm absolutely furious.' His revenge would now be directed against two people.

Just as Les Moonves, the chief executive of CBS, damned *Idol* in an interview as 'a monster' and urged, 'Please kill that show,' Darnell saw the results of the arguments on the screen: Cowell was openly bored and the ratings were falling. The solution, Darnell decided, was Lythgoe's dismissal from the next series. Mortified, Lythgoe had no doubts that Cowell had demanded his removal as a condition for extending his contract in 2010. Cowell denied the accusation: 'I wasn't bothered. I had no part in Nigel's dismissal. I have zero contractual influence.'

Lythgoe was determined on revenge at the very moment Cowell intensified his bid to break out of 'prison'.

During his weekly commute from Los Angeles to London, Cowell switched into conquering mode. The next season of *The X Factor* had been increased by five slots to twenty-seven shows, some staged in the giant O2 Centre and Wembley Arena. The new season of *America's Got Talent* promised to be another winner, and *Britain's Got Talent* had been praised by ITV chairman Michael Grade as 'one of those mood-changing shows', reviving emotional memories of the old-fashioned variety acts. Instead of being shown daily for nine days, Cowell had persuaded Grade to run fourteen programmes over seven weeks. In his search for poignant performances, he had jetted around the country listening to ten hours of auditions every day. Among the 'finds' was Andrew Johnson, a thirteen-year-old choirboy from an impoverished north of England council estate who spoke about repeated bullying at school. His rendition of 'Pie Jesu' had moistened the eyes of everyone in the room. In reality, Johnson did not live in poverty and the 'bullying' had been a single incident years earlier. But 'sob stories' made for good television, which drew viewers and so appealed to Cowell and his producers.

Cowell returned to Los Angeles for the *Idol* final and watched the lacklustre David Cook win in front of a declining TV audience. He jetted straight back to London to wrap up preparations for the *Britain's Got Talent* final on 31 May. His effort attracted 14.4 million viewers – about 54 per cent of that night's TV audience, the highest for an entertainment programme that decade. George Sampson, a fourteen-year-old dancer, won, with Johnson finishing third.

The success of *Britain's Got Talent* and *The X Factor* had transformed Cowell from a performer into a major producer. His contracts with Fox and ITV would expire in 2010 and thereafter, he hoped, he could begin a new chapter in his life. He was on a roll, and among those he expected to suffer were Lythgoe and Fuller. To his surprise, Fuller offered a peace treaty.

Bob Sillerman, the owner of *American Idol*, had earned 'hundreds of millions of dollars' from his $158.3-million purchase of the programme and 19 Entertainment from Fuller in 2005. His sole concern in 2007, when he reduced his stake in CKX to 20 per cent, was getting Fox to extend the contract for *American Idol* so 'it lasts for ever'.

Sillerman had first met Cowell the previous year during a rare visit to CBS's studios in Los Angeles. The stage on Beverly Boulevard was used for *American Idol*'s live shows. Sillerman recognised Cowell as 'a genius' and feared *The X Factor*'s success in Britain. When Cowell's contract with Fox expired in 2010, he suspected, Cowell would be tempted to abandon *American Idol* and introduce *The X Factor* to the US. The danger had been confirmed when Fox paid Cowell $50 million for a five-year agreement for the first option to stage *The X Factor* in America. Sillerman's strategy had been explained to CKX's board of directors: 'I want to combine Fuller's and Cowell's expertise. They're competitors but also friends. I want Cowell in the CKX family, bringing *The X Factor*, the *Talent* programmes and the recording rights to develop the business long-term and build an entertainment empire.'

Getting Fuller's support was effortless. Fuller was concerned about *American Idol*'s future and the threat of Cowell upstaging him. To anticipate Cowell's shift in 2010, Sillerman, with Fuller's support, made a seemingly irresistible offer.

'I'm offering you $300 million to come in with us – a full buyout in perpetuity,' Sillerman told Cowell on his next visit to Los Angeles in 2007. 'That's a ridiculous amount of money,' thought Cowell.

A few months later, in early 2008, Sillerman and Fuller sat for hours in Cowell's home in Los Angeles and his trailer at the studio lot discussing a merger. In Sillerman's opinion, 'It wasn't "if" but "when" and "how".' To finalise the deal, Cowell entrusted the negotiations to his lawyer, Tony Russell.

Certain that he would soon be worth over $500 million and his future would be in America, Cowell urged Terri Seymour, his closest friend in Los Angeles, to look harder for a bigger second home. Money, he assumed, was no object after he was even offered £1 million to advertise Viagra, a proposal he rejected. The ideal house, Seymour reported, was up for sale. 'Who designed this?' asked Cowell after a tour. 'Jennifer Post,' replied the agent. Unfortunately, its owner, actress and singer Jennifer Lopez, had promised the new building to No Doubt's Gwen Stefani.

Seymour finally found a suitable house on North Palm Drive in Beverly Hills, which Cowell bought for $8 million. Seymour agreed to supervise the renovations. After searching through *Architectural Digest* for an interior designer to transform the 12,000-square-foot traditional house into a modern extravaganza, she persuaded Cowell that Jennifer Post was ideal. Eccentric but well respected, Post suggested that Brian Biglin, a local architect, should be hired to 'transform the house into an open and flowing stylised project', retaining the privacy at the front but 'opening up the garden at the back to let the light in'.

Cowell had very specific tastes about everything: the rooms' design; the wood, marble and stone surfaces; the colours – especially dark; the lighting – concealed; his bathroom – vast; the cupboards – plentiful; the kitchen – functional; and the cinema room – comfortable. Only the garden's design remained uncertain.

As the first plans were offered, Cowell began to have doubts. 'Close your eyes,' Post ordered Cowell and Biglin. 'Now open them.' On the table they saw a black toy model of a Maybach car. 'This is your house,' said Post. Cowell was puzzled. Shortly after, he again encountered Post in the house. 'Your T-shirt,' she said, pointing at his usual grey top pulled down below his waist, 'that's your house.'

Sometimes, even Post was confused about her metaphors. 'This is project Bentley,' she would tell Cowell, referring to the standards she expected. 'Like the car, you've got to put all the wood, metal and leather together to make it look seamless.' For the ultimate in luxury there would be cashmere couches, walls covered in Ultrasuede and exterior flooring of black basalt stone – 'The most solid, purest black stone God introduced to the earth,' Post told Cowell.

'I always use the word "Jacometti" in my designs,' she told him, 'but you don't seem to recognise the name.' Nor, it was said beyond Post's hearing, did anyone else. In Post's opinion, New York design was a hundred years ahead of London's, so she embarked on educating her client. 'He didn't know what a fine piece of wood looked like,' Post would say after their relationship crumbled. 'When I said, "We're not going to put Picasso in this house," he asked, "Who's Picasso?" He thought only Frank Sinatra was famous. I told him, "I can't believe it."' Cowell would later explain that he was mischievously teasing Post.

For the initial $3.5-million building budget, Cowell accepted Post's proposals: the interior floors would be covered in 'super slabs' of white Greek Thassos marble lowered into position by cranes; 'elegant but functional' custom-made cupboards throughout the house and kitchen would be supplied by Poliform in Italy; Italian Fenestra windows would be imported to provide a perfect seal against the heat; the lighting would be centrally controlled from the master bedroom by phone; and there would be a cinema room with a fourteen-foot convex screen and a Cat sound system engineered to focus the music at a 'sweet spot where Simon will sit'. The centrepiece would be Cowell's bedroom and 'spa bathroom allowing water to become a feature'. A special custom-made British tub measuring two metres by one and a half was ordered from Zuma, shaped to allow Cowell to relax on a special back rest. The water would cascade into the tub from special taps in the ceiling. Next to the bath was a marble chair for a friend to keep Cowell company while he bathed and watched cartoons.

A shower and steam room with heated marble floors adjoined the bathroom. In the ample cabinet space for his creams, pastes, ointments, sprays, tablets and gels there was no space for 'her' creams, but 'she' would be welcome to use his. Altogether the design created an atmosphere suggesting a temple – a temple of self-obsession, perfect for the worship of Cowell's vanity.

The room assigned as the dressing area was sufficiently

spacious for two people to 'chat while preparing to go out without feeling cramped'. Downstairs, the Miele kitchen was a chef's dream. At the back of the garden there would be two separate buildings: a gym with a treatment room, a big steam shower and an area suitable for a photo shoot; and a separate guest house named Vietnam by Post – 'One large room designed in contemporary architecture like a nice hotel suite,' according to Biglin.

Reconstructing the house on North Palm Drive encouraged Cowell to rebuild his house in Holland Park as well. His incessant demand for change not only applied to his homes, but to his shows as well, including the new *X Factor* series. One hundred and eight-two thousand people, the highest ever, had applied for the auditions.

Sharon Osbourne and her antics were already forgotten. After the final show of 2007, she had issued an ultimatum: she would leave unless Cowell fired Dannii Minogue. Cowell refused. He had already lined up Cheryl Cole, the star of Britain's most successful girl group, Girls Aloud, to take her place. Created in 2002 by *Popstars: The Rivals*, the group had had eighteen consecutive top-ten singles under Louis Walsh's management.

Born Cheryl Tweedy on a council estate in Newcastle in 1983, her family included a brother who had appeared in court over fifty times for theft and vandalism. She too had been convicted after punching a black female nightclub lavatory attendant, and was given 120 hours of community service. In 2006, she had married Ashley Cole, a star Chelsea and England footballer, in a ceremony paid for by *OK!* magazine. Months later, a twenty-two-year-old hairdresser had sold her story to a tabloid, describing her recent one-night stand with the footballer. To Cheryl Cole's distress, that confession provoked other women to sell their stories of sexual encounters with her new husband. But, in 2008, when Cole was revealed as Sharon Osbourne's successor, the two appeared to be reconciled.

Cowell had first met Cole as she waited for him in the cold outside the Wembley studios in 2007 to raise money for Comic Relief as part of the TV series *Celebrity Apprentice*. Cowell was particularly struck that the singer had waited without a film crew, showing her dedication to the cause. 'She's cute,' thought Cowell, and wrote a cheque for £25,000. Weeks later, she accepted his offer to become a judge on *Britain's Got Talent*. However, three days before the show started, she pulled out, explaining that she was 'uncomfortable'. Cowell concluded that she lacked the self-confidence to criticise other artists, and her place was taken by Amanda Holden.

Reconsidering her refusal, Cole told Cowell, 'I made a mistake.' 'Don't worry,' replied Cowell. 'You'll be on *The X Factor*.' At first she again declined, admitting her unease about criticising others, but in the end agreed, joining for £600,000, compared to Dannii Minogue's £500,000. 'Now we've got two toys on the panel,' thought Cowell.

His affair with Minogue was over – 'There were a few bonks and then it petered out while I was in America,' he told a friend – and he was tempted, if the opportunity arose, to enjoy one with Cole. At the same time, he looked forward to playing games with Cole and Minogue. The omens were good. At the reception in a Mayfair hotel to introduce the panel to the media, all the attention was focused on Cole, while Minogue was ignored. 'A bitchy battle of the babes,' thought one of Cowell's aides as they watched Minogue, clearly frazzled by Cheryl-mania. 'That's what the public wants,' agreed Cowell. The media were encouraged to believe that just as Minogue had not spoken to Osbourne, she had no contact with Cole.

Cheryl Cole arrived for the first auditions in mid-June 2008 looking thin after a make-or-break holiday with her husband. Five minutes into the programme, Cowell whispered to his producer, 'A star is born.' By the end of July, he was congratulating himself. Eliza Doolittle from the council estate was perfect casting. Cole had cried during the auditions because, she said, the contestants' hard-luck stories reminded her of her tough youth. 'I wish I could bring someone home to the family,' she said memorably. Increasingly, Cowell included shots of himself together with Cole, often with his arm across her shoulders, and he repeatedly mentioned her in newspaper interviews. Cole's scant knowledge about music – 'She doesn't even know Elton John's "Crocodile Rock",' Louis Walsh told Cowell – was glossed over with Cowell's help.

'Do you fancy him?' Walsh asked the woman who ceaselessly flirted with Cowell. 'I look at Simon as an uncle,' Cole replied. Her detachment inflamed Cowell's interest. Unlike Walsh, who went to Cowell's home after each show to watch a recording alongside the Cowell entourage – with Sinitta and Jackie St Clair competing over who should sit on the sofa next to Simon – Cole returned home 'to look after my dog'. Surprisingly, Minogue showed no jealousy about teacher's new pet. She simply ensured that her clothes outshone Cole's.

By the end of the auditions, Cowell was speaking about 'the strongest season ever'. The tearful stories of poverty, struggle, expulsion from school, marital betrayal and relations dying of cancer were mixed with his barbs and admiration: 'You've got great legs,' he told a transsexual drag queen; 'That's one of the best bodies I've ever seen in my life,' he praised a nude model. His empathy was also edited into a spell-binding exchange with a sobbing twenty-three-year-old as he described his traumatic abandonment by his parents and sexual abuse by a family friend. His story proved to be untrue but the subsequent confession – 'I didn't mean to lie' – was great television. In the trailer, Cowell vowed that the judges were nastier than ever: 'We're going to hell, and I'll be driving the bus.'

Before leaving for his summer holidays, in the same week as

ITV's profits and ratings were revealed to have dropped to a seven-year low, Cowell started a critical fight with the channel's managers. He wanted the network to broadcast the results in a second live show on Sunday nights. Paul Jackson, ITV's head of entertainment, was torn. To save money, some suggested that the results programme should be recorded after Saturday's show. Jackson disagreed and insisted that the programme be live, but was worried about the content and the cost. Cowell's insistence was destabilising.

Jackson's position was precarious. Opposition to Cowell, he knew, usually curtailed careers, but he could no longer tolerate Cowell's 'lunatic level' of self-promotion and his interference in ITV's management of the schedules and even the appointment of the network's senior managers. Unwilling to tolerate critics or those who displeased him, Cowell unhesitatingly expressed his dissatisfaction to ITV supremo Peter Fincham.

'Simon's lost the plot,' Jackson, who had decided to leave, told Fincham. Now free to offer his opinion, he added that there were neither the producers nor the money to make yet another show of uncertain quality. 'The network is too much in hock to Simon. It'll damage ITV because our business is too enmeshed and reliant on him. This is getting out of hand.' In a final warning, Jackson told ITV's executives, 'The deeper we get into the water with Simon, the further we have got to swim back.' On that basis, he also rejected Cowell's latest proposal for a new dance programme.

In Cowell's opinion, Jackson similarly suffered from losing the plot. ITV's salvation, he believed, depended on exploiting the successes he offered. He called Jackson to re-pitch the dance programme.

'Can we stop talking about this bloody show?' snapped Jackson. 'We said we don't want it.'

'I don't like the tone of your voice,' said Cowell calmly.

Jackson apologised to a man whose summer holiday plans confirmed his new status. On Philip Green's advice, he had chartered *Xanadu*, a sixty-metre yacht which could sleep twelve, for one month. Sailing in the Mediterranean with Paul McKenna, Sinitta, Kelly Bergantz and his friends the Silvermans from New York, he met Green, casino boss Steve Wynn and other billionaires sailing on considerably bigger yachts. He was welcomed by all as a star.

Britain's political leaders were also competing for his affections. There was an invitation from Gordon Brown, the prime minister, to Downing Street for drinks, and later he and Piers Morgan enjoyed dinner at Number Ten. With unusual charm, and by waiving VAT on a record Cowell had made for charity, Brown persuaded his guest, a natural Conservative, to consider helping the Labour government raise more money for good causes.

Soon after, Cowell was introduced to David Cameron, the Conservative leader, by a member of the Murdoch family while they were dining at Cipriani's in Mayfair. Cameron appeared for a drink and stayed for fifteen minutes. His easy manner and grasp of Cowell's career secured the star's sympathy. 'He's a regular bloke,' Cowell told his host. 'I like him.' Weeks later, he attended a Conservative ball to raise funds and recruited *Britain's Got Talent* finalists for a party hosted by Cameron at a children's hospital to celebrate the sixtieth birthday of the NHS. Gordon Brown was agitated. Downing Street had been determined to secure the star's endorsement.

The statistics showed that Cowell's show had no rivals, with 10.2 million Britons watching the first episode of *The X Factor*'s 2008 run – 54 per cent of the viewing audience. More watched the launch of the new series – the biggest in ITV's history – than the BBC's *Strictly Come Dancing*. The star was Cheryl Cole, elevated by the public as the champion of abused women struggling, after betrayal by a love cheat, through their crises. 'Just being around Simon and his ego has taught me quite a lot,' sighed Cole. 'He's actually made me a lot more confident and a lot more comfortable. The fact that he respects me means a great deal.' All the ingredients existed, Cowell believed, to launch *The X Factor* in America and challenge *American Idol*'s dominance. His armoury was enhanced, Cowell believed, because he had found another star.

Alexandra Burke, a twenty-year-old girl of Jamaican and Irish parentage – looks which appealed to Cowell – had reached the last twenty-one contestants in 2005's competition. The public was told that she had withdrawn before entering the finals because she was too young, but in reality she had been pregnant. Three years later, after professional coaching, she had shone during the auditions. To promote Cole, Cowell had assigned the singer to be Burke's mentor. But Cole would not be allowed to reach the finals with her contestant without Cowell first 'playing' with his new toy to create some headlines. Inclined to treachery, he provoked those whom he had created.

'You're doing my head in,' Cole snapped at Cowell for disputing her judgement and encouraging an argument with Walsh. 'And you know nothing about girl bands,' she accused her manager, the same Louis Walsh.

To spark more arguments, Cowell probed Dannii Minogue's insecurities, first by questioning her choice of music and then by giving Cole more air time in the edited versions.

'What's your problem?' Minogue asked Cowell during a break.

'I haven't got one,' he replied.

'You have,' she insisted. And then, to Cowell's delight, Walsh reduced Minogue to tears during an argument, allowing Cowell to order the pair of them to 'kiss and make up' live on air.

As the audience increased, Sony began to use the show to promote their artists. Will Young, Take That, Beyoncé, Il Divo and Leona Lewis appeared, and were joined by Mariah Carey, a Cowell favourite, and Cole singing with Girls Aloud. 'That's when I realised Cheryl's a big star,' Cowell said.

His biggest trophy was getting Britney Spears to appear on *The X Factor*. The soap opera of her rise, fall and slow resurrection amid addictions, abuse and hyped relationships had been followed across the globe. In the pop industry, the fineness of the thread separating genius from insanity had destroyed many fame-seekers, but few thrived on attention like Spears.

Cowell appreciated celebrity madness. Those artists who could transcend a decade qualified, in his opinion, to become superstars. 'I like artists who take charge of their careers,' he repeated. 'Game-changers are those prepared to die while trying.' Spears had gone closer to the edge than most.

'She's a plain Jane,' Cowell had said after Spears's disastrous appearance in September 2007 on MTV's Video Music Awards. That was ignored when the singer, in November 2008, searched for slots to promote her latest single in Europe, and Cowell wanted to boost his ratings. But he had not anticipated her antics.

'There'll be no rehearsal,' Cowell was told in the chaos following her arrival. 'She's on medication. The studio must be in lockdown.' Having demanded two Winnebago luxury trailers – every star is normally assigned just one – she took Cowell's old dressing room and refused to meet her host. 'She's frosty and I haven't got a clue why and I don't care,' said Cowell. 'I love all this stuff.' But even he had not anticipated that Spears would also ignore the contestants and mime 'Womanizer', her new single, for three minutes during the live show. 'She forgets her lines,' an aide explained. When Cowell finally entered the diva's dressing room, he recalled, 'She was just staring at me. I said, "Have you ever watched the show?" "No," she said. And I said, "Touch me, I'm human," and I think that broke the ice.' A minute later, Cowell walked out of the room. Her freakish visit pushed the audience to 12.8 million, another record.

Under pressure to increase the viewing figures even further, the publicists picked a new angle every week. At the end of November, they coerced Rachel Hylton, a failed contestant, to curse Walsh as 'a vile old buzzard' and to attack Dannii Minogue vitriolically in a tabloid. 'It's a black thing,' Hylton exclaimed, outraged that 'they were intentionally trying to take the piss out of me' to please 'white middle-class viewers'. Hylton, a former drug addict jailed for violence and the mother of five children (with three in foster care), had been exposed posing in a photograph with a 'gangsta' gun gesture. 'That's how we express ourselves,' she spat. 'I'm from the 'hood.'

As that sensation waned, an attractive contestant expressed her 'shock' that Cowell wanted to spend a night with her: 'He's not really my type,' she said. Walsh then reduced Minogue to tears again by calling her an actress. The following day's newspapers reported his apology and then his breathlessly quick retraction – 'because she *is* an actress'. Finally, in the countdown to the climax on 13 December, Downing Street announced Gordon Brown's personal letter to all twelve finalists advising them not to take Cowell's comments to heart.

Not for the first time, the prime minister had misjudged the nation's real concern. The series had been all about Cheryl Cole: her dignified retort to a love cheat; her uncontrolled sobbing of 'real tears'; and her rehabilitation as 'Our Geordie princess, the nation's sweetheart'. Featured on *Vogue*'s cover, the waif had become a fragile fashion icon. Appearing as a serene and beautiful national treasure, her publicist had persuaded millions of besotted viewers that despite being 'under an enormous amount of pressure during the ten weeks of *The X Factor*, she has worked herself up to get Alexandra Burke ready for the final'.

Even Cowell was glorified for allowing Cole to snatch his popularity. To add grist to the mill, he was simultaneously damned by Minogue as 'the biggest diva on the show', overshadowing even Mariah Carey's demands for rooms, flowers and candles. Playing with his toys, Cowell caricatured Minogue as tortured by jealousy. Eleven years younger and more beautiful, Cole was permanently seated next to Cowell. 'He moved me away from him,' sighed Minogue, 'and now he sits next to Cheryl and is in her ear all the time. It is a snub but I'm fine.' Cowell knew she was not, and that was intentional.

Amid all the emotion, some might have forgotten the contestants. During the finals, Burke, the favourite, sang Leonard Cohen's 'Hallelujah'. 'That was incredible,' said Cowell. 'You've got to win.' Minutes later, Sony released it as a digital download, and it became the fastest-selling song of all time. To maintain the momentum, three days later viewers read that Burke's mother risked missing the show because she required four hours of dialysis every day to prevent a fatal kidney failure. 'Alex will be heartbroken if I don't make it,' said her mother, 'so I'll try my very best.' On the night, joined by Beyoncé on a stage covered with candles, Burke sang 'Silent Night' in an uplifting voice, provoking Cole to tearfully sigh, 'Love you, love you, love you,' and Cowell to pronounce, 'A star has been born.' He hoped that his hunt for a global star – another Robbie Williams – had come to an end.

A record 15 million watched the final and voted for Burke as the winner. Cowell's bonus was that three other contestants, including the boy band JLS, were also signed up to Sony labels. Like the other winners, Burke's prize was £1 million, but she could expect at most £150,000. The remainder would be used to cover her expenses. In the aftermath, Cowell could not resist feeding speculation that Kate Moss, the model who had often sat in his dressing room with Philip Green, might replace Dannii Minogue.

'Yes, possibly,' he winked to the journalist who asked.

13

Media Mogul

In early 2009, Tommy Mottola, the former head of Sony Music Entertainment and the ex-husband of singer Mariah Carey, telephoned Cowell out of the blue.

'I'm in London,' said Mottola, whom Cowell had never met. 'I wanted to come over and say "Hi" and see if we could do something together.'

In the course of a ninety-minute conversation, Cowell trusted his visitor enough to unburden himself of his predicament: 'I'm tired, fed up, there are lots of bills and I'm not sure where this is leading.' His two contracts, he continued – with Fox for *American Idol* and with ITV for *The X Factor* – would expire in 2010. He did not want to continue with *American Idol*, and because *The X Factor* was so successful in Britain, an American offer was certain. If Fox refused to bid, then NBC, thrilled with *America's Got Talent*, would certainly be interested.

Over the past year, said Cowell, everything had become complicated. Since 2008, Tony Russell had been negotiating on his behalf with Rolf Schmidt-Holtz, Sony Music's chairman, and Bob Sillerman. Both offers, Cowell continued, were unsatisfactory. All he had received was an emotional two-page letter from Schmidt-Holtz pleading that Russell should 'not stand between us. You should speak for yourself.'

Now, Cowell felt that possibly he had treated Sony badly. The corporation had offered him $60 million to buy out *The X Factor* and the *Talent* shows, and that was on top of Fox's $100-million contract. Unmentioned was his niggling suspicion that Sillerman's $300-million offer to forge a partnership with CKX and Simon Fuller might be a case of him 'trying to pull a fast one'. Why would Fuller, he thought, want to 'make up and co-operate'? Only recently, Fuller had irritated Cowell by telling a journalist, 'I'm worth more than Cowell. He's in a different league' – by which he meant a lower one.

Aggravating his own discontent, Cowell admitted to Mottola, was monotony: 'I am bored. I easily get bored and I'm hot and cold about the programme.' Mottola's instant analysis crystallised Cowell's thoughts: 'You're not thinking it through. You should own your own rights and be making new shows as the executive producer and owner.' Cowell understood. He needed once again to redefine himself, and he should start by recovering the ownership of the rights to *The X Factor* and the *Talent* programmes from Sony, which he had sold in 2005.

After some thought, he called Philip Green, by then a close friend. 'Help me, I'm overloaded,' pleaded Cowell. 'I can't understand what's happening.' Green drove over to Cowell's office and read through the correspondence between Russell, Sony and Sillerman. 'I can't run a business like Lucian Grainge,' said Cowell, referring to another of the Barbados 'mafia'. 'I'm hopeless.'

'I'll help,' offered Green, recognising Cowell as a kindred spirit who 'needed help'. Cowell, he decided, was 'an honest, hard-working man who woke up in the morning loving his work. I can look after his back because otherwise he'll get hurt.' The added bonus was Green's attraction to showbiz. Particular celebrities intrigued the entrepreneur, especially those who could benefit from his skills.

Green was unconvinced by Tony Russell's efforts and what he felt was his meagre achievement in the current discussions. Pertinently, Sillerman felt the same. Russell, thought Sillerman, was 'smart but inflexible'. He could conduct the single-issue negotiations for his clients or 'the talent', but he was lost when trying to grapple with the big deals. Sillerman was not surprised to hear about the strained telephone conversation when Green terminated Russell's twenty-year relationship with Cowell.

'You twiddle the knobs and I'll do the deal,' Green told Cowell.

Green's next call was to Howard Stringer, Sony's global chairman, who was based in New York and Tokyo. 'You've nearly lost Simon to Bob Sillerman,' he told Stringer. 'Do you want to be part of the deal? If you want to do business about the future of *The X Factor* and *Britain's Got Talent*, let's talk in London.' Green's warning that Sony Music risked losing its most important profit-maker compelled the Sony boss to arrive in London shortly afterwards, on 1 May 2009.

Showbiz contracts and intellectual property rights among celebrities were foreign to Green. So were their lawyers' and agents' methods of negotiation. Having honed a negotiating style which suited the clothing and property market, Green's blunt approach was, said an early victim, 'like a bull crashing around a china shop'. Nevertheless, Stringer's lengthy visit to Green's office in Marylebone with his Sony executives saw them quickly get to the heart of the matter.

'Simon wants to be the owner, not an employee,' Green told Stringer. By the end of the session, Green had established the outlines of a deal for Cowell to recover total ownership of *The X Factor* and *Britain's Got Talent* and also receive a financial windfall. Green was understandably pleased with the result. 'You'll get 100 per cent of the TV programmes from Sony in return for Sony getting a perpetual music licence,' he told Cowell. 'I've also persuaded Sony to consider buying back a part of the new company owning the TV rights, which they've just given to you for nothing!'

'You should be paid for your work,' said Cowell, thrilled – an offer Green dismissed.

On 3 May, Green flew to New York to meet Bob Sillerman. 'My job', he announced, 'is to get all of this cleaned up and tidied.' Sillerman was pleased by the prospect of progress. By contrast, Simon Fuller felt uneasy that Cowell, for the first time, was represented by an accomplished businessman. During their conversation, Green disentangled Sillerman's proposals to discover a non-competition clause empowering Sillerman, if he so wished, to prevent Cowell from appearing on any TV programme. In effect, Cowell could be paid not to work.

The following week, Green flew to meet Cowell in Los Angeles. 'They could park you in the wilderness in a lock-out,' he explained. 'Perhaps Simon wants me off the air,' Cowell told Green, suspicious that the unusual clause could have been Fuller's brainchild. 'This isn't going to happen,' declared Green, sharing Cowell's suspicions. 'They're trying to put handcuffs on me,' concluded Cowell. Both were possibly mistaken. The clause had been inserted, Sillerman would say, at Russell's request, in accordance with Cowell's instructions. 'I don't know if I always want to appear on television,' Cowell had said. 'I want the right to refuse.'

Since Sillerman's sole interest was to capture Cowell, he had agreed without scrutinising the words – or so he would later tell Green when Cowell's suspicions threatened their relationship.

'Cowell was right to be suspicious,' Sillerman would later say. 'He knew Fuller better than me, and he hardly knew me. And I don't understand the business. So Green was protecting Cowell, and I only realised after Green left New York how complicated it was.'

In public, the arguments were unknown. Meanwhile, Cowell was performing to perfection on *American Idol*, telling one contestant, 'You should be a hooker'; to another, 'That sounded like you were drunk, and not on one or two bottles – a whole crate'; while a woman was told, 'It was really boring and I hate what you're wearing.' He also joked on *The Tonight Show* with Jay Leno that he had rejected an invitation to meet President Obama because 'I wasn't available'.

In Britain, while the tabloid headlines featured his confession 'I'd like to kiss Cheryl,' his focus was on the third series of *Britain's Got Talent*. ITV's audiences were still falling and their half-yearly losses had escalated to £105 million. Without Cowell, though, the network risked collapse, and so in 2009 the *X Factor* budget was increased by £5 million to £19 million.

'Will you take over *all* the negotiations with Sillerman and Sony?' Cowell asked Philip Green.

'He's trusted me with his life,' thought Green, and drove across Los Angeles to visit Lucian Grainge and 'sniff out' Cowell's market price. Grainge volunteered that it was more than Sillerman's offer of $300 million, but to extract the higher value Green would need simultaneously to negotiate with Sony, FremantleMedia, Fox and ITV. That played to Green's strengths, but Grainge didn't envy those navigating through the inevitable bombast. At least the survivors would discover Green's talent for creating perfect contractual structures.

Green next telephoned Peter Chernin, the chairman of Fox, and described himself as Cowell's representative. Fox, said Green, had paid to keep *The X Factor* off air for five years and the time had come to negotiate something new. Chernin had already announced his departure from News Corporation and decided not to engage with Green, unexpectedly introducing him to Hollywood's charming ritual of stabbing irritants in the face.

Fighting was natural to Green. In the midst of his negotiations, he suggested to Cowell that they fly to Las Vegas to watch Joe Calzaghe, a Welsh light heavyweight, box against Bernard Hopkins. At the end of a good fight, the two had dinner with Sylvester Stallone, and then Green played roulette at the Bellagio hotel. In the early hours, he won $650,000, but the dealer insisted that the bet had been placed after the wheel began spinning. Outraged, Green demanded to watch the video. The

Cowell's appearance on *Pop Idol* in 2001 launched his sensational career but fractured his relationship with Simon Fuller and even with Pete Waterman (second from left).

After appearing with Paula Abdul and Randy Jackson on *American Idol* in 2002, Cowell became a megastar in the USA.

Produced by Nigel Lythgoe (right), *American Idol*'s ratings soared but Cowell's relationship with Lythgoe soured.

Kelly Clarkson, *American Idol*'s first winner, became a global star and made the show a television phenomenon.

Cowell shared the fame of his shows' other creations: notably Leona Lewis, *The X Factor* victor in 2006, and Susan Boyle, the 2009 sensation of *Britain's Got Talent*.

Bitter arguments among *The X Factor*'s panel – Louis Walsh, Sharon Osbourne, Dannii Minogue and Cowell – generated huge audiences.

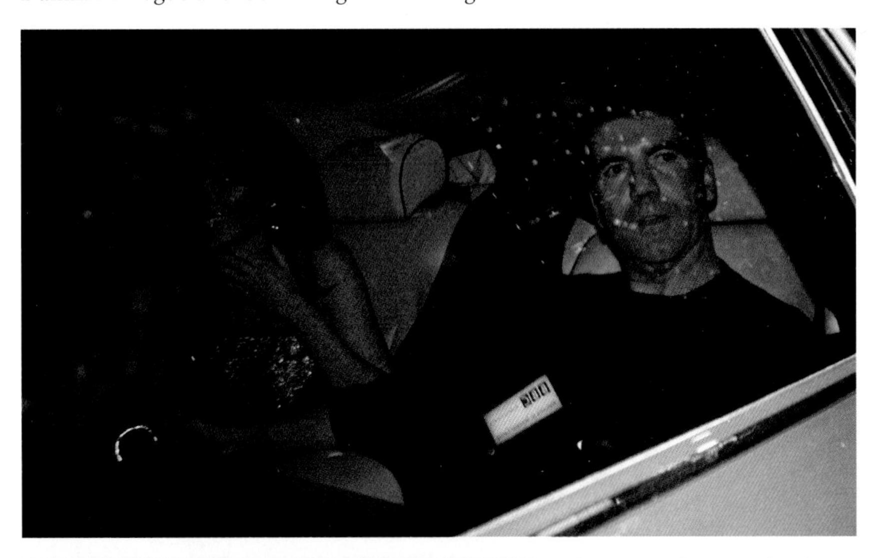

This snap photograph of Cowell holding Dannii Minogue's hand in 2008 sparked speculation about an affair.

After a bust-up with Cowell, Sharon Osbourne appeared only on *America's Got Talent*, NBC's no. 1 show bought from Cowell, also starring controversial journalist Piers Morgan.

Cowell and Ryan Seacrest, the host of *American Idol*, were good friends until the American star staged a photo of their exit from Stringfellows in 2009, provoking Cowell's anger.

Philip Green (far right) became the architect of Cowell's business empire and a peace broker among *The X Factor*'s feuding producers. (From left, Andrew Silverman, Paul McKenna and Steve Wynn.)

Cowell's inclusion among Hollywood's royalty at Oprah Winfrey's farewell extravaganza in 2011 further confirmed his star status, although he appeared uneasy throughout the evening.

Cowell's love for Mezhgan Hussainy, his fiancée in 2011, cooled after experiencing her intolerance of his relentless work ethic. Despite the broken engagement, he still felt affection for her.

To some, Cowell seemed happiest when surrounded by dogs.

After fighting hard to include Paula Abdul and Cheryl Cole in *The X Factor*'s first American show, Cowell tried unsuccessfully after the first auditions in Los Angeles to persuade Cole to return to the British show.

The X Factor USA in 2011 was a mixed success. Cowell blessed L. A. Reid (far left) as a triumph but by the final, won by Melanie Amaro (far right), he'd become unenthusiastic about Nicole Scherzinger and even Paula Abdul. Neither was re-hired.

In 2011, Cowell found happiness on *Slipstream* during a summer Mediterranean cruise.

To wind up the paparazzi in St Barts in 2012, Cowell posed with a banana alongside Sinitta (right), Zeta Graff and Kelly Bergantz.

evidence favoured him and, in the middle of the night, the casino's owner telephoned and agreed to pay the money. Impressed, Cowell became fully committed to entrust his commercial future to the businessman.

On his return to London, Green invited Peter Powell, Cowell's agent and a former DJ once married to TV presenter Anthea Turner, to meet at the Dorchester hotel.

'What's your job?' asked Green.

'I'm on call 24/7,' Powell explained. 'I am his eyes and ears.'

'How come I've never heard of you?' murmured Green, examining the sheet of paper listing Powell's earnings. 'We're not going to need you.'

Another of the old guard had been erased, but Cowell expressed no regrets. Green was firmly responsible for his commercial fate, and Cowell's search for a new father figure had been fulfilled. 'I want you to meet Karren Brady,' said Green, introducing the managing director of Birmingham City Football Club. 'She understands organisation, planning and structures.' Brady's self-introduction as she walked into Cowell's office was blunt: 'You look knackered. You need help.' Some would later interpret those weeks as the passing of the torch.

'Refresh' was Cowell's new mantra. At the outset of the year, he had tried to improve *Britain's Got Talent* by adding Kelly Brook, a model, as the fourth judge in the hope of sparking a new cat fight with Amanda Holden. Chosen just twenty-four hours before the programme started, Brook asked Ant and Dec after their introduction, 'What do you do?'

'Have you ever seen the show?' asked Dec.

'Yeah, bits,' she replied.

'She's out of her comfort zone,' agreed Cowell at the end of the night. His gut instinct had been wrong. After three days she was dismissed, but she kept the £100,000 fee. 'I wasn't sad,' admitted Holden. 'I do like being the only girl.'

To bury the bad publicity, Holden was encouraged to confide, 'I have a crush on Simon. He has this charisma and charm you can't fight.' On cue, Cowell reciprocated: 'Amanda is cute . . . and with a glint in her eye, but unfortunately she is married.' And since in the cause of publicity nothing was too vulgar, he encouraged the *Sun* to report that he had been 'blown away by a professional farter – all the way through *Blue Danube*'. 'You're a disgusting creature,' Cowell told the contestant after approving his inclusion in the programme. 'The show', Cowell admitted, 'is like watching a train wreck. Britain's talent is for rubbish.' He was next seen with Holden cheering at the Ascot races.

Cowell's side-swipe concealed his excitement about another discovery. Watching the edited version of an audition, he noticed that a forty-seven-year-old unemployed spinster looked better on screen than in the flesh. Curiously, his producers had not alerted him to anything special, yet by careful crafting they had polished an average performance by an overweight and frumpy middle-aged woman with unruly hair and a stodgy dress who lived in a council house in West Lothian. The back-story was magical. Afflicted by a lack of oxygen at birth, learning difficulties and bullying at school, the pudgy woman had been urged by her mother until her death in 2007 to audition on ITV. Since then, said the youngest of nine children, she had suffered permanent depression. Despite her illness, she had made her way through the audition process, starting in Glasgow.

'This is a strong story,' said Cowell after rewatching Susan Boyle's appearance. 'She says she's never been kissed and loves her cats. All's good.' But even he could not anticipate the public's reaction on 11 April 2009. Sniggers from the audience could be heard as Boyle stepped forward to sing 'I Dreamed a Dream', from *Les Misérables*, but, before she had even finished, they had erupted with delight. The wild cheering did not surprise Cowell, but 10 million would watch the programme and, within three days, over 30 million would watch her audition on YouTube. Two weeks later, 120 million had seen the online clip and she had been besieged by America's chat shows.

'Is Susan Boyle ITV's saviour?' asked a newspaper. 'She's a little tiger,' said Cowell. 'Get yourself together, sweetheart, for the big one – the semi-final. Shut the door, dye your hair, choose the right song and come back as you are, not who you want to be.' The only public warning about a person whom some were describing as 'a pitiful middle-aged frump with a good voice' came from those who had tracked down Michelle McManus, the 2003 winner of *Pop Idol.* She had just switched on the Christmas lights in Cumnock, East Ayrshire.

Cowell heard the warning about Boyle too late. The pressure, he was told privately, was 'destroying' her. Two days before the final, he invited Boyle and her female friend to his dressing room. 'Do you want to back out?' he asked. Both declined. 'I want to go on,' replied Boyle. Convinced that she would win, not least because of the block Scottish vote and her popularity among the over-forties, Cowell was thrilled. His winning streak seemed unstoppable.

The final show was watched by 19.2 million people, their excited voting adding millions to Cowell's profits. The announcement at the end that the dance troupe Diversity had won, with Boyle second, stunned Cowell. 'Horrendous,' he said as he watched Boyle's face crumble. After quickly congratulating the winners, he sped across the stage to the distraught woman. 'We'll still give you a recording contract,' he whispered in what he would call 'an embarrassing situation'.

As usual, the producers headed from Wembley to The Bar at the Dorchester hotel to celebrate a remarkable series. Cowell arrived, he said later, feeling 'anxious'. 'I had a weird feeling and went home early.' At 2 a.m., he was called. Boyle, he was told, had been taken to the Priory, a private hospital, after suffering a breakdown.

The following day, Cowell was accused by newspapers of failing in his duty of care by allowing a sick woman to remain on the show. The irony that the same media accusers had dispatched over fifty camera crews and journalists to camp outside the Priory in order to snatch a photograph of the patient was ignored by everyone, including Cowell. Controlling his image had always been his strength, so he instantly began telephoning all the tabloid editors. 'We're paying Boyle's bill at the Priory,' he said. 'She's got emotional problems. But have we done something wrong?' No one, he believed, had said that 'I was entirely to blame', but there was criticism that she had been exploited as a freak. He did not disagree. Unnervingly, she called him 'sir' and 'boss' and expressed her fears of being abandoned by Cowell. In his defence, Cowell described the misery of her solitary life before the show: youths had thrown stones at her house; she was tossed into a ditch full of nettles; and she was permanently depressed. However, although vulnerable, she had always wanted to be a singer. He consoled himself with the thought that no one had accused him personally of being responsible. That was questionable, however. There was a resignation at FremantleMedia over the treatment of a clearly disturbed woman, and there were complaints at ITV.

Cowell rebutted the critics. 'I made sure she had a good manager,' he would say. Yet her first manager didn't last long, and Richard Griffiths refused to take up the offer. 'It wouldn't be a pleasurable experience,' he explained. 'She would need too much personal attention.' Griffiths had not anticipated Boyle's continuing success among her middle-aged fan base in mid-America, attracted to a star who said, 'My Catholic faith is the backbone of my life.' On *China's Got Talent*, in 2011, she would be watched on TV by an estimated 510 million viewers while singing in an arena filled with 60,000 fans.

Blessed by the controversy, Susan Boyle's global stardom ratcheted up Cowell's bargaining power with the networks in

Los Angeles, and he returned to the US brimming with confidence. His first stop was to see his house on North Palm Drive. As he entered, the building site was spotless. Although over eighty craftsmen were working, there was hardly a speck of dust.

That was the only source of satisfaction. His relationship with Jennifer Post was proving difficult. She was resisting his demand for a circular staircase to the first floor, insisting that a loft-style staircase was perfect. One completed staircase had been rejected by him and a second had just been assembled. On entering the house, his first glimpse of the stairs evoked anger.

'Pull it down,' he ordered. 'I want a circular one.'

'No way,' Post shouted back. Then, as he walked through the painted building, his mood darkened: 'I don't want any more fucking white in the house.' Every wall and wooden surface was white. Entering the garden, he was blinded by the dazzle. The surface was white concrete. 'This is like an asylum,' he moaned. Post offered alternative dark colours but it was too late and he wanted to move in. 'Build a circular staircase,' he demanded. In the meantime, he lived in nearby Cole Place, which he had rebuilt for $2 million, turning it into an ultra-chic hilltop refuge.

Cowell's principal task in Los Angeles was to crank up his negotiations with Fox for *The X Factor*. With Chernin's departure imminent, he needed to introduce himself to Peter Rice, Chernin's British-born successor. Formerly a senior executive film producer at Twentieth Century Fox, Rice was still basking in the congratulations for his adroit purchase of the film *Slumdog Millionaire* when he arrived for dinner at Cecconi's in Beverly Hills. In Hollywood, Rice knew, TV executives were regarded as second-rate because the best stayed in the film business.

'I've decided to leave *American Idol* in 2010', Cowell said, 'and launch *The X Factor* in America.' Rice's face, partly covered by his horn-rimmed glasses, gave nothing away. He was thinking about the risk to the estimated $850 million which Fox had earned from advertising during the 2009 *Idol* season. 'My departure will be good for the programme,' Cowell continued, his tongue in his cheek. 'You'll get new stars and new energy. And you'll be pleased to see me go. I'm always so late nowadays.' Eventually, Rice replied that he wanted Cowell to remain. 'When my contract runs out, that's it,' repeated Cowell. 'I'm going to launch *The X Factor*.' The question, he wondered, was whether Rice understood the difference between *American Idol* and *The X Factor*. The new programme would include both younger and older contestants and feature the intense competition between the judges in the mentoring of the contestants. Rice, Cowell realised by the end of the meal, 'did not trust me completely'.

Hours later, James Murdoch, the head of News Corporation in the UK, telephoned Cowell and urged him to stay. 'I've done it for ten years,' Cowell replied. 'I've made you a lot of money and now I want to do something new.' No one at Fox took Cowell's threat seriously. Negotiations always started at the extreme.

Soon after, at a party in James's sister Elisabeth Murdoch's home in London, Philip Green approached her father, Rupert. 'You and me will do a deal for Simon,' said Green. What followed has been hotly disputed: Green's critics suggest that Murdoch recoiled from any discussion; Cowell and Green recalled the opposite, with Green reporting the next day, 'I had a great conversation with Rupert.' Either interpretation placed Green at the centre of the negotiations at 2 p.m. on 3 June 2009, when he welcomed the Sony board to his office in Marylebone. By the end of the meeting, Sony had agreed to return 100 per cent of the TV and music rights for *The X Factor*, *Britain's Got Talent* and any other programme he made back to Cowell and settled on increased percentages for all the recording rights – in exchange for absolutely nothing except participation in the new joint venture. Green had built the first block of Cowell's new business.

Gossip about Cowell's plans reached Ryan Seacrest. His

contract as host of *American Idol* was expiring and he decided on a ruse involving a date with Cowell in London. Seacrest's arrival on 11 June raised eyebrows. John Ferriter, the agent who had masterminded his transformation from a Georgia DJ earning $30,000 a year into a $3.5-million-a-year host, was at the time comatose in a Los Angeles hospital. As Ferriter would later complain, 'Ryan didn't drive one mile to visit me but he flew 5,000 miles to meet Simon.' Somewhere across the Atlantic, Seacrest dumped his agent.

The trip was frantic. Within forty-eight hours, Seacrest would be expected at the Gillette Stadium in Boston for the first *Idol* auditions. But, eager to play his game, he entered Green's office with an adviser. 'I want to work with you guys on *The X Factor*,' said Seacrest.

'You've got a contract with *Idol*,' replied Green.

'It's only for one more week, and I've told them I'm not turning up,' retorted Seacrest.

'It's a bad idea not to turn up,' Green told him.

During dinner, Green telephoned Mike Darnell. After explaining the situation, he asked, 'Can I help you? In any case, I'll make sure Ryan turns up tomorrow.'

After the meal, Seacrest suggested to Cowell that they go to Stringfellows. By then, Cowell thought he had persuaded his friend to use Green as his financial adviser: 'He's sorted me out. He would do the same for you.' Seacrest seemed persuaded.

At 5 a.m., the star with the bleached-blond hair emerged with Cowell from the club, covered in lipstick from lusty lap dancers. Camera flashes burst through the darkness. The following day, the photographs were published in the British tabloids. 'It's a riot,' Bob Sillerman told Simon Fuller.

As Seacrest had anticipated, the images sparked Fuller's fear that *American Idol*'s host intended to abandon ship. The next day, Sillerman called Green.

'What are you doing with Ryan?' he asked.

'Monkey business,' replied Green.

Cowell was fuming. He felt he had been used by Seacrest and that the image was damaging. What Seacrest did, however, suffer in common with Cowell was a flurry of malicious false rumours on the Internet about his sexuality, with the suggestion that any association with a woman was a smokescreen.

The following week, Sillerman arrived in Monaco for dinner on Green's yacht. Although CKX's directors opposed his $300-million offer to Cowell as too expensive, Sillerman thought there was a chance to do a deal and to use that success to regain control of his company from the other shareholders.

Unknown to Green, the visit was Sillerman's make-or-break. If he failed, the corporation would be sold. Over six hours, he increased his price by pledging 'a piece of *American Idol* for a piece of *The X Factor*'. The atmosphere was nevertheless uncomfortable. Jews celebrating the Friday-night Shabbat aboard a giant yacht appeared incongruous to the Jewish visitor and, despite 'falling for Tina', Green's wife, Sillerman hated the positioning by everyone around the table. 'You know the old saying about the half-filled glass,' he told his host. 'The optimist says it's half full, the pessimist says it's half empty and the realist says the glass is too big.' That night the glass was not big enough. 'I realised I was part of the problem,' Sillerman would say. 'I was the only man on the planet who liked both Cowell and Fuller. It was like sitting on the electric chair and being asked, "Do you want AC or DC?"'

While Sillerman was flying back to New York, Green was telephoned by Seacrest. 'I've got a new deal for *Idol*,' he said. 'They're paying me $45 million over three years. Up by 80 per cent. Most from Fox but also some from Fuller and Sillerman.'

Soon after Sillerman landed, there was a telephone call from Green. 'Is there something you forgot to tell me?' he asked.

'I don't think so, Phil.'

'What about the little matter of paying Ryan $45 million? Did you forget to tell me that during our six-hour dinner?'

'Well, I promised Ryan not to say anything.'

Green was exasperated. The symbolism of Friday's dinner had been abused by Sillerman's deception. 'I can understand Philip's anger,' Sillerman would later say. Pertinently, Cowell was sympathetic to Sillerman's tactics and could not understand Green's anger.

The last stage of the divorce was Fuller's arrival soon after in Green's office.

'Look, I'm really confused,' said Green. 'I'm trying to do business, so why pay Ryan $45 million?'

'You don't understand,' replied Fuller. 'Things have happened between me and Simon in the past. The deal is done. The train has left the station.'

'We can't deal with you if you don't trust us,' Green scoffed.

Soon after, Green read critical comments about himself, Sony and Fox in the media. He telephoned Julian Henry, Fuller's publicist, to protest. 'He yelled at me,' complained Henry unconvincingly. 'And I don't know why.' Cowell called Sillerman: 'The deal's not going to work but let's stay friends.' One day, he hoped, Sillerman would pay a fortune for his empire.

Cowell had reached another Rubicon. Liberated from Fuller's shadow, he had the energy and inspiration to realise his dream and simultaneously wreak his revenge on Fuller. 'He's the shrinking violet who just got married,' said one of Cowell's aides about his rival. Cowell had not been invited to Fuller's wedding in San Francisco. Instead, he was finally preparing to move into North Palm Drive. Except there was nothing for him to do. After having been banned by Jennifer Post from the property for two weeks as she completed her 'Full Turn-Key Service', he entered his new home to find everything unpacked, the fridge full, the fire burning and not a box in sight. The cupboards were filled with Egyptian cotton sheets, Christofle dinner and tea sets, a sterling-silver tea set, a Dunhill cigar box, nine period decanters and monogrammed black linen table napkins. Black-and-white photographs of Frank Sinatra covered the walls, including a signed copy of Terry O'Neill's famous shot of Sinatra arriving with his bodyguards on Miami beach in 1968. To placate Cowell's dislike of white, Post had even introduced black lavatory paper. Dotted around were sealed packets of Kool cigarettes. Cowell had become accustomed to smoking cigarettes only from newly opened packets so that he would always enjoy fresh tobacco.

Perfection had been delivered for an additional $6 million, with the total value of the house estimated at $22 million. Except that within weeks Cowell was niggling for change. The paint finish, he decided, was unsatisfactory, the rooms were badly designed and he wanted more open-air living space at the back. Architect Brian Biglin was summoned and told to submit plans for adding another 4,000 square feet to transform the garden into a new 'living area'. The initial budget was $2.5 million. 'Simon makes things better,' said Biglin.

'Harry Benson is booked to fly to Los Angeles to shoot the cover for *Architectural Digest*,' Post told Cowell. 'He'll need three days.'

'You're not going to photograph the house,' replied Cowell.

'You can't turn Harry down,' wailed Post, who discovered she had been replaced by Jiin Kim Inoue, a designer based with Finchatton in London. Between regular flights to Los Angeles, Inoue was told to communicate her plans and progress to Biglin and Cowell using three-dimensional drawings. But there were to be no photographs of her work. 'I want my privacy,' said Cowell.

His privacy was protected by increasing his staff. Besides Roxana Reyna, the head housekeeper, there was Zoë, the estate manager, her assistant, two groundsmen to look after the garden and provide maintenance and security, a chef and four housekeepers. (His house in London was looked after by two housekeepers.) Chauffeurs were hired through an agency. His working staff included three personal assistants, an assistant dedicated exclusively to caring for his property and hiring the staff, and another dedicated to supervising construction work.

The excitement of owning two iconic houses in Beverly Hills – he had decided to use one as a home and the other as an office – and the collapse of negotiations with Fuller inspired Cowell to jettison past ambitions. He would no longer be content only to produce the best TV shows; he envisaged creating an entertainment empire. Green, a retail magnate, bestowed credibility on his ambition.

In a public statement, Green announced that he and Cowell had established a joint business to 'build a company bigger than Disney'. Syco, the new holding company, would own Cowell's interests in all TV programmes, talent management and merchandising. Green would be responsible for the multibillion-dollar conglomerate's finance and global strategy and the sale of branded products, such as T-shirts and drinks. The entertainment world was introduced to potentially the world's richest TV mogul. 'You must have a share of the new company,' Cowell told Green. 'I'll take 5 per cent,' replied Green, 'and nothing in writing.' 'Twenty per cent,' insisted Cowell. Green anticipated that once Cowell cashed in, his share would be worth a fortune.

In the expectation that Cowell would one day be earning in excess of $100 million a year, but 'only spending a fraction of what I earn', Green arranged a weekly summary of Cowell's cash position and encouraged him to write a will. 'I'm giving my money to animals and kids,' Cowell said. He liked both but wanted responsibility for neither. Thinking about the fortune which the charities would receive after his death, he sighed, 'I had more fun making money when I earned much less.'

The announcement of Syco's creation sparked a reshuffle among the other players. In July, Sony presented an outline offer which Green judged 'very good'. Next, a summit was called in Los Angeles. The chiefs of FremantleMedia, Sony and Fox – Rupert Murdoch in person – met Cowell and Bryan Lourd, his agent. On Tony Cohen's insistence, Green was not invited. The chief executive of FremantleMedia claimed that during one argument about Syco sharing in the ancillaries' profits – including the £2 million earned from voters' telephone calls – Green became irritated by Cohen's refusal to listen. Green, he alleged, lost his temper and jokingly threatened to throw Cohen off a cliff. Green strenuously denied the accusation. The only relevant truth was all the players' positive responses to Green's orchestration of Cowell's fate.

Murdoch and the Fox executives arrived at the meeting to offer Cowell $130 million to stay on *American Idol* until 2012 and to launch *The X Factor* in the US in 2013. 'That's not enough,' said Cowell. Jeff Zucker of NBC, he explained, had just offered $300 million for *The X Factor* and *America's Got Talent*. 'I won't read or entertain your offer,' he had told Zucker, 'because I don't want Fox to think I'm using you as leverage.' After revealing the NBC bid, Cowell looked at Murdoch: 'It's personal, not financial. I'm attached to Fox. Your people have been very kind, but I want to start *The X Factor*.' Nevertheless, by the end of the meeting Cowell agreed to a phased transition: he would appear on *American Idol* for two years and then launch *The X Factor* USA. The finances were to be finalised by Lourd and Green. FremantleMedia agreed to reduce their interest in *The X Factor* from eighty–twenty in their favour to fifty–fifty, with Sony suggesting a more complicated division of ownership to reflect the fact that 70 per cent of Sony UK's music revenue was generated by artists contracted by Syco.

Green assumed the negotiations were completed, until Rolf Schmidt-Holtz arrived in his office with a group of Sony executives. The company's accountants, it transpired, had protested that handing Cowell 100 per cent ownership of the TV rights, followed by Sony paying Cowell for a share of Syco, the new company, was too disadvantageous to them.

'It's crazy giving this up for free,' exclaimed Schmidt-Holtz.

'It was agreed,' spluttered Green, whose next shock was Schmidt-Holtz's accounting of past income. In particular, he was furious that Sony legally but controversially described Fox's $50-million payment for the *X Factor* option as a profit rather than an exceptional item.

'This is my new offer,' said Schmidt-Holtz, offering a document showing a fifty–fifty split with Syco, substantially less than the 100 per cent he had previously agreed.

'No,' said Green after reading through Sony's proposed contract. 'This is not what we agreed.'

'Yes, but this is my final offer,' Schmidt-Holtz repeated.

'This is outrageous,' said Green excitedly. 'It's not correct. You're a bagel *gonif*.' Schmidt-Holtz did not understand the Yiddish name for a man who steals the hole in the bagel, but he could not ignore Green's anger. Upset, he drove from Green's office to Cowell's home. The German, Cowell noticed, was in an emotional state.

'I won't negotiate with Green,' he said. 'This is my offer and you must sign it whatever Green says. It's fair. We've stood by you. You owe me more.'

Cowell agreed to Sony's offer of a fifty–fifty split, a decision he could live with despite Green's understandable fury.

By then, news of the tortured negotiations had reached Dan Sabbagh, the media editor of *The Times*. On 2 September, he wrote a report that Green was due to fly to New York to negotiate with Fox about the introduction of *The X Factor* to

America, and that NBC was an alternative network should those discussions fail. Sabbagh highlighted that Green's negotiations with Peter Rice had become 'fraught amid a series of differences'. Despite Sabbagh's efforts, Fox had refused to comment, even though the network and the newspaper were both part of Murdoch's empire. Injudiciously, Sabbagh decided at 9 p.m., just as the newspaper's first edition was about to be printed, to fill an unexpected gap on his page with his report. The absence of Fox's comment, he knew, was risky. Minutes after the story appeared in the online edition, Peter Rice became available. Hysterical and aggressive, he told Sabbagh that 'fraught' misrepresented the negotiations.

'That's untrue,' Rice screamed. During the night, successive editions of the newspaper changed 'fraught' to 'fruitful'. Soon after, Sabbagh left the newspaper, saying, 'I felt I was right,' but neither *The Times*'s report nor Rice's overreaction influenced the outcome.

The final deal was that Cowell and Sony would unite in a new joint venture within Syco. Sony would contribute its assets – *The X Factor* and the *Talent* shows – while Cowell provided his exclusive services as the creator of all content and contracted his services as executive producer for five years. Sony advanced $50 million to Cowell, to be set against the income from the programmes and records. Syco, however, did not receive the income from Cowell's appearances on *The X Factor*, the *Talent* shows and in advertisements. That money was deposited with Cowell's private companies in America and Britain, subject to Syco receiving a small fee. The deal, it was colourfully asserted, would earn Cowell $1 billion over the following six years. On Piers Morgan's recommendation, he would appoint Ellis Watson, formerly at Trinity Mirror and transport company FirstGroup, as Syco Entertainment's chief executive.

*

Cowell's agreement, spurred by personal sentiment, was a relief for Murdoch and the Fox producers, but the mood soon soured. On the road for *American Idol* with Paula Abdul, Randy Jackson and Ryan Seacrest, Cowell was feeling more weary than he had anticipated. The contestants were not potential megastars like Kelly Clarkson, and the winners' records were no longer amazing hits. Nigel Lythgoe's absence had sapped energy from the show and sniping with the other judges was no longer fun. In the aftermath of Seacrest's twenty-four-hour dash to London, Cowell's relationship with the show's host was nearly poisonous. 'He's like a young deer at a party,' Cowell told Abdul. 'Young, ambitious and very competitive. He's just signed his new contract, and I just want it to end.' Seacrest's $15 million a year enraged Abdul, who was enmeshed in another personal crisis.

Over the previous weeks, a failed contestant had been stalking her and just days earlier had committed suicide in front of her home. Distressed, Abdul complained that Mike Darnell offered her little sympathy. Now came the gossip that the Fox executives were considering paying Cowell over $300 million, while her annual fee was just $1.9 million. Worse, her request for a new contract was being brusquely ignored by Darnell and Rice. 'It's unnecessarily hurtful and certainly rude,' complained her agent.

As so often in the customary horror of corporate life, the victim was the last to hear the fateful news. In late July, Abdul was waiting for her luggage at Kennedy airport in New York when she switched on her mobile phone to listen to the messages. Ken Warwick, Lythgoe's replacement, had left one in which he flippantly mentioned that there would be a fourth judge on the show. Shocked, Abdul called Warwick back.

'This is not good news,' she said, feeling 'really crappy'. 'What's his name?'

'He's a she,' replied Warwick, 'and you won't know her.'

'If she's a songwriter,' snapped Abdul, 'it's Kara DioGuardi.'

There was a long silence from Los Angeles. 'How do you know?' asked Warwick.

'I started her career,' said Abdul. 'I picked her off the street in New York, moved her into my home and with my help she got a number-one hit. Then off she goes and I don't hear from her for four years. Do you mean she didn't tell you?'

'No.'

'How do you think I feel to be the last to know about this? And about someone no one has ever heard of? Even the lighting man probably knew before me.'

Warwick was contrite. 'It was Simon Fuller's idea,' he said.

Abdul was shocked. She couldn't quite remember how many times she had spoken to Fuller, but she knew they could be counted on the fingers of one hand. Nor could she understand why Cécile Frot-Coutaz and Mike Darnell, possibly encouraged by Lythgoe, had treated her so poorly, unless by creating insecurity they hoped to make her feel paranoid.

Kara DioGuardi, she suspected, would prove to be hopeless, and as for Ellen DeGeneres, another prospective replacement, no one, said Abdul, was mentioning her recent marriage to her girlfriend, Portia de Rossi.

DioGuardi joined the auditions and, as Abdul predicted, her performance was poor. Backstage, their mutual dislike climaxed in a fight outside Abdul's dressing room. Darnell's purpose, Abdul raged, was to dampen her demands for an increased fee. She had originally asked for $10 million; in response, Fox offered $3 million for one season. Eventually she reduced her demand to $5 million, and Fox offered $4.5 million. Now, Fox refused to compromise, even over such a small amount, and, on 5 August, Abdul announced her immediate departure. Fuller, Abdul assumed, was delighted. 'Creatively,' said Cécile Frot-Coutaz enigmatically, 'no one wanted Paula to leave *American Idol*.'

Victoria Beckham, alias Posh Spice and Fuller's client, was inserted as her replacement. Cowell's apparent enthusiasm was contradicted by an overnight media report that he had found her 'wooden'. The following day, Posh arrived incensed and refused to accept Cowell's insistence that the report was fictitious. The chemistry of the panel had failed to materialise.

Cowell immediately telephoned Abdul. She spoke about life in the wilderness and 'the end of my career'. 'Don't worry,' said Cowell. 'Just hang on. Things are happening and you'll be back with me.'

The X Factor's prospective American launch in 2013 spurred Cowell to keep the show at the heart of Britain's national conversation during the new season. Boosted by the success of Leona Lewis and JLS, the increased budget had changed the programme. For the first time, the contestants auditioned in front of an audience rather than a soulless room, and he arranged for Ashley Cole, the cheating husband, to sit in the front row so that he could witness Cowell's barbs with the 'wronged woman' loved by millions of Britons. 'Footballer's wives', Cheryl Cole had written in 2006, 'are just as bad as benefit scroungers – it's just a higher class of scrounger.' Playing with emotions gave the show edginess. 'Cheryl Cole and Walsh Mock Cowell's Judgement' was the *Sun* headline encouraged by Cowell. 'I like the show to be in the press,' he said.

Taking his cue, Louis Walsh picked an opportunity to make a confession in a newspaper interview. Cowell, he explained, had told the fifty-seven-year-old, 'Darling, we should get the eyes and teeth done. Do some cosmetic maintenance.' The result was surgery on Walsh's eye bags and gleaming porcelain caps in his mouth.

'What's the difference between God and Simon Cowell?' asked Walsh during the interview. 'God doesn't walk around

Knightsbridge thinking he's Cowell.' Cowell loved harmless carping so long as nothing disturbed his magic. His personality, he hoped, would silence the critics and secure adoration for himself as the universal hero. One obstacle was *The X Factor* itself, whose attraction at the outset depended on the humiliation of certain contestants.

Newspapers were led to Katrina Lee, a twenty-three-year-old Belfast shop worker whom Cowell had told five years earlier that her voice should ideally be 'in someone else's body'. Since then, she had lost two stone, paid for laser treatment on her face and dental surgery, and had dyed her hair red. 'Your comments nearly wrecked my life,' she told Cowell in the edited version of an audition, referring to her developing shingles and an eating disorder. 'He seemed really shocked about how his comments had affected me,' she said later. Cowell understood the tabloid readers' appetite for stories of anguish, and her colourful trauma kept *The X Factor* in the tabloid headlines for days, helped by the *Mirror* finding Hollie Steel, a failed contestant who after crying on the stage likened Cowell to a playground bully. 'Don't do it again,' Cowell told journalists in personal telephone calls. 'Hollie admits it's not true.' Unfair criticism of himself, he explained, was hurtful. 'I've ordered the judges to be kind,' he said, feeding the tabloids' interest further.

The enjoyment he was getting out of being the executive producer extinguished Cowell's lingering interest in *American Idol*. The combination of Fox's treatment of Abdul, Seacrest's behaviour, Fuller's omnipresence and the frustration of performing rather than producing turned him against staying longer than necessary. With hindsight, he realised that observing Green's negotiations had solidified his antagonism.

At 2 a.m., he telephoned Green. Accustomed by then to being awoken during the night, Green assumed Cowell needed another therapy session and prepared to doze while Cowell spoke. But the first words broke through Green's semi-consciousness: 'I know it's all done but I'm not doing *Idol* after this season.'

'Getting the deal has taken ten months of my life,' growled Green.

'I know, but I'm mentally done. I want a clean break, starting in 2011.' Cowell continued, 'The issue is what *I* want to do. For the first time I'm going to take a risk. It's a red or black moment. I want more on the back end from Fox, dependent on ratings, rather than big bonuses up front.'

This was, Green knew, a seismic change in Cowell's life. Until then, he had always wanted a guarantee of cash up front. Now, he was gambling to beat Fuller. Green replaced the receiver. 'He got the tuts,' he told himself.

Green next called Peter Rice. 'My horse has broken its leg fifty yards from the finishing line. You'd better come to London.'

Eight weeks into his new job as Fox's chief executive, Rice was soon sitting with Green at the Dorchester, uncertain why he had rushed overnight from Los Angeles. Cowell arrived late.

'I don't want to do *American Idol* any more,' he announced.

'Really?' gasped Rice, visibly stunned. His Hollywood career had not prepared him for the loss of Fox's biggest star, the foundation stone of the network's success.

Minutes passed and no one spoke. Cowell steeled himself against breaking the silence. 'It's so quiet I can hear a pin drop,' thought Green, who would describe what followed as 'the most fascinating moment in my business career'.

Rice broke the silence: 'Is that it?'

'This is very personal for me,' explained Cowell. 'I've worked nine seasons for you. I'm not entertaining any other offers. It's important for me to be separate now, and I don't feel comfortable doing both shows.' Rice, he could see, was distressed. He did not want *The X Factor* muddying the waters. This was nothing more than the mutual denigration of two British egos, Cowell's and Fuller's. They were engaged in a gladiatorial contest, with Fox haplessly uncertain of the outcome on their own turf.

Normally, Cowell was a plate spinner, a man on the wire occasionally close to falling off, but now his self-confidence was cast-iron and he was unusually decisive. He did not imagine how strenuously his judgement would be tested over the following weeks.

After fifty minutes, Rice went for a walk with Bryan Lourd in Hyde Park and then flew back to Los Angeles. Within hours, Fuller called Cowell urging him to stay on *Idol*. 'It's not personal,' Cowell said with an unseen smile.

His income that year would be at least $27 million from *American Idol*, about £9 million from ITV and at least £25 million from Sony Music. With at least another £10 million from other interests, his annual income was heading towards £70 million and would only increase. Fuller's was considerably less. Cowell intended to take a gamble and agree that his fees from Fox should depend on *American Idol*'s audience ratings.

'This is a big turning point in your life,' Terri Seymour told Cowell as he approached his fiftieth birthday. 'Every decade,' Cowell agreed, 'is a milestone and a new challenge.' Somehow it was appropriate that the celebrations should be organised by Tina Green. In their daily telephone conversations, Philip Green was serving as Cowell's unpaid mentor, adviser and confessor, so his wife automatically agreed to stage an extravaganza for his birthday. After first suggesting that Cowell 'rent three jumbos and fly everyone to New York', Green retreated to something more modest in England. The venue, Tina Green decided, should be Wrotham Park, an eighteenth-century mansion in Hertfordshire, and, after consulting her husband, she chose Cowell's vanity as the theme. Banana Split, the party organisers, were given a budget of £2 million.

Unsurprisingly, Jackie St Clair was not prepared to abandon her own plans to celebrate Cowell's birthday. Two hundred people, including many of Cowell's former girlfriends, had been summoned to her home in Holland Park. Among the definite exclusions was Louise Payne, his ex-fiancée, and among the diffident invitees were Terri Seymour and Sinitta. St Clair lived much of her life through Cowell and loved stepping into the limelight with her friend. Aggressive in defending her territory, she disliked her rivals, especially Sinitta, but conceded that Cowell enjoyed the competition for his attention. Most of the guests obeyed her request to bring a mirror as a present, and at the end of the evening there would be 179 stacked in a room.

'I've got a present for you,' Cowell said at the outset of his speech, looking at St Clair. 'It's a picture of someone I greatly admire.' Ripping open the paper, St Clair found a life-size portrait of Cowell. He also gave her a Lowry. Anticipating his self-deprecation, St Clair organised that Dannii Minogue, Amanda Holden, Louis Walsh and Bruno Tonioli, a *Strictly Come Dancing* judge, should sing 'You're So Vain', all wearing Cowell masks. The Greens, not invited to St Clair's 'private party for old friends', were surprised to hear that vanity should also have been chosen as the theme, but Cowell had amusingly told the guests after singing some Beatles songs that '80 per cent of you are not invited to my official party'.

That guest list of 450 people included most of the stars associated with his programmes, his media allies, his family, friends and a contingent of his office staff, accountants, lawyers and professional advisers. Over dinner at London club Les Ambassadeurs two weeks before the party, Philip Green moaned to Cowell about the absence of a seating plan. 'If you didn't have thirty-nine ex-girlfriends, it would be easy. And it's growing weekly. They all phone up and ask a variety of "Can I sing? Can I jump out of a cake? Can I jump off the roof?" You can't imagine.'

One week later, Tina Green had still not received a table plan. Her husband called Cowell. 'You're crazy,' he shouted. 'We don't know the people. You've got to tell us where everyone sits.' 'I can't do it,' said Cowell. 'Can't get my head around it.' The following day, he disappeared, resurfacing in the penthouse of the Setai hotel in Miami, one of his favourite haunts. 'I couldn't be bothered,' he later said. 'I didn't want to do it. There were too many fights, so I fled the country to get chilled.' Miami was Cowell's natural playground. Latino girls in the nightclubs threw themselves at the generous party animal, and within days he had recovered.

Forty-eight hours before the party, he returned to London. On Friday night, 2 October, Philip and Tina Green arrived at Cowell's home to find their friend enjoying a facial massage in his bathroom. At first, Tina sat on the bathroom floor asking about each name for the table plan. Then, while Cowell immersed himself in a bath, the Greens continued the argument in the adjoining bedroom, spreading the name tags over Cowell's bed. At around midnight the chore was completed.

The next day, before driving to Hertfordshire, Cowell took half a milligram of a sleeping tablet. 'I wanted to be slightly dreamy because I was stressed by the thought of nearly 500 people,' he would say. 'I would have to go to the tables and be nice to everyone. I can't bear crowds. It was almost unbearable. The tablet made me relaxed.'

In the dusk, Wrotham Park was bathed in a coloured projection of him with a cigarette. Entering the mansion, he was greeted by waiters wearing Cowell masks and top hats. Peering into the dining marquee with Philip Green, Cowell was impressed by what his money had bought, although the budget had increased to £3 million. Huge blue satin curtains covered the walls and the curved tables were covered with gold and silver, transforming the room into a kind of debauched boudoir. The waitresses were wearing hot pants and acrobats were hanging from the rafters. The tablecloths were decorated with a profile of the birthday boy, and the name plates were cherubs wearing G-strings and gold crowns. Cowell's own table was decorated with two porcelain males wearing bondage gear and gold angel wings. Hovering over the guests was a replica of Michelangelo's *Creation of Adam* painting on the ceiling of the Vatican's Sistine Chapel, the image of God replaced by one of Cowell.

'Oh my God,' exclaimed Cowell. 'How camp is this?' Terri Seymour was watching from the side: 'He looked so uncomfortable. He'd lost his usual composure. I expected the evening to be much worse than it was.'

Clutching glasses of Cristal champagne and dressed in long, low-cut couture dresses, some of London's most beautiful and best-known women lit up the room, representing, in Cowell's mischievous calculation, 'half of Britain's Botox consumers'. Amid riotous laughter and, inevitably, the best music, guests were served with soup decorated with 'Simon' written in cream, followed by fish fingers and shepherd's pie, two of his favourite dishes. Everyone was encouraged to smoke.

All of the guests knew about their host's love and support for his mother Julie, who was seated by her son. Whenever he was in London, he arranged to meet her every week, usually for Sunday lunch. Some knew that beyond the glowing interviews she gave to newspapers about her son, there was also criticism: she revealed that his nickname as a child was 'Mummy look at me'; a journalist was told that 'Simon gave me a Porsche for Christmas, I wanted a duvet'; and she commented that 'My best Christmas presents ever were my grandchildren by [his brother] Nick.' The insiders suspected that Julie's frustrated ambition to be a star sixty years earlier was behind her enthusiastic public appearances beside her son.

'It's gone full circle' was Cowell's conclusion. 'When I was a child I loved my mother providing access to Robert Mitchum at parties. And now, because of me, she gets what she wants: the same.'

Julie was scrutinised in particular by the table of journalists, including Rebekah Brooks, of the *Sun*, and the *Mirror*'s Richard Wallace.

'This is like *The Godfather*,' said the *Mirror*'s editor. 'It brings to mind the First Holy Communion party in *Godfather II*, a family event for Michael Corleone's son – a gathering of self-interested parties, and not all of them wishing the host well!'

The entertainment was eccentric. In a recorded speech Carly Simon joked that her 1972 hit 'You're So Vain' was written about Cowell; there was a film of his mother, his brother Nick and other friends auditioning on the set of *Britain's Got Talent*, mixed with Cowell's derogatory comments; disco legends Earth, Wind and Fire had been flown in from New York; there was a rendition of Wayne Newton's 1963 syrupy ballad 'Danke Schoen', described by Cowell as 'my favourite song'; there were also shocks, especially for Julie Cowell, as The Box, burlesque artists from New York dressed as giant vaginas, performed a sex routine; and, finally, there was Nick Cowell's speech.

His brother had expected 'payback for what I did to Nick at both his weddings'. At Nick's first wedding to Kim, Cowell, during his best-man speech, had quoted from Nick's teenage 'diary': 'Off to Paris to meet a nice boy; went off with him. Met a nice donkey in the bedroom.' Next, Cowell read a 'letter for a job application' explaining why, as a boy scout, Nick had been found giving mouth-to-mouth resuscitation to another scout in a dark room. Then he had quoted 'personal letters' describing Nick's love for boys. In the middle of the speech, Kim's father had tried to unplug the microphone.

Undeterred, at Nick's second marriage to Kate, Cowell had again read a series of 'letters' sent by a dating agency during their worldwide search for a bride, which climaxed in finally unearthing Kate in Eastern Europe. While speaking, Cowell could see Sinitta first hold her head in her hands and then hide behind a column. Booing broke out, and Kate's parents would delete his speech from the marriage video.

'I took it too far,' Cowell admitted, 'and was meaner and ruder than I intended. They have never forgiven me.'

After those humiliations, Cowell was expecting his brother's revenge. None of his guests had been forewarned.

Nick's body language as he mounted the stage was combative. 'Revenge is a dish best served cold,' he started. 'At my wedding Simon made a dreadful speech, and I was going to wait until his wedding to make this speech. But until they make a law that you can marry yourself, I won't get the chance, so I'll make it now.'

His theme was not only his brother's vanity, but also his homosexuality. 'Simon's favourite animals as a child were elves, goblins and fairies, and he still likes fairies today,' he began, 'and his favourite group was the Pet Shop Boys.' Then he added, 'Simon couldn't believe that Terri could be a girl's name as well . . .'

The side-splitting laughter among the insiders was mixed with bewilderment from the likes of Philip Green, who was stunned by the brother's venom. Sitting next to Green, Cheryl Cole was left open-mouthed. And since Nick ended without any profession of love, Green wrongly assumed that he had not even wished his brother 'happy birthday'. Looking around the marquee, Green perceived stunned silence and an emotional vacuum. He rose and made an impromptu speech to fill the void.

'Nick was really bad,' admitted Cowell, 'but I got off lightly.' In his own speech, he made no reference to his brother. Most notable was his warmth towards his guests, including the journalists, 'who have been kind and balanced', and to Pete Waterman, Lucian Grainge and Simon Fuller, who was noticeably thrilled with the namecheck and Cowell's comment 'I hope we remain friends for a long time.'

The huge birthday cake symbolised Cowell's passion: carried by two beefy men stripped to the waist, it was adorned by a near-naked lap dancer.

The party ended in disarray. 'The best party I've ever been to,' said many guests as they left at 3 a.m. Some guests, including David Hasselhoff, needed help to leave; others cavorted with the scantily dressed waitresses or offered Cowell oral sex and more in exchange for a record contract. Some behaviour, especially by Katie Price, alias Jordan, was so colourful that newspaper editors spiked the stories.

'I enjoyed the official party enormously,' Cowell told friends over the following days, although some were not convinced. Cowell did not like big parties and the final bill was over £3 million. 'I had to earn over £5 million [before tax] to pay for the seven hours. It was too much but it was one of the best nights of my life.'

Cowell did not normally suffer from self-delusion. Beyond his public persona, his confidants knew, was a man who feared toppling into the abyss. His smugness concealed a nightmare. Etched upon him since his humiliation at school and Arista was an irrefutable law of showbiz: artists' fortunes were either rising or falling. If he was ever to fail, his downfall would be applauded by those on whom he had vowed to take revenge, including some of his birthday guests. But for the moment his ascendancy seemed unstoppable. The music industry had recently bestowed upon him their highest awards and nominated him for more, but he understood the danger of complacency. After receiving gongs, there was always emptiness: 'I went home depressed,' he said after one ceremony. 'It means nothing to me when things are based on something that has happened. I am only interested in the future and what I am going to get. Getting there is more fun than being there . . . I love the journey.' Few could understand.

The birthday party had coincided with the audiences for *The X Factor* hitting new highs. Cowell credited his triumph to manipulating the audience's emotions, but continued success, he repeated, depended on reinvention: 'The moment that you start assuming that the audience is happy to see the same show again, you're dead.' Over 200,000 people had been auditioned for the next series, but not a single contestant had shown star quality. He feared failing to find another Leona Lewis. Like *American Idol* post-Kelly Clarkson, *The X Factor* had hit a talent plateau.

More than ever, the programme depended upon slick editing and quietly dropping contestants who had won a unanimous 'yes' from the judges. They had only 'won' to create a feel-good atmosphere but, according to the rules, could be dropped at the producers' discretion. The alternative to talent was using a bad singer's 'personality' as entertainment fodder until a winner emerged. In 2009, the combination of Cowell's ceaseless ascendancy and the dearth of talent sparked a crisis.

As usual, the early programmes had featured hilarious flops: a fat, tone-deaf, middle-aged man, screeching youngsters and singers chosen for their 'stories' of abuse, drugs, poverty and tragedy. All were vulnerable to Cowell's 'honest' assessment. As the show cross-cut between the judges' smiles and scoffs and cutaways of sobs and hugs by anxious families backstage, an Irish duo had emerged as favourites after what the tabloids called a 'shock win' at the end of October, although they were fourth.

John and Edward Grimes were outrageously dressed and unable to sing. 'If they win,' said Cowell, shuddering at the twins' extravagant hairstyles, 'it will be a complete and utter disaster. I'd probably sulk for six months and get on a very fast plane out of the country.' With the help of the tabloids, Cowell's 'worst nightmare' scenario incited Britain's political leaders, anticipating the imminent general election, to add their voices to the public debate about the twins' fate. After Gordon Brown, the prime minister, announced, 'I don't think they're very good,' Conservative leader David Cameron described himself as their supporter, 'nailed to the chair' as he waited for 'the terrible twins to appear'.

With *The X Factor* at the centre of a national debate, Cowell fuelled the controversy by damning the duo as 'vile little creatures who would step on their mother's head to have a hit'. In early November, Lucie Jones, a Welsh teenager, was tipped as a winner of that episode, but 16.6 million watched Cowell promptly oust the girl and 'save' Jedward, as the twins were now called. Overnight, thousands of fans, including a punter who lost £10,000 betting that the twins would lose, complained that the programme was 'fixed', and the tabloids started a campaign against 'public enemy no. 1' for smirking while Dannii Minogue, who had championed Jones, was in tears. On 21 November, the twins were voted out, but Louis Walsh and Sony offered them contracts to produce a song for the following year.

The purists' outrage filled the airwaves and the Internet. Pop music, they said, was not about singing – that's opera – but about character, sincerity and the truth. Unlike Bob Dylan, Leonard Cohen and Morrissey, who could not sing but were authentic, Jedward were fakes lacking personality, integrity and real human soul.

The *Mirror* denounced the programme for mixing the background vocals to drown the worst aspects of Jedward's voices.

'Fox will be worried,' Cowell told Richard Wallace, the paper's editor, in a telephone call protesting about a 'false' story.

'That's not my concern,' replied Wallace, insisting on the truth of the report.

The controversy was more profound than merely the

promotion of talentless singers. In the days before the *X Factor* final, Jedward's contract was blamed for fracturing and even destroying the music industry. Creative young aspiring artists who produced proper music, fumed Cowell's critics, were being marginalised on the fringes of the Internet, reliant on downloads, while *The X Factor*'s mediocrities prospered thanks to Cowell's malign influence. He was, they complained, the wrong man in the right place at the right time.

Cowell was pragmatic. Even good artists, he believed, survived for only two to three years. The very greatest could dominate the scene for about ten years, but thereafter their music was no longer played on the radio and they were kept alive on nostalgia. The best – Elton John, Rod Stewart and Barry Manilow – prospered in Las Vegas, appearing in $125-a-ticket concerts, hoping to promote themselves with guest appearances on *The X Factor*. The irony, as the argument about the soul of music escalated, was ignored.

Even Pete Waterman blasted 'the Cowell show' for 'ruthlessly' caring only about viewing figures: 'Simon has one fixation, and that's being successful, and he'll cut through anything.' Waterman was not critical of *The X Factor*'s winner singing an overproduced, saccharine version of a popular song; he was irked by 'the villainous pantomime host's' influence, especially because the favourite to win the current series, Joe McElderry, a toothy Geordie, was mediocre.

'Fed up with Cowell's latest karaoke act being Christmas number one?' asked Jon and Tracy Morter, an Essex couple, on their Facebook page. 'Me too. So who's up for a mass purchase of the track "Killing in the Name"?' Opponents of *The X Factor* could download the Rage Against the Machine song, first released as a single in 1992, knowing that their purchase would register on the charts against McElderry. Cowell did not underestimate the challenge mounted by the Morters. 'It's stupid – a cynical campaign aimed at me which is going to spoil the party,' he cursed during a two-day sulk. 'All these musical snobs have ganged up against Joe. It's a teenager being attacked by a huge hate mob . . . a kid being bullied.' His outrage, he hoped, would deter the critics who damned *The X Factor* as 'the home of misfits' and 'mediocre bordering on lousy'. He underestimated social networking and the anger against himself.

His consolation was that 19 million Britons watched the show over two nights, with live performances by Paul McCartney and George Michael in front of a studio audience that included Prince Harry and his girlfriend, Chelsy Davy. Genuine royalty and pop royalty had accepted his invitation to witness 'the nation coming together in an explosion of gloss, glamour and glitter . . . creating good feelings in shameless, mass-market entertainment'. As predicted, McElderry won, with Louis Walsh gushing, 'Joe, you've got everything. You've got the walk, the attitude, the charm. You're a small boy with a big voice.' Cowell added, 'This is the closest competition I've ever been involved in,' although McElderry secured 61.3 per cent of the vote. Fortunately for Cowell, his hyperbole was rarely remembered and never thrown back at him.

That night, inhabiting a bubble, Cowell deceived himself. Over 500,000 people bought 'Killing in the Name', outselling McElderry's 'The Climb' by 50,000. For the first time in five years, *The X Factor* had not produced the Christmas number one. Cowell's anger was not shared by Sony, however. The company also owned the Rage Against the Machine song, effectively increasing their profits.

Cowell was stung by the criticism. 'We're getting fat, arrogant and lazy,' he told his producers. 'This is a wake-up call.' Although Leona Lewis and Susan Boyle had sold millions of albums, the programme had still not produced a global star like Robbie Williams or Britney Spears. McElderry was certain to disappear. However, there was just a chance, Cowell thought, that Cheryl Cole could evolve into a megastar. Since her appearance on *The X Factor* all her albums had been number-one hits. 'People love her,' Cowell enthused. 'She's unstoppable.' Tiffs and teases about her clothes and performance had provoked tears and even a playful punch at Cowell during one break, raising her profile and adding strength to his negotiations with ITV. Her dissociation from her philandering husband was hailed as inspiring conduct by her adoring female fans.

The 2009 season had beaten all records since the launch of *Pop Idol*. ITV had earned an estimated £75 million from advertising and telephone calls. The following year, they were promised more from sponsorship deals and enhanced advertising campaigns. Cowell would demand an additional £3 million for the budget, giving him £1.7 million for each weekend and making *The X Factor* by far the most expensive entertainment programme on British television. He also expected ITV to increase Cole's £1.2-million fee. Professionally, his demand for perfection made the show seem unassailable, but he sensed exhaustion. 'A lot of things are going to have to change next year if we bring the show back,' he declared. As Christmas presents, he gave his three co-presenters vouchers for Botox treatment at the Urban Retreat in Harrods. Only change and renewal could guarantee their survival.

'I've walked through a lot of walls to get to the end of the journey,' said Cowell as he prepared to fly to Barbados for Christmas. The 'end' was not only his last season on *American Idol*, but also the prospect of a major change in his bachelor lifestyle.

14

True Love

'He's madly in love,' thought Julie Cowell when she saw her son arrive in Barbados with Mezhgan Hussainy.

Cowell had met the Afghani make-up artist seven years earlier on the *American Idol* set. While living with Terri Seymour in 2006, he had enjoyed a secret relationship with her, but they had only started dating openly in December 2009. Described as thirty-six years old – although others would unkindly suggest she was forty-one – Hussainy had fled her homeland with her parents at the age of nine and in her early twenties had been forced into an arranged marriage with an older carpet-seller. Since her divorce, the attractive brunette had enjoyed life in Los Angeles and, to Julie Cowell, seemed keen to have children.

'Before I go,' Julie told her son, 'it would be nice if I could see you settled down.' 'Yes, mother,' replied Cowell with sincerity.

Mezhgan Hussainy was special. During the last months of filming *American Idol*, he later explained, 'Mezhgan was helpful in allaying my stress. It was difficult in the *Idol* team, and she was always at my side. I could confide in her and she was supportive. So we created a real bond.' Her presence at his fiftieth birthday party, he agreed with his mother, was 'important'. Others repeated gossip from the *American Idol* team that Hussainy is 'like a kitten and knows what to do in the bedroom'. Smitten by the woman's looks and sex appeal, Cowell invited her to join him after Christmas on his chartered yacht.

Exhausted by the prospect of endless conversations with the crowds who flocked annually to Barbados's Sandy Lane hotel and irritated by the nonchalant staff at Cove Spring House, which he had rented, Cowell decided to stay with his mother only until New Year's Eve. Desperate for privacy, and to avoid going out every night, he had chartered *Slipstream*, a new 193-foot, $45-million yacht. He planned to leave the island with Hussainy in the early hours of New Year's Day and sail south. Among his guests were Kelly Bergantz, whom he had recently employed to develop a new TV series, and Paul McKenna. He had arranged to meet Philip Green on *Lionheart*.

Their rendezvous in the Caribbean became the gossip on the moguls' grapevine. During the first week of January, a gaggle of billionaires' yachts anchored off Tobago Cays, five uninhabited islands in the Grenadines. Looking from his deck, Cowell could see *Rising Sun*, the world's biggest yacht, owned by David Geffen, the Hollywood film and record producer. Green was on *Lionheart*, while his sparring partner, Stuart Rose, the chairman of Marks and Spencer, was a guest of Elisabeth Murdoch and her family on their own boat. Alongside them was James Murdoch's *Angle Share*, a 130-foot yacht, and in the middle was Rupert Murdoch's vessel. His guests included Rebekah Brooks, the former editor of the *Sun* who had recently been appointed News International's chief executive in London. Near by, on board *Hamilton*, was Charles Dunstone, the owner of Carphone Warehouse and a sponsor of the British *X Factor*. And among that gaggle of super-rich was *Slipstream*, a testament to Cowell's ambition to rise from multimillionaire to billionaire.

To taste the elite's lifestyle, Cowell, Hussainy and McKenna inspected Geffen's *Rising Sun*, a 453-foot-long craft with eighty-two rooms spread over five floors.

'What's the one piece of advice you've got?' Cowell asked Geffen.

'You've got to know when to leave the fair,' replied Geffen. 'You've got to know when it's time to go.'

After a two-hour tour, Cowell sheepishly returned to his 193-foot minnow. 'I prefer ours,' Hussainy told her depressed host. 'It's cosy.'

One billionaire's fantasy began before Cowell awoke. Rupert Murdoch stopped by *Slipstream* on his tender delivering that morning's newspapers, published by News International in Britain, America and Australia. They had been reproduced on a printing press installed on Murdoch's yacht. 'The world's most expensive newspaper boy,' Stuart Rose had quipped, digging for a coin to tip the deliverer.

The surreal party was capped by an evening game of Trivial Pursuit between the guests on Dunstone's and Cowell's yachts. As the tension rose, the game, dubbed 'public school versus showbiz', required Rebekah Brooks, acting as quiz master, to mediate between the screaming contestants. At one game each, the final game would be decided by whether the Dunstone team could name the composer of the *Pink Panther* film score. The entrepreneur was stumped, while Cowell was bursting.

'I know,' shouted Cowell. 'Give up.' But at the very last moment, one of Dunstone's team took a wild gamble: 'Henry Mancini?' Cowell was devastated as Brooks declared Dunstone's team the winners.

Realising the pleasure to be had from owning a boat, Cowell regretted depositing £17 million for a house to be built on a prime site adjoining the Four Seasons hotel in Barbados. His neighbours would be Lucian Grainge and Andrew Lloyd Webber, who had recently criticised Cowell's programmes. 'We nurture, we don't torture,' Lloyd Webber had said, attacking 'Cowell's gimmicks'. A few days later, he had apologised. Out of Cowell's circle of super-rich friends, only Philip Green had refused to invest in developer Robin Paterson's scheme. 'I don't like the look of it,' he had said. Cowell and other investors would complain that they lost a lot of their money.

During that voyage, Cowell's relationship with Hussainy intensified. For the first time, their relationship was no longer clandestine. The furtiveness of their meetings in Los Angeles was abandoned and, in his usual way, Cowell became, his friends noticed, 'hot and heavy'. Content to listen for hours to Cowell's agonised monologues about his plans, disputes and confessions, Hussainy's sympathetic responses drew the two closer together. 'She makes me happy,' he thought to himself, especially when she ran around the bedroom in her exquisite lingerie. 'She's sexy and she's great,' he told his friends on the yacht as he flirted endlessly with her.

The big hiccup occurred during a conversation on the trip about their future. If he refused to commit himself, Hussainy intimated, she might end up accepting an offer from another person to whom she had become close. To his surprise, Hussainy was suggesting that he had a rival. Seizing her mobile phone, he read messages confirming the existence of another relationship.

Cowell would interpret that scene as banter or 'winding each other up', but others believed that he was angry. In any event, momentarily he was no longer genial. To his friends, he appeared unusually vulnerable as he reassessed his position. He spoke to his closest women friends about his fears. They were puzzled by his infatuation and equally bewildered that Hussainy, for no reason, appeared to regard them as enemies. But Cowell, his friends knew, preferred simple, good-looking women who indulged him and enjoyed 'fun'.

The attractions of Cowell for Hussainy were obvious, and she counted her blessings. He possessed enough money to provide luxury for the rest of their combined lives, and he planned to have even more. For his part, fearing that she could leave, he had persuaded himself that Hussainy's presence during the next stage of his life would be ideal.

Introducing *The X Factor* to America meant that he would

centre his life in Los Angeles rather than London. 'I like Los Angeles because of its positivity,' he told Hussainy. 'I like driving everywhere with the hood down in the sunshine in my Bugatti or Bentley, with girls waving at me.' The shouts from strangers on the pavements and the inviting stares from wannabe starlets – even Los Angeles's dippy, self-obsessed airheads – were irresistible. 'I like the architecture and the great people around me for the shows and hosting great dinner parties for fourteen or sixteen people. I have to pinch myself as I drive into the Fox studios.'

In the near future, he would also use a Ferrari being assembled in Italy. The last Ferrari he had driven, on loan from a dealer in London, had ended up in a ditch in the Oxfordshire countryside, the casualty of a reckless reversing manoeuvre. Forsaking London's miserable weather would be a pleasure and he could rebuild North Palm Drive to live and work in the fresh air. The downside was the city's unfriendliness. Strangely, although he was one of the city's most famous stars, he had few genuine friendships. Other than Paul McKenna and Randy Jackson, there were no men he counted as close pals other than Maurice Veronique, a friend from Windsor Technical College, but even they rarely spoke. His friendships with women, however, were special. Besides Terri Seymour, Sinitta and Jackie St Clair, he leaned on Kelly Bergantz and Lauren Silverman. Late at night, he spoke animatedly and honestly about his life and loves knowing that he could rely on their discreet candour. Mezhgan Hussainy could join the stable. She suited his criteria: tall, dusky, fun-loving and, most importantly, tolerant of his needs. She was, in sum, a true friend upon whom he could rely.

His most basic requirement was relief from a niggling fear of loneliness. Although constantly surrounded by people and compelled to resist the pressure from others demanding his attention, he was sentimental about his parents' happy marriage and half wanted the same. So far, he had chosen women for fun rather than the intimacy of sharing his life. His success while pursuing his specific goals had depended upon freedom from girlfriends' interference. But now, on the eve of establishing a global empire, he was unusually depressed. Life on *American Idol* had been oppressive. Numbness had replaced his normal excitement. Lacking drive, he was at best on autopilot, relying on Hussainy for comfort.

On his return from the Caribbean, Cowell's anxiety reached a new peak. On 11 January 2010, he was due to appear at the Pasadena Civic centre for the start of his final *Idol* season. The media were accurately speculating that Cowell would leave the show, and Fox was under pressure to make a public statement. Negotiations for *The X Factor* USA had been complicated, especially obtaining from Fox guarantees that the programme's unique features, including the judges' mentoring, the wider age range of the competitors and huge audiences at the auditions, would not be adopted by *American Idol*.

Cowell's anger with Fuller had not abated. On the one hand, as he told Claudia Rosencrantz, he had sent a letter of condolence to Fuller after his mother's death. In telling the story, Cowell explained his horror of any mother's death. Rosencrantz was impressed. Considering how Cowell hated Fuller, his sentiments showed the way his good nature overcame his deep resentment. But those sentiments and the ones he had expressed at his birthday party of friendship had disappeared. Now, he was fulminating to Fox's producers about Fuller's treachery. To the incredulous, Cowell explained, 'I was in the mood at the party but not any more.'

As he drove from North Palm Drive down Santa Monica Boulevard towards Pasadena for the *Idol* presentation, his lawyer called.

'Where are you?' he asked.

'Highland,' replied Cowell. 'I've just left.'

'Do a U-turn and go back,' ordered the lawyer. 'The contract's not finalised.' The last-minute hitch was Fox's insistence on owning all of *The X Factor* USA's digital rights. Cowell wanted a 50 per cent share.

'Simon's turned round,' his lawyer told Fox chief Peter Rice.

'OK, fifty–fifty,' agreed Rice.

'Do another U-turn and get down to Pasadena as fast as you can,' Cowell was told.

Just after midday, Cowell appeared on the stage. The atmosphere in the hall, he sensed, was bad. 'There's been a lot of speculation,' he began, knowing every word was being carefully scrutinised by journalists in the building, 'partly because we didn't have a contract agreement. We reached an agreement formally at about half past eleven this morning.' *The X Factor* USA, he announced, would launch in 2011, and he would be leaving *American Idol* in May. 'I was offered a lot of money to stay on but I wanted to do something different. I wanted a new challenge.'

The perceptive among the audience understood that Cowell was establishing his own media empire and had declared war against Fuller. None, however, grasped the extent of Cowell's ambitions. He would be satisfied with nothing less than Syco matching Aaron Spelling's corporation as Hollywood's foremost entertainment producer.

Thereafter, he did little to conceal his irascible boredom on *Idol*. In what he anticipated would be a poor season, he even criticised good performers, exceeding his own vitriol by describing one contestant in Orlando as singing 'like a lawnmower' and watching bemused while his angry victim was forcibly removed from the stage in handcuffs.

Four weeks later, he was back in London to record *Britain's Got Talent*. Coincidentally, St Valentine's Day was approaching.

Cowell's attitude to marriage had not changed since he had broken up with Louise Payne nine years earlier. Marriage, he had often repeated, was an 'outdated contract. The truth is you get married and in a year or two they clean you out.' But the prospect of bachelor life was no longer so appealing, especially if he could find a woman who, while independent in her own right, was not too independent of him. 'You want someone who's not needy' was the reassuring summary of one of his female confidantes. 'Someone who's feisty and challenges you, but who's not too independent and doesn't blow smoke up your ass.' There was, he believed, little time to lose.

Vitamin injections, special fruits, intravenous drips, piles of pills, Botox, massages, dyes, chest waxing, tooth caps and cosmetic surgery had limited the evidence of ageing, but passing the fifty-year mark had made a bigger difference than Cowell had anticipated. The milestone had stirred unusual restlessness, aggravated by the relief of leaving *American Idol* and risking his career on the successful launch of *The X Factor* in the US. During those tense weeks he had relied on Hussainy in order to preserve his sanity. His hunger for change had been sated, at a cost, but now he felt liberated and, most importantly, happy again. The permanent cure, he suspected, was not only marriage but parenthood. In his search to replicate his parents' happiness, he admitted to himself, 'I need to have little Simons running around. Now is the last moment for children or it will be too late.' Without confiding in anyone, he took a momentous decision.

At 10 p.m. on 14 February – St Valentine's Day – he was in his bedroom in his London home with Hussainy. Days earlier, during the *Britain's Got Talent* auditions, the manager of Graff, the Bond Street jewellers, had brought six engagement rings for Cowell to see. He had chosen a rectangular six-carat diamond set in platinum costing £250,000. 'I was happy and I wanted her to be surprised,' explained one of Hollywood's eligible bachelors, who enjoyed boasting about his own selfishness. While he lay in bed with Hussainy, he got up, collected the ring from his dressing room and proposed marriage.

'Will you marry me?'

'Oh, yes,' she replied, thrilled. 'Yes, yes.'

The following evening, Julie Cowell arrived as usual to stay in his Holland Park home. Although he had occasionally become impatient listening to her complaints, they remained close. Their love did not extend to Cowell discussing his girlfriends with her, and he later denied that his life-changing decision had been influenced by his mother.

'I've got engaged,' Cowell told her.

'Have you bought a ring?' Julie asked suspiciously.

'I've bought the ring and I've given it to her. And I'm really going to get married.'

'I'm so delighted,' gasped Julie, relieved that her son had finally decided to 'settle down'. The ceremony, she imagined, would be held within months in Los Angeles, Barbados or Brighton, and more grandchildren would follow. Two days later, Cowell began telephoning friends.

'I've proposed,' Cowell told Lauren Silverman.

'Proposed what?' asked his best friend in New York.

'To marry Mezhgan.'

There was a brief pause. Silverman was 'completely flabbergasted'. Even Cowell's close friend had not 'seen it coming'.

'Congratulations,' she said, with little conviction but not betraying her fears. At the end of the call, she told her husband Andrew, 'The whole thing is wrong.'

'Guess what?' Cowell asked another female confidante before revealing his engagement. Uniformly, all their congratulations were somewhat contrived. None could quite understand. 'I feel I'm losing a friend,' sighed another of his holiday companions.

Julie Cowell's doubts began even while her son was telephoning with the news. Unlike Terri Seymour, Hussainy appeared to make only limited attempts to draw closer to Cowell's family and, bewilderingly, she never appeared before three o'clock in the afternoon. 'What are you doing up there?' Julie would ask. Her future daughter-in-law's replies provoked Julie to suspect peculiar habits caused possibly by jet lag. 'She's the only American I've ever met', she observed, 'who comes to London and doesn't want to see Buckingham Palace and the Tower of London.' On another day, Julie exclaimed, 'She doesn't seem to be interested in anything.' She said nothing to her son about her concerns. His happiness was paramount and she assumed the best.

In public, Julie played the game: 'Turning fifty has changed him. I'm delighted that he's finally settled down.' She also blessed the bride: 'She's a lovely woman, she's got a great personality and is perfect for him.' Her son would be a 'great dad' to their children.

Excited and in love, Cowell and his fiancée returned together to Los Angeles on a private jet and travelled on to meet her parents in Mill Harbor for their blessing. At the end of that day, Cowell was convinced that he had found the perfect wife from an ideal family. He called Terri Seymour. 'It's because you're fifty, isn't it?' she asked. 'Yes, and why not?' he replied, adding, 'We'll see what happens.' Meanwhile, Hussainy energetically summoned Los Angeles's wedding experts to arrange her celebrity nuptials.

The event deserved a momentous publicity blast to prove there were no doubts. 'She's very special,' Cowell told Piers Morgan on his nightly CNN television show in late February. 'You know when you've found someone very special. I'm smitten – I think she's "the one".' In later interviews, he mentioned how she admired his performance in bed, which he rated as nine out of ten. 'She makes me look so handsome,' he said of the make-up artist who had by now moved into North Palm Drive. In anticipation of marriage and children, Cowell called Brian Biglin, the architect. The new extension was to be made even larger.

Six weeks later, the doubts began. In April, Julie Cowell arrived to stay for a week in North Palm Drive. Her son's departure from *American Idol*, she discovered, had created a crisis between Cowell and some of the Fox producers. Every night he returned home late for dinner and, to Julie's distress, Mezhgan Hussainy was angry. 'Don't say anything,' she advised Hussainy on the third night. 'When he comes in, just give him a kiss and smile and say, "Hi, I missed you." Just don't nag him.'

Instead, Cowell's arrival sparked a barrage of abuse. 'You're late. I thought you'd be here by now,' shouted Hussainy.

Cowell's solution was to find himself some 'space'. Sitting in the garden, he listened to music, smoked a Kool and drank a beer, interrupted only by texts and telephone calls.

'What are you doing?' Hussainy asked repeatedly.

Hussainy, he realised, was not a feisty woman after all. She was suffocating him. She did not understand that she could neither change nor control him.

'The tension was horrendous,' recalled Julie. 'The way Mezhgan behaved made my stomach churn.'

As they sat down for dinner, Cowell's mobile rang.

'Who is it?' asked Hussainy in a fiery tone. 'Who are you texting now?'

A violent argument erupted. Hussainy got up, screamed abuse, ran upstairs and slammed the bedroom door.

'Charming,' said Julie.

'Sit down,' Cowell told his mother. 'We'll eat alone.'

'Something's wrong here, Simon. It's not what we thought. I was very happy and now I'm not.'

'There's a problem,' agreed Cowell.

Hussainy, they concluded after lengthy analysis, had clearly not understood that work was her fiancé's priority, and there was also a lack of trust.

Soon after Julie returned to London, the Silvermans arrived from New York. Hussainy, they realised, was clearly unhappy. 'There's a lot of tension,' Lauren noted. The regularisation of their relationship into a daily routine had exposed irreconcilable flaws. Neither the Silvermans nor Cowell could envisage a solution.

Cowell had reached a moment of truth. Late one night, he told Hussainy, 'I will always turn my back on you, and you won't like it. You have to understand that having a fling with me is different to living with me. Work is my mistress.' Eager for her lover's complete attention, Hussainy could not understand Cowell's mood as he switched off from her and focused on work. Unlike other men, he did not need to live with a soulmate. He needed and trusted her as a close friend, but living together had proved too difficult.

The impasse was interrupted by a telephone call from Rebekah Brooks in London. Britain was in the final stages of a general-election campaign, and Brooks was looking for famous personalities to endorse David Cameron's challenge to the Labour government in the *Sun*. The tabloid prided itself in determining the outcome of British elections, and Rupert Murdoch had switched allegiance from Gordon Brown to the Conservatives. Brooks's request placed Cowell in a difficult position. His commercial fate depended upon Murdoch and he was a natural Conservative, yet he had never openly declared his political allegiance. In fact, Cowell was so apolitical that he had never even voted in any election. However, ever since he had first met Gordon Brown at the Pride of Britain awards in 2007, he had grown to like the prime minister. Prompted by Piers Morgan, a Labour supporter, he had twice accepted Brown's dinner invitations in Downing Street and responded to his regular telephone calls seeking support for charities. His decisive participation in the appeal for the victims of 2010's earthquake in Haiti had produced a huge response and had been warmly praised by Brown.

'I felt he was a good man with a good heart and sincere,' said Cowell after they had 'done a lot of charity together'. Keen to garner star support for the prime minister's beleaguered administration, a Brown aide mentioned to the *Mirror* that Cowell might expect a knighthood after the election. Cowell felt there was every reason to believe the *Mirror*'s report. 'Sir Simon', he thought, 'has a wonderful resonance' and would irritate his critics. He also learned that Brown was sensitive about their relationship. Hours after he was seen in Westminster with David Cameron, Brown personally telephoned Cowell to check whether the Tories had sought his political endorsement. Reassured that the meeting related to a charity for hospices, Cowell got the impression that the prime minister's aide had repeated the suggestion of an honour.

In the week before the general election, the outcome had become uncertain. Every vote now counted in order to avoid a hung parliament. Hoping that Cowell could swing a few votes, Rebekah Brooks asked that he give a few quotes to a *Sun* journalist in support of the Tories. Assuming his words would be part of a long piece inside the newspaper, Cowell said from Los Angeles, 'I like Cameron. I trust him. He has substance and the stomach to navigate us through difficult times.'

On the eve of the election, he awoke to find the *Sun*'s front page covered by a long article, supposedly written by himself, urging *Sun* readers to vote Tory. 'Tomorrow's election must change Britain,' he 'wrote'. 'That endorsement lost me the knighthood which Brown would have given to me,' Cowell lamented. 'Sir Simon has a nice sound, although I would never use the title.'

At least Cameron, after becoming prime minister, responded to Cowell's plea for an £11-million grant to the Chase hospice in Surrey.

Ten days later, Cowell celebrated the final *American Idol* programme: 'It was my last season and everyone was in an uncomfortable position. I just wanted the series to end.' The sour mood was aggravated by Ryan Seacrest.

A few days earlier, Seacrest had been asked in a TV interview how Cowell would cope with marriage. 'I hope that if they are building a life together,' replied Seacrest, 'there aren't too many mirrors around to distract him from his girlfriend. He's so self-centred.' Asked to identify his wedding present, Seacrest replied, 'My presence. No, I'm teasing. I don't know that there is a wedding.'

Seacrest's perception was followed by his ridicule of Cowell's sexuality live on *Idol*. 'Back off,' Cowell warned later. 'You're trying to set me up.'

On the penultimate programme, Seacrest had again bantered on air about Cowell being in the closet.

'You crossed the line,' spat Cowell as the opening titles began rolling for the final show on 26 May 2010.

'What will you do?' hissed Seacrest sheepishly. 'You'll soon see,' threatened Cowell. 'I'll do it live.' As the programme started, Cowell jumped in and created what he called 'an awkward moment', telling Seacrest to 'forever stay out of my space'.

Cowell's relief as the credits rolled at the end of nine seasons was dizzying. 'It's been a blast,' he told the theatre audience. 'I want to thank you from the bottom of my heart for the support, the fun and your sense of humour.' Cowell felt bullish as everyone headed for the party at the Mondrian hotel on Sunset Boulevard.

Without him, he expected *Idol* to decline, an unspoken

opinion shared by Simon Fuller, who looked edgy when they met at the party. Fuller disliked Cowell's life in the spotlight, always encouraging dramas which were detached from reality. Nevertheless, his own pretence of staying in the shadows was somewhat contrived: Julian Henry, his personal publicist, employed more than ten people to cultivate his image.

Visitors to Fuller's headquarters on Sunset Boulevard – formerly *Playboy*'s main offices – were regaled by Fuller's description of his global interests in TV, fashion, film and the Internet. Proud of his 'seven homes on four continents', he encouraged his profilers to describe him as the softly spoken but ruthless negotiator with over one hundred staff, compared to Syco's eleven employees. In a recently published book called *American Idol*, written with Fuller's help, he was portrayed as the cool power broker mobbed by Hollywood's top agents, who were desperate to get world-famous artists adopted by his international empire. By comparison, Fuller told an American newspaper, Susan Boyle was 'a freak'. Cowell was personified as the fiercely ambitious underdog intent on imitating Fuller's trajectory.

Most people who spotted the two men chatting at the party that night would have believed that they had reached an armistice, but a subtle tension still plagued their relationship. Only one curious bystander overheard the heartfelt spleen Cowell unleashed on Fuller: 'All I've done – *Britain's Got Talent*, *The X Factor* and much more – is revenge for what you did to me. And there's much more to come.' Fuller stared at him, speechless. It was a defining moment. Fuller's own vulnerability was evident. An early draft of the *Hollywood Reporter*'s 'Power List' had for the first time placed Cowell ahead of Fuller. However, thanks to representations on his behalf, Fuller's occupation had been recategorised and the embarrassment avoided. A new reality was emerging, as Cowell was generating considerably more revenue than Fuller, not least because Fuller's collaboration with Bob Sillerman had failed to fulfil its original billing.

In theory, their plan to buy the intellectual property rights of famous icons was inspired. On the basis that 'content is king', they planned to unlock the artists' 'brand value' to market a catalogue of images and sounds. CKX had bought an 80 per cent stake in Muhammad Ali's name and image and a major interest in Elvis Presley's estate. There were plans to acquire Marilyn Monroe's image and to buy the 'name' and music catalogues of Elton John and Rod Stewart. Unexpected problems, however, had arisen. Living stars resisted Fuller's offers for their estates because CKX, as a public company, would be compelled to disclose their financial secrets. Fuller also discovered that the number of iconic stars amenable to his plan had been exaggerated. Instead of a flow of major acquisitions, enhanced by a network of production houses, boosting CKX's share value, the corporation's ambitions had withered since 2005.

Although Fuller's original puff about a master strategy was unrealised, Sillerman had not lost out. Thanks to *Idol*'s success, 19 Entertainment's profits had doubled, justifying his original risk. Over forty countries had bought the format, and Fuller had personally maintained its quality. However, there was nothing to buy with the cash Sillerman was accumulating. At the heart of his dilemma was showbiz's immutable teaser: was Fuller a one-trick pony?

Fuller's only new invention was *If I Can Dream*, a series sponsored by Pepsi and Ford to be shown on insignificant TV stations across the US. Contestants living together in a house wired with fifty-six cameras would be shown trying to excel at their various specialities. However, after a stuttering start, the show would be abruptly halted in October 2010. His ambition to build an empire was frustrated by the absence of another big idea.

Fuller's parallel strategy, based within XIX, his new

corporation, was to become a super-agent for stars. His stable was limited to Andy Murray, the Scottish tennis player still awaiting his first major title; the Beckhams, the iconic but fading footballer and his thrusting wife; and Lewis Hamilton, the frustrated Formula One driver. To understand Hamilton's business Fuller had visited Bernie Ecclestone, the Formula One supremo, but the meeting had been unexpectedly curtailed. 'I'm not wasting my time teaching you about Formula One,' Ecclestone had said, bidding his visitor farewell. Fuller would fail to produce a single new endorsement for Hamilton.

In music, he had done little better. Over the previous ten years, he had failed to pitch any idea with the instant appeal of *Pop Idol* successfully. By contrast, Cowell, as even ITV boss Paul Jackson acknowledged, remained 'a brilliant creative producer'.

Days after the *American Idol* party, Fuller unveiled his new strategy: to buy CKX and recover ownership of *Idol*. He had resigned from CKX in January but was retained as a consultant for *American Idol* and another reality show, *So You Think You Can Dance*, for which he received 10 per cent of the net profits, an annual fee of $1.5 million and an advance of $5 million. His departure followed his failed attempt in 2009 to buy the corporation for $560 million. In May 2010, after Sillerman had also resigned, Fuller renewed his bid, offering $600 million. 'You don't mess with Sillerman,' observed Cowell, calling him 'a friend, a class guy'. After Fuller's offer was again rejected, Sillerman, who owned just over 20 per cent of the shares, made a counter-bid which, amid controversial media coverage, also failed. Cowell identified Sillerman as a possible future purchaser of Syco.

Eventually, after cutting their overheads, CKX would be sold for $500 million to Apollo, a private-equity investor based in New York. In Cowell's opinion, Fuller was bruised. Without a new idea, his rival risked being beached. Although Fuller claimed to be worth $340 million, the source of the additional

$200 million since the sale of 19 Entertainment was unclear, not least because of the losses that had been incurred.

By contrast, in what Paul Jackson described as 'a dick-measuring contest', Cowell's empire was growing. Unlike Fuller, Cowell was churning out ideas. Twenty-six countries had bought the *X Factor* format and over forty had bought the *Got Talent* programme format. Half the income went directly to Cowell, and he earned royalties from all Sony's record sales and his personal endorsements.

His dominance could no longer be ignored. At the annual BAFTA ceremony in May, Britain's film and television industry presented a 'special award' to Cowell. Walking onto the stage without a planned speech, he impulsively thanked the 'person who had made applause and cheers possible. This is long overdue,' and named Claudia Rosencrantz as the begetter of his good fortune. She was not in the theatre. His critics, however, seated in front of him, questioned whether the Susan Boyle phenomenon could be repeated. His success in attracting 19.2 million viewers had embarrassed the BBC into pledging to spend more money to recapture viewers from ITV. Cowell's critics willed the corporation to succeed.

Many doubted whether his producers could find sufficient new talent to generate gossip around the water coolers. Although ITV had invested another million pounds to improve the stage design, the knockers declared, 'The talent pool is dry.' Even Cowell looked bored watching a burping accounts clerk, a retired teacher impersonating a gibbon and a woman force-feeding a parrot with mashed potato. Rolling his eyes, he showed little enthusiasm about another dancing dog and four flabby naked men, alias The Cheeky Boys, holding balloons over their manhood. 'It was what it was,' he said dismissively and agreed that 'The pond has been fished dry.' Yet, thanks to Ant and Dec oozing charm and the skilful editing of contestants 'wanting it' and parading their 'journey', 14 million viewers watched a non-entity win the final.

Cowell had flown to London alone, having decided not to invite his fiancée. To his closest friends he admitted, 'I've made a big mistake.' In his Los Angeles home, they noticed, he had become unusually silent, as if trapped and uncertain how to escape. Strangely for the self-confident performer, he begged them not to leave him alone in his house with his fiancée. 'A light seems to have gone out,' thought Lauren Silverman. 'He's walking on eggshells.'

In London, Cowell reflected on his fate. He was in the midst of his biggest challenge – launching *The X Factor* in America and refreshing the British version. London was a sanctuary from his emotional stress but, professionally, the hecklers were voicing familiar doubts about the revival of *The X Factor* in Britain. Starting in August, the show would inevitably dominate the autumn schedules, but the legacy of 2009 raised doubts. Since December, the only release by Joe McElderry, the risible winner, had been a press announcement about his sexuality. His fate mirrored the antics of previous contestants who had been given contracts. Even Jedward had been dropped by Sony, although they still became millionaires. The public's imagination had been captured by dance, rap and R&B artists and Lady Gaga, who did not appear on *The X Factor*, but Cowell's defence was defiant: 'Few new artists are signed by labels. We've done more good for the music business by turning up interest in music among the young.' The previous Christmas, Cowell had pledged, 'A lot of things are going to change.' Now, he knew, everyone would scrutinise the programme's reinvention.

Cowell's publicists promised a revolution. Sob stories were curbed, 'journeys' were outlawed, some songs were banned and contestants were better groomed. But the cynics smelled desperation. There was a 'crisis' because Dannii Minogue was temporarily absent on maternity leave, Cheryl Cole had fallen sick with malaria and Louis Walsh had been 'fired' for appearing on a 'stupid TV programme' and then rehired after giving 'a grovelling apology'. The drama among the early contestants was predictably tawdry and, compounding the frustrations, Cowell had still not signed a new contract with ITV. On Cowell's behalf, Philip Green was demanding a three-year agreement, with an additional £6 million, but with no commitment that Cowell would appear on the programmes; and an extra £3 million for the programme budget, with a proviso that ITV could cancel the programme if ratings fell.

Peter Fincham's leverage for ITV over Cowell was limited. Huge crowds had appeared for the first *X Factor* auditions in Birmingham; 10,000 hopefuls had queued for auditions in Dublin, which had been abandoned by Cowell in 2006; and nearly 20,000 fans had watched the auditions at the O2 arena in London. During the intervals, Syco had sold merchandise, including programmes, the *X Factor* magazine, glitter caps, foam-rubber hands, music downloads and tickets for the *X Factor* national concert tour. The juggernaut was irresistible. Fincham agreed a £100-million deal for *The X Factor* and *Britain's Got Talent*, including ITV showing the American versions of both shows. Each *X Factor* show on Saturdays and Sundays would be extended to two hours, with ITV expecting to sell a thirty-second advertising slot for £150,000. The network's loss was Cowell's refusal to appear in Britain. 'I never begged him to stay,' Fincham would say. 'We calculated that *The X Factor* would work without Simon.'

To justify the package, Cowell promised new twists to produce a genuine star. He was certain one would emerge. The 'dry pool' argument was, he thought, 'rubbish'. Every year, more teenagers emerged with ambitions to become singers, but as a safeguard he dispatched talent seekers to the usual venues and decided to form a new group from the contestants. That was one advantage of running *The X Factor*: record producers risked a fortune to create boy bands, never certain of the result; Cowell's lucrative bonus was to be able to do the same cost-free. 'On the spur of the moment' he had spotted five young boys who had entered the competition individually and put them together as a group. 'Think of a name for yourselves,' Cowell told them. 'One Direction,' they eventually replied.

Once his scheme was publicised, the fate of his former groups was excavated. Michelle Barber, a survivor of Girl Thing, recalled how Cowell 'dumped us. Simon just vanished in a puff of smoke.' And, although Il Divo had sold 40 million albums since 2003, their only performances in 2009 had been in Abu Dhabi, Lebanon and Vietnam. One Direction risked the same fate, predicted the critics, forgetting that their mockery goaded Cowell to wreak revenge. 'Embrace the madness' was his slogan. Privately, he called it 'playing with my toys'.

The chemistry of the judging panel was as inflammable as that previously engineered between Dannii Minogue and Sharon Osbourne. 'He's gone slightly mad this year,' Cheryl Cole told a journalist. 'He definitely has a glint in his eye, and it's spreading. His influence on people has made them crazy.' Sitting next to Cowell on the show, his arm firmly around her, the singer's personality had been transformed as Cowell dismissed Louis Walsh and Minogue with disdain. His emotions were sparked. 'Cheryl is complex, and I don't understand her,' he said with honest awe. 'She is distrustful of others, but she does trust me.'

As the arguments during the programme increased, Cole frequently appeared in Cowell's dressing room. He was mesmerised: 'She came in dressed in her tracksuit and slippers, dropped her eyes and played the soulful victim to get around me. She did play me.' With the roles reversed, Cowell was vulnerable: 'When she walked over, I felt I was the mouse with a beautiful cat. I adored her. And as she got her own way, it drove Louis mad.'

'These girls are actresses,' Walsh warned Cowell. 'They'll get you to do what they want.' Walsh, Cowell scoffed, failed to understand the wonders of an 'intriguing and complex' woman.

'I would have liked an affair with Cheryl, but she was uninterested,' he admitted in 2011. 'She'd broken up with Ashley, and her boyfriend lived in Los Angeles.' That, of course, was no barrier to a man who still adored the chase, especially for a woman he deemed to be intriguing. Others would interpret her mournful silences as evidence of a vapid woman with nothing to say, but that conclusion would be rebutted by her shimmering performances on air.

During the programmes, Cowell's affections changed by the hour. In the battle between himself and the others about the fate of their acts, and especially One Direction, he accused Walsh of being 'nasty' and 'unpleasant', before unexpectedly swinging against Cole: 'You've not really got the hang of it this year, have you, pet?' Having generated newspaper coverage about the judges' histrionics and recrimination, he then fostered a barrage of abuse from Walsh and Cole and stormed from the studio. In the national conversation, the tears and tantrums appeared spontaneous, but others saw 'The triumph of ersatz working-class culture over real culture. We are all Cowell's children now.'

The timing was perfect for Mike Darnell and other Fox executives to visit London. Knowing the history of those who had criticised Fox for staging an identical rival to America's most popular show – especially Simon Fuller – Cowell had urged Darnell, 'You have to taste *The X Factor* to see the difference.' Darnell was coming to watch the programme, discuss Fox's requirements for the American version and sign off on the budget. Cowell was nervous about their forty-eight-hour visit.

'Oh Christ, what a day,' Cowell wailed on the morning of their arrival. 'Fix Factor' had dominated the tabloid headlines that morning. 'They always say it's fixed, but why choose today?' he said. The test was which genius would emerge on top – Cowell or Fuller?

At least Fuller had recently changed his tune, describing *Idol* as a boxing match to *The X Factor*'s wrestling bout. 'I like wrestling,' Cowell told Darnell in Sony's west London offices. 'We're a fun jungle compared to *Idol*'s manicured, polished, protected show where the performances are nice and the pressure is gentle. It's the purity of a meadow versus a showbiz jungle.'

On Cowell's agenda was persuading Darnell to hire Cheryl Cole. 'I've seen the amazing reaction when she walks into an arena,' he told Darnell. Ever since her 'spectacular' solo performance on *The X Factor* in 2009, Cowell had coached his protégée. 'I want to make Cheryl a star,' he said.

Six weeks earlier, Cole had met Darnell and FremantleMedia's Cécile Frot-Coutaz at Cowell's office in Beverly Hills. To Cowell's delight, the pop icon had executed a flawless performance, combining amusing banter and professional maturity. Darnell had become infatuated and, after watching some DVDs, excitedly texted Cowell about 'this new girl', brushing aside her anonymity in the US. The only shadow was Cole's decision to hire will.i.am, a member of the Black Eyed Peas, as her agent. Cowell was puzzled but said nothing.

On the eve of Darnell's arrival, Cole had been on edge. Excited by the prospect of working in Los Angeles, she imagined that with Cowell by her side there would be little difference to appearing in Britain. Nothing was said about the cultural differences, especially America's more demanding audiences. 'She looks amazing and is amazing,' thought Cowell as he watched the singer 'parade her assets in front of Darnell'.

Cole targeted a man whose eyeline was level with her breasts. 'She's in top form and Mike [Darnell] has been blown away,' concluded Cowell. The former actor had already rationalised Fox's dilemma of staging both *American Idol* and *The X Factor* USA: 'Whichever programme wins, Fox wins,' he thought. Competition appealed to Darnell. By the end of the visit, Joe Earley, Fox's head of marketing, was equally excited and the network's boss, Peter Rice, whom Cowell had originally suspected, had become an ally.

The dinner for twelve people at the China Tang restaurant in the Dorchester hotel sealed the relationships, although there was one casualty: Ellis Watson, the new chief executive of Syco. Appointed on Piers Morgan's suggestion after their long relationship at the *Mirror*, Watson had argued with Philip Green during the dinner. He sealed his fate when, at the end of the meal, he idly spun the lazy Susan in the centre of the table, causing a lump of ice cream to spin off a bowl, land on Green's face and fall onto his suit. 'I think we'll get the bill,' said Green, with Darnell's warm farewell confirming that Cowell's future in America had been secured on his terms.

The following morning, Watson's removal was demanded by Ged Doherty, chairman of Sony Music in Britain. Watson, it was politely announced, had 'left for family reasons', but insiders spoke about a man unable to cope with competing interests and personalities. His replacement was Charlie Garland, who until 2006 had been employed in the same position by Simon Fuller. In the music industry's small world, Garland had been the best man at RCA chief Jeremy Marsh's wedding. The bloodshed did not stop there. Sony Music CEO Rolf Schmidt-Holtz retired and his replacement, Doug Morris, the seventy-two-year-old head of Universal Music, was urged to reverse Schmidt-Holtz's 'dead hand' and improve Sony's music output. Fashioned as 'The Godfather', Cowell hailed Morris as 'the smartest man in the world and a genius. He knows how to make records. There's no bullshit.' Shortly after, Morris fired Ged Doherty.

Survival in the music industry required luck, talent, networking skills and brazenness. Those with only three of the four qualities would inevitably fail. To climb to the very top like Cowell also required single-mindedness, selfishness and a sprinkling of stardust. BAFTA's acknowledgement of his uniqueness was replicated in November in New York, where Rupert Murdoch presented Cowell with an International Emmy Founders Award for having 'reshaped twenty-first-century television and music around the world'. Posing for the photographers, Cowell clutched Mezhgan Hussainy's hand. He had invited her to come to witness his success and, at the same time, to quash rumours of a split. In New York, the embarrassed woman found his lack of commitment hard. 'We're still engaged,' she told a journalist, adding, without anticipating the reaction, 'as far as I know'.

Cowell believed their relationship was irreconcilable, but she was unpersuaded even after she was sent alone from London to Los Angeles in early summer. A few weeks later, to the surprise of the holidaying Cowell and his usual gang of friends, she appeared in the south of France to join them aboard *Slipstream*. The terrible tension, observed a member of the crew, was aggravated by Hussainy remaining locked in her cabin for long periods, emerging only to engage in arguments. 'Simon feels guilty,' Lauren Silverman and Kelly Bergantz agreed. Hussainy's wedding plans were put on hold.

There was a perfunctory kiss as the couple parted, she to return to Los Angeles and he to London for *The X Factor*. As he suspected, during the series no potential star emerged, but the competition between Rebecca Ferguson and Matt Cardle, a decorator, was tight. Neither would be worth promoting, he thought. The certain commercial victor was One Direction. Nevertheless, building on the tabloid frenzy about the judges' warfare, ITV's publicity campaign attracted 19.4 million viewers – one-third of Britain's population and 60 per cent of the TV audience – to witness Cardle's narrow victory amid strobing lights, dry ice, fireworks, confetti and raunchy dancers. In truth, everyone was a winner. However, Cowell calculated that Cardle's glory would be short-lived, while he could make money out of Cardle's fellow contestants Cher Lloyd, Rebecca Ferguson and One Direction within a year. The principal questions posed by the tabloids were which girl was sleeping with Cardle and whether Cowell or *Strictly Come Dancing* host Bruce Forsyth would receive a knighthood in the New Year Honours list. The disappointing silence about the award of an honour registered after Christmas, as Cowell and his friends darted between the Grenadines, Mustique and St Barts for three weeks aboard *Slipstream*. Hussainy, in a bad mood, stayed for two of them.

The other irritation was spread by Nigel Lythgoe. Cowell's departure had eased the Briton's return as *American Idol*'s producer. In a carefully placed interview while filming the auditions for the next series, he had observed that *Idol* was a 'lighter' place with a happier atmosphere since Cowell had quit. Incensed, Cowell telephoned Lythgoe. 'Nigel, even if you feel that way, you've got to remember that I put nine years of my life into that show and that was the reason it became such a hit. You're unprofessional, disrespectful and it's not what you should be doing as a human being and as a producer. It's unnecessary, so just stop it.'

The tension before the outbreak of war was irrepressible. Cowell's taste for revenge had never felt more acute, and Lythgoe and Fuller shared his sentiments.

15

8 May 2011

After a tortuous night, Simon Cowell awoke before midday on 8 May 2011 in a suite at the Peninsula hotel in Beverly Hills. *The X Factor* USA's first audition was due to begin that afternoon, and the previous days had been dominated by brinkmanship which had jeopardised the launch. To relieve the tension on the big day, he called for a masseuse and, while his breakfast was perfectly choreographed, read his text messages and watched cartoons.

Less than one mile away, Mezhgan Hussainy was awaiting his call. She had moved into Cole Place, his hilltop home, just before the builders had arrived at North Palm Drive. Inevitably, she had not been consulted about the plans for the house's latest expansion – this time to 15,000 square feet. Cowell, she now understood, forbade any interference in his life, but his need for uncomplicated relationships was being compromised by the weary baggage of an uncomprehending woman. Her requests for attention and refusal to acquiesce peacefully to her total exclusion quite naturally sparked tumultuous arguments. Amid tears, she had demanded a date for their wedding. Eventually, feeling unusually guilt-ridden, Cowell admitted that he was reneging on his promise and moved to the Peninsula 'to have time without her'. If there was a choice between power, sex and money, Cowell's priority was power.

Secure in his 'space', Cowell knew precisely how he would extricate himself. His plan was, with the best of intentions, to 'bring Mezhgan to the same relationship I have with Terri'. In other words, they would not sleep together but would remain the very best of friends. His idea was to 'let things happen naturally and make sure she felt secure'. To protect himself from embarrassment and his fiancée from misery, he pledged to provide all her material needs: 'I'd put her in the public eye and attracted a lot of attention to her. I had to be sensitive about her position and I didn't want to hurt her family, with whom I had become close.'

In Cowell's opinion, he bore a responsibility to provide the luxury to which she had become accustomed. To that end, he promised to transfer the ownership of his $8-million hilltop house in Beverly Hills to her. She would laugh when he later joked, 'I've found the ideal place for you. I just drove past it.'

'I know what you're thinking,' she replied.

'Yes,' he laughed, 'Forest Lawn.' The cemetery in Hollywood Hills is a celebrities' favourite.

The loss of the $8-million house was, in Cowell's opinion, a price worth paying. Over the previous months, liberated from *American Idol* and now Hussainy, he had expunged his demons. 'You've weeded out the bad,' concluded one of his confidants. 'You've grown up a lot, let go of your fears and paranoia, and now you're really excited and happy again.'

'I know,' replied Cowell, 'this is going to be a great year.'

To assuage Hussainy's fear of humiliation, they agreed to conceal their separation. At the outset, the deception was not difficult. They met frequently because Cole Place was also his office; and, because she remained a talented artist, she was hired to apply his make-up for the auditions in Los Angeles. On that morning, she waited demurely, aware that over the previous twenty-four hours Cowell's threats to abandon his dream had reached a climax.

'Unless she's confirmed today, we're not filming,' Cowell had warned Cécile Frot-Coutaz. Thirty years of experience had encouraged him to raise the stakes. Having wagered his reputation on *The X Factor*'s success in America, he would not allow the FremantleMedia boss to exclude Paula Abdul from appearing as a fellow judge in the $100-million series.

Ever since Abdul had left *American Idol* three years earlier, Cowell had pledged to rescue her from the wilderness. 'I promised her that she would be on the new show,' he told Frot-Coutaz. Viewers, he told the French woman, had been besotted by their fiery relationship and would be excited by their reunion: 'I want to get back to those times. Stuff it. Give her a contract.'

'Do it with the three of you,' countered Frot-Coutaz, meaning that Cowell could start with the two other judges, Cheryl Cole and L. A. Reid, a famous New York-based music producer.

Frot-Coutaz did not believe that firing Abdul had been a mistake. She had disliked the hard-nosed bargaining games from an unreliable artist who on one occasion had been asleep while her make-up was being applied.

'No,' said Cowell, pulling emphatically on his cigarette. 'This deal can be done. Or else cancel the filming.'

In the intervening years, Cowell had regularly telephoned the singer to offer reassurance. Once Fox had bought *The X Factor*, his call was decisive: 'I need you on the show.' Loved for her vulnerability and empathy, Abdul was an essential ingredient.

'They're not keen on me,' sighed the diva. 'They don't want to go back to the old. They fear it'll be a retread. They're not negotiating.'

Cowell was adamant. The survivor of humiliation and hubris in showbiz's bitchy jungle trusted only his own judgement. To exact revenge on his foes, the odds needed to be stacked in his favour. Mike Darnell had been as adamantly in favour of Cheryl Cole as Cowell was for Abdul. The compromise, he told Darnell, was to hire both.

At the end of four hours of telephone conversations the previous day, squinting in the sunshine on the terrace of Cole

Place, Cowell stubbed out his cigarette, took a final sip of his tea flavoured with a slice of lemon, and drove his black convertible Rolls-Royce down the winding road to Santa Monica Boulevard. Less than a day before the first auditions, Abdul's fate still remained undecided.

Even in a hotel suite, Cowell's routine rarely changed. To relieve the tension, he enjoyed a steam bath followed by a massage and finally spaghetti bolognese, a favourite. The meal was interrupted by a telephone call. Darnell and Frot-Coutaz had capitulated: Paula Abdul would be given a contract. Frot-Coutaz would later say that she was never in any doubt a deal could be done with Abdul, but only on satisfactory financial terms.

Cowell was relieved. Aged fifty-one, he had asserted his primacy as a television mogul, a worthy successor to Aaron Spelling. His dream team was in place.

At lunchtime the following day, Cowell's stretch black Rolls-Royce Phantom was waiting outside the hotel. Polished every week, the limousine had been driven from a vault and sprayed with wax to increase the dazzle. Across Los Angeles, on the fringe of a college campus, over 4,000 excited Californians were queuing in the heat at the Galen Center. Amid Cowell's endless last-minute concerns, the most pressing were whether the audience would understand the process and his team's unconvincing assurances about the talent waiting to be auditioned.

He chose a white T-shirt, the second he had worn that morning, and tugged it hard at the bottom. He liked new T-shirts to appear slightly worn, and he would change twice more during that day. The last tweaks were honed to a soundbite intended for transmission across the country: 'We're here to find a star and give him or her $5 million, the richest prize in TV history. If we fail to find a star, we'll pack up and go home.'

To feed the media, Cowell would arrive last in the choreography of arrivals. Abdul was first. Perched on six-inch stilettos and wearing a light chiffon dress, her appearance provoked screams from the hundreds of women corralled behind barriers: 'Paula, we love you!' Chanting fans provide a celebrity's oxygen, and Abdul smiled with relief. 'America will get who I am,' beamed the survivor as she disappeared among twenty cameras. 'I'm thrilled, exhilarated – beyond exhilarated – and terrified,' she gushed. 'It's awkward and wonderful and beautiful all at the same time.' Then she headed into the vast convention centre. In synchrony, another limousine came to a halt by the barriers restraining over a hundred journalists.

Silence greeted the emergence of Cheryl Cole, the English icon whose megastardom owed so much to Cowell. 'She has been fantastic to work with,' Cowell had recently said. 'She is also a complete brat.' Unknown in the US, Cole had been persuaded by Cowell that her fortunes would soar on his new programme. Her first moments in front of the cameras challenged that promise. Dressed in excessively long purple flares designed by Diane von Furstenberg and a peach-coloured frilly shirt, her head was cocooned in a strangely over-egged hairstyle favoured, quipped an observer, by Chewbacca in *Star Wars*. Another suggested that she had mistakenly dressed for a night out at a Newcastle disco. 'I didn't have a contract until yesterday,' she volunteered to the press, confirming the last-minute chaos. Criticised in the media for being an unknown speaking in an incomprehensible accent, Cole also defied Hollywood's mantra for immaculate preening. 'I won't be changing my accent,' she replied in her soft Geordie lilt. 'I'd be crucified if I did. Americans will understand me.' Focus groups commissioned by Fox had confirmed that Cole's accent was not a barrier to success.

The third judge, L. A. Reid, arrived to no fanfare. Dressed smartly in a dark suit, white shirt and tie, the producer of the Island Def Jam label was famous for discovering Justin Bieber, the young global star, and producing Kanye West, Usher and

Rihanna. But as a 'face' he was unknown. *The X Factor* USA, he hoped, would also turn him into a celebrity. 'I was happy to get the call from Simon,' he said later. 'It was good for my career at that time.' He and Cowell had first met in 1999, at a BMG music conference at the Beverly Wilshire hotel. 'When I first saw Simon, I saw a star,' he swooned appropriately. Before Cowell's telephone call, Reid had criticised *The X Factor* as 'microwave stardom' that challenged his faith in nurturing talent. 'We've never produced a global artist,' Cowell had told Reid. 'Selection and mentoring have got better, but we've reached the end of improving people. We've got to find someone special.'

Like the other three judges, Reid had seen and heard thousands of aspiring and established singers. Instinctively he knew good from bad. He had been lured away from a lucrative contract with Universal by Cowell's promise of his own label within Sony and a share of the profits from their new stars. The world's best singers, both believed, were American.

To deter Reid's defection, at the last moment Lucian Grainge had offered the producer a place on *American Idol* and over $10 million. Cowell was shocked. Grainge, his old friend, had clearly forged an alliance with Simon Fuller against him. A peace meeting had been brokered by Philip Green at the Dorchester hotel in London. 'You can compete,' Cowell told Grainge, 'but play fair. I don't like your alliance with Fuller against me. Come into TV with a positive attitude. It's just air time. Have fun but don't share Simon's obsession to destroy me.' They had parted as friends but also rivals.

The next test of Reid's loyalty to Cowell came directly from Fuller. Reid was not only offered Cowell's place on *American Idol* and a huge financial package, but also his own new label at Universal Music.

Reid was familiar with Fuller's methods. In 2000, he had taken over Arista from Clive Davis and among the artists on his books was Fuller's client Annie Lennox. Every month, he had called Fuller to arrange a meeting, and for eighteen months he had not received a reply. Eventually, Fuller agreed to visit Reid's New York office. He arrived late.

'You didn't take my call for eighteen months and now you come in two hours late,' said Reid, irritated by Fuller's nonchalant, even pugnacious 'So . . .' replies to his placid comments. There was a silence as Reid assessed the situation. He then rose and opened his door: 'I'd like you to leave my office right now.' Startled, Fuller rose but said nothing.

After Fuller left, Reid called his deputy. 'I've just kicked Fuller out of my office. Tell Fuller I mean that he should leave the building – now.' Lennox's contract with Arista was terminated, but Reid did not regret the departure of an artist in decline. Nor did Cowell.

'A monster' was Cowell's verdict on Lennox when he heard the story of her departure, having suffered his own run-in with the singer in the past. Nor was he surprised by Grainge's and Fuller's fury after Reid finally rejected their offers. 'I've made up my mind,' Reid told them. 'I'm going to Simon Cowell.' Those left behind at Universal cursed Reid as driven by narcissism. 'He just wants to be famous on the street,' grumped one executive, pledging his revenge.

As Reid disappeared into the Galen Center, the gala's architect was gliding towards his own grand entrance. Ten years earlier, he could have walked down Oxford Street unrecognised. Now, the Cowell 'brand' guaranteed thunderous cheers as he stepped from the Rolls. Across the city, he knew, were many who wished him ill fortune. Some, he suspected, had even conspired to block Abdul's contract. Bursting with a mixture of relief and anger, his honest sentiments to the cameras did not celebrate his triumph. 'I couldn't have started without Paula. I would have looked ridiculous,' he told the journalists. At the eleventh hour, he explained, protecting his relations with the producers, 'she decided to play hardball. It's a little nuts.' Cowell did not deny the possibility of failure. 'It's the good, the bad and the ugly in a reality show where so much is made up on the spot. Exciting and unpredictable. That's why we won't know if it's a success until it's done.'

Selecting the panel of judges, he continued, was like arranging a dinner party. 'It's all down to the chemistry. They haven't all met yet. All the girls get sulky. We'll see if it works within thirty minutes, and then it must last for three months. And it will only succeed if it's special. It'll either be great or a train crash.' As an afterthought, and a reflection on his inner turmoil, he said with a smile, 'I could walk out in six hours' time and throw myself off a bridge.'

Inside the Galen Center, an energetic warm-up man was whipping up frenzied excitement among the audience. Teenage girls dressed in party clothes had been packed in behind the judges, in full view of the cameras. Older people were slotted into the darkness on the sides. In the large 'judges' room', Cowell was introducing Abdul and Cole to each other and to L. A. Reid.

A special bond united Reid and Abdul. In 1998, Abdul had given Reid his big break by paving the way for his first songwriting contract, worth $100,000, with Kenneth 'Babyface' Edmonds. The bond between Cowell and Abdul was also special. 'Only we understand our relationship,' Cowell told Reid and Cole. 'Initially I was very shocked by his rudeness and couldn't stand him,' said Abdul. 'As an artist I thought it was wrong to be critical of other artists. But since then I've grown to love Simon as my hero. He's taught me a lot.' Meanwhile, Cole sat silently, her glacial expression deterring Reid and Abdul from assuming any familiarity. None of the three doubted Cowell's dominance. As the owner and executive producer of the show, he expected them to perform to his requirements. In London, his technique had been monitored by producer Alan Boyd, a champion of *Pop*

Idol. In PowerPoint presentations, Boyd had described Cowell as 'the benevolent dictator manipulating the judges' whose 'golden rule' was 'authenticity to keep the public's trust'.

'Right. Ready?' asked Cowell thirty minutes after the deadline to start the show. Punctuality was not his priority. Standing unseen on the edge of the auditorium, beneath tiers of seats, he steadied himself. 'I go in as a performer, not a producer,' he said to himself as he signalled their entry. 'Simon, we love you,' women began to scream, while others embraced Abdul. The uproar relieved his tension. Unlike *American Idol*, where the auditions are conducted in a small room with just three judges, his extravaganza, he hoped, would attract 20 million viewers from the outset and eventually reach 30 million, the same as *Idol* at its peak.

Standing on the stage between Cole and Abdul, casting around the 4,000 spectators, Cowell enjoyed being the object of women's fascination. Underlying his charisma was the inscrutability of his sexuality as he picked up a microphone: 'Hello, everyone. Thanks for coming. I've come here to find a star. Not someone who wants to be a star but someone who is a star. Five million dollars is at stake.' Each of the three judges introduced themselves hesitantly. None knew what to expect. Nor did the first contestant, who was greeted with deliberate silence as she walked onto the huge empty stage.

Over the previous months, a dragnet had been drawn across the US in a search for the talent missed by *American Idol*. In six cities, over 100,000 people had queued for hours to sing in a booth for two minutes, hoping to advance to the next stage. Eight hundred hopefuls passed through a single booth every day, and in each venue there were about twenty booths staffed by Syco employees. The process was identical to *American Idol*'s. In addition, Cowell had encouraged aspiring contestants to apply via YouTube and in MyStudio booths. Leaving nothing to chance, talent scouts had also been dispatched to clubs, gigs and schools to find singers prepared to humiliate themselves but potentially good enough to humble *Idol.* Some of the scouts had met with Cowell beforehand to discuss their strategy for finding better contestants over the following days. By May, six hundred contestants were booked to audition on stages in six cities.

Frequently drinking water from a large Pepsi beaker – a reward for the sponsor who had pledged $50 million – in each city Cowell would pose similar questions to each of the one hundred contestants in order to test their grit: 'What would you do with $5 million?'; and 'This is chance of a lifetime. What gap in the market are you going to fill? Who are you going to knock out of the game?' Charmless bores were abruptly cut off. He intended to live up to his 'Mr Nasty' image with a succession of barbs as he crushed dreams in front of millions: 'You should be singing at home when your children are asleep'; 'It was lazy and whining'; 'You're limp and forgettable'; 'I thought it was totally hideous, total torture. I was waiting for it to end.' Appeals for mercy – 'I love you, Simon, and have your picture in my kitchen' – were crushed. 'You were singing and you looked like you've swallowed poison.' To an oddball woman who introduced herself hesitantly, 'My name is Carlo but my friends call me Angel,' Cowell asked, 'Why?' 'Because I used to be a guy,' she replied. There was no mercy: 'Imagine the biggest corn field in the world and multiply that by a million and that's how corny you are'; 'In five minutes I'll have forgotten you'; and 'You were born in the wrong body.' Hungry for drama, he began ribbing Abdul. On cue, she snapped. 'Leave me alone, Simon. You're starting already.' 'OK, Cheryl, see if you can do better.' 'No, I can't,' she replied. Sneering humour was *The X Factor*'s bedrock, but Cole was struggling, unengaged. 'You're the cutest thing I've ever seen,' she repeated to several contestants.

At the end of the evening's second session, played out in front of another 4,000 spectators, Cowell returned to the hotel.

After a bath, he ate some vegetable soup, drank the first of four Sapporo beers, lit the first of nearly twenty cigarettes and began four hours of telephone calls with his producers, publicists and Fox executives. Cole, everyone agreed, appeared uneasy.

'She's got a great chance and isn't taking it,' said Cowell.

'Cheryl's fantastic because she's so sensitive,' Shu Greene, the heart of Cowell's production team, said reassuringly. 'But she does seem to lack confidence. She's got self-doubt.'

The following afternoon, they agreed, Greene would urge Cole to recall her own days auditioning as a contestant. To boost her self-esteem, the *Sun*'s headline the next morning was 'America Loves Cheryl Cole'. In the '10,000-seater arena', wrote the paper's US editor, Cole had 'dazzled America with her *X Factor* debut'.

At five in the morning, Cowell took two sleeping pills. His last thought was of a showdown that evening if Cole failed to 'up her game'.

With the same fanfare, Cowell paraded triumphantly into the scream-filled auditorium for the second day's auditions. 'We're offering $5 million and don't want a karaoke singer,' he told his fans. The venom started soon after. 'You're like a goldfish trying to be a piranha,' he told a young girl. After an untalented female singer was booed by the audience, Abdul said, 'I could kill her. I want to hear someone worth $5 million.' 'This isn't the singing business, it's the entertainment business,' said Reid with authority. 'People with the X factor are like rough diamonds.' Cool and savvy, he played the game without revealing that he was on a steep learning curve as he watched Cowell and Abdul.

There were also some stunning performances. 'You're thirteen,' Cowell told one young hopeful, 'and I like your cocky confidence. I like your incredible arrogance, which I relate to. It's like looking at me when I was thirteen.'

On cue, a contestant announced he would sing an Adele song.

'As a matter of fact, she's here,' said Cowell. Five thousand spectators cheered as the English star acknowledged the applause. *The X Factor*'s critics would cite Adele as the opposite of reality TV's products: she was a real, honest woman who wrote her own songs reflecting genuine emotions. Her fleeting presence proved the importance of associating with Cowell: not by coincidence, she was contracted to Sony.

At the end of the afternoon session, Cole was seated in the long, windowless production room with her younger brother and an assistant, picking at a tasteless salad. Speaking occasionally in a timid voice, she had chosen to sit apart from Reid and Abdul. Reid looked across and noticed how she had isolated herself and was keeping everyone at a distance, a glazed expression on her face. 'It's doing my head in,' she had recently said in reference to her domestic crisis, adding that since her divorce she preferred the social company of women. To some, the outburst underlined the stress she was suffering following the break-up of her marriage. The producers were more generous. Recalling her success in Britain, they assumed she needed help in becoming accustomed to her new environment. 'Find out what's wrong,' Cowell ordered. 'She was glued to my hip in England,' he laughed. 'Is that the problem?' Sitting at her table, his producers tried to fathom whether the problem was the seating. Cowell was now seated beside Abdul and was noticeably cheering and sharing comments with her and not Cole. Was Cole, the producers wondered, suffering because she was no longer physically and emotionally close to Cowell during the recording?

Near by, perched in his make-up chair and eating a turkey sandwich, Cowell was listening to Mike Darnell. Dressed in his trademark high-heeled snakeskin boots, torn jeans and cowboy jacket, Darnell had been impossible to miss during the afternoon session. Defying his stature, he had frequently jumped onto the judges' plinth and animatedly commanded their attention with his opinions about the contestants and the music. Sensitive to the network executives' power, Cowell had laughed at Darnell's jokes and maintained his rapt attention, despite Darnell's disregard of the floor manager's shouts that the taping had started and the show was under way.

More than ever, Cowell needed Darnell's support. *American Idol*'s ratings for the new season, despite Cowell's absence, were higher than anticipated and rising to a five-year peak. Cowell's battle against Fuller had assumed a new dimension. He could not afford any defects, especially a weak judge, and no time could be wasted. The next auditions would be five days later in Chicago, and he needed an immediate solution.

At nearly midnight, after the second day's auditions had ended, Cowell summoned a meeting of the producers, Darnell and Cécile Frot-Coutaz in a side room in the deserted Galen Center. 'Cheryl's quiet,' said Cowell in a neutral tone. 'She doesn't look comfortable.' Everyone agreed. Cowell wanted a showdown with Cole. 'Let's leave it a couple of days,' said Frot-Coutaz, a late convert to hiring Cole. Focus groups, she continued, reported a positive reaction to the Geordie accent. 'America will fall in love with her beauty, her accent and her incredible chemistry with Simon Cowell,' she puffed. Darnell agreed: 'We should boost Cheryl's self-confidence,' suggested a man who would not deny publicity whispers that 'Mike has the hots for Cheryl.' 'Right,' said Cowell, 'we'll announce, "The good news is that Cheryl and Paula have bonded together."'

Still troubled, Cowell seized the first opportunity to pour out his concern to Philip Green in London. Green was not surprised by the early-morning call. Coincidentally, his wife Tina had been visiting Los Angeles during the auditions and after the first day had reported her own impressions and those of the production team to her husband. 'They say that Cheryl's unhappy and would be happier in England,' Philip Green agreed. 'I can read the tea leaves. It's time to act the Kissinger and get everybody in place in case she comes back.'

The timetable was tight. The opening auditions for the British *X Factor* would be ten days later in Manchester, the same day as the next auditions in Chicago. Pleased to offer his services to 'manage the accidents' or, as he also put it, 'act the wicket-keeper to help things along', Green suggested that they 'cancel Manchester and see how she does in Chicago'. 'Very clever,' said Cowell. He hated confrontation and hoped that the others would electrify Cole. After conference calls with all the players – Fox, FremantleMedia and ITV – the *X Factor* trucks were ordered not to drive to Manchester.

As usual, Green spent the weekend of 14 May with his wife on *Lionheart*, anchored in the bay for the Cannes film festival. Knowing that Cheryl Cole would be visiting the festival to promote L'Oréal – 'You know you're worth it' was the caption over her photograph – Green sent a text to her saying that he was outside her hotel and would she like a drink? The billionaire waited for a reply. Puzzled by her silence, he received a call after midnight from Seth Friedman, one of her agents in Los Angeles. 'She can't meet you,' said Friedman without any explanation.

'It doesn't feel right,' Green told Cowell, who was not surprised. Cole would not expose herself to difficult meetings. But the truth could not be avoided. In the past, he had targeted Sharon Osbourne, Piers Morgan and others with 'the same complaints, so I did not think a conversation would be unusual'. In Cowell's opinion, 'Cheryl's position is no different to that of the contestants whom she is paid to criticise.'

Their relationship was, however, special. During her first season on *The X Factor* in Britain, she had given him a £50,000 watch for his birthday. Its diamond-encrusted gold case was unique. The following year, she had given him a Jaeger watch. In 2010, she had hired a group of dwarfs to follow him around the studio singing 'Happy Birthday'. All that was proof of their special chemistry, and yet she was so difficult to read. To his regret, they had not even enjoyed a 'K&C' – a kiss and a cuddle – and that made her all the more attractive. He called her in the late morning.

'Are you OK?' he asked. 'Look, Cheryl, we've worked together a long time. I've got to be honest with you: I've looked through the LA tapes and I've got to tell you, you're not as sharp and focused as before. This is a different country. America is different to England. You've got to raise your game. Once you're in the hot seat there are pluses and minuses. I want you to be as focused as you were when you sang for the first time in *The X Factor*.' After a pause, Cole asked, 'Do you think you've been as good?' 'Probably not,' replied Cowell, 'but I think I'll get there.' After some further talk, Cowell delivered his bombshell: 'Do you think you'd be happier if you went back to *The X Factor* in Britain?' Again, Cole paused. The idea was not unattractive, she replied, but 'I want to come to Chicago to give it another go.' If anyone else had been involved, Cowell would have spoken about 'no job is safe' and 'no one should take me for granted'. Had Louis Walsh similarly failed, there would have been no mercy. But this was Cheryl. He smiled at the thought of those seductive eyes and agreed to try Chicago.

In London, Peter Fincham received a late-night call from Richard Holloway, who had just returned from Los Angeles. 'Cheryl's not working in America,' the producer told Fincham. 'Simon wondered if she could come back to *The X Factor* here?' After registering surprise that Cowell had so quickly condemned his own decision, Fincham speculated whether the British show should be a refuge for damaged goods. But since no decision was expected yet and Cole was to be given another chance at the next auditions in Chicago, it was agreed to 'wait and see'.

*

Paula Abdul was waiting for Cowell at Los Angeles's Van Nuys airport at 3 p.m. the following day, Sunday 15 May. Minutes after entering the private plane to fly to New York, Abdul showed Cowell the result of some minor cosmetic surgery on her face. 'It doesn't show,' soothed Cowell in the friendly manner of a man who would later say, 'I saved her career.' Bubbly and laughing, Abdul walked to the back of the plane to sit with Mezhgan Hussainy, hoping that any uncertainties caused by the recent break in Hussainy's three-year relationship with Cowell had been healed by her receiving the house and sufficient money to maintain her lifestyle. As the plane took off, Abi Doyle, Cowell's executive assistant, delivered the audience ratings of the previous night's Eurovision song contest in Britain, which had been broadcast at the same time as *Britain's Got Talent*. Clearly upset, Cowell fumed about Eurovision's ratings victory. 'I'm angry,' he said. He had watched the Eurovision show live on a Russian station. The German producers, he conceded, 'have taken it from the Premiership into the Champions League by using ideas from *The X Factor*'.

Reviewing *Britain's Got Talent* again on an Apple Mac while the jet climbed away from Los Angeles, he condemned his own production: 'Boring. It looks provincial.' Abi Doyle was summoned to send a message to Shu Greene expressing his unhappiness and demanding a discussion that night about improvements.

Top of his agenda were production changes to improve *The X Factor* USA's appearance. He was irritated by the design of the stage in Los Angeles. 'It was no good,' he said. 'It's blue and flat, and the sound is poor because there's only one mixer.' Sipping a constantly refreshed cup of PG Tips with lemon, he ate a turkey sandwich and some carrots. 'It's all too gloomy,' he concluded about the staging. He wanted a global extravaganza to compete against Eurovision.

Successful shows, he knew, always hit a peak and then fell into a slow decline. *Britain's Got Talent*, he complained, had become 'too formulaic'. Like all stage performers, Cowell feared failure, but since TV producers can be counted on to recognise trends in advance of an audience, his concerns could be rectified. For the moment, though, his anger went unanswered. Surrounded by employees apprehensive of his grumpy reaction to any contradiction, no one would put the programme's slide into perspective. He was the centre of a flat organisation of 'yes' men bereft of delegated power.

Taking some medicine from vials laid out in a row next to his seat, he suggested a conference call in New York at 1 a.m. With a compulsive need to telephone around the clock, regardless of the local time in America or Britain, he demanded instant responses. His only relief before reaching Teterboro airport in New Jersey, near New York, was Fox's promotional clip for *The X Factor* USA. He laughed loudly about the reference to his turbulent relationship with Abdul.

Fox's financial lifeblood depended on the choreographed 'upfronts', the network's showcase to advertisers of the best attractions in the coming year. On Monday 16 May, amid a heavy downpour, Cowell arrived at a dilapidated but packed Broadway theatre. Walking into a cramped space backstage, he noticed that Abdul and Cole were unintentionally wearing identical red dresses. 'Hysterical,' thought Cowell, especially because both women were patently embarrassed. 'I'm cold,' whispered Cole, who had just returned from Cannes. Randy Jackson, still a judge on Fox's *American Idol*, put his jacket over her shoulders. Despite the disquiet about the colour clash, Cowell was pleased by Cole's new hairstyle.

'Cheryl's a fighter and wants to win,' he confided to an associate, 'so she agreed to a make-over.' Although he regarded her as a friend, with so much at stake there was no place for anything other than candour. Cole barely acknowledged Cowell's arrival.

Near by stood Nicole Scherzinger, the lead singer of the Pussycat Dolls, who had just arrived from a show in Scotland. Cowell regarded the dusky beauty as another 'toy' whose professionalism and hunger for success made her 'like a panther' but also 'the biggest diva I've ever met. She has her water served in a thimble so that it's always the right temperature.' In an aside to her female assistant, Scherzinger confessed, 'I've never been so nervous and all I've got to do is walk onto a stage and wave. My lips are so dry.' Scherzinger and Steve Jones, a Welshman, had been chosen as the hosts of the programme.

To cheer everyone in the countdown to their appearance on the stage, Cowell joked as they climbed the steps, 'Ready to make animal sacrifices on stage?' The stage lights were dimmed. A voice introduced Cowell as 'the best-looking reality man on TV, and that was just five minutes ago'. The lights were reignited as the four *X Factor* judges, along with Jackson, emerged through clouds of tacky dry ice. 'Randy, you've come to the wrong show,' Cowell quipped weakly, ordering him off the stage. He then stepped forward and spoke confidently: 'We have just come from LA, where the two days of auditions were, in my opinion, two of the best I've seen. *The X Factor* is going to be fun and this is going to be different.' He concluded with an obligatory 'special thanks to Pepsi for sponsoring the show'.

There was a heavy downpour as the judges headed for Fox's party in marquees set up at the Wollman Rink in Central Park. 'This is like a zoo,' complained Cowell, peering into a gloom that was relieved only by dozens of tiny girls perched on stiletto heels. 'I'm not staying for more than an hour.' In his perpetual campaign to make *The X Factor* USA America's most popular show and beat *American Idol*, Cowell engaged with inebriated advertisers and agreed to repeated requests to be photographed with them. Next, he was led to a line of television cameras.

'We make the show up as we go along,' laughed Cowell as

he worked his way down. 'If it fails, we're out of a job.' Before replying to a question about Cole, he noticed that the singer looked disturbed by his bantering with Abdul. 'I choose people I like with egos,' he said, introducing Abdul. 'I gave ammo to Cheryl,' added Abdul to extinguish the doubts about Cole, 'and she's given ammo to me to make Simon's life difficult.' Cole looked on uncomfortably.

As the rain turned to drizzle, Cowell escaped from the dank atmosphere and headed for the airport. On the chartered plane to Chicago he watched once again the rushes of the Los Angeles auditions. 'The set', he dictated to Abi Doyle, 'is too flat. It's got the wrong feel. It feels old-fashioned. It should feel more like a spectacular, with a documentary sense. I want filmic quality.' After a moment's thought, he added, 'The performances are disappointing. I want a more ruthless feel, as if someone's got to win. I want losers to feel gutted.' Next, he listened to a selection of songs for the contestants in the semi-finals of *Britain's Got Talent*, followed by clips of *Australia's Got Talent*, featuring Dannii Minogue. 'It's very good,' he said. The Australian versions of *The X Factor* and *Talent* would become the template. Finally, he dictated a memo that Syco should bid for the opening music of the London Olympics, before relaxing with a beer and a heaped plate of spaghetti bolognese. 'Simon would then like a sliced apple,' Doyle told the plane's attendant. 'Make sure there's no peel.'

Unmentioned during the flight was his unease about Cole. The focus in London, he had been told as he got onto the plane, was on Dannii Minogue, who was still in Australia. Journalists were asking whether she had been dropped as an *X Factor* judge. The media, Cowell knew, delighted in any damaging news. Someone at ITV, he suspected, had hinted that Cowell disliked Minogue. 'We're loyal to people,' he insisted, casting his dismissal of Louis Walsh four years earlier as 'a glitch'. The reality, he knew, was that there was turmoil in Minogue's private life. She was reluctant to travel with her baby, and there were 'boyfriend problems'. But, for the moment, Cowell directed that his publicist express his ignorance of Minogue's last-minute refusal to fly from Australia to London. 'Say, "We were talking to Dannii Minogue's agent and we've changed the dates to avoid a conflict with her appearance on *Australia's Got Talent.*" And then, if the conflicts can't be sorted, say, "We're talking about other projects."'

Quietly, he had already lined up a substitute for Minogue. To minimise the criticism, he ordered the publicist to arrange telephone interviews with the tabloid journalists the next day.

Cowell awoke in Chicago with a bad migraine. He took a pill to control the pain and abandoned the conference call with journalists in London. At three o'clock in the afternoon, dressed in a grey sweatshirt and jeans, he took another painkiller and left the Peninsula hotel for the United Center on the outskirts of the city, accompanied by a beefy bodyguard who had just secured the security contract for the duration of *The X Factor* and Abi Doyle, who repeated the details of the day's events. After twenty-five years, Oprah Winfrey, America's most successful TV celebrity, was retiring, and Cowell had been invited to feature in *Surprise, Oprah! A Farewell Spectacular*, her final show.

'I don't like parties,' griped Cowell. 'I don't know many celebs or Hollywood stars, so I don't know why I bother to go.' By the time he arrived at the giant arena, feeling unsteady, he expressed disbelief that the celebration was not at Oprah's regular Harpo Studios in front of a regular invited audience, but instead was being staged in front of 15,000 adoring fans.

As Cowell was escorted to his dressing room, a large corporate box overlooking the arena, he passed the rooms assigned to Hollywood's royalty: Tom Hanks, Tom Cruise, Madonna, Beyoncé, Aretha Franklin, Stevie Wonder and Maria Shriver. He was, he murmured, unprepared for such an extravaganza.

'I feel a bit of a fraud,' he told Terri Seymour on the phone, repeating that he felt awkward around celebrities. An uncomfortable room, lit by incense candles and decorated with a large photograph of himself standing beside Oprah, was testimony to his own status: the only non-American invited to participate in the homage to a heroine. 'It's all about number one,' he said, contemplating his standing as Hussainy – having arrived separately – poured herself a glass of champagne. 'Talking to celebrities is too much effort. They all think the same.' He recalled meeting Madonna at an Oscar-night party and how it was 'too much' as she brushed past him; and how, at another party in 2009, he had said 'hello' to Annie Lennox, who, after staring at him, turned around and walked away without a word. 'She just snubbed me,' he recalled with a pained smile.

'I'm no good with prompters,' he told the producer who presented the script he was expected to read off the autocue. 'And I'll have to wear glasses, which I hate.' While he read the script and drank a cup of tea, Hussainy was repeatedly adding make-up. His head was throbbing. 'I'm going back to the hotel,' he announced, to the organisers' distress. 'I'll be back at seven.' Two hours later, he returned to the dressing room feeling refreshed. Peering through the black curtains at the audience as they screamed their replies to the warm-up men, Cowell was unusually quiet. 'Oprah's pretty incredible,' he mused. 'She's going to be very emotional tonight.'

His fascination with Oprah's magnetism turned to irritation as he compared her stage with *The X Factor*'s set. 'I like the way they combine the two colours – blue and the pink. I want that,' he dictated. 'And who's their sound guy? Get his name. How come they can make a stadium work and we can't?'

'Their sound man's called Jeremy,' Doyle reported within minutes.

'Get a number for him,' ordered Cowell. 'And who does their lighting?'

'Terra,' replied Doyle, anticipating the enquiry.

'Tell them I'm blued out,' he ordered, referring to the labours of his British production team. 'I don't want it any more. They should use a bit of red.'

Peering through the curtains again, he saw thousands of glowing Knuckle Lights – used by joggers – waving in the darkness as the audience obeyed the order to move their arms in synchronisation. 'Get those too,' ordered Cowell, eager for wide shots on a thirty-four-inch screen to 'show the money' that would be spent and overruling his producers' passion for close-ups. Simultaneously, Hannah Lamden, his second assistant, was sending images of the stage from her iPhone to *The X Factor*'s producers with the latest instructions: 'I want more lights on the judges' desk. And a different colour for every city.'

To the sound of the Black Eyed Peas hit 'I Gotta Feeling', Tom Hanks and Oprah walked onto the stage to open the show. Successively, Hanks introduced Tom Cruise, one of Oprah's favourites, Madonna, actress Dakota Fanning, country band Rascal Flatts and many more. All were appearing without a fee, their costs paid personally or by their record companies, who were eager for the publicity. Oprah's eyes were glistening. 'It's an incredible story, isn't it?' sighed Cowell, gazing at an American coronation. 'It looks amazing. Amazing. They're the best producers in the world.'

Retreating to his room, he carried on watching the show on TV, eating carrots and celery and dragging on successive Kools. Diane Sawyer, the famous journalist, was announcing that 25,000 oak trees were to be planted in honour of Oprah's twenty-five-year campaign to encourage reading. 'I won't even get a bush when I go,' said Cowell. 'All I'll get is a nettle patch.'

Irritated by his script, Cowell asked for an 'and' to be deleted and walked towards the stage. On the way, he silently passed Maria Shriver, who was heavily made up to conceal her emotional state. The previous day's media had disclosed that Arnold Schwarzenegger, her husband, had fathered a son with the family's trusted housekeeper. 'Hello,' said Cowell as he saw Tom Cruise and his wife Katie Holmes, who was holding their daughter's hand. Cruise's smile appeared forced. Waiting in the reception area, Will Smith and his wife Jada Pinkett Smith eyed Cowell warily. Beyoncé looked away. 'I've been critical of her, that's why she's frosty,' admitted Cowell, referring to his recent comments about the singer being 'out of tune'. But, he added, 'she was fantastic'.

He had reached a dimly lit, cavernous waiting room behind the stage. The grim atmosphere was broken by a tiny blonde, Kristin Chenoweth, hugging Cowell. 'You caused a lot of trouble on *American Idol* kicking your legs in the air,' laughed Cowell, referring to her guest appearance on the show. 'That was only for you,' Chenoweth replied, hoping for an opportunity to appear on *The X Factor* USA. At the side of the room, Tom Hanks appeared to be deciding whether to approach Cowell. Finally, he summoned up the courage to introduce himself. To the actor's obvious relief, Cowell was friendly. 'Can we have a photograph together?' asked Hanks, as Patti LaBelle, the singer, approached for an intimate conversation. Admired by Cowell, Labelle was also hoping to make an appearance on *The X Factor*.

Moments later, Hanks walked onto the stage to introduce Stevie Wonder playing 'Isn't She Lovely?', followed by comedian Jerry Seinfeld. After four minutes of high-quality jokes, Cowell walked nervously onto the stage to the backing of the Lighthouse Family's 'Lifted'. His task was difficult: following the music, humour and emotion, he had been cast as 'Mr Nasty' to introduce Rosie O'Donnell singing 'Fever'. After a fluff that left him cursing his poor eyesight, his words on the retake were not appreciated by O'Donnell: 'Oprah, I'm not so sure that this is the most talented group of singers you're going to see tonight . . .' He left the stage more nervous than during his entry and was led towards a line of television cameras for interviews.

'What's it like walking onto a stage in front of 15,000?' he was asked.

'Terrifying, seriously very intimidating. That's why I sit down for a living.' The female interviewer kicked off her shoes to be photographed with Cowell at his height.

After the finale, Cowell stood in the backstage area, obviously pleased to be mingling with Hollywood royalty. He did not anticipate that no British newspaper would include his name in their reports about the extravaganza. Led by his bodyguard, he headed towards his fleet of gleaming black 4×4s and drove past the cheering fans. Hussainy departed by herself. 'Our journey should take twenty-five minutes,' said an assistant.

'"Journey" is a forbidden word,' joked Cowell, reflecting his weariness of a term used by *X Factor* contestants before they recited their dysfunctional lives. 'We say "trip" now.'

Back in the hotel, a young woman guest was prevented by his bodyguard from stepping inside the lift with him. 'I looked terrible,' he complained to his assistant about the incident. 'It made me look awful.'

The following afternoon, his mood deteriorated even more. English newspapers wrote that Cowell would need to appear on the British *X Factor* and *Britain's Got Talent* in order to reverse the falling ratings. Meanwhile, in Chicago, the media reported that over 20 million had watched the semi-finals of *American Idol* and 75 million votes had been registered, with some people voting more than once. That unexpectedly high audience was eclipsed by the news of the triumphant debut of *The Voice*, a new competitor to *The X Factor* and *American Idol* from NBC that copied the former's mentoring style. *The Voice*'s 10 million audience and good reviews put Cowell in a bad frame of mind as he was driven, at 4 p.m., to the Sears Centre outside Chicago, where the *X Factor* USA auditions would be held the next day.

During the hour's journey, Cowell watched the latest edits of *Britain's Got Talent* on his laptop and issued a stream of criticisms for the producers in London. 'The quality of the programmes around the world must be improved,' he said. *The X Factor* and the *Talent* shows, he believed, needed to appeal more to youth, but the prospect of endless discussions with the network executives was unattractive. Bored, he began cursing again the lighting on *The X Factor* USA. The comparison with Oprah's set rankled, and he anticipated an argument with the stubborn technicians at the Sears Centre. Previously, he had lost his patience, but he now decided to be less truculent.

Overnight, his British production team had responded to his stream of orders and had accommodated his preference for purple and gold lighting on the gigantic set and more illumination on the four judges. However, squeezing into the mobile studio-control truck, Cowell instantly expressed dissatisfaction. 'It's still too much like a TV studio. I want scale of enormity, like a huge concert.' The camera angles were 'wrong', he continued, and 'the floor looks dull. I want it shining.' With barely time to inhale he damned a set of yellow spotlights: 'I hate them.' To his relief, the surliness he anticipated from the technicians did not materialise and, within minutes, riggers were climbing sixty-foot ropes to adjust the spotlights at the top of the scaffolding.

During the return to the hotel, Cowell listened through headphones to selected songs for future *X Factor* shows. 'I'm worried about his taste,' he complained about an assistant in London who was supplying him with CDs every day. 'Every night my bed is covered with them. It's impossible to take an evening off.' He did not equate his tortuous attention to detail and the resulting enormous workload with his refusal to delegate.

Over the following two days, Cowell concealed his bad mood

from the 17,000 spectators who packed into the Sears Centre. The original fear that *The X Factor* could attract audiences only if they were paid – with their consequent sullenness – had gone. Paula Abdul was mobbed by women eager for an embrace and a kiss, and dozens of mobile telephones recorded Cowell's face as he walked amid thunderous cheers to the dais. 'I sense an evil crowd, and I like that,' he said as he introduced himself. 'This will be a long three hours. We have barricaded the doors to keep you here. The judges don't know who they will audition. Some will be great, others will be terrible. We'll deal with it. Let us know. You, the audience, are the fifth judge.'

More cheers greeted Abdul, who titillated the crowd with amorous advances to Cowell and then introduced Cheryl Cole. 'This is my first time to Chicago,' said Cole, 'and I'm really enjoying it. And next to me is the amazing and, some say, legendary L. A. Reid.' Reid matched her effusiveness: 'I'm sitting next to the amazing Cheryl Cole, and we're here because I believe there is a superstar still to be found.'

'This is a three-minute audition worth $5 million,' Cowell told the first contestant. 'Three minutes to change your life. Show me you're worth $5 million.'

His barbs over the two days never faltered as his search for a star was frustrated by freaks and sob stories. 'You walk better than you sing,' he told one, while to a woman who said, 'I've been a singer all my life,' he replied, 'Then it's time to choose something else.' Prompted by the producers, he asked a fifty-five-year-old, twice-married corn farmer's wife from Missouri, 'What happened to your first husband?' 'I killed him,' she replied. 'He went for a gun, so I went for my gun and shot him.' Her fate after the killing was left unexplained. Cowell professed not to know.

Equally unexplained was Cowell's late arrival on the second day. 'I wouldn't expect him to apologise,' said Reid, who was gossiping with Abdul, while Cole morosely ate a salad across the room. Below, 3,400 people had waited for nearly two hours. 'Hi,' smiled Cowell, concealing his unhappiness. 'I was knackered,' he later explained. 'I don't like travelling and shooting in different cities. I got up dreading the day's filming. And I didn't like the contestants the previous day. There was so much on my mind.' The four of them headed down to the auditorium.

'I appreciate your artistic work,' Cole told a flashy contestant, 'but you're camp.' The man's face was blank. 'Do you understand "camp"?' asked Cole. The man was clearly puzzled. So was the audience. 'What's the American for it?' Cole asked Cowell. The obvious answer was not forthcoming and, after an embarrassing pause, she pressed on. 'I like your package,' she said to the man, who was wearing tight jeans. The double meaning was not lost on the prim Chicago audience. Stung by a few boos, Cole was isolated, and Cowell did not come to her rescue.

'I'm a shameless capitalist record executive,' Reid was telling the contestant, 'and I'm going to say "no".' Reid, thought Cowell, 'is very competitive. He hates it if I've picked up a point which he has missed.' Abdul began sparring with the man, alluding to his life 'journey', which had been assisted by substance abuse. Her understanding of his torment appealed to Cowell. 'Paula, you're an LA child,' he laughed. 'You've always lived among rainbows, mountains and flowers.' He silently compared her to Cole: 'Paula's a great survivor, with someone always snapping at her heels. It's tough in LA, but she's got her confidence.'

Cole's personal assistant suddenly appeared at the dais to push a paper plate heaped with Maltesers and another with fruit gums towards her employer. The comfort food reflected Cole's distress. 'She wrongly thought that appearing in America would be just like Britain,' opined Cowell later. Her failure was to prepare for the harder challenge. Wilting as her self-confidence drained away, Cole lacked the strength of character and intelligence to rectify her plight.

The session ended, and the judges returned to their room for dinner. In London, Philip Green's watch showed it was just after 3 a.m. when Cowell rang to report that Cole had performed badly in the first session. 'It's a big mess,' he said.

'Whatever happens,' Green urged, 'promise me that at the end of the show you don't have a conversation with her. That you'll go home, have a sleep and think about it.'

Cowell agreed and returned smiling and waving to the auditorium for the final session. Unusually, not only was the media unaware of the crisis, but Philip Green, often likened to a bull in a china shop, had become the mediator, the only person who could bring the disparate parties together. 'Simon', he would say, 'is my only outside interest.'

During the break for dinner, Nicole Scherzinger had approached Cowell. 'In here,' he had said, diving through a curtain into a back room. For ten minutes, the singer hosting the show pitched for Cole's job. She had proved her credibility, she argued, the previous year in the British *X Factor*, when she had stepped in while Dannii Minogue had been having a baby. 'Nicole wants reassurance that she's important' was Cowell's explanation for the huddle that night. 'She wants more involvement in the programme.' If Cole was fired, Scherzinger was placed to be her successor. Cowell did not commit himself, but his few words were enough for Scherzinger.

At the end of the second audition, the judges were asked to remain to record a promotional video. 'Chicago is a great music town,' Reid told Cowell, 'a place which changes music, but some of the greatness did not come out. I'm disappointed.' Cowell offered reassurance. 'We only need two or three potential stars from Chicago, and we've got that. And we've got between five or six great hopes from LA.' Reid was not reassured. 'If we can't find one star', continued Cowell, 'out of the 80,000 people applying, then we're not doing our job.'

Reid still looked doubtful. Cowell explained that the competition process itself turned the raw material into stars. 'Kelly Clarkson justified *American Idol*'s 2002 competition, and we'll do the same.' Even Reid, a highly regarded producer, could not quite imagine Cowell's formula for the judges to mentor their contestants and turn them into professionals.

'Cheryl's gone,' Abi Doyle told Cowell. 'She just left. It'll just be the three of you recording.' Cole's unexplained disappearance reminded Cowell that she had attracted some bad reviews in the previous season's *The X Factor* in Britain. He wondered whether his personal affection had blinded him to her faults.

The driver lost his way to the airport while Cowell wrestled with Cole's fate. 'Cheryl has still to find her feet,' he told an assistant. 'She's instinctive and she's enjoying herself. But here it's hard. She has to start again. In London, she's like Princess Diana arriving, but here every Brit that's hired is hired as a complete dick, and Cheryl is the first one who's nice.' His voice trailed off as the car finally arrived after midnight for the private charter to Luton. Up until three years earlier, Cowell had commuted across the Atlantic on British Airways, but ever since being mobbed by fans at a shop in Heathrow he had flown privately, sharing the cost with Fox.

Throughout the seven-hour flight, Cowell could not sleep. 'Do I pretend it's OK,' he asked himself, 'or do I do what in the long term is best for everyone?' Eating an Irish stew and drinking a Sapporo, Cowell discussed Cole's fate with Richard Holloway, who was seated across the aisle. Their relationship had recently recovered from a breakdown initiated by Cowell lasting nearly a year. Since then, the producer had become more keen than usual to oblige Cowell. He agreed that a possible solution would be for Cole to return to *The X Factor* in Britain. If necessary, he would approach her, although he was fearful of the media reaction. Holloway then let his chair fall back and fell asleep.

Just before the plane arrived on Saturday lunchtime, Cowell revealed that he had not slept during the night and was still undecided. Whisked away from the foot of the aircraft in his Rolls-Royce, he anticipated immersing himself in the steam room of his Holland Park house and enjoying a massage before going to bed. 'It's all playing on my mind,' he said to himself before he finally collapsed at 8 p.m.

Eight hours later, he awoke. By early evening he had decided, 'It's crazy to delay any longer.' Later he would explain, 'No one is regarded as having more judgement than me. I had substitutes waiting. I didn't want them to feel second best. I knew that no one else would take the decision. If you're too afraid of the consequences, you'll just get a horrible slow decline. You'd never change and get new people, and it would be a boring world. I had to drop a pebble in the water and take the consequences.' He would take responsibility even if the decision proved to be an embarrassing mistake.

His first calls would be to Mike Darnell and Cécile Frot-Coutaz. Neither, he suspected, would completely understand his reasons, but they shared his 'consciousness that she wasn't happy'. He hoped they would agree that Cheryl should be 'eased back into the UK'. No one ever agreed 100 per cent with him, but he expected generosity. Compared to others, he had been 'a loyal pussycat' towards Fox and FremantleMedia by rejecting the 'biggest offer in TV history' from NBC. Frot-Coutaz, Cowell suspected, would be more difficult to persuade than Darnell. Politics and cost rather than quality were her priority. Her usual response to any suggestion was to look down at her shoes and say, 'Well, if that's what you want, but Syco will have to pay.' *The X Factor* USA's success, she had originally feared, would be at the expense of *American Idol*, another programme produced by the FremantleMedia machine. Now, she hinted indifference to Cowell's torment.

'We're going to make a decision for Cheryl's sake,' said Cowell, setting the mood of the conference call. She would be replaced, he continued, by Nicole Scherzinger. To his disappointment, both Darnell and Frot-Coutaz hesitated and seemed unwilling to move from the corporate script. After a long discussion, however, they shifted. Survival in their world meant keeping talent like Cowell happy, and Cowell was emphatic. In the end, both knew that success would also depend on instinct and luck. 'It's worth a try,' Darnell agreed.

Next, Cowell called ITV boss Peter Fincham. Cole, he explained, would make a surprise return to Britain and should be paid more money. Fincham was doubtful. He was excited by the two women already lined up – Kelly Rowland of Destiny's Child and Tulisa Contostavlos of N-Dubz – and doubted whether Cole would accept being a pawn on a chessboard.

By the end of Sunday, Cowell was gloomy: 'I could feel a sense of unease. I'd done enough shows to know that people were worried. No one said, "We must keep her on the US show," and I was clear she would be better in the UK. But no one said, "Great, go for it."' The burden was placed on Cowell. As a courtesy, and to protect Sony's interests, Cowell also called David Joseph, the chief executive of Universal Music, Sony's rival, who had taken over the music rights at *American Idol* and to whom Cole was contracted.

Richard Holloway was delegated to do the dirty work and head to Cole's temporary home in a hotel in Hadley Wood, Hertfordshire. 'There were no tears,' Holloway reported. 'She admitted her disappointment but would think overnight about returning to *The X Factor* in Britain.' Cowell was optimistic. 'I had expected Cole to look at it logically. I had given her a good TV break, produced her well. She would be happier and better in Britain.' The deadline for her final decision was Wednesday.

Cole's conversation with Cowell on Monday afternoon started

frostily. 'Can I have your dressing room at Wembley?' she asked.

'Yes,' he agreed, allocating to her the largest dressing room in the Fountain studios.

'And I want to keep it quiet,' she said, 'so I can surprise everyone by appearing live at the auditions in Birmingham.'

'I love that,' said Cowell.

The conversation ended. He believed he had averted a crisis. 'She'll walk onto the stage and be revealed as a hero,' Cowell told everyone, assuming that Cole had accepted his plan.

Later that day, will.i.am, Cole's agent, called for the beginning of three days of negotiations. The introduction was strained. Cowell was accused of deliberately undermining Cole by reducing the volume of her microphone. The performer turned agent, Cowell believed, did not understand that his responsibility was to put his client's interests first. Instead of understanding both sides of the argument, will.i.am was riding his own ego. For his part, the agent insisted that, despite Cowell's anger, he was acting solely in Cole's interests. Eventually, Cowell pacified him and by the end agreed that Cole's fee for *The X Factor* in Britain would be increased. 'No one from her side has said she wants to stay in America,' Cowell reported.

Late on Tuesday 24 May, Cowell received a shock. The celebrity-gossip website *TMZ* was reporting from Hollywood that Cheryl Cole had been fired from *The X Factor* USA. The game had completely changed.

'Will doesn't understand the pressures we're under,' Cowell was told as the media's demands for information grew.

'So what's the problem?' he asked. 'A leak is not the start of World War III.' Cowell doubted the publicity was damaging. After all, Louis Walsh had been fired and then returned. That was a trademark game he enjoyed playing.

'She's taken her phone off the hook,' cursed Richard Holloway. Cole had cut herself off from any calls, while her agent screamed furiously for twenty minutes to Cowell on the telephone, 'I've been mugged.'

'He doesn't realise we're trying to help them,' an aide said to Cowell.

'I've met Will many times,' replied Cowell, 'and I thought we had a good relationship. He even asked me whether he could be a judge in the British *X Factor*. I refused.'

By the end of Wednesday, even Cowell was frazzled by the media storm of speculation that the British tabloids' favourite had been ridiculed in America and was a casualty of Cowell's ruthlessness. Navigating around the industry's reptiles was truly horrendous.

'The leak to *TMZ* was deliberate sabotage by a rival,' he concluded. Some speculated that the culprit was Universal, who had a vested interest in getting Cole off *The X Factor* and onto NBC's *The Voice*, for which they had the contract to sell the winner's records. 'They won't have shed many tears about the leak,' said Cowell, admitting that he was 'naïve to rely on the discretion of agents and managers to keep quiet'. Others suspected the culprit was Cole's agent or someone associated with Nicole Scherzinger, the person who had most to gain by Cole's departure.

The finalising of Cole's fate was delayed for twenty-four hours after a tortured conference call at 3 a.m. London time between Cowell, Holloway, Philip Green and Seth Friedman, one of Cole's agents, about some simple legalities. Finally, the hurdles were resolved and Cowell believed Cole was cleared to return to Britain. The offer was generous: she would receive $2 million to pay up her American contract and a further £2 million for appearing on the British programme.

'Right,' Green told Friedman, 'we can have a contract finalised in thirty minutes.'

'I haven't spoken to my client,' replied Friedman.

'Why not?' exploded Green. 'It's 4.45 a.m. Go and talk to her.'

Friedman was never heard from again, and will.i.am took over. 'Can Cheryl have equity in *The X Factor*?' he asked.

'It's not mine to give,' said Cowell. 'But I'll raise her fee from £2 million to £2.5 million, with a bonus for ratings, and I'll give her the "executive producer" credit that she wanted.' He added, 'I'm doing this for her own interest, so we can do this cleanly and quickly.'

Again, Cowell assumed a deal had been reached and that she had agreed to return to Britain. 'I'll consider other options,' replied the improbable agent, seeming more interested in himself than his client. Cowell was puzzled. He got on well with Cole. They were personal friends and he understood her vulnerabilities, albeit there were barriers forbidding any discussion about her boyfriends and marriage. Considering her disappointing performance, he was offering her a generous deal, so he texted her: 'Despite the publicity this is all positive. If you like, I'll come over and see you.' There was no reply. Cole's attitude was a mystery.

As the tabloids heard about her refusal to talk to Cowell or anyone else, they abandoned any reticence about criticising television's most powerful personality. The headlines were hysterical about her mistreatment. Although she refused to speak, that did not prevent her family and friends briefing journalists about her 'deep depression' while she lived in America, her 'major sulk', the tears because 'she feels hurt and let down' and her 'humiliation' – an irony, some would think, considering she was paid £2 million to tell *The X Factor*'s contestants unpleasant truths.

'Cowell under pressure' was the media's kindest description of a man who over the years they had accused of slyly manipulating audiences, aggressively promoting his commercial partners, plugging clients like Leona Lewis, and doing favours for friends like Piers Morgan. Some believed that Cowell, on the eve of his return to British television for the semi-finals of *Britain's Got*

Talent, was again manipulating the publicity. Cowell could only wish that for once events were under his control.

Cole's refusal to consider returning to Britain had disrupted plans. The British *X Factor* auditions were due to start on 1 June in Birmingham, and the deadline for the judges to be contracted was Saturday 28 May. Under pressure, Cowell could no longer hide behind a screen of publicists. He needed his version to be properly presented.

'My Cheryl Guilt – A Cowell Exclusive' was the *Sun*'s front-page headline on the day of the deadline, confirming the collapse of a miscalculated plot. 'I'm sorry it didn't work out,' Cowell admitted to the world. Except that Cowell later denied the confession. 'I haven't a clue how they could say "my guilt",' he would say, 'because I didn't speak to the *Sun*. I knew I was getting a bashing, but I didn't talk.'

The rival *Mirror* attacked the 'manipulator'. 'Cowell's monumental blunder', reported the newspaper, arose from his 'seat-of-the-pants style of management'. The damning quotation from Cowell – 'She doesn't travel well. We've made a terrible mistake' – was accurate.

'Are you OK?' his friends texted. 'I'm not reading the papers,' Cowell replied tongue-in-cheek. 'Just as well,' they agreed. Since outsiders could not understand the root of the crisis, the *Mail on Sunday* identified Mike Darnell as the culprit. Under the headline 'Axed by Fiendish Rumpelstiltskin', the report erroneously depicted Darnell as the monster who ruined England's sweetheart because her accent was incomprehensible. 'They picked on me because of my height,' Darnell laughed, but with the problem slipping out of the control of so many interested parties – Syco, Fox, FremantleMedia and ITV – he was diving to avoid the flak. He suspected that the *Mail* had been briefed by Cowell's publicists. 'We're not passing the blame,' Cowell told Darnell. 'Just don't read the papers.'

Cowell was now chain-smoking. The British *X Factor* auditions, delayed by two weeks, would start on Wednesday in Birmingham, but the judges could only be announced at the last moment. *The X Factor* in America seemed to be a mess, and the *Britain's Got Talent* finals seemed lacklustre.

The media were struggling to pinpoint Cowell's position in the public's feelings. 'You always get *X Factor*-crisis stories,' Cowell told his staff, 'but the only crisis will be when people stop watching.' His intimate circle witnessed a different story: a man heading towards the edge, hating the delight Simon Fuller would draw from his embarrassment as *American Idol*'s ratings rose above 22 million. But even Fuller could not assess Cowell's real vulnerability.

Over that weekend, a new solution surfaced from Los Angeles. Darnell and Frot-Coutaz told Cowell that Cole should return to America and appear at *The X Factor* USA's next auditions in Newark.

'This is completely crazy,' said Philip Green. By then, Cowell was relying on the billionaire to solve his problems, and his trust was shared by the other players. 'Is this for real?' Green asked Cowell, bewildered by the about-turn.

'You call Mike and Cécile,' replied Cowell, shying away from confrontation.

The conference call was fractious. 'We want her to return to Newark,' said Frot-Coutaz.

'Why?' asked Green.

'Because we're paying her.'

'It's a $100-million production,' exclaimed Green. 'Why are you causing so much trouble about a measly $2 million? What about you, Mike?'

'I agree. She should come back.'

'Mike, what are you smoking? Why is everyone behaving like this? Can we be sensible?'

Darnell, apparently scared and powerless, was unforthcoming.

'Mike, where is this going?' Green scoffed. 'You're four foot already. Do you want to be three foot? Fuck it, I'll pay her.'

The call ended without resolution. Cole was still ignoring all telephone calls but had, according to her family, vowed never to speak to Cowell again. 'She feels so badly treated,' said one relative, 'that she has had enough of the showbiz world.'

On reflection, Cowell recognised his weakness in America. Without a hinterland, influential allies or a top-gun American executive, he could only bow to two fearful and superstitious corporate employees who were proposing a ridiculous solution. Quite simply, unlike his earlier arguments in Britain with ITV's chiefs, he lacked any firepower to push through the obvious solution. In the future, he realised, he would need to reinforce Syco's and Sony's authority or else sell out. In the meantime, he could only act as a meek firefighter.

'48 Hours to Save *X Factor*' was the *Sun*'s front-page headline on Monday 30 May. 'Cowell fears for ratings.' Rupert Murdoch's newspaper, usually a cheerleader for Cowell, could not resist knocking the man who too often had prevented the publication of an embarrassing story. 'Simon has clearly dropped a massive clanger,' wrote Gordon Smart, the paper's showbiz editor, 'and he should be saying sorry.' Cowell was described as 'shattered' by the end of his friendship with Cole, admitting, 'It's a cock-up.' Cole herself, 'too fragile' because of Cowell's bad treatment of her, could not consider starting the British auditions on Wednesday. Peter Fincham had allegedly 'flown in' to save Britain's *X Factor*. In fact, he was participating in telephone conferences from Calgary in Canada, but all of them were baffled at being outwitted by manufactured indignation. As Cowell read the newspaper at lunchtime, he anticipated heading four hours later towards the Wembley studios for the finals of *Britain's Got Talent* and his first public appearance since Chicago. Over the previous days, he had ordered the production team to re-edit the taped portions exhaustively.

That afternoon, Cowell chose his clothes carefully. In the midst of a crisis, with the excited audience anticipating a drama, he abandoned his jeans and T-shirt and dressed in a grey suit and a white shirt undone to his waist. 'They want to see me taking a huge kicking,' he said nervously as he entered the Fountain studios. 'There's a bloodbath going on.' In the event, there was only one catcall.

'Can you understand us?' joked Ant and Dec, the two hosts, in deep northern accents similar to Cole's.

'Am I missing something here?' asked Cowell. 'I have just got back. Otherwise, what's been going on?' The answer, Cowell knew, was the prospect of a poor show. 'There are too many old acts,' he admitted. 'It could have been better.'

Despite the efforts of his scouts, the contestants were dreary. The show had deteriorated. The only spark was Ronan Parke, an engaging twelve-year-old singer. 'At least that answers the cynics who say everything is fixed in advance,' said Cowell.

The following day's newspapers reported that his right eye was drooping. Inadequate Botox was blamed. On edge, Cowell explained that the make-up woman had solved the 'droop' by removing 'hair below his eye', but the damage was done. The only good news was Louis Walsh's excited report that the new *X Factor* panel had done 'very well' on its first day, without Cowell and Cole.

Cheryl Cole's exclusion from both *X Factor*s seemed inevitable until a night-time conference call on Wednesday 1 June. 'I'm not comfortable with Nicole,' Cécile Frot-Coutaz told Cowell. 'Mike and I want Cheryl back in the US.' Cowell suppressed his exasperation. Frot-Coutaz, he suspected, was still bothered about paying Cole if she failed to appear, and at the same time she had not seen Scherzinger's glittering performance on Britain's *X Factor*. Corporate animals sometimes advocated ridiculous solutions to control potential internal damage.

'I don't want anyone to feel compromised,' Cowell replied. 'I want a clear-headed decision. If she comes back, OK. If she can get her confidence back, I'll look after her.' While the conversation continued, Cowell thought how to remedy the awful lighting on *The X Factor* USA set.

'Right, that's agreed,' he concluded. 'Cheryl's coming back.' Frot-Coutaz, it was agreed, would write to Cole asking whether she wanted to return to America, and will.i.am would be told that arrangements had been made for his client to go to the American embassy in London on Friday to obtain a new work visa. The crisis, the voices from Los Angeles confirmed, was over.

Cowell's peace was short-lived. When he awoke later on Thursday morning, he was told by Ann-Marie Thomson, his spokeswoman, that JustPaste.It, a Polish website, had posted a damning blog allegedly written by a Sony Music executive. The anonymous blogger, claiming to work closely with Cowell, described how he had become 'increasingly uncomfortable' with the 'fixing' of *Britain's Got Talent*. In particular, he asserted that Ronan Parke, the favourite, was not a normal contestant who had worked his way up but was the beneficiary of a 'grooming and manipulation process to prepare Ronan for stardom'. The blogger claimed Parke had been secretly selected by Cowell's scouts two years earlier as part of a strategy to crack the preteen market. Ronan's grooming, wrote the former 'executive', not only involved singing and elocution lessons, but also the supervision of his hairstyle, clothes and poise, and even management of his appearances on YouTube, Twitter and Facebook. Accordingly, wrote the blogger, all the 'oddities, freaks and mentally ill people' who flocked to the auditions at personal expense were being deceived just like the television audience. Even the telephone voting, he claimed, was 'manipulated' by those saying, 'The public need to be told who to vote for.' About 140,000 people had read the wholly false vitriol of a malicious oddball before Syco's lawyers managed to ensure its removal.

Cowell's return to the front pages of the newspapers – involuntarily because of Cole and the blogger, and deliberately to promote *Britain's Got Talent* – reawakened anger that his huge fortune, estimated at £400 million, had been earned by manipulating the public's taste. To some, the latest sensation about a repeated theme, regardless of its veracity, suggested that Cowell was too powerful and too rich. The row, some even suspected, was contrived by Cowell to increase the viewing figures.

Cowell feared that a bad week could be followed by an even worse seven days. 'Don't give me the newspapers or tell me what's in them,' he ordered his staff, giving the impression that he would remain unswayed by the media. In reality, he regularly looked at his iPhone to read the Google alerts of his name. Everything written was taken to heart.

The blog had left Cowell distraught, and he suspected a conspiracy. While ITV's and Cowell's lawyers hired specialist investigators to track down the crank, he telephoned Ronan's mother.

'Have we ever met? Did we ever help Ronan?' he asked.

'No,' she replied. 'I always wish we had met, but we never did and you never helped Ronan.'

The media were guided to the woman for interviews. 'It is libellous and lies,' she confirmed.

Within twenty-four hours, Syco's executives were convinced the culprit was living in Germany and his arrest was 'just a matter of time'.

In Holland Park, Cowell told the ever-present Jackie St Clair, 'I've become public enemy number one.' The compensation was the certainty of more viewers when he appeared live on *Britain's Got Talent* the following day, Friday 3 June. His bid to make a live statement at the outset of the programme was rejected by Fincham. 'Don't get dragged down into the tabloid morass,' advised Fincham. 'It's all hullabaloo.' After a brisk discussion, Cowell agreed to confine himself to a short denunciation. 'This is a deliberate smear campaign,' he told 11 million viewers, 'and it is my job to make sure that whoever this liar is, he is exposed and this kid is treated in the same way as everybody else.'

Back home after the show, Cowell had his normal massage and steam bath followed by a burger and chips. 'I'm floating,' he confessed, buffeted by the media outcry and confused by mixed messages from Los Angeles. 'I've got to the point where I've had enough.' In public, his staff spoke only about 'helping Cheryl' and 'wanting the best for Cheryl', although all agreed that 'In this crazy world no one knows what she wants.' Darnell, Cowell believed, was offering little help, but in fact the producer was angry at being dragged into the debacle. Officially, Fox's publicity machine was silent, but Darnell's spokesmen refused to dispel stories about Cole's depression, love torment, homesickness, unconfident performances, incomprehensible accent and poor bonding with Paula Abdul. To complicate matters, a tape had been released on YouTube showing Cole articulating confident judgements in the auditions.

At 2 a.m., Cowell began a conference call with Darnell and Frot-Coutaz. Unexpectedly, the mood music from Los Angeles was buoyant. Unburdened by any American media coverage about Cole, neither could grasp Cowell's distress. Although Cole had neither replied to Frot-Coutaz's message two days earlier nor collected her work visa, Frot-Coutaz was optimistic. 'I'll text Cheryl,' she volunteered, expecting a positive reply. They set a deadline of midnight on Sunday, the following day, allowing her just enough time to arrive in New York for the auditions.

After daybreak on Saturday, Cowell finally went to sleep. 'I must stay focused on the show and not read the papers,' he promised himself. Usually he loved publicity, but now he admitted, 'My life is like reality TV – live TV and live consequences. My private life and business is shared with the world. I'm in a stressful position, trying to make the right decisions. Whatever I do has huge consequences and becomes a massive story.'

'It's been an awful week,' Cowell admitted as he arrived at the Fountain studios in Wembley Park on Saturday 4 June, ready to record *Britain's Got Talent*. 'I've spent the whole night on the phone, until 7.30 this morning.' In the auditorium, his friends and executives were crowded onto uncomfortable seats listening to a limp warm-up by a former policeman. 'I want you to stand and scream and clap,' he urged the audience. Some were already weary at the prospect of yo-yoing up and down over the next three hours. Glancing in the contestants' 'holding room', Cowell was overcome by 'a huge wave of depression. This is a moment of total pressure. There's no sense of fun. I don't know what's going to happen in the next hour.' As a joke, he added, 'In TV now there aren't any hard drugs, just prescription drugs to stave off depression. There's not much laughter.'

Concealing his exhaustion, Cowell entered the studio. He hoped Ronan Parke would win, although in his predictions, to be revealed after the show, he had picked New Bounce, four black teenage boys whom he knew had no chance of success, even against dreary dancers, an unamusing comedian and a clutch of tuneless singers. Between the acts, he glanced at his phone. A message from Colin Myler, the editor of the *News of the World*, asked him to ring before the newspaper's deadline.

Slipping out of the studio, Cowell made the call. 'I've been told by a source in New York that Cheryl's going back to America,' Myler said. 'I called Philip Green, and he said, "Be careful. It's not over until the fat lady sings." But I think it's happening. Is your gut feeling that she'll be in New York on Wednesday?'

'Not 100 per cent,' replied Cowell, 'but there's a good chance she's coming back, so yes.'

Myler ordered the following morning's front-page headline to report Cole's certain return to New York. Cowell was unconcerned about the report's veracity. The public speculation and the pantomime of the nation holding its breath could only enhance his status.

During the show's critical interval, while the peak audience of over 14 million was voting, Cowell rested in his dressing room with his mother and friends, dipping potato chips into tomato sauce. 'There is a twist to the Cheryl story,' he confided to his entourage. 'A surprise,' he smiled as he returned to the studio for the results. How many viewers had voted remained, for the moment, a closely guarded secret, known only to the government's regulator to prevent any malpractice.

As the dross got eliminated and the final choice was between Parke and Jai McDowall, a pedestrian Scottish care worker with a good voice but no star appeal, Cowell closed his eyes. His head jerked with shock when the Scot was named the winner. 'It's a dream come true,' said McDowall, pledging to use the £100,000 prize to buy his house. Clearly disappointed, Cowell praised McDowall as a 'worthy winner' and consoled himself with the fact that Susan Boyle lost the same competition two years earlier. As he hurriedly stepped over cables and past the cameras towards his Rolls-Royce waiting in a bay next to the studio, he accidentally bumped into McDowall. 'You know who you are and where you're going,' said Cowell, summoning polite encouragement. The victor nodded mutely to Cowell's offer to 'look after him' at the Royal Variety Performance.

While the other three judges and the programme executives headed to the Dorchester hotel to celebrate, Cowell was driven home, ostensibly for a bath. His more serious purpose was to reply to a text from will.i.am. Thankfully, the agent wanted a conversation.

'She should come back on the American show,' said Cowell.

'How do I know this isn't a trick to avoid paying her in case she refuses to turn up?' asked the agent.

'This is ridiculous,' exploded Cowell. 'Who cares about $2 million? What does she actually want? Does she want to come back on the show?'

'That isn't your concern,' replied the agent.

Cowell's suspicions were roused. 'Her agent's winding her up,' he thought, but he ended the conversation positively. The deadline was a conference call scheduled for Sunday at 9 p.m., London time.

Cowell then set off for the Dorchester, convinced that 'It's a complete mess.' The *Britain's Got Talent* party was limp. Having fulfilled his duty to thank everyone, he returned home after less than an hour.

At 9 p.m. the following evening, Cowell, Darnell and Frot-Coutaz dialled in for the conference call.

'Are you there, Will?' asked Frot-Coutaz. There was silence.

'I don't know why he's broken off,' said Cowell. 'Perhaps he's negotiating to get her onto *The Voice* in America or even the following year in Britain. She's missed the deadline. That's it. We sign Nicole.'

To a man accustomed to winning, Cole's tactics were a novelty. Cowell was gearing up to retaliate. Four months later, he would gloss over the agony and tell a newspaper, 'I had Peter Fincham on the phone saying, "We'll have her back, we'll pay her more money."'

The headline in Monday morning's *Sun* appeared a day late: 'Cheryl Cole . . . You Have 24 Hours to Save Your Career'. The offer to 'salvage her career' was described as 'her lifeline to return to the US *X Factor*'. During that day, Cowell sought to salvage his reputation. 'I'm not a monster,' he told the *Mirror*, 'but I did the right thing . . . she was out of her comfort zone . . . I was just protecting her.' He continued, 'The hardest thing to accept is that everyone has painted me as a monster because I embarrassed her, but the truth was I was protecting her.'

No one understood the problems, he believed, and few took notice of another story published that day about an investigator having tracked down in the north of England the Internet imposter who had posed as the 'Sony executive' and exposed how *Britain's Got Talent* was rigged. The man made a public apology.

Cowell had read the newspapers before he arrived at the Harrods executive terminal at Luton airport to fly to New York. Throughout his life, he had rarely displayed vulnerability after a setback, seemingly able to shrug off humiliation and move on. This time, he was uncertain about the consequences of the previous two weeks. While twenty-six suitcases were loaded onto the plane, he asked rhetorically, 'Have I been damaged? When the general public see what else is happening, they'll see I haven't done a bad thing. The critics aren't producing shows. Every decision depends on audience acceptance, and I know when I've done something bad. The impression is that Cheryl was my decision alone, but it was a group decision. I've had to take the blame. I've had to be the fall guy, taking the flak. There's always only one name in the firing line. I'm the one sitting in the editing bay and at every audition.'

As he walked through the plane he spotted the day's newspapers on a table. 'Get the *Daily Mail* off,' he told Abi Doyle. Hannah Lamden dropped off two bags of fruit in the cabin. 'This is just in case Simon asks for a smoothie,' she told the hostess. Ever since Cowell had read about their life-enhancing powers in a newspaper, he had placed a regular order for rare fruits to be air-freighted to London or Los Angeles. He changed into a tracksuit, asked for his smelling salts, which he passed under his nose, and continued his discourse: 'The public will love Cheryl even more now. She's still a hot property. She can walk onto any show right now.' Then he laughed. 'The madness this week was unbelievable. They all think I'm manipulating it. I wish.'

As the plane crossed the British coastline, he began dictating his latest proposals for new shows in a bid to move away from reality TV. He complained that his latest programme, *Red or Black?*, bought by ITV, was poorly produced. Fearful of deterioration or rivals producing better shows, he urged his handful of staff to rejuvenate his programmes with the aim of building an empire so, like Aaron Spelling, 'I can earn money while I'm asleep. Aaron Spelling understood good casting, and he broke stars. He never hired established stars.' In the background, Hannah Lamden and Jennie Paine, a third assistant, were searching for the name of the Russian masseuse he had used last time he was in Miami so they could book her for his upcoming two-week stay there, following his stops in New York and Chicago. 'She had dark hair,' Cowell said helpfully. There was no plan for Mezhgan Hussainy to join her fiancé on the east coast.

Finally, Cowell gave brief thought to the following day's *X Factor* USA auditions in Newark. In the state of Frank Sinatra's and Bruce Springsteen's birth, he needed to dispel the gloom. Nicole Scherzinger had won the prize, but Paula Abdul, he anticipated, would bid to grab the limelight. Cheryl Cole was now merely a ghost.

'After a bumpy week, today is a new beginning,' Cowell said, greeting his battered troops. 'Enjoy yourselves.'

Abdul had arrived in the gloomy judges' room to find a large bunch of flowers. The card contained warm greetings from Cole. Sensitive to showbiz turmoil, Abdul was genuinely grateful. In the distant darkness of the room was a basket of fruit for L. A. Reid. The following day, when the circus moved on, the basket and the card from Cole remained, untouched.

16
Crisis

Although his private jet was parked less than twenty yards from the executive terminal at Luton airport, Simon Cowell made the short journey in his black Rolls-Royce. Not out of convenience but to make a statement. To step out of his limousine at the foot of the aircraft steps reconfirmed his fame and wealth.

Two minutes later, the plane was taxiing towards the runway, ready to begin the eleven-hour flight to Los Angeles. Lighting up a Kool, Cowell sipped a cup of tea and told Abi Doyle to start up two laptops. Stretching back, he left his seatbelt undone and began watching recordings of the forty-five female singers due to perform at the Pasadena Civic centre four days later, on 20 July 2011. Out of the 100,000 who had been originally auditioned in six cities, just 262 men and women aged between thirteen and seventy-six had been invited to the 'boot camp'. After five days of auditions, only thirty-two would survive.

Pulling on the Kool as the jet lifted off the tarmac, Cowell spoke enthusiastically about his search for a global star who would separate *The X Factor* USA from the imitation programmes sprouting across American television. The countdown had begun to enrich Sony and himself.

'She's pretty and can sing,' he commented about Caitlin Koch, a blonde rugby coach from Buffalo, New York.

'I must have been in a good mood that day,' he dictated, terminating the chances of a brunette from Chicago with a flick on his pad.

'Cari Fletcher from New Jersey, she's got potential,' he told Doyle.

'She's not going anywhere,' he said after two seconds of another brunette, pushing the fast-forward button.

'Dani Knights: sexy, good name. I like her a lot.'

As Doyle inserted new DVDs into the computers and the plane crossed the British coastline, Cowell grimaced: 'They're commercial but they're choosing the wrong songs.' On reflection he realised his own error: 'The ones I thought were good aren't sounding so good, and those who weren't on the radar are much better than I realised.' In Cowell's business, so much depended on impulse on the night, but Stacy Francis, a forty-two-year-old living in Burbank, remained his Susan Boyle 'replica'.

At the end of the viewings, his favourite was an eighteen-year-old blonde from Seattle. 'It'll all change,' he smiled, noting a few girls who could be forged into a group. Hammering inexperienced singers into four different groups, he decided, would be Paula Abdul's summer chore. The collapse since 2003 of the Dixie Chicks, America's most popular female country band with sales of over 30 million albums prior to their anti-Bush comments, had left a gap in the market. Before the start of the live *X Factor* programmes in October, Abdul would select four attractive girls from the dozens heading to Pasadena to shape into a group.

As he ate the dinner sent ahead by Helen, his cook in London, Cowell speculated on the panel's chemistry, especially Abdul's relationship with Nicole Scherzinger. 'Nicole', he said with glee, 'has become like a panther ready to strike, which Paula hates because she fears the competition.' Their relationship, he envisaged, would crack once they began to disagree about the contestants. 'I'll encourage it because otherwise the show will be boring.' Twenty million Americans, he was sure, would turn on to watch the cat fights, down 10 million from his summer prediction.

Cowell's second stretch Rolls-Royce Phantom was waiting outside US immigration's small concrete block at Los Angeles international airport dedicated to passengers on private jets. After shaking two officers' hands in the empty room, he drove to the house he was renting in West Hollywood. As usual, Abi Doyle had given him $50 in cash, his tip for the driver. Cowell rarely travelled with money.

His first appointment the following day was in North Palm Drive to see the builders' progress on his house. To his neighbours' distress, about a hundred workers had been arriving daily since February to transform the exterior, refurnish and redecorate the interior and expand the house into the garden. The total budget had escalated towards $14 million.

At 2 p.m., Cowell drove his Bentley convertible onto the black basalt forecourt. Anticipating his arrival, Zoë, the house manager, had directed four housekeepers and three groundsmen to clean the building site until it was spotless. Cowell was delighted by his first impression. Over the previous five months, all the white wooden surfaces in the exterior and many interior shelves and frames had been sanded down and covered with a custom-prepared greeny-black oil paint. The last of fourteen coats was being applied. After each coat had dried, the wood had been sanded and another coat painted on.

'It's completely unique,' swooned architect Brian Biglin about the art-deco style.

'It's great,' Cowell agreed.

Since it was Sunday, the usual noise and dirt from the excavators and jackhammers was absent. Nevertheless, over forty tradesmen were working, many in the garden.

Cowell's idea was to have an outdoor living space surrounded by plants, water and fire. Three rooms had been extended to create exterior loggias covered by retractable push-button roof shades if the sun was too strong, and retractable skylights for when it rained. Electric heaters in the beams staved off any night chill, and live fires blazed from iron grates. Regardless of the weather, Cowell could sit outdoors.

Along one of the new extensions was a 'living wall' for plants. Amid green foliage, white and magenta flowers would grow vertically as a piece of art, watered via permanently moist foam attached to the wall. If Cowell so desired, the wall garden could be changed within a day. Opposite the living wall was a waterfall gurgling into a submerged basin lit up by flames emerging from the bubbling water.

To cross between the two seating areas opening into the garden, Biglin had designed a walkway that seemed to float on the water. Cowell and his guests would step on apparently drifting stones linked to black tiles illuminated by concealed lighting.

At the rear of the garden, in front of the separate gym and guest house, was a fifty-foot reflecting swimming pool lined with Italian Bisazza stone tiles. Coloured black with a hint of purple, the water mirrored the surrounding buildings, the foliage of the nine specially planted mature palm trees and the tubs and planters made from black Absolute granite from Europe. 'Mine will be the only house in Palm Drive with palm trees,' chortled Cowell.

The unique omission for a Californian home was a barbecue. 'I can't stand them,' he had declared, ordering instead two Italian brick pizza ovens. Near by were racks for various types of wood, each of which infused the food with a particular taste. Once completed, his chef would fly from London to confirm that pizzas could be baked perfectly in the new ovens, and then return to Europe. Soon after she fulfilled that task, Cowell decided to employ another cook.

A new feature in the garden was the paving surrounding the lawn. Seven thousand square feet of limestone had been cut from a quarry in Vancouver, Canada. Found by Biglin after a long search, Cowell liked the grey colour, which in sunlight became dark grey with blue veins.

Persuading the quarry owners to cut the stone in a precise thickness and shape had been difficult because the process would inevitably cause breakages. In anticipation, Biglin had ordered 40 per cent more stone than required. But, in the event, so much stone broke that the quarry lost money on the contract and vowed never to repeat the process.

Creating this extraordinary garden had irritated Cowell's neighbours. Not only was the quiet road disturbed by noise and dirt, but it was clogged daily by over seventy vehicles. Protests had persuaded the local authority to ban all building temporarily, until Biglin organised a shuttle to the site for the workers. 'They're neighbours from hell,' scoffed Cowell. To fashion reconciliation, he offered the complainants spa treatment and cakes. They would at least be spared his plan to build studios and an office block in Los Angeles if *The X Factor* and *America's Got Talent* were recommissioned.

'When can I move in?' he asked.

'In eight weeks,' replied Biglin. 'Mid-September.'

Five minutes later, Cowell had crossed Sunset Boulevard and was driving up Loma Vista, a steep climb into Beverly Hills. Patrick Dantolario, his property manager, had found a replacement for Cole Place, which was being legally transferred to Mezhgan Hussainy. At the end of a winding road, the house at the peak of Trousdale Place cost about $11 million. Isolated above the city, the uninterrupted view from the shady garden guaranteed a paradise even greater than North Palm Drive. Bought from a music producer, the 7,000-square-foot house was ornately furnished and lit by crystal chandeliers.

'Get rid of all that,' Cowell told his manager.

'It's valuable,' he replied.

'Just get it out,' insisted Cowell.

The house, to be used as an office, was to be rebuilt as 'an 8,000-square-foot Asian retreat', which to Biglin meant it would be 'warmer, creamy, natural and relaxed with a lot of water and wood like a home in Bali'. Cowell asked Hussainy to supervise the renovation. 'It keeps her involved and happy,' he believed. She was also efficient. He had seen an $18,000 invoice for a month's supply of flowers. Hussainy had negotiated an immediate 30 per cent reduction, eventually cutting the monthly bill to just $280. 'Great,' said Cowell. 'I can't stand flowers.'

At 7 p.m., Cowell returned to his rented house. His producers had been summoned to discuss the five days of auditions. Led by Tim Byrne, Syco's creative director, the British contingent dominated the meeting. Byrne, a former television music producer, had featured Cowell's Fanfare records on ITV's Saturday-morning programmes, especially promoting the hit 'Yell' by Instant Replay. Reporting to Byrne were the programme's producers, music directors and sound technicians. To tilt the odds in his favour, Cowell had drawn the best talent from Britain, at the expense of the British *X Factor* show. Thrilled to be responsible for a cast of experts and technicians supporting twenty-four cameras – all at his beck and call – he had hired choreographers, vocalists, stylists and music experts to produce a spectacular as different as possible from *American Idol.*

'I'll either be praised as a genius', he told his producers, 'or get screwed.'

Three days later, Cowell arrived at the Pasadena Civic centre, an imposing theatre built in 1931 with over 3,000 seats. The 260 contestants, staying in two local hotels at Fox's expense, were standing on the huge stage facing the empty auditorium. Cowell's introductory sermon was chilling: 'Over the next twenty-four hours, you're being tested to see if you're a star. We're going to test your attitudes to team work, hard work and if you've got talent. We will separate the good from the not so good. There'll be no feedback, except that half of you will be going home tomorrow.' The inevitability of expulsions cast a pall. 'And more of you will leave over the next days,' he added. The gloom was punctured by a promise: 'One of you will get $5 million.'

The harsh tone was uncompromising. 'There's one winner up there,' said L. A. Reid. 'But it's a competitive environment.'

'You're competing against one another,' agreed Paula Abdul. 'This will be a stressful week. Stay true to yourselves. But be amazing. Put your nerves aside. Be bold, daring, unique. There's always a winner, but we are determined to find a star.'

'Years ago,' concluded Nicole Scherzinger, 'I started up there on *Popstars*. This is your time to shine.'

Gathered behind the judges was the evidence of Cowell's resolve. Choreographers, vocal coaches, stylists, songwriters and Sony executives were watching to spot whether any of the raw material bore signs of potential stardom.

Even on *The X Factor*, genuine stars could not be entirely manufactured. The experts searched for talent and character. Within two minutes, they could distinguish between actors and those using a song to define their interpretation and identity. Some of those experts spoke about an artist's body as an instrument, with true artists using their bodies to hook the audience. The intense auditions were a pressure cooker, and those overwhelmed by the experience because they lacked talent and character would be separated from those using the expertise provided to grow in spurts into a professional.

'I need to see you fighting for the $5 million,' Brian Friedman, the choreographer, was saying as he walked among the contestants. Since his abrupt departure from Britain's *X Factor*, Friedman had been reborn as a teacher. 'Set your bar really high, and your goal must be to go even higher,' he continued. 'You must call attention to yourself through the music. It's not about dancing, it's about using the stage.' Only a few understood his message.

The first fifteen contestants walked onto the stage to perform.

'Don't stand there like a pencil,' Cowell snapped at a hapless male from Dallas. 'This was your moment. You've lost it.' He called a break.

Smoking in hot sunshine outside his Star Wagon trailer, Cowell looked at eight pots of anti-ageing cream placed on a wall for his approval. Then, after a few words with Tim Byrne, he walked back into the hall to address the contestants. Alongside him was L. A. Reid.

'The first fifteen were no good,' he told the hushed crowd. 'They were standing like doughnuts. You've got two minutes. You need to start thinking about entertaining us. Because a lot of you are going home tonight.'

'On the basis of what we've seen,' Reid added, 'I don't know why we said "yes" to anyone.'

Once the auditions resumed, Cowell's mood darkened. Instead of listening, he and Abdul were engrossed in conversation.

'Thank you for putting me into the show,' she told Cowell for the umpteenth time. 'It's such a warm, wonderful atmosphere. I feel so appreciated. It's so much better than *Idol*. That's slow, lazy and underproduced.'

On stage, a twenty-two-year-old's fate had been decided. Turning his back to speak to the experts, Cowell expressed his frustration.

'These were good people but they're performing badly. They haven't prepared themselves.'

Yet their hunger could not be disputed. One girl stood singing on crutches, two were pregnant, a man sang hours after hearing that his brother had just died, and Stacy Francis performed rather than go to her father's funeral that same day. 'That wasn't good' was Cowell's verdict on her performance, and she burst into tears.

*

'Crunch time,' announced Cowell just after 11 p.m. at the end of the second day. The first decisions had been made. Outside the auditorium, 170 contestants were being directed down an empty corridor. Dragging their suitcases, all wore long faces and, anticipating the worst, some were in tears. Like doomed refugees in a wartime drama, their movements were funereal.

Elsewhere, the remaining ninety-two were being corralled into holding areas. While they waited in anguish, the producers discussed the deployment of the cameras to record images of joy and despair.

In a sideshow, four young girls had been taken to a room with their parents to meet all four judges. The group, the Lilas, were being told by Cowell that because one of the girls was one month too young, the group would unfortunately be excluded. Six cameras recorded their howls and tears. Such was their distress that Abdul and Scherzinger also began crying. The recorded drama was electrifying but excessively emotional. 'We can't use that,' Cowell declared, knowing the limits of the public's taste, and headed back into the theatre.

Ninety-two contestants were on the stage. 'This is not easy for any of us,' said Reid, describing the inadequacy of some performances and the rigour of the competition. All believed they were about to be sent home. 'But the good news', continued Reid, keeping a poker face, 'is that you're through to the next round.' The stage exploded with cheers.

'I still haven't seen a star,' Reid told Cowell at 1 a.m. 'I hope we haven't wasted our time.'

'Don't worry,' replied Cowell, heading for home and four hours on the telephone.

At 6 a.m., the survivors were woken up and divided into thirteen groups. Following Cowell's master plan, Paula Abdul, supported by choreographers and vocalists, gave them songs to learn and then instruction on how to sing and dance.

At 5 p.m., Cowell appeared. The groups entered the stage and, while singing together, each contestant stepped forward for a forty-second solo while the remainder provided a choral background. The raw material had been transformed into a disciplined troupe providing compelling entertainment, the beginning of an intensely micro-managed production process. Cowell would leave nothing to chance.

Spontaneously, Cowell, Abdul, Scherzinger and Reid burst into animated hugs and high fives. The gaggle of professionals in the vast theatre was mesmerised. 'We've got some real stars,' they screeched. Reid was mightily relieved. There were, he realised, at least six potential stars. Finally, he grasped Cowell's insight. There was light at the end of the tunnel.

At 11.30 p.m., after an hour of negotiation, another thirty-two were isolated and brought to the stage. 'It's the end,' they were told by Abdul. Hurried into a large room, they were filmed crying and even screaming obscenities at Cowell.

Unaware of those scenes, the remaining sixty were summoned back onto the stage. 'It's not good news,' sighed Cowell mournfully. Twelve cameras recorded misery. Then: 'It's great news. You're through.' After four minutes of recording, Cowell took the microphone: 'Tomorrow we start again. At the end, half of you will also be out of the competition. To stay in, you have to create magic. Think of the $5 million. Study the songs. Be true to yourselves. In the meantime, we've arranged a party. Enjoy yourselves.'

'I'm not going to the party,' he whispered to an assistant. 'I might do something I regret.' One pretty girl might prove too attractive to resist.

Twenty-four hours later, just thirty-two out of the original 100,000 hopefuls remained. Divided into four sections – girls, boys, groups and over-thirties – they would be 'mentored' over the summer in a 'judge's house', which in reality were rented homes in superb locations. Cameras would record the training and the emotions as the judge chose which four would go through to the live shows in Los Angeles in October. Four female country singers who all looked like Taylor Swift were chosen to be trained by Abdul. They decided to call themselves Lakoda Rayne. Optimistic about the attractive girls, Cowell never understood whether the name had a meaning.

In a good mood, Cowell flew with his friends to Nice to board *Slipstream*. During August, his producers would edit the first eight programmes. The news from London was excellent: 11.4 million people – 48 per cent of the TV audience – had watched the British *X Factor*. The new panel of judges – Gary Barlow, Tulisa Contostavlos, Kelly Rowland and Louis Walsh – had set a new record. 'There's great energy on the show,' Cowell concluded. 'It's a happy ship.' ITV, he noted, 'cannot get the press releases out fast enough'. Peter Fincham, he heard, was pleased that Cowell had proven to be dispensable.

Over two days, Cowell commuted between the yacht and the rented 'judge's house' in St-Tropez where six *X Factor* USA girls – flown in from America – battled for a place on the live programmes. At the end, among the two rejected by Cowell was Melanie Amaro, a nineteen-year-old from Florida.

Cowell's next stop was London. *Red or Black?*, a game show with a daily prize of £1 million for the winner, whose only skill would be to choose the right colour, was starting on Saturday 3 September. Commissioned from Syco by ITV as part of the 2010 contract for *The X Factor*, the programme was scheduled nightly for one week. Claudia Rosencrantz and other seasoned television executives were surprised that ITV had commissioned a mindless contest which she had unhesitatingly rejected, while Fincham was reminded of Paul Jackson's warning that ITV had become too reliant on Cowell.

By the second day, the most expensive game show in British

TV history, costing about £15 million, was already mired in scandal. The first winner, whose single talent had been to utter a one-syllable word, was exposed as an ex-convict, jailed for brutally assaulting a former girlfriend. By the fifth day, as Cowell again boarded a jet at Luton heading for Los Angeles, the audience had fallen from 7.2 million to 3.9 million. Cowell's reputation was knocked, but he did not appear concerned.

Minutes after take-off, he did, however, make a confession. As the jet crossed the Irish coastline and headed towards the Atlantic, he twice watched Melanie Amaro's performance in St-Tropez on his laptop. 'My greatest mistake was not putting Melanie through,' he moaned. 'It was insane. I don't know why I didn't put her through. I'll bring her back.' Shortly after, he flew to Florida and, in a specially taped encounter, invited the tearful girl back into the competition.

His other woman problem that day had also been self-inflicted. Speaking on Howard Stern's radio show, he admitted to having once enjoyed a threesome with two girls, avoided confirming his intention to marry Mezhgan Hussainy, and finally confessed his everlasting love for Terri Seymour. The conversation with the shock jock embarrassed Hussainy and outraged Sinitta. 'Why did you say you love Terri and not me?' she had wailed over the telephone.

Having pacified Sinitta, Cowell planned to tip off 'the paps' that he and Hussainy would be walking along Rodeo Drive, Los Angeles's expensive shopping area. 'That should wind them up,' he thought. A few hours later, he abandoned the idea. Instead, his fiancée would be invited to the *X Factor* USA screening party on 21 September.

Sitting down to dinner in Los Angeles, he cast aside what he considered to be trivia and considered his challenge during the autumn. With three big shows in Britain – *The X Factor*, *Britain's Got Talent* and another series of *Red or Black?* – and the launch of *The X Factor* USA, he would be stretched. Simultaneously, he would be supervising the franchises of his formats in over forty countries and also Syco's music producers. Overshadowing all that was the resilience of *American Idol*, which was still attracting over 22 million viewers. Normally he loved competition, but the criticism of his power to dictate public taste in television and pop music had become irritating. Too many were speculating whether cracks would soon show.

Among his latest critics were Lohan Presencer and James Palumbo at the Ministry of Sound. The record producers complained that Syco had without their agreement seized 'Collide', a song written by Swedish DJ and producer Avicii, to relaunch Leona Lewis. Cowell denied their claim, and the dispute was destined for an expensive High Court battle. The more profound issue, Cowell knew, was the argument about Lewis's artistic integrity. Compared to Adele, who wrote her own songs, Lewis lacked an intimacy with music and, like an actor, relied entirely on others.

Presencer and Palumbo were trenchant opponents of *The X Factor*'s manufactured pop. Lewis's inability to write her own music, they argued, and her unmemorable interviews guaranteed a 'short play' for her career. *The X Factor*, wrote Palumbo, is 'a cruel illusion that karaoke crooners can become stars'. Lewis, he predicted, would 'soon be finished'. Her first album had sold 7 million copies, her second 1 million and the third, he predicted, would crash.

Both 'snobs' infuriated Cowell. 'How many songs did Frank Sinatra write?' he asked rhetorically. His opponents had briefed the *Guardian* and *Daily Mail* to publish prejudiced reports about the Avicii dispute under the headline 'Rip-Off Factor'. Unfortunately, Lewis's relaunch singing the Avicii song on *Red or Black?* had failed. The song was poor, confirming Lewis's problem that no one was writing suitable music for her.

Commercially, however, her fate was unimportant to Cowell. Cher Lloyd, a runner-up in the last season of *The X Factor*, would be a hit by Christmas. The truncated careers of pop stars caused him little concern.

In the bigger picture, Palumbo was a mere pinprick for Cowell. The real challenge was posed by Lucian Grainge. Cowell's old friend had successfully planned with John de Mol, the Dutch producer of reality-TV shows, to sell *The Voice* to the BBC, starting in 2012. 'I bit like a dog on a bone when I got the offer,' admitted Grainge. Eighteen months after becoming Universal's global chief, he was proud to have become Cowell's principal rival, owning the international music rights for *American Idol* and now *The Voice*.

Sipping a red smoothie on the plane, Cowell spoke dismissively about Grainge's previous failures 'with his other TV shows – *Fame Academy* and *Britannia High*'. He was also flippant about the failure of *American Idol* and *The Voice* to produce hit records in 2011. '*The X Factor* USA', he pledged, 'will produce stars.'

Cowell was, however, irked by the BBC spending about £24 million of licence payers' money to pitch *The Voice* against him. 'The BBC is obsessed with destroying one of my shows. That's why I'm going back to Britain. I'm going to throw everything at them.'

One irony was not lost on Cowell. Twenty years earlier, he had had difficulties at Arista thanks to Nigel Grainge. Now Grainge's estranged brother had declared war, and Cowell mischievously speculated that Simon Fuller might be lurking in the shadows as an adviser. Eager to get his own revenge, Fuller might have encouraged will.i.am and Will Young to join *The Voice*'s panel in Britain. Whatever the truth, having fought against him for ten years Fuller had once again become part of Cowell's life. Dragging on a Kool, he predicted that 20 million viewers for *The*

X Factor USA on 21 September would silence Grainge, Fuller and the rest. 'It's got personal,' he said. 'I'm going to kill them.'

As his chauffeured Rolls-Royce drove north up Interstate 405 from Los Angeles airport, his self-confidence was boosted by the huge billboards along the freeway promoting the *X Factor* USA launch and featuring his photograph. Even Ryan Seacrest had sent a text admitting his irritation at Cowell's looming presence across the city.

The countdown to the first night was a lavish party for 1,500 guests at the ArcLight cinema in Hollywood to premiere the first programme, followed later that night by a second party for 200 at the Redbury hotel. By 3 a.m., even hardened critics spoke admiringly about *The X Factor* USA's 'European edginess compared to *Idol*'s schmaltzy, shameless pulling of heart strings'.

At 5 p.m. on 21 September, the programme's producers and stars met at Syco executive Simon Jones's home in the Hollywood Hills to watch the live transmission on a big screen in the garden. The forty guests left in high spirits, boosted by the Twitter reaction on the east coast. Early the following morning, the same people were reeling. Only 12.2 million had watched and *The X Factor* USA had ranked only as the third-most popular programme that night.

'I feel bruised,' Cowell told Bryan Lourd in one of his first calls.

'You've set your bar too high,' replied his agent. 'Twenty million for a new show in the fall was impossible.'

'I wish I'd kept my big mouth shut. I should have been less lippy.'

'If it falls by 30 per cent tonight,' warned Lourd, referring to the results programme, 'you've got real problems.'

No one else, Cowell steeled himself, would be allowed to see his unease. During a hastily summoned meeting, he urged his producers to 'work hard to put on a good show'. The problem, he announced, was not *The X Factor* itself but fatigue with singing competitions and similar formats. *American Idol*, he consoled himself, had started without any competition.

'It's hard to accept that there are people who will celebrate your failure' was his only concession of vulnerability.

Unlike earlier crises, he could cope with the fear of failure but, when his team departed, he admitted to a confidant: 'If it's bad tonight, we're toast. It'll be the end of my TV career in America.'

Other channels were swiftly cancelling series like *Pan Am* and a remake of *Charlie's Angels* 'on air' after a few episodes. Even Cowell was shocked by the brutality. Still blistered by his failure to secure 20 million viewers, he mentioned to his confidants his genuine fear of a similar fate if his audience collapsed. Bitter memories of his Arista days returned but naturally remained unspoken. Only his father could have understood his unseen pain and now no one else would sympathise with a man whose fame relied on nonchalance towards the downfall of others.

At 6 a.m. the following morning, Cowell telephoned Mike Darnell. To his relief, the ratings were steady. Not only had nearly 12 million watched, but, critically, *The X Factor*'s audience was top of the 18–49 demographic which advertisers targeted. The collapse had not occurred.

The relief was short-lived. The news from America about Cowell's failed prophecy had encouraged his critics in Britain to ask, 'Who needs Simon?' Cowell interpreted the reaction as 'the media are waging a vendetta against me'. Even Louis Walsh fuelled the fire: 'Everyone's happy because it's [*The X Factor*'s] really working. There's less pressure because Simon's not here.'

The reports, Cowell admitted, were 'not great for the ego. I always thought it would happen one day. I'm not feeling sorry for myself.' *America's Got Talent*, too, was under the microscope. Even though it had received the highest summer ratings, judge Piers Morgan's contract would not be renewed by NBC and he would be replaced by Howard Stern, the radio shock jock. NBC cited Morgan's duties for CNN in election year as the reason, but in reality they wanted Stern to increase the advertisers' target audience of eighteen- to forty-nine-year-olds. To win that demographic, NBC were prepared to spend an additional $20 million to move the production to New York so they could feature the American star. 'He's too dangerous for a family show,' Cowell had told the NBC executives. 'We could lose sponsors if the pressure groups start going.' But after Stern's assurances – 'I know what I can and what I can't say,' he promised – the move to New York was agreed. The presenter would be paid just over $10 million for the season.

Seeking a break, Cowell flew to Miami to celebrate his fifty-second birthday. In a conference call with his *X Factor* producers, he agreed, 'I'll change the programme on the basis of feedback but I'm sticking to the principles I believe in. We must do what interests me, and I won't be swayed.' At issue was nothing less than Cowell's micro-management of every aspect of the programme: not only the lighting and sound, but also the contestants' appearance and music. At later stages he would allow them and their 'judges' to choose their clothes and songs, but his showbiz-extravaganza production values were, he believed, essential. No one dared to contradict him and voice the concern that the show risked appearing overproduced, thus undermining its credibility.

Despite his absence, Cheryl Cole hired a plane to fly over North Palm Drive trailing a banner delivering barbed congratulations: 'Simon Cowell is 52 today. Ha ha ha! Love Cheryl xoxo.'

'I must admit the show is incredible,' she texted Cowell.

He was thrilled. Always intrigued by the woman who had eluded him romantically, he immediately telephoned her. During an hour-long conversation, she confirmed that she wanted to resume their working relationship.

'Thanks for making me look so good on the show,' Cole said,

grateful that her brief appearance on *The X Factor* USA had been well edited. Taking her cue, Cowell hoped she could be persuaded to return to one of his programmes.

'Come back to *The X Factor* in London,' he said. 'It'll be your Princess Diana moment. You'd do a great entrance.'

'OK, I'll do it,' agreed Cole. Will.i.am, her agent, did not pursue the idea.

The rebuff incited Cowell to consider retaliation. If will.i.am was to appear on the BBC's version of *The Voice* in early 2012, he would appear against him on *Britain's Got Talent*. He called Cole again. Would she, he asked, like to join him? 'No way,' she replied.

His next call was to see if Dannii Minogue was interested. 'She's a real man's girl,' he thought. 'Very feminine. I miss her.' The conversation was positive. 'She's like a greyhound out of a trap,' he chuckled. All that remained was a conversation with ITV boss Peter Fincham to agree on the judges.

The possibility of easy negotiations disappeared at the end of the week. The pincer came from two fronts. In Britain, *The X Factor*'s audience for the live shows had fallen by 700,000 in one week and it was about to fall 500,000 below the BBC's *Strictly Come Dancing* for the first time in four years. Most commentators blamed Cowell's absence from the programme as the reason.

'I can see the trap they've fallen into,' said Cowell, watching the British show from Los Angeles. 'They've chosen the wrong songs, wrong styling and choreography. I can't change the problem of the talent.' The contestants, everyone agreed, were uninteresting.

On 15 October, he spoke to each of the judges for thirty minutes, then to the producers and finally sent detailed notes. 'I need 10 per cent improvement each week,' he concluded. 'But I can't be too hard on them because it wouldn't be the best thing to do.'

The following day, the tabloid headlines dramatised Cowell's 'explosion' after 2 million viewers had switched off.

'This series of *The X Factor*', said Fincham grittily, 'is still the second-most popular series in its history and is still getting the same advertising revenue.'

Battered in Britain, Cowell was receiving a painful lesson about the cultural differences between UK and US audiences, not least among teenagers. 'It's obvious it's going wrong,' he admitted. Ratings in the US remained stubbornly below 12 million. His bid to attract younger viewers had alienated the middle-aged, and *The X Factor* USA had little appeal among the mid-American audience, especially as appropriate family viewing. Most of the contestants came from the two coasts and there was not enough country music.

In the US, the momentum of the recorded shows, Cowell acknowledged, was slipping. The show's appearance and even the songs were 'wrong'; the recorded programmes were predictable and lacked suspense; the contestants seemed too similar; and the audience were unable to see any difference from other shows.

'There have been a few blunders and I'm learning from the mistakes,' said Cowell. 'I thought I could start where we ended in the UK. It was arrogance on my part. We're adapting, not panicking.'

He was reconciled to the fact that an audience of 11 million for a new show was respectable but pledged that 16 million would watch the final in December. The turning point, he hoped, would be the first live two-and-a-half-hour show on 25 October.

The day before, he arrived in his Bentley for the dress rehearsal at the CBS studios. He parked outside his new double-decker, $1.6-million trailer, hired in the confident days of a star anticipating 20 million viewers.

'It's all worse than I've ever seen,' he exclaimed at the run-through. 'It's not what I wanted.' The graphics and sound were 'wrong'. The lighting – the most complicated ever constructed on a CBS set – was 'awful'. The music was 'badly mixed'. The contestants, he protested, looked phoney. 'I don't want stylists jumping all over them, sucking their identities out of them. The kids won't buy into acts if they're changed out of reality.' His problem, he thought, was working with strangers – like the lighting director – so 'messages were mixed'. Twenty hours before the live show began, he spoke about 'meltdown'.

The burden was entirely on Cowell. Although L. A. Reid was 'my rock. He's amazing,' only Cowell could save his show. 'As producer, I've got to do all the work. Everything depends on the feel on the night when I walk into the studio.'

Over twenty people were summoned to his trailer. 'We came to America to raise our game,' he started. 'I feel let down. We've got to improve.' Over five tense hours, he unpicked and rebuilt every aspect of the programme. 'I don't want the show to be an identikit to the UK's. It must be different. I want the set to be like an infinity pool so you don't see the beginning and end.'

The team was dispatched to work through the night, while he returned to his rented home. After two beers, he called with a new list of improvements.

'This isn't the usual karaoke with just one good singer,' he told Tim Byrne. 'We've got six great potential stars. I want them all to look different. They mustn't sound like a talent show. We've got to play to their strengths. Think hard what they should sing.'

Once he ended the conversation, he became maudlin: 'I'm learning on the fly. I'm learning something new – that you don't win in America unless you deserve to win. I'm working under difficult conditions. I've got sharper awareness than before. But I feel freer than I have for a long time. We're going to make it with this group of people.'

At 2 p.m. the following day, Cowell returned to CBS's Television City. Overnight, another crisis had erupted in Britain. Kelly Rowland had argued with her fellow *X Factor* judge Tulisa Contostavlos and had abruptly flown to Los Angeles. She was pleading that sickness would prevent her returning to London.

The tabloids were also speculating that Louis Walsh would be fired as the programme spiralled down.

'I have not arranged for the judges to argue,' Cowell scoffed. 'I don't want a panto.' But, as usual, he regarded the drama as a godsend: 'I love it. We're all at war now.'

Nor was he worried by the bad publicity. Fincham might complain about the 'tabloid morass', but the speculation about Rowland's antics would add to the ratings. He texted Walsh with some reassurance and called Cheryl Cole to beg her to return for a guest appearance on the British show. 'No way,' Cole replied, changing her mind once again. As he predicted, the headlines did push the British show back up to a peak audience of 13.5 million. His self-confidence was restored. Even when he had been down, Cowell had never revealed his anguish.

'What shall I wear?' he asked himself, looking at six suits and six white shirts hanging on a rail in the trailer.

'I'm going to touch you up,' said Carola Gonzalez, his new make-up artist, who was hovering near by. Cowell laughed. Looking down, he realised that he had just completed a magazine interview with his flies undone. The attractive female journalist had said nothing while he chewed a raw carrot.

'Ginger tea, please,' asked Cowell. A short conversation had recently persuaded him of the medicinal benefits of strong herbal tea, now made with bottled water brought from his home. Gonzalez had talked him into buying a Kangen water filter. 'It makes your skin a lot better,' she had promised. 'It filters all the toxins out of the water and adds vitamins and alkalis.' For $4,800, plus $130 for each filter, Cowell had snapped up yet another anti-ageing remedy.

At 4.50 p.m., the studio was packed, the audience was going wild and the programme was ready to go live. Cowell's favourites to win were constantly changing. On that evening, his male choices were Chris Rene and Astro, a fourteen-year-old black rapper from Newark – 'The most arrogant kid I've ever met, and he looks like a star.' He was no longer sure about Rachel Crow – 'probably too sweet', he thought, 'and doesn't love pop music like Justin Bieber' – and was hankering for Melanie Amaro and fourteen-year-old girl singer Drew Ryniewicz. 'Stacy's probably going home,' he speculated.

Just why he had shifted his allegiances regarding Crow and Stacy Francis was baffling. 'I'm a bit of a flake,' he admitted in his trailer. 'One minute I love someone and then I switch. It's easy to fall in and out with a contestant. They're bubble moments. In the auditorium, the song is good, the audience are on their feet and you lose your sense of perspective. I didn't realise the difference between a TV moment and a future star. At the beginning, Stacy was OK, and then it was "You're getting on my nerves now. You're too whimsical and misunderstand the audience." Eventually, there are too many TV moments, and the public saw limitations which I didn't.'

The real test was the public's verdict on himself. For the umpteenth time, Cowell looked at himself in the mirror: 'If I go down, I'll go down in flames.' He walked in the sunshine towards his fate.

The following morning, the world had not changed. The show's audience had barely increased and media interest was muted. Unlike in Britain, there were no raging tabloid headlines highlighting a scandal to generate new interest. Despite all his efforts, *The X Factor* USA was static.

On the eve of the following week's show, Cowell had dinner with Fox's Peter Rice and Mike Darnell. Unexpectedly, he was told at the end that the network would commission the series again for 2012. He returned home 'bouncing'.

At the end of the show, he had received another bonus: Brian Biglin, his architect, had called to say, 'Your house is ready.'

Cowell drove straight to North Palm Drive. Frantically, his staff had removed every last wrinkle and, on 3 November, he entered a perfect home.

'Bouncing around like a kid,' said Biglin, as Cowell rushed around 15,000 square feet of bliss. Everything, he declared, was 'great', except the grass in the garden. 'It's too smooth, like for bowling.' He ordered it to be ripped out and replaced with normal grass.

Keen to share his pleasure, he summoned Terri Seymour and Mezhgan Hussainy. Within minutes, both drove down from the homes he had bought them in Beverly Hills. In a surreal snapshot, Cowell showed two rival ex-lovers his stunning home. On cue, both admitted their admiration, with both chanting their demands for similar furniture and features in their own houses. After a time, their paymaster's enthusiasm for his guests was exhausted and he bid them farewell. Thankfully, alone again in his house, he could enjoy the solitude of his 'space'.

At 1.30 a.m., he was linked to the *X Factor* contestants in London by Skype. 'The contestants are not being given enough guidance,' Cowell had said. 'They need renewed confidence.' Even Denise Beighton had told Cowell's music executive, Sonny Takhar, that the independent labels were not interested in the contestants. The only choice, some were suggesting, was to bury the series and start afresh in 2012.

Cowell had wanted to fly the contestants to Los Angeles from Britain, but Fincham had vetoed the idea.

'I don't want Cowell interfering,' he said. 'The show should stand on its own feet.' Cowell's return to *Britain's Got Talent* the previous summer, Fincham thought, had been disruptive and any future comeback would be 'part of a big conversation'. 'Cowell is spinning too many plates,' Fincham told his staff, who were also irritated by *Red or Black?*. The crisis was growing. Even the *Sun* was hostile.

'We're not going to bury the show,' announced Cowell. 'I'm going to do something to get it back on the road. We fight to the end.' If Fincham blocked the trip to America, he would find another way to speak directly to *The X Factor*'s remaining contestants. He imagined a jokey fifteen-minute session on Skype.

The images on the huge screen in his new media room shocked Cowell. Staring back at him from London was a surly group. 'Why are you hiding your face?' he asked one male with a hood over his head. 'That's disrespectful.'

'Why', he asked another, 'don't you speak to me?'

Then there was Frankie Cocozza, a nineteen-year-old who could neither sing nor dance but whose sex life and drug use made him as attractive as Johnny Rotten – with matching publicity.

'Why are you putting your hand up to speak to me?' asked Cowell, perplexed by the lack of attitude. 'You all need to get your game up.'

When one of the Little Mix girls asked, 'What should we do?' Cowell could not swallow his anger. 'The Spice Girls never asked, "What should we do?" They said what they were going to do. If you don't know, you're lost.'

At the end of ninety minutes he cut the link.

'This is the worst group of contestants there's ever been,' he told his producers. 'We need a complete change.'

At 5.30 a.m., he took a sleeping pill and went to bed in his new house. At midday, he woke up and tried to open his bedroom door. Concealed bolts – installed for his protection – prevented his exit. Locked in the room, he called his housekeeper. 'There's a hidden button to release the bolts,' he was told. Concerned for his safety, he had already pledged to buy two Dobermanns to supplement the permanent security guard.

After drinking three glasses of filtered water and three smoothies, followed by a small plate of pills, oatmeal and other nutrients, at 3.45 p.m he summoned an emergency meeting of producers at his house. Overnight, the shock from London had sparked doubts about the American show.

'It's all bad,' he told his employees standing in the garden. 'Last night was the worst programme I've ever been on.' Not only was the music and lighting 'bad', but he was disappointed that L. A. Reid and Nicole Scherzinger were unengaged. 'They need to work hard for their artists,' he ordered. 'The show must have more star appeal, and more American appeal.' Steve Jones, the Welsh host, was, he declared, incomprehensible to Americans and should not be rehired. Everything needed renewal.

The crisis, however, was no reason for Cowell to abandon life's pleasures. To celebrate the twenty-ninth birthday of Kelly Bergantz, the executive producer responsible for developing new programmes with Cowell, he flew her and Ben, her boyfriend, along with Lauren and Andrew Silverman, to Las Vegas by private jet. Casino owner Steve Wynn had allocated villas in his private compound to the group. He also provided five bodyguards to escort them to a Halloween party at the XS nightclub. They proved insufficient to fend off the dozens of women who threw themselves at Cowell, who repeatedly agreed to pose for photographs and be kissed. At 2 a.m., in the midst of a rousing party, he led the way to the local Spearmint Rhino. For three hours, three lap dancers focused on him. As he left at 6 a.m., he appeared to be attracted to one of the girls. 'Leave them,' ordered his friends. 'You don't need any bad publicity.'

Earlier that week, after a good evening at Drai's nightclub in Hollywood, he had taken a girl back to his bungalow at the Beverly Hills hotel. He had drunk too much vodka and mixes and had awoken in the morning to discover not only the theft of money, but also his laptop, which was filled with confidential information. The local police, using images from the security cameras at the club and the hotel, had traced the girl, who was persuaded to return the computer in exchange for keeping the cash. No one thought it worthwhile to repeat the risk in Las Vegas.

'It's warfare in the jungle now,' he said, surveying his fate on his return to Los Angeles. Amid the post-mortems and plans to increase *The X Factor* USA's audience, Cowell had separately met with Ryan Seacrest, for an uneasy dinner, and with Nigel Lythgoe, which was 'relaxed', but both failed to rekindle the old friendships. Meeting the enemy, however, had reignited his quest to understand his mistakes.

Frustrated that his producers could not provide the answer, he had paid $250 for Mezhgan Hussainy's fifteen-year-old nephew to write a merciless critique of the programme's failures. The unorthodox report was damning. The contestants, he was told, failed to connect with the audience, the 'reality' was unreal and, most importantly, he had mistakenly assumed that American audiences would immediately understand what had taken seven years to develop in Britain. 'It's taking too long to sink in,' realised Cowell. His British producers, he concluded, were excessively remunerated and 'too safe and too cosy'. The four girls of Lakoda Rayne symbolised the problem: 'They've got no clue who they should be, and no clue about the music business.' They would rightly be voted off the programme, he decided, because 'they look too manufactured'.

In the weeks before the finals in Britain and America, he had taken the criticism to heart. He would need to renew everything for the following year: producers, judges and the entire format.

17

Revenge Is Sweet

As Rachel Crow collapsed sobbing onto the stage after being unexpectedly voted off *The X Factor* USA, Cowell rushed towards the helpless thirteen-year-old. The audience in the CBS studio – already hyped up by an energetic cheerleader – spontaneously erupted. Screams filled the vast hangar. Even for Cowell, the split-second drama was unexpected.

Crow, he knew, was convinced she would win. In the backstage area, she and her mother had skipped around, confident about her destiny. Enjoying the fussy attention of the wardrobe, make-up and personal assistants, Crow had assumed the demeanour of a star. Now, she risked self-destruction.

'Her mum's going to have a nervous breakdown,' Cowell said as he watched the crumpled teenager being helped to her feet.

'You promised I would win,' Crow howled reproachfully at her mother.

The girl's fate, Cowell knew, would be decided within seconds. Any mistake as millions watched live – and countless more on the web later – could destroy a talented artist who over the previous weeks had played the media, in his words, 'incredibly well'.

The broadcast cut to a video showing the highlights of Crow's past performances. In the studio, the tension was near breaking point.

'I can't breathe,' Crow cried out. 'I was supposed to win this. I was going to make history.'

With seconds to go before the live transmission resumed,

Cowell formulated a harsh message. Viewers saw him speaking to the stricken girl. None could have imagined his precise words: 'Stop crying. You can't change anything. You were at the bottom of the votes. Now you must act like the person every record company wants to work with. Disney will not want to work with a sore loser. Say something gracious. It'll make you more interesting, darling.'

Mercilessness rather than compassion would have reduced others to renewed hysteria, but Cowell understood the girl, whom he described as 'an actress with a thirty-year-old's mind'. Crow quickly recovered as Nicole Scherzinger, whose vote had triggered her expulsion, mounted the stage. As boos from the audience resounded across the studio, Scherzinger tearfully apologised. Crow now hugged and consoled the singer. Puffing out his cheeks, Cowell stood transfixed. 'Bloody hell,' he repeated to himself. 'I hope she says the right things.'

On cue, Crow looked into the camera and sweetly but tearfully told the audience 'I love you' and various other platitudes. The broadcast ended and the wounded were led from the spotlight into the darkness of backstage.

Ten minutes later, searching for Crow, Cowell arrived in Scherzinger's dressing room. The two girls were together, the target of a hyperactive photographer. 'The room's soaking wet,' said Cowell, smiling. 'Mostly from Nicole.'

The drama, Cowell knew, was TV magic. The viewers had been hooked. This, he hoped, would be the breakthrough on the way to a bigger audience. Instead, *The X Factor* USA's ratings the following week stayed stubbornly below 11 million.

'I misunderstood America,' Cowell admitted yet again. 'I cocked up.'

He had arrived in Los Angeles accompanied by his prized British production team. Together, they convinced themselves, they would beat *American Idol*. But on the eve of the final programme on 22 December, with the audience now below 10 million, Cowell acknowledged a heap of mistakes.

The programme had too many gimmicks, dancers, strobing lights and bursts of flames. What it lacked in a saturated market were contestants who grabbed mid-America's interest. In a series of late-night telephone calls, he blamed himself for overproducing and preventing the contestants from 'being themselves'. To please the advertisers, he had focused too much on teenage stars who pulled in a young audience, but he had ignored mid-America's passion for country music.

Even chasing the youth audience had not been an outright success. Fourteen-year-old singer Drew and Rachel Crow had originally been among his ideal winners, but both had been expelled, first by the audience's votes and then by Paula Abdul and Nicole Scherzinger voting for deadlock.

'At least it proves I don't fix the shows,' he said without bitterness.

Now he pondered over whether both judges should be dropped from the next series. Scherzinger, cursed by what he called 'her flakiness', had attracted no extra viewers, and even Abdul's initial attractions had waned. To Cowell's surprise, during live performances his old partner had been using her phone to read suggested comments composed by a scriptwriter. He would never allow sentiment to interfere with his decision on whether to part with Abdul but, as usual, he would not decide until the last moment. He enjoyed cultivating people's insecurities. Instead, his focus was on the final.

Even before Crow's departure, Cowell had switched his support to Melanie Amaro, a nineteen-year-old from Florida. At first, he had been suspicious about the girl's ability to engage. A good voice was not enough. Genuine artists won an audience's sympathy by displaying their understanding of music through their character and personality. Gradually, he noticed, Amaro was beginning to understand his message. Unlike the others, she was learning particular tricks from her coaches and, more importantly, displaying the will power necessary to become a star.

The change had started six weeks earlier. Concerned about Amaro's attitude, Cowell had invited the girl from a poor background to visit his house – now revalued at $34 million – for a pep talk over tea. 'Start working hard,' he told her in the loggia flanked by the living garden on one wall and a waterfall on the other. 'Get into your head that you're going to win. You've got to show how much you want to be a star. Kelly Clarkson has had a ten-year career because she's a killer.'

Unfortunately, during the competition Amaro had ballooned two sizes and required three corsets and elastic tights to constrain her figure. Despite her exceptional voice, making her attractive to America would be a challenge, not least because her music was unfashionable. Songwriters were not offering diva ballads for singers like Leona Lewis because pop radio stations refused to play those kinds of records. Finding hit songs was a challenge, Cowell decided, that L. A. Reid would have to overcome to relaunch Epic, his new label. At least, during the last days of the competition, Amaro had fully understood Cowell's lessons and convinced herself that she could become the new Mariah Carey. By contrast, her two male competitors, Josh Krajcik and Chris Rene, lacked serious commercial potential. Their music would not attract big sales.

In Britain, Cowell's problems were worse. The *X Factor* winners, the four Little Mix girls, were, many thought, unattractive, uninteresting and could not sing. Sales of their Christmas single, which normally would have been an automatic number one, were bad. 'Before I decide what to do with them,' said Cowell, 'I'll have to look into their eyes.' Compared with the dazzling American show, Britain's *X Factor* was dowdy and no longer the country's number-one programme. The BBC's *Strictly Come Dancing* had snatched that prize after *The X Factor* had attracted only 13.7 million viewers for its final, compared to 17.7 million in 2010. Cowell's absence was blamed for that decline. He had now decided to drop at least two of the judges, replacing Gary Barlow with a former record executive. 'I need someone who naturally understands production and the music business,' Cowell said, disdainful of Barlow's performance, which to Cowell felt more scripted than spontaneous.

In both London and Los Angeles, Cowell's critics were revelling in his misfortunes, but he shrugged off the doomsayers. Both *X Factor*s and the *Talent* programmes remained top-rated shows and, after thirty years in the music business, he knew how to cope with setbacks. He already had plans for major changes to the programmes' formats – and to Syco's staff. Too many of his producers – British and male – had become complacent and were reluctant to embrace radical change. He needed younger, wittier and less predictable producers in his team.

Confident that he could fix the problems and increase the ratings over the following two years, and certain that he still enjoyed the support of the broadcasters and sponsors, Cowell refocused on those who were relishing his discomfort.

Simon Fuller, he concluded, was no longer his principal rival. Without a successful new programme on the US or British networks for ten years, he spoke about Fuller as the past. '*Idol*'s in decline,' he mischievously told Fox's executives. The new target, he explained, was NBC's *The Voice*. 'That's the new kid on the block', he told Peter Rice, 'which threatens *Idol*'s supremacy in 2012.' American TV, he continued, with a diminishing pool of talent, could not sustain three major music reality shows; there would, he said, be a battle for survival and one show would be axed. 'There's going to be a bloodbath,' he predicted, but *The X Factor* USA would emerge on top if, and only if, he could persuade Fox 'to prioritise *The X Factor* in its battle against *The Voice* – and let *American Idol* wither'.

His reasoning was clear. Unlike *Idol*, *The X Factor* USA and *The Voice* were reinventing themselves, using the shows to sell more than music. According to *The Voice*'s rules, artists under contract to a record label would be allowed to participate in the competition. Theirs was no longer a talent contest for amateurs. Cowell would consider the same for his revamped shows in 2012. In his battle for supremacy, his biggest rival had become Lucian Grainge and Universal Music, associated with *American Idol* and *The Voice*. 'I've now got two TV series', Grainge had boasted, 'against Simon's *X Factor*.'

Cowell was looking for what he called a 'game changer'. *Pop Idol* and its successor programmes had replaced radio as the key marketing tool for pop music. Now, he believed, was the moment to develop a new format as an alternative to *The X Factor* and to revolutionise the business.

To plan the future battle, he invited fifteen managers from Sony's global music business to a meeting on 2 December 2011 at Soho House in Hollywood. There would be a presentation about what Cowell described as a 'defining moment' for Syco. Across the world, sales of *The X Factor*'s format had overtaken *American Idol*'s. About forty broadcasters were buying *The X Factor*, compared to about fifteen sales of *Idol*, down from thirty-five; the *Got Talent* format was sold by FremantleMedia in thirty-six countries. Depending on the size of the country's population, in 2011 Syco earned between $30,000 (in Estonia) and $3 million (in Australia) from each broadcaster for *The X Factor* and the *Talent* shows. In addition, *The X Factor* USA was broadcast in 130 countries, bringing Syco about $15 million, a small amount compared to the huge income from the sales of the Sony and Syco records promoted by the show. That was the principal difference between music reality shows and other TV output: the former spawned profits through the sale of music. Increasing that income was the reason for the meeting in Soho House.

Over ten years, Cowell had built a sustainable business, but he had now reached a crossroads. His challenge was to avoid becoming a casualty of the industry's appetite for sucking out the best talent and then discarding the corpse of a fading star. His longevity depended upon not being a 'lollipop' – slowly disappearing with consumption. The future, he decided, lay in using music reality shows to exploit Sony's electronic products and those of his sponsors, Pepsi and Verizon. But first he needed to reassess his relationship with Sony, a damaged corporation recovering from serial hacking of customers' IDs and the Japanese earthquake. 'Sony's become too passive,' he complained.

Syco's agreement with Sony, negotiated by Philip Green in 2010, was due to end in 2013. At that stage, both sides would have the option to sell their 50 per cent stake. Cowell was toying with the idea of selling out if Sony did not become more aggressive against Universal. His business, he calculated, was worth around $700 million.

'You must take an interest in the battle to support *The X Factor*,' Cowell urged Sony's managers. '*The Voice* has given us a kick up the ass. The battle is international. The common enemy is Universal Music. To beat *Idol* and *The Voice* we must take control of the music from FremantleMedia and defeat Universal.' If Sony failed to engage in the battle, he hinted, he would sell his 50 per cent to Apollo, Bob Sillerman or another investor and start afresh. Unspoken was his idea to manage *Idol*, *The X Factor* and the *Got Talent* programmes as a director of Apollo.

An opportunity to engineer a dramatic change came about during a chance meeting backstage at the Oprah Winfrey show in May. Subsequently, Cowell had become impressed by Jada Pinkett Smith, the wife of Will Smith, the actor. Pinkett Smith had spoken about her idea for a new music show. 'We must work together,' Cowell suggested. 'I'll give you 50 per cent of anything we do.' Soon after, as a token of her affection, Pinkett Smith gave Cowell a Can-Am three-wheeler motorbike. 'My latest toy,' he chirruped as he roared around Beverly Hills. In return, he sent Pinkett Smith a custom-built Smart car, similar to one he had just bought for himself and equipped with gull-wing doors and leather seats supplied by Bentley. He also gave her an idea to develop.

The result was unveiled on the eve of the *X Factor* USA final in Cowell's trailer on CBS's lot. *In the Mix*, explained Pinkett Smith, was a competition to find the best disc jockey in America and Britain. Music's new stars were the handful of DJs commanding $1 million for a single night's session. *In the Mix*, she explained, would be a competition between those DJs as they played music to 3,000 clubbers invited either to Sony's studio in Culver City or to one of the fifty major nightclubs in the US and Europe. To save money and enhance the visual experience, virtual stages would be generated by computer for the TV viewers.

'The tribes in the clubs', Pinkett Smith told Cowell, 'will rate the DJ's music by the amount of noise they generate, by clapping, shouting and stomping.' Between the dancing, the DJs would reveal their life stories. On the back of the shows, Sony would sell not only music, but also equipment to clubbers wanting to be DJs themselves.

'I think it's genius,' trilled Cowell. 'I'm blown away.' Fearing competitors would steal the idea, he wanted a formal proposal written by January. 'We'll have a few days to develop it. Sony can either come in or sell out,' he believed. Fizzing with excitement, Cowell was sure he had seen the future. (In early 2012, their relationship would acrimoniously crumble.)

A hundred yards away, the three contestants were finishing

rehearsals for the next day's *X Factor* USA finals. Cowell walked confidently to the studio from his trailer. Anyone taking his passion for fun, money and celebrity for flippancy would be mistaken. One of his strengths was to disguise the seriousness of his ambitions.

From the stage, Melanie Amaro's powerful voice filled the empty studio. In six months, she had been transformed by Cowell's team. Sitting among his producers, stylists, choreographers, singing coaches and record executives, Cowell wondered whether his latest manufactured star could become as credible as Adele. Amaro's new steely resolve certainly glossed over the emptiness of reality TV.

There was nothing phoney about her singing, but no one in Cowell's entourage at the rehearsal could predict with certainty that the likely winner from the original 100,000 applicants had the depth to become an enduring $5-million star. Rather, they spoke about the short term. Amaro and her two male competitors would undoubtedly earn profits for Syco through their recording contracts. And Cowell also expected income from Drew, Rachel Crow, Astro and one of the expelled groups. That alone, said Cowell, was far better than the miserable revenue earned by the winners of that year's *American Idol* and *The Voice*. At the end of the day, he could launch at least six artists from the series, at zero cost to Syco and Sony.

Cowell had left nothing to chance. Despite his professed disdain for gimmicks, he had included every trick to make the final a breathlessly exciting show: the dancers had been encouraged by Brian Friedman to be 'real sexy'; there were also strobe lights, shooting flames, knuckle lights for the whole audience and a ton of tinsel cascading from the heights. The show also featured performances by Alanis Morissette, Justin Bieber, Stevie Wonder and R. Kelly. Dazzling, loud, humorous and tense, the producers had conjured up a true spectacular, but for many the night lacked emotion. Amaro was declared the winner with 42 per cent of the 40 million votes, with between 11 million and 12.5 million viewers watching the show over the two days, lower than all his predictions. 'Thank God she won,' sighed a Cowell aide, 'otherwise Simon would have been in a grump for three months.'

At the end, the atmosphere backstage was one of relief rather than excitement. Cowell had secured credibility for the next series but had failed to make himself or *The X Factor* the hot topic in America's conversation.

Back in his trailer after the finale, he was joined by Peter Rice and Mike Darnell as a bottle of champagne was hesitatingly opened. Cowell appreciated the support of Fox's executives.

'Mel's mother's home has been foreclosed,' Cowell revealed, referring to the winner, 'so the $5 million will save them.' His guests nodded. 'I make popular dreams come true,' Cowell said. He truly believed it. The singer, he had decided with L. A. Reid, would be sent to a health spa for a month to lose weight and enhance her appearance. Then the nurturing would begin.

'There have been a lot of references to *The X Factor* in Fox's meetings this week,' muttered Rice, using corporate jargon for 'congratulations'. Cowell crunched a carrot while the glasses were raised, putting his down without drinking a drop. All three had reason to be satisfied. Cowell could be relied upon to improve the ratings in 2012.

Outside the trailer, Nicole Scherzinger was standing with a carton of expensively wrapped presents for the two executives and Cowell. Rushing to get away, all three were underwhelmed as she distributed the boxes. Without opening his gift – a specially made pair of *X Factor* cufflinks – Cowell chuckled as he walked towards the waiting media. 'I know what you're thinking,' he told a friend. Scherzinger's fate had been sealed long before.

After a raucous wrap party at Drai's in Hollywood for 500 people, Cowell returned to his house at 4 a.m. Several women had waited for an invitation to accompany him but, more self-confident and relaxed than previously, he was not in the mood for a one-night stand. He did not exclude at some stage the possibility of a permanent relationship. 'But', he said without regret, 'it's no use looking.' (A few weeks later, he would abandon the idea.)

Underneath the Christmas tree were about twenty parcels of all sizes. 'They're all for me,' said Cowell jokily. There was unusual mayhem in the house as he was preparing to depart for Barbados later that day. Among his many calls was one to Peter Fincham at ITV. He needed Fincham's agreement to offer Alesha Dixon, a star on the BBC's *Strictly Come Dancing*, over £300,000 to appear with him on *Britain's Got Talent* in early 2012. 'We've got to beat *The Voice*,' argued Cowell. He himself would be returning to the programme on his terms in order to resurrect his status as British TV's number one. Everything had to be tilted in his favour, ready for the next battle. Just as he expected, Fincham finally agreed, but his relationship with ITV had become uneasy.

Delayed by the calls and last-minute instructions, Cowell eventually left his Los Angeles home and headed for the private jet. He would not return until May. Among the crowd waiting for him in the Caribbean was Lucian Grainge, his old friend and new enemy.

'Come for tea,' Cowell suggested to Grainge when they met in Philip Green's suite at the Sandy Lane hotel.

When he arrived at Cowell's rented apartment, Grainge looked somewhat suspicious. Cowell was deliberately emollient. The music business was tough, both knew, and Cowell wanted to disarm his rival by dangling the possibility of Grainge joining Syco.

'You won't be working at Universal for ever,' said Cowell, hinting about the inevitable corporate power struggles. 'We're friends, so don't rule out that one day we'll be working together.'

'We'll see,' replied Grainge warily. Like Cowell, he was looking forward to the next round of the battle in Britain, aware that one of them would certainly be humiliated by defeat. Cowell's cheery self-confidence was irritating, but Grainge was reassured by the BBC's commitment to win the battle.

'I know what works,' said Cowell. 'I can do it better.'

Their conversation was not continued at the Sandy Lane's New Year's Eve party. 'The best ever,' agreed Cowell and his friends. Unlike previous years, Cowell remained long after midnight and continued celebrating in his apartment. The following afternoon, he bid farewell to his mother and flew to St Barts to board *Slipstream* for a three-week cruise around the island. Joined by Sinitta, Zeta Graff, a hilarious Greek divorcee, Lauren Silverman and Kelly Bergantz, he appeared more relaxed than for many years.

'I feel free,' he told his friends. 'I've got my energy back and I'm not frightened any more. Not even of the paparazzi.' Looking over the blue sea, he reflected that he was finally in command of his own destiny. He knew how to improve *The X Factor* in America; *Got Talent*, he was certain, would beat *The Voice* in Britain; he had found enough potential stars to score hits in the charts; and he would rebuild his organisation to meet his challengers. Above all, he felt that he had taken his revenge on Fuller.

At the end of one high-spirited night at the island's yacht club, fuelled by champagne and vodka, he had invited a group of Brazilian girls onto *Slipstream*. By 5 a.m., he was intimately embraced with Anna Paula, a well-known international socialite. At teatime later that day, she had flown back to São Paulo on a private jet and had texted her intentions. 'She's coming to London soon,' he announced at dinner. 'That should be fun.'

Over the last days of his holiday, he bought a reconditioned blue vintage MG sports car for spinning around London, posed on *Slipstream*'s sun deck speaking into a banana for an invisible paparazzo, and confirmed his first appointment after returning home: a forty-minute session of colonic irrigation. 'It's so cleansing,' he told his friends sitting on the boat's aft deck at 3 a.m. 'And it makes my eyes shine brighter.'

His first business meeting would be with Philip Green to plan the expansion of his empire. 'I know I can do the shows better than anyone,' he repeated as Frank Sinatra sang 'Witchcraft' and he lit a Kool. 'The wheel is going to be turning faster than ever. I'll win.'

Sources

I first took an interest in *The X Factor* just before Christmas 2010. A friend, knowing about my track record of writing about men with power and money, had suggested I should write Simon Cowell's biography. 'Why not watch the final with me', she suggested, 'and see what you make of it?' Shortly after, I started serious research for an unauthorised biography. Then, out of the blue, I received a telephone call. 'Would you like to meet Cowell?' I was asked. Subsequently, I accepted his offer of co-operation, subject to the condition that I would publish both criticism and any evidence of wrongdoing. After May 2011, we met regularly in London and Los Angeles or spoke for hours on the telephone at all times of day and night.

Although Cowell answered my questions in his own fashion and did arrange for me to meet several members of his family and some friends, there were limits to his co-operation. He accepted my stipulation that he had no copy approval and certainly would not be able to read the book until publication. He did place barriers to my access to some people, which I did my best to overcome. Sometimes I was successful but on other occasions I discovered that individuals who had worked with him were just too fearful of the damage to their own reputations to speak to me, and sometimes their fears were understandable because they had treated him badly. Others feared his wrath if they risked speaking.

He was particularly sensitive about his relationships with certain women, especially those confidantes who still hear his intense confessions about his fears and phobias. Fortunately, the obstacles he raised were not always successful. To his credit, when I did ask for a comment about any embarrassing information I had discovered, he answered my questions without any rancour.

As time passed, I realised how many mysteries remained. After experiencing showbiz's many pitfalls, Cowell is more careful than most to protect his reputation. One false move, he knows, could end a remarkable career. Despite the constant glare of the media, with whom he actively co-operates, he has successfully preserved many secrets in his life. Occasionally, when I asked for a confession about a particular 'skeleton in the cupboard', he created a shield of perplexed innocence, but eventually he did admit to 'unknowns' which are unravelled within this book. Considering that he had no control over the outcome, he was remarkably candid.

Even under scrutiny, Cowell is good company. He likes to be entertained and is himself entertaining. Our relationship was harmonious. Many may suspect that Cowell is simply an outstanding manipulator, but after a forty-three-year career chasing criminals, cheats and con men, I don't think Cowell fits into any of those categories. Nor am I vulnerable to the charm of a man who is undoubtedly civilised but who describes himself as 'odd'.

Significantly, Cowell did not steer me initially and help me to understand his quest for revenge. On the contrary, at the beginning he refused to speak about his enemies and rivals. He waited until I had accumulated the evidence from others, often without his knowledge. I arrived unaided at my own conclusions. Only then did he explain to me his motivation and offer information which was until then unknown.

Irrefutably, he is a master of our celebrity culture. He also has ambitions to become a TV mogul with an empire stretching across the globe. At the moment, his quest seems realisable. How he achieved that status is the essence of this story.

I have not listed the individual sources for this book. Unless indicated to the contrary, most direct speech was obtained by me in interviews. I have naturally relied on the huge volume of reports in the newspapers and other media. I am grateful for the insight provided by the following books:

Carter, Bill, *Desperate Networks* (Doubleday, 2006)
Cowell, Simon, *I Don't Mean to Be Rude, But . . .* (Broadway Books, 2003)
Dannen, Fredric, *Hit Men* (Times Books, 1990)
Goodman, Fred, *The Mansion on the Hill* (Times Books, 1997)
Newkey-Burden, Chas, *Simon Cowell* (O'Mara, 2009)
Rushfield, Richard, *American Idol: The Untold Story* (Hyperion, New York, 2011)

As usual, many sources wish to remain anonymous, and to them and those I can mention I express my genuine gratitude. The others include:

Paula Abdul, Denise Beighton, Brian Biglin, Keith Blackhurst, Alan Boyd, Iain Burton, Tim Byrne, Mike Darnell, Clive Davis, Stephen Ferrera, Marc Fox, Cécile Frot-Coutaz, Tanya Gold, Hugh Goldsmith, Diana Graham, Lucian Grainge, Nigel Grainge, Richard Griffiths, Chris Herbert, Chris Hill, Claire Horton, Denis Ingoldsby, Simon Jones, Jonathan King, Jeremy Lascelles, Ian Levine, Camilla Long, Ron McCreight, Jeremy Marsh, Korda Marshall, Ashley Newton, Lohan Presencer, John Preston, Steve Redmond, L. A. Reid, Claudia Rosencrantz, Richard Rushfield, Dan Sabbagh, Terri Seymour, Robert Sillerman, Nigel Sinclair, Marty Singer, Rav Singh, Mike Stock, Louis Theroux, Maurice Veronique, Louis Walsh, Pete Waterman, Tom Watkins and Paul Williams of *Music Week*.

I am very grateful to Robin Denselow, Helen Dann and Adam White for their help at the beginning.

Robert Barrett produced outstanding research about the Cowell family history. Thanks also to Mark Hollingsworth for research.

I am grateful to all members of the Cowell family. Among Cowell's close friends, I am grateful to Lauren Silverman, Kelly Bergantz and Jackie St Clair. Among his staff, thanks to Abi Doyle, Sarah Jane Ingram, Hannah Lamden, Jennie Paine and Ann-Marie Thomson.

In Los Angeles, the staff of the Petit Ermitage, especially Chris, Josh and Lena, made my stay very comfortable.

As always I owe a lot to the publishers. Angus Cargill, Ian Bahrami and Will Atkinson at Faber and Faber in London and Pamela Cannon at Random House in New York were all invaluable.

David Hooper has been my libel lawyer since 1987. Thanks to him, so much truth which others would have suppressed has been courageously published. He is a champion of free speech.

I owe a similar debt to Jonathan Lloyd, my agent at Curtis Brown. Always in a good mood, he combines friendship with honest criticism.

Above all, I owe so much to my family. My mother Sylvia, my children and, especially, Veronica, an amazing friend and supporter.

Illustration Credits

Page 1: Photos © Lauren Silverman.
Page 2: Photos © Julie Cowell. Reproduced with kind permission.
Page 3: (top left) © Julie Cowell. Reproduced with kind permission); (top right) © Lauren Silverman; (bottom) © Julie Cowell. Reproduced with kind permission.
Page 4: (top) © Alpha; (bottom) © Rex Features.
Page 5: (top) © Alpha; (bottom) © Jackie St Clair.
Page 6: (top) © Redferns/Getty Images; (bottom) © Getty Images.
Page 7: (top) © Haydn West/PA Archive/Press Association Images; (bottom) © Getty Images.
Page 8: (top left) © Mirrorpix; (top right) © TeamCamera/Rex Features; (bottom right) © Fiona Hanson/PA Archive/Press Association Images; (bottom left) © Yui Mok/PA Archive/Press Association Images; (centre) © TeamCamera/Rex Features.
Page 9: (top) © Getty Images; (bottom) © 20th Century Fox.
Page 10: (top) © Alex Tehrani/Corbis Outline; (bottom) © Lucy Nicholson/AP/Press Association Images.
Page 11: (top) © FremantleMedia Limited/Simco Limited; (bottom) © FremantleMedia Limited/Simco Limited.
Page 12: (top) © FremantleMedia Limited/Simco Limited; (centre) uncredited; (bottom) © NBCU Photobank/Rex Features.
Page 13: (top) © Copetti/Photofab/Rex Features; (bottom) © Lauren Silverman.

Page 14: (top) © John Gress/Corbis; (bottom left) © Lauren Silverman; (bottom right) © Julie Cowell. Reproduced with kind permission.

Page 15: (top) © Startraks Photo/Rex Features; (bottom) © Startraks Photo/Rex Features.

Page 16: (top) © Lauren Silverman; (bottom) © Eliot Press/bauergriffinonline.com.

Index

Index